SMITHSONIAN INSTITUTION
BUREAU OF AMERICAN ETHNOLOGY
BULLETIN 188

Shonto: A Study of the Role of the Trader in a Modern Navaho Community

By WILLIAM Y. ADAMS

U.S. GOVERNMENT PRINTING OFFICE
WASHINGTON : 1963

LETTER OF TRANSMITTAL

SMITHSONIAN INSTITUTION,
BUREAU OF AMERICAN ETHNOLOGY,
Washington, D.C., March 30, 1962.

SIR: I have the honor to submit the accompanying manuscript entitled "Shonto: A Study of the Role of the Trader in a Modern Navaho Community," by William Y. Adams, and to recommend that it be published as a bulletin of the Bureau of American Ethnology.

Very respectfully yours,

FRANK H. H. ROBERTS, Jr.,
Director.

DR. LEONARD CARMICHAEL,
Secretary, Smithsonian Institution.

II

CONTENT

ILLUSTRATIONS

PLATES

(All plates follow p. 316)

1. *a*, Tsegi Canyon, typical of the topography of the Shonto region. (Courtesy Parker Hamilton.) *b*, Betatakin ruin, Navajo National Monument. (Courtesy Christy G. Turner II, Museum of Northern Arizona.)
2. *a*, Winter in Shonto Canyon: the trading-post grounds. *b*, The road into Shonto Canyon from the west.
3. *a*, The Government corral, Shonto Canyon. *b*, In Shonto Canyon. (*a*, *b*, Courtesy Bud DeWald, Arizona Days & Ways, The Arizona Republic.)
4. *a*, Modern Navaho material culture, illustrating the influence of the trading post. *b*, Pawning a belt. (*a*, *b*, Courtesy Bud DeWald, Arizona Days & Ways, The Arizona Republic.)
5. *a*, Setting of the trading post. (Courtesy Christy G. Turner II, Museum of Northern Arizona.) *b*, The trading post. Warehouse to left, store in center, living quarters right. Electric gasoline pump installed, 1957. (Courtesy Bud DeWald, Arizona Days & Ways, The Arizona Republic.)
6. *a*, Entrance to the store. (Courtesy Bud DeWald, Arizona Days & Ways, The Arizona Republic.) *b*, Shipping cattle from the Government corral.
7. *a*, In the pawn vault. Rugs taken in trade are also stored here. Dial telephone installed, 1956. *b*, Inside store, looking toward the grocery counter. (*a*, *b*, Courtesy Bud DeWald, Arizona Days & Ways, The Arizona Republic.)
8. *a*, *b*, Trading at the grocery counter.
9. *a*, Navajo National Monument, a source of employment for Shonto Navahos. *b*, Police visit to Shonto Trading Post. (*a*, *b*, Courtesy Bud DeWald, Arizona Days & Ways, The Arizona Republic.)
10. *a*, Listening to speeches at community meeting. *b*, Indoor community meeting at Shonto. (*a*, *b*, Courtesy Arthur H. White.)

TEXT FIGURES

MAPS

CHARTS

The field investigations upon which this study is based were carried out between 1954 and 1956, and the report itself was completed in the following year. No changes or additions have been made to the text since it was originally written. The reader of today will thus find no mention of many important events and developments that have occurred during the past 5 years.

The years since 1957 have brought dramatic changes to the Navaho country, some of which were foreseen when the Shonto report was written, while others have come as a surprise, at least to the author. Today an expanding network of paved highways criss-crosses the Navaho Reservation, and such pioneer settlements as Tuba City and Kayenta are being transformed into typical American crossroads towns, with their clusters of filling stations, cafes, motels, and even movie houses. A paved road passes within 10 miles of Shonto itself, and a new, 300-pupil boarding school will soon be completed on the rim of Shonto Canyon. Within a few years one of the main power transmission lines from the Glen Canyon Dam will pass almost directly over Shonto Trading Post.

Far-reaching economic and social changes are once again taking place in the Navaho world. Railroad way labor has almost disappeared from the economic picture, and has been replaced by local wage work on construction projects financed in many cases by the Navaho tribe itself. In the administration of this new program and countless others, the Tribal Government has shown a capacity and foresight that have compelled Navahos and Whites alike to regard it with far more respect than they did 5 years ago. Perhaps symbolic of the new role of tribal government is Shonto's new stone chapter house, currently the most impressive building in the community.

In many of its details, and particularly in the field of economics, the present study is already out of date. It may be said to describe a pattern of economic integration which remained relatively stable throughout the western Navaho country in the decade and a half immediately following World War II. In the future this economic period, like the weaving and livestock eras before it, may be of historic interest as one of the successive steps in the economic assimilation of the Navaho.

The importance of the trader, at Shonto and throughout the Navaho Reservation, has undoubtedly diminished since 1957. Nevertheless, the trading post is not yet an obsolete institution. It remains a fixed point in the constantly shifting spectrum of Navaho-White relations, as it has been for over half a century, giving a measure of direction and stability to the process of Navaho cultural adaptation. As such its importance is likely to persist at least for another generation before it finally and fully gives place to more up-to-date enterprises.

W.Y.A.
Wadi Halfa, Sudan

August 1962

SHONTO: A STUDY OF THE ROLE OF THE TRADER IN A MODERN NAVAHO COMMUNITY

By WILLIAM Y. ADAMS

INTRODUCTION

DEFINITION AND DELIMITATION

This is not a community study in any ordinary sense of the term (see, e.g., Steward, 1950); nor is there any such geographical or social reality as Shonto community. Throughout the northwestern reaches of the Navaho Reservation, settlement is scattered but at the same time more or less regular, so that it is impossible to identify any significant structural unit of population larger than the kin-determined residence group (see Social Structure," pp. 54–65). In this respect, as in nearly all others, Navaho society in the Shonto region is a true folk society (cf. Redfield, 1947; Miner, 1952).

The 100 Navaho families whose activities are recorded and analyzed in these pages are not set apart from their neighbors, particularly to the north, west, and south, by any visible boundaries, either social or geographical. Among all the Navaho on the reservation, their sole collective distinction is that they are the most frequent and regular customers of Shonto Trading Post, in whose vicinity they live. In other words, this is a study of a trading community—a clientele.

Even in this regard a considerable amount of selection has been exercised, such that the delimitation of the group is largely arbitrary. Frequency and regularity of trading are, of course, matters of degree. If all the Navaho individuals who had ever been customers at Shonto Trading Post were numbered as clientele, their aggregate would certainly come to over 2,000. At least 1,000 persons appear at the store with sufficient regularity so that their names are known to the trader. Of this latter group, however, about half live closer to other trading posts than to Shonto, and hence are likely to do a good part of their trading elsewhere. Such divided trading relationships precluded the gathering of the sort of detailed and complete information, particularly with regard to economic activities and income (see pp. 94–148) which were considered essential to the present study.

1

The trading community of Shonto, hereinafter designated as the community, is confined to those Navaho individuals who are considered by the owner of Shonto Trading Post to be "Shonto Navvies." These are the families who trade exclusively, or nearly so, at the one store, and thus enable the trader to observe every phase of their economic life. As delimited for the purposes of the present study, this group was originally found to include 103 households and 39 residence groups. For the sake of symmetry and statistical simplicity, it was then decided to eliminate the three most uncertain households (constituting a single residence group), so as to reduce the total number of Navaho households studied to an even 100. The group is collectively designated as "Shonto community" in succeeding pages solely for want of any other appropriate term, and with no intention of suggesting a visible social identity.

The 100 Shonto households selected, with their 568 individual inhabitants, constitute the entire Navaho universe of this study. They have not been selected, nor are they advanced, as being in any way a sample or even "typical" of a larger social whole. On the contrary, considerable pains have been taken in later pages to show how and why Shonto differs from other parts of the Navaho country, and particularly from those which have been the scenes of recent studies by anthropologists. The investigation of Shonto and the present report are confined to the problem of determining the structural interrelationships and the processual interaction of a single American-inspired and American-operated trading post and its Navaho clientele. As for a wider applicability, the present research can serve only to frame a hypothesis, not to test it (cf. pp. 305–307).

GENESIS OF THE STUDY

Like many other anthropological projects, this one arose from an original interest in a specific sociocultural situation rather than in a more theoretical social or cultural problem. It was the situation at Shonto which drew attention to the general problem of the role of the entrepreneur in culture contact—not vice versa. In other respects, however, the personal and professional circumstances under which the study evolved have been sufficiently deviant from the usual experiences of anthropologists that it seems not only justifiable but necessary to set them down in considerable detail.

FIRST ACQUAINTANCE WITH SHONTO COMMUNITY

I got my first view of Shonto Trading Post, in the capacity of an ordinary tourist, during the summer of 1948. I had just received my bachelor's degree in anthropology from the University of California, and was spending the summer with my family on the Navaho

Reservation. Our family home at that time, as during much of my
boyhood, was at Window Rock (see map 1). As a result, I had
sufficient first-hand acquaintance to be thoroughly fascinated with the
more obvious features of Navaho life and culture. I had also a fair
personal knowledge of the Navaho Reservation, although I had never
before had the opportunity of visiting its far northwestern reaches.
My brother and I spent the summer of 1948 in making up for that
deficiency by exploring the regions from Monument Valley to Rainbow Bridge as much as we were able, in the course of which we visited
Shonto on several occasions. I still recall being impressed particularly with the old-fashioned and primitive flavor of the trading post,
by comparison with those I knew, and also by the high prices.

During the 3 years which followed, I pursued graduate studies in
anthropology at the University of California, and during each of the
three summers I returned to Shonto at one time or another to renew
and extend my acquaintance with the community. In 1949 I was
engaged in archeological excavations in the Flagstaff area, but found
time to visit Shonto late in the summer. In 1950, having conceived an
interest in post-war changes in the Navaho economy (cf. "The Outside
World," pp. 49–51), I accepted complementary grants from the University of California and from the Placement Division of the Bureau
of Indian Affairs (Window Rock) to make a study of the effects of
wage work on Navaho society. I chose District 8 (Kayenta-Oljeto-
Dennehotso-Chilchinbito) as my "sample." In 1951, I was engaged
in an extensive archeological reconnaissance of the lower San Juan
drainage, in the course of which I made frequent use of Navaho information and assistance. All these summer activities contributed directly or indirectly to my knowledge of Shonto community and its
native life, although I had at the time no thought of ever making any
use of such knowledge.

ASSOCIATION WITH SHONTO TRADING POST

During my travels through and around the northwestern Navaho
country, I had naturally made the acquaintance of a number of traders,
including the owner of Shonto Trading Post. In the fall of 1951,
I was approached by the Shonto trader with the offer of a position which I found myself unable to resist. The trader was at that
time preparing for the annual lamb drive to the railroad (cf. "Commodity Exchange," pp. 172–175), and because of extreme drought
conditions he had determined to abandon his accustomed route to
Farmington and instead to drive via Black Mesa and Leupp to a
shipping point on the Santa Fe near Winslow. Being himself unfamiliar with the territory, he asked me to take charge and direct
the drive in the field, a matter of overseeing a handful of Navaho
herders and some 2,800 head of lambs for 6 weeks. Suppressing the

fact that my acquaintance with the territory south of the Hopi Village was even less than that of my employer, and that I knew virtually no "Trader Navaho" (see "Communication," pp. 212–214), I readily accepted his offer. Certainly I was attracted to it more by a vague sense of adventure than by any professional consideration, and I made no records or analysis of my experience or my relations with the herders.

If I had no other qualifications for the assignment of range boss, I had at least sense enough to let the Navaho herders run things their own way without any interference from me, with the result that the drive was a success from my employer's point of view. It began, for me, a period of association with Shonto Trading Post which has continued through the succeeding years and has culminated in the present study. After 1951, I had a standing invitation to return to Shonto and take charge of the sheep drive every fall. I did not avail myself of the opportunity in the following year, but in 1953, having terminated my studies at the University of California, I returned to the Navaho Reservation. I worked for a short time at Navajo National Monument (see map 3), and then once again I made the drive to the railroad with Shonto's lambs. Immediately upon completion of the drive, I went to work full time as the regular trader at Shonto Trading Post, commencing an intermittent experience which continued over 3 years and largely formed the basis of the present study.

TRADING EXPERIENCE

During my first weeks as a trader, I was much too busy learning the endlessly complicated "ropes" of trading (cf. "Staff," pp. 163–164), and struggling to communicate with the customers, to be aware to any extent of what went on beyond the trading post door. As I began to master the routine and feel at home behind the counter, however, I also began to see a new world of anthropological experience opening up before me. I was, I realized, seeing a side of Navaho life and a series of intercultural relationships at which I had only guessed before, and which, I am convinced, have been fully perceived by few observers of the Navaho scene.

To begin with, I quickly learned that the postwar Navaho economy was very different from what I or anyone of my acquaintance had supposed (see pp. 94–148). I saw clearly that my 1950 survey had not sufficiently penetrated to the purely native roots of the Navaho economy, with the result that I had in some ways overestimated and in others underestimated the significance of wage work. Most clearly of all, I saw that I, along with many another student of the Navaho, had ignored the paramount influence of the trader in the Navaho economy. Finally, I became aware that I was involved in a situation of culture contact which manifestly was not operating to produce assimilation, but rather to perpetuate Navaho cultural and social differentiation.

In short, it seemed to me that the role of the trader in Shonto community opened up new vistas not only in the study of recent Navaho culture history, but also in the analysis of culture contact in general. I became so intrigued by the anthropological possibilities of my experience at Shonto that I determined to carry out a formal investigation of the relationship of trading post and Navaho society and economy. Considering that such a study would comprise a satisfactory doctoral dissertation, I made plans to continue my education toward the Ph.D. Having received generous encouragement in this direction from Drs. Haury and Spicer of the Department of Anthropology at the University of Arizona, I selected that school for my studies.

My decision to work toward a Ph. D. was made in January 1954. Although I had at that time no very clear perception of the direction my study would take, I began keeping notes and compiling records of trader-Navaho relations, and especially of the purely economic aspects of trading. Some of these notes and records have found their way into the present report, particularly in "Retail Trade," pp. 184–214, and "Community Services," pp. 214–230. I continued in my overt capacity as trader at Shonto, coupled with my covert status as economic and social observer and recorder, until the end of August 1954, when I resigned to enroll in the Graduate College at the University of Arizona to pursue work toward my doctorate in anthropology.

THE TRADER IN LITERATURE

One of my first undertakings was an examination of the literature on Navaho life for any material which would confirm my own observations and experience. I found, as I had expected, that there was virtually nothing, and that my earlier ignorance concerning the role of the trader was not due to unfamiliarity with the literature. There can be no doubt that both anthropologists and informed laymen have interested themselves in the Navaho primarily for their native religion, and accounts of Navaho life, both technical and popular, have emphasized this sphere of activity at the expense and often to the total exclusion of all others. Of all the areas of Navaho life, however, none has been more consistently ignored or even misrepresented than the economic field. I was not surprised at this state of affairs, since I was and am convinced that Navaho economics, and especially the supposedly "traditional" Navaho economy, could not be understood without making an intensive study in and of the trading post, and to my knowledge no such study had ever been made.

Anthropological studies of the Navaho fall largely into three basic classes, corresponding in a rough way to chronological phases in the development of such studies. The earlier works, beginning in the 19th century and continuing until about 1940, are for the most part purely ethnographic—concerned with precontact Navaho culture and especially with religion. In this category are the pioneering investigations of Washington Matthews, the long series of social and religious studies undertaken by Gladys Reichard and especially by Father Berard Haile, and the varied ethnographic potpourri from the pen of W. W. Hill. (A full enumeration of relevant titles published by these four students alone would fill several pages of bibliography. For titles and full documenation, the reader is referred to Kluckholn and Spencer, 1940.) Although culture historians in this period concerned themselves with Navaho culture contact and change in pre-Anglo times (e.g., Farmer, 1941; Hill, 1940 b; Kroeber, 1928; Luomala, 1938), such studies uniformly ignored the phenomenon of modern culture contact and its consequences.

Popular and nonanthropological works during the same period were somewhat more concerned with the realities of modern Navaho life, although Lipps (1909) found himself able to describe the Navaho economy of his day without any mention of the trader. It was not until 1930 that the role of the trader even in the "traditional" Navaho economy was recognized in print, and then only in a popular work (Coolidge and Coolidge, 1930, pp 67–69). The Coolidges (1930, p. 67) described the trader as "far and away the most important White man on the Navajo Reservation, outside of government officials," yet devoted only three pages of their study of current Navaho life to him.

It was Amsden's (1934, pp. 172–182, 191–204) painstaking history and analysis of Navaho weaving which first gave the trader his due as a historic influence in the Navaho economy. Amsden's account has been widely quoted by later students (e.g., Luomala, 1938, pp. 65–70; Underhill, 1956, pp. 185–190) and seems to remain at the present time the standard source on the historical role of the Navaho trader. The structural-functional significance of the trading post received significant attention for the first time in 1937, when it was studied by Youngblood at the behest of the Indian Bureau. The report appeared only in the form of a paper appended to the transcript of a senate subcommittee hearing (Youngblood, 1937) and has received little attention from anthropologists, although it is quoted by Luomala (1938, p. 5) and Sanders et al. (1953, pp. 231–234). Youngblood's account is the only important title on Navaho-trader relations to appear among 11 pages of entries on "Navajo relations with Whites" in the Kluckhohn-Spencer (1940) bibliography on the Navaho.

The turning point in Navaho studies was reached in the 1940's, and is marked by the various works and particularly the brilliant descriptive integrations of Kluckhohn and the Leightons (e.g., Kluckhohn, 1944; Leighton and Leighton, 1944; Kluckhohn and Leighton, 1946; Leighton and Kluckhohn, 1948), with their penetrating insights into modern culture contact and its consequences. These studies have opened the door to a whole new school of Navaho investigations, with emphasis on the here and now. Nevertheless, and amazingly, they are little better than their predecessors in dealing with the Navaho economy. Kluckhohn and Leighton's (1946) magnificent "The Navaho," which in other respects is certain to remain the definitive work on modern Navaho life for years to come, presents a picture of Navaho economy and income which was distinctly out of date even at the time of publication, and is doubly so today (ibid., pp. 13–41, especially pp. 24–26). The work, moreover, devotes only 4 pages (38–39, 78–79) to the trader and his role, as compared with 6 pages (80–85) for the missionary, 28 pages (33–37, 85–100, 105–111) for the Federal Government, and 8 pages (36, 100–105, 111–112) for other contact agencies. The companion volume (Leighton and Kluckhohn, 1948) does not mention traders at all.

The most recent phase in Navaho studies comprises the investigations carried out by the successors to Kluckhohn and the Leightons, which follow the general direction laid down by them. These are the numerous studies of the Navaho in the Ramah area, published variously as "Reports of the Ramah Project" and "Reports of the Rimrock Project" in the Peabody Museum Papers of Harvard University, plus a number of titles published elsewhere (for an enumeration of these see Roberts, 1951, pp. viii–x). They have emphasized various loci of Navaho-White culture contact and conflict, such as the armed forces (Vogt, 1951), missions (Rapoport, 1954), and the presence of White settlers (Landgraf, 1954). Like their predecessors, they have uniformly ignored the trader as a force in culture contact. Even Hobson's (1954) examination of Navaho acquisitive values has nothing to say about the possible influence of the trader thereon (cf. "Perceptions and Values," pp. 281–287).

Not until 1956 has any general account of Navaho life, popular or technical, given more than passing attention to the role of the trading post. However, in her most recent history of the Navaho people, Ruth Underhill (1956, pp. 177–195) not only devotes a whole chapter to traders, but bestows upon them the not wholly inappropriate sobriquet of "Navajo Shoguns" (ibid., pp. 180–181). In keeping with the nature of her work, she is actually speaking primarily of the historical influence of the trading post, particularly in the development of the Navaho rug, and she draws a large part of her material from Amsden (1934).

Although individual traders have been the subject of several popular biographies (Coolidge, 1925; Gillmor and Wetherill, 1934; Faunce,

1934; Hannum, 1946; Schmedding, 1951), these have failed to recognize the trader in general as anything more than a purely personal force on the Navaho scene. They have consistently dramatized his life and relations with his Navaho neighbors without providing any real cultural insight into them. From the standpoint of straightforward information the best of the trader biographies, although the least known, is that of Schmedding (1951). It is, also, the only genuinely autobiographical account.

In sum, I found that existing literature provided little insight into the cross-cultural problem which I had come upon more or less accidentally through my experience at Shonto Trading Post, and which I now proposed to investigate. Consequently, it has been necessary for me to work out my own field methods and systems of analysis as best I could on the basis of my own previous experience. And if the resulting report is far longer than either the members of my faculty thesis committee or I had anticipated, it is because in many areas of intercultural relations there has been no existing body of knowledge upon which I could draw. In dealing especially with the Navaho economy, as the reader of "Navaho Economics" (pp. 94–148) will discover, I have had to start from absolute scratch.

REFINEMENT OF THE PROBLEM

At the time of my enrollment at the University of Arizona, I had only a series of vague and half-formulated ideas as to how I should go about studying trader-Navaho relations. It is true that when I returned to Shonto a year later I still had not ironed out a good many of the details, but in the intervening months I had at least sharpened my perception and refined my definition of the problem to a manageable point. Credit for this achievement belongs very largely to Dr. Edward H. Spicer, my faculty advisor and the chairman of my thesis committee, with whom I had a series of conferences as well as a seminar on anthropological field methods which allowed me to work out some of my own theoretical and methodological problems.

As an initial step it was necessary to establish the fact that there was such a thing as an institutionalized "role of the trader" apart from the personal role of any given trader. On this point I had no doubt whatsoever. My acquaintance with my employer and with many other traders in every part of the Navaho Reservation convinced me that all of us, although with various degrees of sophistication, had closely similar perceptions of Navaho life and of our own place in it. I found also that the nature and limits of our relations with our Navaho customers and neighbors were closely comparable. Most important of all, in my years of association with Shonto Trading Post I recognized clearly that I had come increasingly to share the values of my employer, particularly in regard to Navaho-White relations, and had acquired a sense of superior status despite my intellectual principles. I began by doing and saying things of which I did not approve, because I was paid for it, and ended by justifying them to myself and others in the same terms as did the other traders of my acquaintance. Clearly, our behavior and our role were being determined for us, in spite of enormous individual differences in personality, education, and experience, by constant factors in the structure of our social milieu.

In the most immediate sense our social milieu was the Navaho community as it had evolved under a century of direct and indirect Anglo-American influence, and my first objective was to trace the course of this evolution (cf. "Background," pp. 30–53) and describe its end product as it stood in 1955 ("Navaho Life," pp. 53–94). I would be particularly concerned with community economics, as the phase of Navaho life which most directly concerned the trader. In any case I had always intended to undertake a detailed description and analysis of the modern Navaho economy, simply because it constituted one of the great gaps in the anthropological literature. (This intention was duly carried out, and comprises the section "Navaho Economics" of the present study.)

The factors conditioning the trader's behavior are obviously not confined to the Navaho community in which he lives. He himself is a member of another sociocultural system which impinges on him particularly in his professional capacity as a businessman. As an agent, in a sense, of the modern American industrial and mercantile economy, he is subject to numerous limitations imposed by them. It was necessary, therefore, to ascertain the place of the trader in the modern American society and economy, and its effect on his behavior (see pp. 167–184).

In the broadest sense, the social milieu of the trader is the whole complex of Navaho-White relations of which he is a part. The interrelationship of the two sociocultural systems is thoroughly structured both at the community level (pp. 184–214 and pp. 214–230) and at the level of the total society (pp. 231–267), providing the trader with numerous behavioral mandates which I would have to discover and define. Finally, I would have to ascertain the operational motives of the trader himself and determine how and in what ways they affected his behavior (pp. 267–296).

THEORETICAL FOUNDATIONS

In short, my problem was to reduce the total phenomenon of Navaho-White contact to the scope of a single, arbitrarily but rigidly delimited social system involving members of both groups (i.e., a "contact community"). I had then to study the internal structure of that social system with particular reference to the status of the trader, and to study its internal interaction in terms of the role of the trader, and with special attention to his own motivations.

This structural analysis of culture contact in terms of interaction within a single discrete social system involved no new departure in anthropological theory. Shortly before I began refining my own problem, the report of the Social Science Research Council Summer Seminar on Acculturation (1954, p. 980) had appeared, carrying the statement that—

The patterns of conjunctive relations may be conceptualized as intercultural role networks that not only establish the framework of contact but also provide the channels through which the content of one cultural system must be communicated and transmitted to another.

A number of earlier works were cited in which this type of analysis had been employed: those of Fortes (1936), Ekvall (1939), Gluckman (1940), Mandelbaum (1941), and Honigmann (1952).

The same report went on to say:

Cultures do not meet, but people who are their carriers do. As carriers of traditions such contacting individuals never know their entire cultures and never convey all they know of them to one another. That part of their cultural inventory which they do transmit is conditioned primarily by their reasons for making the contact, that is, by the cultural concomitants of the role that they assume in dealing with an alien group. [Summer Seminar on Acculturation, 1954, pp. 980–981.]

Here were expressed many of the underlying assumptions upon which I proposed to base my own study. Essentially the same view had been taken by Radcliffe-Brown (1940) and Malinowski (1945, pp. 14–18) a decade earlier.

The structural analysis of culture contact amounts essentially to the study of a cross-cultural social system (or "contact community") according to the principles of social analysis developed in particular by Talcott Parsons (cf. especially 1949, pp. 3–16; 1951, pp. 3–23) and a few other students of social structure (e.g., Merton, 1949; Levy, 1952). Although formulated in recent years by sociologists, this "actor-situation" approach (cf. Levy, 1952, p. 18) is built to a considerable extent upon foundations laid by Durkheim (1897) and later by Linton (especially 1936). It is expressed in the statement of Parsons (1951, p. 5) that—

a social system consists in a plurality of individual actors interacting with each other in a situation which has at least a physical or environmental aspect, actors who are motivated in terms of a tendency to the "optimization of gratification" and whose relation to their situations, including each other, is defined and mediated in terms of a system of culturally structured and shared symbols.

In the analysis of culture contact at Shonto I have found all of these formulations useful and suggestive in their way. I did not find, however, that in and of themselves they furnished satisfactory models for the study of the situation at hand. It was apparent in the case of Shonto that status and role have quantitative as well as qualitative aspects. The American sociocultural system was and is represented in the community by a series of separate agencies working more or less independently of one another, and the effect of these is felt very unevenly in the community. It was clear to me that the trader in particular had opportunities to influence Navaho behavior and responses which are not shared by other White agencies. This fact, like the qualitative aspect of the trader's role, I was able to account for in terms of the history and structure of culture contact (see pp. 231–267).

In order to deal with this quantitative aspect of role, I have conceptualized a general condition of subordination of Navaho society to White society, which is maintained through a cross-cultural power structure in which the position of Shonto Trading Post is preeminent. That is, I have taken the position that owing to their differentiated historical and structural positions, different White agencies have differential capacities to influence Navaho behavior—that of Shonto Trading Post being the greatest.

I find that this notion of variable "cross-cultural influence" in itself is not new. It was hinted at in the first Social Science Research Council acculturation memorandum (Redfield, Linton, and Herskovits, 1936, p. 150), and is implied or suggested in one way or another in various analyses of culture contact (e.g., Linton, 1940, p. 498; Radcliffe-Brown, 1940, p. 202; Malinowski, 1945, pp. 73–76; Summer Seminar on Acculturation, 1954, p. 981). To my knowledge it has not, however, been explicitly formulated, or analyzed in terms of component factors. This is perhaps a consequence of the fact that up to the present time too little attention has been focused on the differential and not infrequently conflicting motives of the different agencies which may be involved in culture contact, particularly where a thoroughly compartmentalized (e.g., Euro-American) culture comes in contact with a folk one (cf. Malinowski, 1945, p. 15 and Summer Seminar on Acculturation, 1954, p. 981). There has been instead a tendency to conceptualize culture contact in terms of the interaction of two complete and internally consistent sociocultural systems.

SUMMARY OF THE PROBLEM

In stating clearly the underlying assumptions upon which the study of Shonto Trading Post was based, I have to some extent distorted the actual sequences of development of the project. Like many another anthropologist going into the field, I did not have my basic assumptions clearly in mind myself when I headed for Shonto in July

1955. I had at that time the sort of acquaintance with the works of Parsons, Malinowski, Linton, and others which is acquired in the course of preparing for doctoral examinations, and my present more intimate familiarity with these works has come about through the necessity of analyzing and classifying the results of my fieldwork. I have not found this kind of experience to be uncommon among my anthropologist acquaintances.

At the time when I began the formal field study of Shonto Trading Post and Community I conceptualized my problem in terms of three basic objectives:

(1) To analyze and describe the total sociocultural environment of the trading post, including all of the institutions of both Navaho and American society which would necessarily bear upon *any* trader in it.

(2) To record, classify, and analyze the total range of behavior of the trader toward his Navaho clientele.

(3) To account for (2) in terms of (1). This would, to my mind, constitute a full description and analysis of the cross-cultural role of the trader in Shonto community, according to the definition of *role* upon which I had determined (see "The Definition of Role," pp. 268–269).

EXECUTION OF THE STUDY

CONDITIONS OF FIELDWORK

My wife and I arrived at Shonto to begin our study on July 1, 1955, and took up residence in a hogan behind the trading post (see fig. 1, H, p. 157). It had been my original intention simply to station myself in the store to observe and record behavior, and later to augment this information with direct interviews around the community. However, this did not prove to be initially feasible. In the first place, no financial support for the project had been obtained, and by this time, I had already determined that the single summer period originally allocated to field study was entirely too short and that I should remain at Shonto at least until the end of the year.

Accordingly, when my wife and I arrived at Shonto I had already made arrangements with the owner to resume my old duties as trader. I stepped back immediately into my accustomed status and role, and continued so throughout the summer and early fall. My actual employment terminated with the lamb drive in October, which I once again conducted, accompanied this time by my wife.

After the lamb drive, I remained at the store and continued to occupy my quarters and receive subsistence, in exchange for assuming all the duties of building, utility, and auto maintenance on the premises (see "The Trading Post Today," pp. 161–165). I had no other responsibilities, and was therefore left free to devote the greatest part of my time directly to the study. This period, beginning about the first of November and lasting until the middle of December, was spent almost entirely within the store building, in observing and recording the behavior of my successor. I was able to use for this purpose the trader's desk behind the counter (see fig. 3, p. 162), in such a way that my note taking was fairly unobtrusive. When convenient, I interrupted my observations for such small services as delivering mail and making small cash sales, hoping thereby to perpetuate as much as possible my status as trader and to distract attention from my anthropological activities.

My covert status as investigator was never at any time acknowledged to the Navaho community. Fortunately, I had since my earliest association with Shonto Trading Post shown a lively curiosity about Navaho society and culture, and had bombarded the customers and particularly the Navaho hired helper with a steady though unsystematic series of questions about them. I had thus acquired a general reputation as being considerably more interested in native life and lore than were my employers, therefore was allowed some leeway in my covert investigations. My employers, as well as my successor, were, of course, informed that I was "studying the store," but they never showed any particular interest in the nature of my investigations, and never looked over my material. They were unaware that their own behavior was being examined and recorded.

At the beginning of 1956 I was persuaded to interrupt my Shonto study long enough to undertake a field survey of Navaho health conditions on behalf of the Bureau of Ethnic Research at the University of Arizona. This enterprise kept me away from Shonto throughout January and February of 1956. However, it had been decided that some of my Shonto data might appropriately be employed in the health study, and therefore Dr. William H. Kelly, the director of the Bureau of Ethnic Research, kindly made arrangements for me to return to Shonto and continue my investigations in such a way as to benefit both the health survey and my own project. I therefore spent a good part of March 1956 at Shonto in assembling and systematizing the income data which I had already gathered, and which appears on pages 94–148 of the present study. I was also enabled to pull together a great deal of my material on social organization and to add significantly to it (see "Social Structure," pp. 54–65). Both of these activities I had intended to postpone until after my return to Tucson; the fact that I was enabled to complete them in the field allowed me to fill many gaps which otherwise would have gone unrectified. Participation in the health survey also gave me the opportunity, not originally contemplated, of investigating the relations of Shonto people with the Tuba City Hospital as revealed in the latter's admission records.

At the conclusion of the health survey on the first of April, I resumed the duties of trader at Shonto for the third and last time. I was not, fortunately, kept particularly busy until the first of May, when wool buying commenced in earnest. I was able to make use of this period for further observation and recording of relations in the store, concentrating this time on the extent and circumstances of Navaho utilization of the trading post for noncommercial purposes. Much of this information is found in pages 184–230. My fieldwork as well as my formal association with Shonto Trading Post came to an end early in May 1956, when my wife and I left the community for the last time.

METHODS

It should be apparent that the primary technique involved in the study of Shonto Trading Post and community was that of participant observation (see F. Kluckhohn, 1940). Since my role of anthropological investigator was never openly avowed to Navahos, it was necessary for me to do most of my recording "after the fact" and in private. This was true in particular throughout my periods of actual employment as trader, when I would not in any case have had time to make sustained notes. The best I could manage was to scribble short phrases of mnemonic devises on the backs of paper sacks or in empty account books, and stuff them into my pockets. These were then expanded into respectable notes during lunch periods and especially evenings in the privacy of my own hogan. As I also had to keep the store accounts every evening, my work day was fairly prolonged. However, my wife rendered invaluable assistance both in making and transcribing notes.

My investigations in the store, even while employed as trader, were not confined exclusively to the silent observation of behavior. Since I had virtually no opportunity to circulate in the community outside the store (see "Role," below), it was necessary for me to obtain straight ethnographic data largely by inquiry. The information contained in "Navaho Life," and to some extent in "Navaho Economics," of this study was obtained partly by direct observation, but even more by a disconnected and ingenuous series of questions addressed to Shonto's Navaho clientele when and as the occasion permitted. As will be apparent in later pages ("Interpersonal Relations," pp. 287–290), the social atmosphere of the trading post freely allows of such exchanges between trader and customer, particularly during the long, quiet periods when there is no actual trading to be done.

Most of the information contained in pages 167–184, as well as historical data in pages 30–53 and 149–167, was obtained by querying Shonto's owner and other traders in the same disinterested and unsystematic way. As in the case of information from Navahos, this information was later recorded in the privacy of the hogan.

In keeping with my determination not to deviate from the role of trader in my relations with Navahos, I did no formal interviewing of any kind. Even my position as health investigator for the Bureau of Ethnic Research was not revealed to the community. I was and am convinced that in an uncompartmentalized folk society (cf. Redfield, 1947) such as Shonto, any outright change of role, unless consecrated by some sort of crisis rite, is impossible, and that any attempt on my part to alter my relations with the community would have been met with confusion and suspicion such as to impede my further investigations. I was not, in any case, primarily interested either in health statistics per se nor in the sort of ethnographic data normally gathered by anthropologists, but in the special economic data which is accessible only and specially to traders, and which therefore flowed to me more or less automatically as long as I did not compromise my accepted status.

The compartmentalization normal to American life made it possible for me to change status somewhat more freely in my relations with my White neighbors. Even here I did not find it advisable to reveal or to discuss the true nature of my study. Fortunately for me, none of my associates took it very seriously, since I did not give the impression in public of working at it very assiduously, and in other ways strove to make light of it. On the other hand, I felt free to take advantage of my temporary status as a health investigator to do a certain amount of formal interviewing of my White neighbors which would have hardly been possible for me as trader. Although I already had ample information on Navaho incomes through the channels of information which are structurally inherent in trading (see especially pp. 184–214), I was able to corroborate and amplify it through direct interviews with the Shonto schoolteachers, the superintendent at Navajo National Monument, and the chief of the Nava-Hopi Unit of the State Department of Public Welfare. I also used the interview technique to obtain genealogical data from the teachers, and medical histories from officials at the Tuba City Hospital. During the earlier phases of the health survey, I also interviewed a number of traders in other parts of the Navaho Reservation, and obtained valuable comparative material data. Throughout this work, as well as at Shonto, my wife rendered invaluable service and conducted numerous additional interviews, particularly with women.

<h3 style="text-align:center">INFORMANTS</h3>

Inasmuch as the study of Shonto was conducted largely by observation rather than by inquiry, it is true in a sense that all of the community's 568 Navaho inhabitants have been my informants. A few individuals, however, have also contributed heavily through verbal response to my numerous queries as well as by giving all kinds of unsolicited information, and these must be reckoned my principal informants. They would not, I hope, recognize themselves under that appellation.

Outstanding among my informants has been the Navaho hired man at Shonto Trading Post, with whom I was in daily contact for an average of 9 hours, and with whom I shared the noon meal. The nature of the Navaho trade (cf. table 36, p. 203) is such that we had the store all to ourselves on numerous occasions for as much as several hours, particularly during the long and severe winter storms when heavy snow all but blocked the store door. We occupied such periods alternately huddled over the stove or pricing, marking, and stocking merchandise, as the occasion demanded. Our work was nearly always accompanied by lively conversation, which consisted principally of idle queries from me and lengthy replies from the hired man. On most occasions he was quite as anxious to gossip about the lives and loves of everyone in the community, including himself, as I was to listen to it, and on quiet afternoons I had only to "open the tap and let him run."

Shonto's Navaho hired man has certainly contributed verbally more to my ethnographic studies of the community (see pp. 53–94) than all other Navaho informants combined. He is a man of fairly high status in the community, not because of his connection with the store but because he is well-to-do in sheep and other property and because he is in all respects a thoroughgoing cultural conservative. He has never been to school, speaks no English, wears long hair, and by his own admission has been off the reservation only twice in his life. In all of these respects he is, of course, a thoroughly untypical trading post hired man, and his duties are necessarily confined to manual labor and to making cash sales. (The ability to add and subtract and to operate the cash register are his only job skills, although, like nearly all Navahos, he can also read numbers.) Fortunately for his contribution to the study, he was sufficiently aware of the limitations of my "Trader Navaho" (see "Communication," pp. 212–214) as to limit his own vocabulary accordingly, with the result that I never had any difficulty in understanding him.

Other important Navaho informants have been the sheepherders with whom I have been associated for periods of several weeks on three occasions (see "Association with Shonto Trading Post," above). Here, as in the store, conditions have often been conducive to ethnographic inquiry as well as to observation, particularly during the long evenings in camp. Here again communication has been confined largely to Trader Navaho, as the store makes a policy of hiring older and more experienced—therefore less educated—Navahos as herders.[1]

---

[1] If the character of the hired man, the sheepherders, and other Navahos occasionally employed at Shonto Trading Post are considered, it becomes immediately apparent that the major qualifications for employment at the store are *lack* of education and accultura-

I have had frequent and close contact with the Navaho employees of Shonto School and Navajo National Monument, as well as with the local tribal councilman. All of them have contributed measurably to the study. Communication with all except the latter has been largely in English. My wife has made friends among the Shonto women, who have contributed additional information.

Although I myself was employed as trader at Shonto during most of the time when my study was carried out, the reader should not assume that I am presenting an analysis of my own behavior. So far as I am able, I have omitted all of my own actions and attitudes from the pages which follow, simply because I am incapable of objective evaluation of them. This is not to say that another or more disinterested student would not have found my actions and attitudes generally comparable to those of other traders.

Throughout most of my employment at Shonto Trading Post, the owner of the store also was present at least one day a week (as required by his duties as claims agent—see "Railroad Work," pp. 129–133). On many occasions he was on hand for the better part of a week. I have therefore had ample opportunity to observe his behavior and relations over several years, and he has been my principal White informant. He has, however, been far from the only one. In the periods between and to some extent overlapping my own employment I have had the opportunity to observe closely and to associate on intimate terms with four other "hired traders" (like myself) at Shonto, and all of these have played their part in my study.

Shonto's owner is a man of about 40, who is married and has three young children. The entire family lives in Flagstaff during most of the year so as to allow the children to attend school. Like many another trader, Shonto's owner was born and had lived much of his life in the town of Farmington, some 200 miles east of Shonto. He holds an A.B. from Colorado State College of Education at Greeley, and was for some years a high school teacher and coach in Farmington. Subsequently, he became associated with one of the wholesale houses in that town, and through it with the Indian trade. His father-in-law, a trader for most of his life, helped set Shonto's owner up in his first store at Oljeto, which he ran for 7 years before buying Shonto in 1945.

Hired traders whom I have known and observed at Shonto have included a retired small businessman and his wife from Prescott (who came to the reservation for the adventure and were hired by Shonto's owner in the service of Freemasonry) ; a young former logger from

---

tion, in marked contrast to all other White agencies employing Navaho help. Shonto's owner professes contempt for long hair as a symbol of inferior status, but he has not had a short-haired Navaho employee for years. This is part of the special role of the trading post with its emphasis on preservation of the status quo—see pp. 290–296.

Datil, N. Mex., and his Navaho wife; a student of anthropology fresh out of college (another one, that is) ; and a very silent bachelor, who has spent most of his adult life running trading posts in every part of the Navaho country, but has never owned one. This last was my immediate successor and the individual whose behavior I was able to observe in special detail during November and December of 1955. However, I found the role behavior of all of them to be closely similar in spite of their extremely disparate backgrounds, and all of them are a part of the composite which in later pages is designated as "Shonto's trader." [2]

Other traders in every part of the Navaho country have contributed, for the most part unwittingly, to the study of Shonto. The trader at Inscription House, some 20 miles to the west (by road—see map 3) has been of special value in many ways. He is the father-in-law of my employer at Shonto, and at the time of the study was in partnership with him in the Inscription House venture. Thanks to this connection, I have had a long association with Inscription House as well as with Shonto, and I have "filled in" as trader there for periods of several days on a few occasions. The Inscription House trader is a native of the Farmington area who has had over 40 years' continuous experience in the Navaho trade—greater than that of any other still-active trader. I have made frequent use of his historical insights and judgments in the pages which follow.

Other traders whom I have known, both personally and professionally, and who have contributed their part to this study are or were those at Navajo Mountain, Coppermine, Cow Springs, Red Lake, Tuba City, Kayenta, Oljeto, Dennehotso, Chilchinbeto, Mexican Hat, Chinle, Lukachukai, Ganado, Fort Defiance, Gallup, and Carsons. Many of these were my friends and neighbors as well as informants.

Far and away my most valuable sources of verbal information have been my employer at Shonto and his father-in-law at Inscription House. As with my Navaho acquaintances, they are accustomed to my curiosity on all manner of subjects, which is no doubt appropriate in a "college kid," and freely answered my various questions about stores and store operation. They are largely responsible for the local historical data which appear toward the end of "Background" (pp. 30–53) and especially on pages 149–167), as well as for most of the financial information in "Trading Post Economics."

I have also had a few White informants who were officially such during my temporary health survey stint. Shonto's owner furnished me with economic and income data from past years, which I lacked.

---

[2] The reader may infer from these statements that personnel turnover at Shonto Trading Post is extremely high. This is a condition which is invariably encountered among hired traders—i.e., in every trading post which is not actually operated by its owner.

The schoolteachers in the community gave me invaluable genealogical data, as well as information on the nature and frequency of adult Navaho contacts with the school, and income figures for school employees. The superintendent at Navajo National Monument provided the same information about his Navaho employees. The Shonto missionary gave me information about his activities, particularly in transporting local residents to the hospital. The admissions clerk at the Tuba City Hospital gave me invaluable information about Navaho use thereof, and the medical officer in charge gave me the purely medical side of the picture. The district supervisor at Tuba City (with jurisdiction over Shonto) provided information about Navaho contacts and relations with other Government agencies. The director of the Nava-Hopi Unit of the Arizona State Department of Public Welfare (himself briefly a trader at Shonto) supplied overall income figures for Shonto welfare recipients. Finally, the assistant to the general superintendent at Window Rock furnished me with his own computations of total Navaho income for 1955. These appear in tables 26 and 27 (pp. 146–147) and have since been published in Young (1955, p. 65).

RECORDS AND DOCUMENTS

In addition to my human informants, I have had access to various written records of Navaho life at Shonto. The contribution of most of these has been supplementary, but a few were absolutely basic to the study—so much so that it could hardly have been successfully concluded without their aid.

First and foremost are the various routine economic and income records kept at Shonto Trading Post as a regular part of its business operation. These have furnished the great bulk of the data in pp. 94–148, and nearly all the financial data in pages 184–214. They include ledger books, current account books, pawn accounts, duplicate records of old accounts and of commodity and barter transactions, notations of credit limits, wool and lamb purchase books, cash register tapes, and above all those capsule histories of trading post life, the day sheets (cf. Carson, 1954). They include also the paycheck stubs, payroll records, correspondence from the Railroad Retirement Board, and other data on railroad earnings which accrue to the trader in his capacity as claims agent (see "Railroad Work," pp. 129–133). Additional income data have been obtained from the records of Shonto School, Navajo National Monument, the Railroad Retirement Board, and the Arizona State Department of Public Welfare.

Of almost equal value has been the painstakingly accurate school census compiled by Shonto's White schoolteachers. Since my position as trader never allowed me the opportunity to circulate freely in the community (see "Role," below) or to do informant work openly, it provided me only with such vague and often incorrect information about families and relationships as I could gather from silent observation. The school census, however, more than made up the deficit; it furnished me with information which it would have taken me weeks to accumulate through my own endeavors. Relationships between separate households and especially residence groups have been further clarified by the 1936 Official Navaho enumeration, a very battered copy of which has somehow found its way into the hands of the Shonto trader. These two documents, the school census of 1955 and the tribal census of 1936, provided the foundation upon which has been built the mass of information on social organization presented in pp. 54–65. The map compiled by the teachers in connection with their census is also the basis for map 3 herein.

Admission records at Tuba City Hospital, to which I was given free access, furnished me with invaluable data on the nature and frequency of Navaho use of the hospital. Because of the incompleteness of the data, however, they did not permit me to make valid statistical compilations. Also of value were the Navaho income figures compiled at Window Rock and furnished to me through the courtesy of the assistant to the general superintendent.

I have, of course, made extensive use of the published literature for such historical and comparative material as I could find. Two little-known works deserve special mention in the former regard: Richard Van Valkenburgh's "A Short History of the Navajo People" (coauthored by John C. McPhee, 1938) and his "Dine Bikeyah" (1941). Both of these contain a mass of local historical data carefully compiled from a wide variety of Government archives (cf. Kluckhohn and Spencer, 1940, p. 70) and not found to my knowledge in any other source.

Prior to my own investigations, Shonto had not been the scene of any ethnological studies (although local antiquities have received widespread attention from archeologists). The neighboring and closely similar community of Navajo Mountain, however, was investigated in 1938 by Malcolm Carr Collier. Unfortunately, this material has never been published. It is summarized briefly in Leighton and Kluckhohn's (1948, pp. 139–145) "Children of the People" under the caption "The People of Navajo Mountain: Harmony in the Backwoods" and as such remains the only published material on any community close to or comparable with Shonto. Ethnologists, who usually show a marked preference for the "backwoods," have for some reason avoided them in the Navaho country.

SUMMARY OF SOURCES

Background (part 1): Information on the physical setting is based on my personal familiarity with the region plus a few published sources. Earlier phases of Navaho history are extracted from the literature, while more recent information comes from first-hand observation supplied largely by Shonto's owner.

Navaho life: Account of social organization is based heavily on the school census, augmented by the tribal census of 1936 and by a great deal of verbal information supplied by many Whites and Navahos in the community. My wife obtained some of the information through direct interviews. Remaining portions of this section are based largely on my own observation, various random inquiries of Navahos, and comparable published material.

Navaho economics: Data on economic structure and function in opening pages is essentially ethnographic and was obtained in much the same way as ethnographic data in the preceding section. Income figures and detailed information on various economic pursuits are based on my own observations and especially on the numerous and varied economic records kept at Shonto Trading Post by myself and others. They were slightly augmented by income figures furnished by other agencies from their files.

Background (part 2): Historical data is derived to some extent from the published literature, but much more from first-hand information furnished by traders at Shonto and Inscription House. Descriptive material comes from my personal familiarity.

Trading Post economics: This discussion derives very heavily from my own observations and from information supplied wittingly and unwittingly by my employers, the trader at Inscription House, and salesmen for the off-reservation general wholesale houses. It owes little or nothing to published sources. Modern economic analysis is consistently processual rather than structural, the latter approach being confined to ideal models presented in elementary business textbooks (e.g., Beckman and Engle, 1951; Comish, 1946; Nystrom, 1930). As for actual descriptions of retail operations similar to Shonto Trading Post (e.g., Atherton, 1939; Carson, 1954), they tend to be flavored with a kind of contrived nostalgia which renders them practically useless for straight comparative purposes.

Retail trade, Community Services, the Structure of Contact, and Cross-Cultural Role: Based almost entirely upon my own observations, records specially devised and kept by me, and standard trading post records.

The Entrepreneur in Culture Contact: Contains no new material on Shonto.

ROLE

Unlike anthropologists who work openly, I cannot claim that I have gained the confidence and the sympathy of the natives to a degree not accorded other White men. To the best of my knowledge and belief, I remain in the eyes of Shonto nothing more nor less than a trader, and neither better nor worse liked or trusted than the run of other traders. Certainly, I do not possess any superordinate personality traits which would enable me to obtain special information which does not normally accrue to a trader.

Throughout the study of Shonto my status as anthropological investigator was suppressed as much as possible among both Navahos and Whites, but especially among the former. I attempted in every way possible to sustain my status as trader even when I was not actually employed as such. My purpose in this was aided by the fact that I continued to reside on the trading post premises and to take my position behind the counter in the store (see fig. 3, p. 162), a prerogative normally reserved for the trader. It was and is my belief that the special type of information which I sought would accrue to me most readily by maintaining the trader's role throughout.

My relations with my Navaho neighbors at Shonto were, therefore, exactly such as are described throughout the study which follows. This is not to imply that it is a study of my own behavior, but simply that, had it been undertaken by anyone else, it could well be.

The special advantages of the trader's status as an observation point from which to gain a fresh and different view of Navaho life, and particularly economic life, have already been dwelt upon at considerable length. Some of its disadvantages must also be made clear. To begin with, every trader is physically a prisoner of his store day and night—the endless complex of activities connected not only with operating the business but also with looking after the physical plant at Shonto (see "The Trading Post Today," pp. 161–165) were such that I had no opportunity to leave the store premises (see fig. 1, p. 157) for weeks at a time. The close personal familiarity with other parts of Shonto community upon which I have drawn in succeeding pages was gained almost entirely during periods when I was not working at the store, and particularly in the course of my archeological surveys. During the entire period of my trading post employment, I never had the opportunity to attend a Navaho ritual performance of any kind in the community. For an anthropologist living on the Navaho Reservation, this must constitute some kind of a record.

Behavior appropriate to the trader's role has inevitably been determined to a considerable extent by the various individuals who have actually occupied it—my fellow traders and their predecessors. This has placed some additional restrictions on the present study. Most modern traders have shown themselves personally indifferent and contemptuous toward native Navaho beliefs and practices, although accepting them as appropriate for Navahos (cf. pp. 267–297). This position has perhaps been taken deliberately, as a means of emphasizing the separate and superior status of the trader (see "Trader Behavior," pp. 210–212). At any rate, I found that as a trader I could not inquire too openly and persistently into native culture patterns without being suspected of ulterior purposes. Beyond a certain point, my inquiries were likely to meet with a suspicious "What do you want to know for?" which is the common experience of traders and Government officials as distinguished from at least the more adept anthropologists.

Finally, there is no occasion upon which a trader may legitimately employ an interpreter. On the one hand, the area of Navaho culture in which he is specifically interested (i.e., economics) is entirely amenable to discussion in the Trader Navaho jargon, which has been developed for that precise purpose (see "Communication," pp. 212–214). On the other hand, his interest in other areas of Navaho life is not supposed to carry to the point of spending his own good money for an interpreter through whom he can inquire into them. In consequence none of the information contained in the present study was obtained through an interpreter.

In sum, the trading post offers the worst possible base of operations for ethnographic research. In addition to trained anthropologists, both Government officials (e.g., Reagan, 1934) and missionaries (e.g., Haile, 1935, 1938 a, b, etc.) have contributed to some extent to the literature on Navaho culture, while traders have contributed virtually nothing. These limitations will be apparent throughout the present work, which, so far as I know, contributes nothing new to the study of native lore and customs. Religion in particular will be found to have received perhaps less attention here than in any other study of the Navaho of comparable length.

Insofar as I had any individual role apart from that of trader, I am unable to evaluate it. To the best of my knowledge and belief, my age, appearance, dress, and speech, no less than my behavior, were well within the conventional limits for traders. My physical appearance is in some respects similar to that of Shonto's owner, particularly in the dimension of circumference, and this circumstance caused us to be frequently associated in Navaho speech. He was habitually designated as *nimazi* (the spherical one) and I as *nimazi yazhi* or *nimazi bik'is* (the little spherical one or the spherical one's kinsman). Whether or not this latter implication was ever taken seriously, I do not know.

Throughout my earlier association with Shonto Trading Post, I believe that my one personal eccentricity in the eyes of the Navaho community was my lack of a wife. Jokingly, and perhaps seriously as well, this was attributed to avarice—it was not, at any rate, considered normal. In 1956, after my marriage, I found my acceptance in many situations to be considerably improved.

My White neighbors at Shonto School and at Betatakin (see map 3) were close personal friends, with both of whom my wife and I had frequent and reciprocal visiting relationships. Relations with these individuals were purely personal. My relations with my fellow traders, on the other hand, were somewhat more complex and compartmentalized. I have been employed as trader at Shonto three times, have filled in on several occasions at Inscription House, and have also been offered the trader's job at Oljeto, Cow Springs, and Coppermine. I take this as signifying that from a purely professional point of view, my behavior has been well up to trader standards. On the other hand, my education and my academic orientations, both of which are undoubtedly manifest in my speech, are such as to prevent my being fully accepted personally. (Aside from our common social and enviromental situation, the two interests which I principally shared with my employer were politics and baseball, and throughout 3 years our casual conversation was largely confined to them—although in both cases our individual persuasions were somewhat at variance.)

Among my trader associates, I never attempted to play down or to belittle my college associations, although I recognized that they were a mark of differentiation between them and myself. On the contrary, I found that my status as a "college kid" allowed me considerable leeway in pursuing interests which would not otherwise have been appropriate. At the same time, it has undoubtedly stood in the way of full acceptance by traders as "their kind of people."

My purpose in undertaking the Shonto study, and in setting down my observations and conclusions hereinafter, has been to draw down upon the trader neither approval nor disapproval, but only the attention which I believe to be his due. It is my earnest hope that nothing I have said will be interpreted as an exposé, or as implying censure of the trader. It is necessary for me to reiterate that I also have engaged in credit saturation, delaying checks, tampering with the mail, misrepresenting the outside world, and all the other devious devices by which the trader maintains his position in the community (see pp. 267–297). If I had not done these things I would not have been a trader—and this study could never have been made.

BIASES

Five important agencies of White contact with Navaho life are traders, Government officials, missionaries, residents of off-reservation towns, and anthropologists. At one time or another in the past 10 years, I have found myself in, or closely associated with, all but one of these. I grew up in an Indian Service family, and in addition worked on behalf of the Bureau on my economic survey in 1950 (to the extent of sporting that ubiquitous status symbol, the Government car). I traded at Shonto off and on from 1953 to 1956, and lived in Flagstaff for a time in 1949. Also, during all this time, I was striving for acceptance as an anthropologist.

It is my hope, therefore, that the biases which are inherent in each of the statuses with respect to all the others have to some extent canceled each other out. I do not feel, for example, that I have the common trader's prejudice against the Government (cf. Schmedding, 1951), nor the predisposition of the average Flagstaff resident against the anthropologist. To the best of my ability, I have tried to maintain some sort of balance in dealing with each of these in the pages which follow.

On the other hand, I have never been closely associated with missionaries. I am conscious, moreover, that I share in the general prejudice against them that is harbored by all of the other functionaries whom I have named, and particularly by many anthropologists (e.g., Kluckhohn and Leighton, 1946; pp. 82–85; Reichard, 1949). Among all the contact agencies whose activities are chronicled herein, therefore, it is probable that the Shonto missionary has fared worst at my hands.

I also hold to some extent the prejudice of Government officials and especially traders toward the Navaho tribal organization (cf. "Intracultural Relations at the Contact Level," pp. 253–256), although I like and admire its present chairman. My general antipathy arises out of a personal dislike and disapproval of a good many councilmen of my acquaintaince, at Shonto and elsewhere.

I am conscious of a vague sense of liking Navahos collectively, as neighbors and as a people, perhaps somewhat better than White Americans as a whole. I do not, however, admire them for possessing any special virtues or qualities not found in White people, and it is more than probable that my liking for them stems from a sense of my own superiority rather than theirs. My personal relations with Navaho individuals, insofar as my status as trader allowed me to have any, run the gamut from friendship to hostility and are about evenly divided in either direction. However, probably because of my institutionalized role as trader, there are no extremes in this range of variation—no Navaho individuals whom I either like or dislike nearly as much as I do some White people.

My attitude toward Navaho culture, like that of a very large number of White residents of the Navaho Reservation, is ambivalent. It is derived less from my participation in any one pattern of culture contact than from the fact that since early boyhood I have considered the Navaho Reservation as my home. I have never favored the preservation of Navaho ways of life for their own sake, or because I felt that there was anything intrinsically superior about them. On the contrary, I believe that Navahos must adapt themselves however they can to the White world around them sufficiently to support themselves by their own efforts. On the other hand I have thoroughly enjoyed life on the reservation as I have known it, and I resent at least personally any threatened change. I, too, am haunted by the vision of my favorite canyons and mesas littered with papers and bottles; of endless rows of roadside curio stands vying with each other in sheer hideousness; and of an unending procession of casual and unappreciative visitors in slacks and sunglasses. These things to me are a threat to a cherished way of life—yet I recognize that they are only the incidental though inevitable byproducts of a fabulously high material standard of living.

Personally, I like old-fashioned, "unacculturated" Navahos better than most of their more educated offspring, and I appreciate and value the hairknot as their symbol (see "Dress and Ornamentation," pp. 79–81). My attitude stems largely from the fact that the older folk do not manifest the symptoms of culture conflict, such as drunkenness and hostility, often found in their descendants. It is also, perhaps, due to the fact that they seldom challenge my superior status.

The greatest danger of personal bias to the present study is that it may have led me to overestimate and overstate the importance of the trader in Navaho life and in Navaho-White relations. If this is so, it must be because I have not even yet entirely shed my own role as trader. It is something which only other and more disinterested students of the Navaho scene can determine.

PREPARATION OF THE REPORT

The report on the Shonto study, which occupies succeeding pages, has been prepared entirely in residence at the University of Arizona. This undertaking has occupied most of the period between September 1956 and September 1957. It has been made possible by a Wenner-Gren Pre-Doctoral Fellowship Grant and by additional assistance from the Colonel McClintock Education Fund and from the Eban Comins Fellowship Fund, all of which are herewith gratefully acknowledged.

This study was originally submitted to the Faculty of Anthropology in the College of Letters and Science at the University of Arizona, in partial fulfillment of the requirements for the degree of doctor of philosophy.

I am indebted to Barton A. Wright, of the Museum of Northern Arizona, for preparation of the maps, charts, and text figures, and to Messrs. Bud DeWald, Parker Hamilton, Christy G. Turner II, and Arthur H. White for supplying several of the photographic illustrations that I have included.

PERSONAL ACKNOWLEDGMENTS

So far as is possible without compromising the principles of either clarity or courtesy, I have followed the policy throughout this study of not mentioning names. A great many individuals, both White and Navaho, have contributed significantly to its development, and these will, I hope, recognize themselves as described in preceding pages. I trust that they will also recognize and accept this anonymous acknowledgment of their assistance, as well as the considerations which have made it necessary.

In a folk society such as still exists on the Navaho Reservation, however, professional and personal relations are often inseparable. Throughout the years since 1946 I have come under heavy personal obligation to a very great number of individuals for their generosity, hospitality, and assistance in ways too numerous to mention. All of these people deserve nothing less than citation by name, and it is my hope that they will find themselves included in the lists which follow.

I cannot begin more appropriately than by avowing my incalculable indebtedness to my mother, Lucy W. Adams. By bringing me to live on the Navaho Reservation at an early and impressionable age, she set me, albeit unwittingly, on the course which has led irrevocably to the present study and to my chosen career. To her and to my brother Ernest, who was my closest companion not only in boyhood but for years afterward, I owe much for the stimulation of sharing my earliest and still some of my most vivid experiences with the Navaho world.

Personally as well as professionally, I am deeply indebted to the numerous Navaho traders and their families with whom I have been associated over the years. Foremost among these in every way are Mr. and Mrs. Reuben Heflin, Mr. and Mrs. O. J. ("Stokes") Carson, and Mr. and Mrs. David M. Goss. Other traders whom I have known and liked, and whose hospitality I have often enjoyed, are or were Mr. and Mrs. Coyt Patterson, Mr. and Mrs. Floyd Boyle (deceased), Mr. and Mrs. Ed Smith, Mr. and Mrs. Willard Layton, Mr. and Mrs.

Ray Hunt, Mr. and Mrs. Bennett Hyde, Mr. and Mrs. Elvin Kerley, Miles Hedrick, Sam Drolet, and H. T. Donald.

My fellow White residents of Shonto community have been the finest kind of neighbors, and remain among my closest personal friends. Among these are Mr. and Mrs. Foy L. Young, Mr. and Mrs. John A. Aubuchon, Arthur H. White, Eddie Thompson, and Gloria Jones.

I am especially indebted to a few of the outstanding Navaho personalities at Shonto for their special contributions to my work and to my insight into the "Navaho mind." Individuals who, if they knew any English, might or might not recognize themselves in the pages which follow are Dick Brown, Bob Black, Pipeline, Jerry Salt, Joe Reese, Greenstone, Mike Calamity, Sam Edgewater, Dan Cly, Percy Shootinglady, John Manheimer, Jim Teamster, Hubert Laughter, and Beshii. Notable among the weaker sex are Nancy Fuller, Mary Black, Della Calamity, Ruth Adakai, Janet Talker, Helen Hudgens, and Fanny Blackgoat.

I have several educated Navaho friends, whom I admire for their ability to move freely and with confidence in two worlds. Among these in particular are Dana Natani Begay, Rudolph Russel, John D. Wallace, Howard Hawthorne, Leigh Hubbard, and Bert Tallsalt. All of them have also given me insights into the "Navaho mind." I have a strong conviction that if there is any enduring collective future for the Navaho people, it lies in the hands of men such as these.

Government officials at Window Rock and elsewhere whose friendship as well as whose information I have valued are Robert W. Young, Howard Johnson, Rudolph Zweifel, Jack South, Gene Ellison, and Lisbeth Eubank. From my youth I also remember with affection the Fred W. Croxen family, and my recent reacquaintance with the entire family has done much to refresh my memory of conditions on the Navaho Reservation as they existed 20 years ago.

Throughout the years when I lived and worked in the Shonto area, I have maintained close and cordial relations with the Museum of Northern Arizona in Flagstaff. I should like to express my appreciation not only of the museum as an institution, but also and particularly for the friendship, hospitality, and stimulation which I have received from individual members of the staff. Outstanding among these have been the director, Harold S. Colton, as well as Mrs. Colton, and Mr. and Mrs. Malcolm F. Farmer.

In the academic world I am conscious of an incalculable collective obligation to the faculty of the Department of Anthropology at the University of Arizona, and of a pride in my association with them. To Dr. Emil W. Haury, chairman of the Department, I am indebted for his encouragement and optimism at every phase of my career at the University of Arizona. My greatest intellectual debt is to Dr. Edward H. Spicer for the wisdom, sympathy, and permissiveness with which he has guided the Shonto study, to say nothing of my general intellectual development, from beginning to end. I am under obligation also to Dr. Harry T. Getty, Mrs. Clara Lee Tanner, and Dr. William H. Kelly for their specific contributions and suggestions. I am further indebted to all of the above and to all of the other members of the anthropology faculty at the University of Arizona for the pleasure and stimulation of their association in what has certainly been the most enjoyable educational experience of my life.

Nettie, my wife, has not undertaken the arduous clerical work involved in this report, nor has she presumed to correct my grammar and spelling. Her contribution throughout every phase of the work has been of a far higher order.

PART 1. THE COMMUNITY

BACKGROUND

The far northwestern reaches of the Navaho Indian Reservation, spanning the Arizona-Utah boundary east of the Colorado River and south of the San Juan, probably need little introduction for most readers. Through the pages of Arizona Highways, The National Geographic Magazine, and a host of other travel books and articles, the region has become one of the best known, photographically, in the Southwest. Outstanding attractions such as Monument Valley, Rainbow Bridge, Navajo Mountain, Tsegi (or Segi, Sagi) Canyon, and the spectacular Betatakin and Keet Seel cliff dwellings have received a measure of nationwide recognition.

MAP 1.—Northeastern Arizona and adjoining States.

Renowned along with the natural features of the region is its
Navaho Indian population, believed by photographers and travelers
to be exceptionally picturesque. Scattered Navaho settlements from
Kayenta to Kaibito and from Black Mesa to the San Juan are served
by a string of isolated and more or less primitive trading posts (see
maps 1 and 2), the last outposts of Anglo-American penetration in
Navaho Land. Among these is Shonto Trading Post, focus of the
present study.

PHYSICAL SETTING

Primary access to the northwestern Navaho country is afforded by a
graded road leaving paved U.S. 89 sixty-five miles north of Flagstaff, Ariz., and proceeding northwest for 13 miles along the Moencopi
Valley to Tuba City (see map 1). This little community of some 200

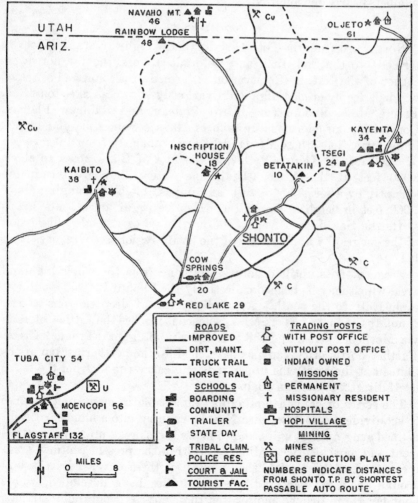

MAP 2.—Northwestern Navaho Reservation.

persons, originally a Mormon farming colony, is the principal administrative center for the western Navaho area, and includes the area's only hospital, court, and jail, as well as its largest Indian school and numerous other facilities.

Beyond Tuba City an inferior graded road continues northwestward for 75 miles, skirting the northern scarp of Black Mesa and passing through the narrow defile of Marsh Pass, until it reaches Kayenta, the crossroads of the northern Navaho country (maps 1 and 2). This community, founded by John and Louisa Wetherill in 1909 and subsequently made famous by them (cf. Gillmor and Wetherill, 1934), is the site of a large new Navaho boarding school, which opened in 1954 and is rapidly gaining importance on the strength of recent uranium developments to the north and east. Its present population numbers nearly one hundred.

GEOGRAPHY

Northward from the Tuba City-Kayenta "highway" (as it is locally termed) to the San Juan and Colorado Rivers, the far northwest corner of the Navaho Reservation is formed of a connected series of wooded, deeply eroded highlands, variously known as Skeleton Mesa, Paiute Mesa, Shonto (or Shato) Plateau, and Rainbow Plateau. Comprising an enormous upwarp of Navajo Sandstone and underlying formations, these highlands rise continuously from an elevation of 5,600 feet in Klethla Valley, at the foot of Black Mesa, to about 8,000 feet at the Arizona-Utah line. Here they are terminated abruptly by a series of gigantic and impassable cliffs, ranging above 2,000 feet in height. Beyond, a broken series of much lower mesas skirts the San Juan River to the north. (For extended discussion of the geography and geology of the entire region, see Gregory, 1916, 1917.)

Because of its uptilted nature, drainage from the whole highland area, which may be termed collectively the Shonto Plateau, is almost exclusively to the south. A parallel series of deep canyons carries runoff to the foot of Black Mesa, whence it reaches the Little Colorado via Moencopi Wash and the San Juan via Laguna (Tyende) Creek. Farther north, other canyons have cut into the northern scarp of the plateau at their extreme upper ends and carry runoff from the scarp itself directly to the San Juan.

The series of canyons and cliffs, impassable in many places, serve to subdivide the northwestern Navaho country into a number of well-defined geographical units, and in many cases break up Navaho settlement and movement accordingly. Within the present century, trading posts have been established in each of these restricted areas, and around them regular trading communities have developed, whose boundaries are defined more often than not by geographic barriers.

Among them, the Shonto trading community occupies roughly the southwestern quarter of the total Shonto Plateau highland.

Shonto Trading Post is located in the central of three parallel canyons draining the Shonto Plateau to the south, about 8 miles upstream from its mouth. The area regularly served by it, termed the Shonto Community in this study, is delimited to the east and west by the first and third of the canyons—the deep and almost impassable Tsegi to the east and the much smaller Cow Springs Canyon to the west. To the north and south, respectively, the extreme limits of the community are set by the northern scarp of the Shonto Plateau at Cow Canyon (not the same as Cow Springs Canyon), and by the northern scrap of Black Mesa at Klethla Valley. The irregular area thus defined has very roughly the shape of a highly elongated triangle, with its long dimension north-south and its base at the south. Maximum dimensions are about 30 miles north-south and 15 miles east-west.

Adjacent to Shonto on all sides are other trading communities, each called after the store which supplies it. To the west, the area between Cow Springs Canyon and Navajo Canyon is the Inscription House area; beyond Navajo Canyon lies the Kaibito community. Northwest of Shonto, the Navajo Mountain community occupies the Rainbow Plateau and Paiute Mesa. Far to the northeast, the Oljeto (or Oljetoh, Oljato) area includes Cow Canyon and the low mesas north of it. Many of the people here traded at Shonto, coming up from Cow Canyon on a very rough horse trail, until their area was made accessible from Oljeto by construction of a uranium road in 1953. Skeleton Mesa, the connected highland northeast of Shonto, remains uninhabited. Further south, Tsegi Canyon and adjacent Marsh Pass and Long House Valley belong to the Tsegi area served by a small Navaho-owned store in Marsh Pass. The lowland areas east of Marsh Pass trade at Kayenta, where three trading posts are now located.

Due south of Shonto, the northern portion of immense Black Mesa is unique in having no trading post of its own. The widely scattered Navaho population trade principally at Shonto, but also at Red Lake, Cow Springs, Tsegi, and Kayenta, all located at the foot of the mesa. Cow Springs and Red Lake, jointly owned and operated until recently as a single enterprise, are located southwest of Shonto. Both serve the heavily agricultural settlements of lower Klethla Valley. Beyond them lies the Tuba City community.

TOPOGRAPHY

The Shonto area spans the entire width of the Shonto Plateau from north to south, and its elevations and topography are such as have been described for the region in general. In addition to the overall north-south slope, there is a secondary slope from the rim of Tsegi

Canyon at the east to Cow Springs Canyon at the west. Besides its three major canyons, the plateau is incised with innumerable small watercourses, all tending in a southerly or southwesterly direction, toward Klethla Valley. Surface contour throughout most of the Shonto area is fairly irregular, marked by numerous small detached mesas, ridges, bluffs, and rocky outcrops. Only in the extreme south, on the Klethla Valley floodplain, is there an extensive level area.

GEOLOGY

The entire Shonto Plateau is capped by a stratum of Navaho Sandstone 200 to 300 feet in thickness. The region was at one time denuded of all soil cover, presenting an unbroken surface of naked rock such as may still be seen in areas to the east and west. Except in its three major canyon drainages subsequent deposition has been chiefly in the form of coarse wind-blown sand, which now covers the more level portions of the plateau to a depth of 1 to 5 feet. However, many small expanses of exposed bedrock remain throughout the Shonto area, and nearly all slopes are devoid of soil. It is doubtful if the soil cover anywhere exceeds 5 feet in depth.

Because of the peculiar geology, the common type of gully erosion found throughout the Navaho country does not occur in the Shonto area, except in Klethla Valley. Small watercourses on the Shonto Plateau tend to have sloping, sandy walls and rock floors. Of the major canyons, Shonto and Cow Springs both present steep, unbroken sandstone walls 150 to 250 feet in height. Much deeper Tsegi is cut down through the Navajo into underlying sandstone formations, so that its steep walls descend in a series of terraces, having a total height of nearly 800 feet.

The floors of Tsegi and Cow Springs Canyons are formed by shallow alluvial deposits, frequently overlain with aeolian sand and cut by deep arroyos which reach bedrock.[3] Shonto Canyon, by contrast, is unique among the canyons in the Navaho country in that its alluvial floor is aggrading instead of eroding. At some time in the past the mouth of Shonto Canyon was blocked by an enormous rockslide, with the result that most of the canyon became deeply filled with alluvium. The slide has served to impound water as well as soil, and the floor of the canyon is today so waterlogged that Shonto Trading Post is able to pump its water from a depth of less than 10 feet. Extensive marshes occur farther downstream. As a consequence, the small permanent stream in upper Shonto Canyon flows upon the alluvial surface, free of any natural channel. It is confined by artificial banks and by plantings of cottonwood.

Aside from the canyons, alluvial deposits in the Shonto area occur only in Klethla Valley, the broad floodplain at the southern margin of

---

[3] For a detailed description of the geology of Tsegi, see Hack, 1945

the Shonto Plateau which is formed by downwash from Black Mesa, and overlies the Navaho Sandstone. It is constituted of the heavy blue adobe, familiar to travelers in the northern Southwest, which results from the decomposition of Mancos Shale on the side of the mesa above. Klethla Valley exhibits the typical pattern of gully erosion found in adobe soils everywhere, and is totally unlike any other portion of the Shonto area.

WATER SUPPLY

Permanent surface streams occur only in Tsegi Canyon and the upper reaches of Shonto Canyon. Elsewhere, drainage is intermittent, but the rock bottoms in most watercourses permit a maximum of conservation in small pools, waterpockets, and impounds. Supplementary water supply comes from a couple of small dams in Cow Springs Canyon and from numerous stock tanks on the plateau. There are, in addition, four deep wells, with the conventional windmill pumps, in various parts of the area. Shonto Trading Post, with its electric pump and unfailing water supply, is the most important single water source in the Shonto area.

VEGETATION

Vegetation varies with altitude, as in the Colorado Plateau generally. The lowest portions of the Shonto area, in the south, support only a cover of bunchgrasses—principally gramma—and hardy shrubs, prominent among which is Mormon tea. At about 6,500 feet elevation, the complex is joined by a dense growth of sagebrush which covers the greater part of the Shonto area, extending upward to about 8,000 feet. With sagebrush comes a scattered growth of juniper, which is augmented by pinyon at a slightly higher elevation. In the vicinity of Shonto itself, the country presents a savannalike appearance, with piñon, juniper and oak clustered densely along ridges and slopes, and open stretches of sagebrush and tall grass in between. A little farther north, the woody cover becomes dense, extending to the northern limits of the Shonto area. At its extreme upper end, juniper has ceased, but the heavy stand of large piñons is augmented by a few Ponderosa pine and two small groves of aspen, as well as numerous thickets of Gambel's oak.

Watercourses exhibit, in addition, willow and numerous woody shrubs. Cottonwoods have been planted in Cow Springs and Shonto Canyons, and occur near springs in one or two other places.

CLIMATE

Meteorological records have been kept for several years at Navajo National Monument (Betatakin), within the Shonto area. A 10-year average, from 1940 to 1950, reveals a mean annual temperature of 49.9°, with extreme monthly means of 71.9° in July and 29.6° in

January. Extreme average maximum and minimum temperatures are 87.5° in July and 19.3° in January. The highest temperature ever recorded is 100°; lowest −12°.

The annual precipitation averages 12.80 inches, distributed remarkably evenly throughout the year. The lowest average month is June, with 0.35 inches, and the highest August, with 1.62 inches.

Traces of snowfall have been recorded in every month of the year. However, 90 percent of snow falls in the 4 months from December through March. The average annual snowfall is 52.3 inches. The highest average month is February, with 14.9 inches. Freezing temperatures have occurred in every month save July and August, and the growing season averages little more than 100 days. A mean 4.5-inch precipitation is received during the growing season. A generalized description of the climate of the Navaho country is that of Field (1953).

HISTORICAL SETTING

A curious anomaly of the Shonto country is the fact that its prehistory seems to be considerably better known than its recent history. The rise and fall of the Puebloan people who occupied the area a thousand years ago have been charted in detail through the work of numerous archeologists. By contrast, the history of the Navaho settlement and even of European penetration into the same area remain shrouded in mystery which persists into the present century.

PREHISTORY

Among anthropologists, the Shonto area is chiefly famous as the original homeland of the Kayenta branch of the Anasazi or prehistoric Pueblo people. Relics of their prehistoric occupation are found upon almost every acre of the region, and include the celebrated Betatakin and Keet Seel ruins. The prehistoric farmers perhaps sought out the deeply incised highlands deliberately, as the best watered portion of the lower San Juan basin. Following the tremendous social amalgamation which occurred in Pueblo life during the 12th and 13th centuries, however, the limited soil resources of the highlands proved incapable of supporting concentrated agricultural populations. Throughout the Pueblo area at about A.D. 1300, there was a general abandonment of eroded mesas in favor of downstream floodplains, as soil rather than water became the critical need. The Kayenta people removed themselves from the Shonto area to the broad floodplains at the southern foot of Black Mesa, where their descendants survive as the Hopi of today.[4] Prior to the present century, then, the Shonto area supported its heaviest population nearly 1,000 years ago.

---

[4] This theory of the prehistoric population and depopulation of the Tsegi area is set forth at length in Adams, MS.

What happened at Shonto after the departure of the Kayenta people centuries ago is not clear. At some subsequent time there was a certain amount of marginal penetration south of the San Juan by bands of Southern Paiute, some of whom were farmers along the river itself. Escalante and Dominguez (1776), traversing the area in the vicinity of Kaibito in 1776, met both Paiute and Havasupai; the latter were frequently encountered in the region until a century later. A few Paiute families remained around Navajo Mountain and elsewhere along the lower San Juan as late as a generation ago, and have given their name to such features as Paiute Canyon, Paiute Mesa and Paiute Farms (north of Oljeto). At what date the Shoshoneans and Yumans entered, and what their numbers were, cannot be determined, as archeological evidence of them has not come to light. It is doubtful if they ever represented a significant occupation.

NAVAHO SETTLEMENT

No one knows when or why the Navaho first moved westward beyond Canyon de Chelly. As early as 1700, a European work on native America (De l'Isle, 1700) indicates "Apaches de Navaio" located northwest of the Hopi, and possibly even beyond the Colorado River. In 1706 their territory is described as extending "as far west as the Moqui [Hopi]" (Cuervo y Valdez, 1706). Beyond Hopi, however, Escalante met only Paiutes and Havasupai ("Cosninas") on his journey of 1776 from the vicinity of Navajo Mountain to Oraibi. He found the Hopi in regular intercourse with the Navaho to the east, but not to the west or north. Escalante had been stationed for many years in Santa Fe and undoubtedly knew a Navaho when he saw one, and there is no reason to suppose that he failed to identify correctly the aboriginal groups that he encountered.

Several documents mention Navahos in the Hopi area between 1776 and 1781 (letters between Anza, Croix and Galvez translated *in* Thomas, 1932, pp. 142–148, 221–239). A map published in 1775 (Jefferys, 1775, map 5), probably copied from De l'Isle, again shows "Apaches de Navajo" northwest of Moqui. From that time onward for 80 years there is no mention of Navahos anywhere north or west of the Hopi. In 1859 a United States scouting party from Fort Defiance penetrated Marsh Pass as far as the eastern limits of the present Shonto area (Van Valkenburgh and McPhee, 1938, p. 16). The party, on its return journey, found no Navaho habitation on Black Mesa except at its extreme eastern edge.

Within a very few years, however, Mormon pioneers pushing south into the Kanab area began meeting groups of Navahos not only west of the Hopi but west of the Colorado River. Sporadic warfare ensued until in 1871 an agreement was reached setting a boundary at the Colorado, and in effect recognizing the region east of the river as Navaho territory (McClintock, 1921, pp. 59–80; Corbett, 1952, pp. 148–311). There can be little doubt that the century from 1775 to 1875 saw the Navaho extend their dominion almost to its present limits, including the modern Shonto area.

It has commonly been held that repeated military campaigns against the Navahos in the east between 1860 and 1864, and especially the Kit Carson campaign of 1863–64 which resulted in removal of a large part of the Navaho tribe to the Pecos River, were primarily responsible for Navaho westward expansion. This theory is given weight by information from Shonto. Of the three basic population groups within the community (see "Social Structure," pp. 54–65) the largest and apparently longest established lineage occupies the territory south and west of Shonto Trading Post. Its interrelations are to the west, with the Inscription House community and the inhabitants of Navajo Canyon. It is impossible to trace this group back to any other location in the past. Two informants assert that it is descended from a band of Navaho who fled into the virtually impregnable reaches of the Navajo Canyon system to escape the Carson campaign, and who continue to occupy the canyon and areas immediately to the east and west.

A second element at Shonto occupies the area to the south and east of Shonto store, including Klethla Valley, and has close relations with the neighboring population on top of Black Mesa. Malcolm Farmer believes this group to be a remnant of what he terms the Black Mesa band of Navaho, who are thought to have moved westward from the Canyon de Chelly area for the purpose of preying upon the Hopi.[5]

According to Van Valkenburgh (1941, p. 145) a portion of the Black Mesa band was captured near the Shonto area in the campaign of 1863 and sent to Fort Sumner. It is believed that the band originally occupied only the summit of Black Mesa, farming in the numerous small interior valleys. Drying up of water sources on the mesa and expanding population have more recently forced considerable numbers to move down into Klethla Valley and across it onto the southern margin of the Shonto Plateau, as far as Shonto itself. This colonization of the Shonto area by Black Mesa people seems to have taken place between 50 and 60 years ago, according to informants in the community.

The high northern half of the Shonto area, north of the trading post, has apparently been colonized only within the last two generations. It is occupied today by a related group of families who

---

[5] Personal communication. Farmer's elaborate reconstructions of Navaho population groupings and movements are now in preparation for publication. He believes that the Navaho in the early historic period were grouped in bands similar to those of the Western Apache. Cf. Garrido y Duran, 1786.

are still in the procees of moving southward from Oljeto and Navajo Mountain. As a group, they can be traced back to the celebrated Hoskinini band which, under the leadership of Hoskinini, fled into the mesa country west of Oljeto in 1863, incidentally overrunning the straggling Paiute farming population along the San Juan River. Beginning on Hoskinini Mesa near Oljeto, this group has expanded to occupy most of the Oljeto area, Paiute Mesa, Navajo Mountain, and, latterly, the northern half of the Shonto area. On the upper Shonto Plateau only Skeleton Mesa now remains unoccupied, and, under the constant pressure of expanding population, it may well be the next area of colonization.

Whereas the various population elements at Shonto have close ties in other trading communities to the north, west, and south, there appears to be a sharp population division to the east, at the line of Tsegi Canyon. No families at Shonto are said to have originated in the Kayenta area, and few have relatives there. It is further notable that not a single Shonto resident claims an ancestor who under-went the "long walk" to Fort Sumner, while stories of the "long walk" are common around Kayenta. This circumstance strongly suggests that the entire isolated highland area west of Marsh Pass was an effective refuge zone whose inhabitants largely escaped the Carson campaign, but that the refuge area did not extend east of Marsh Pass. The broad expanses of the Tyende and Chinle Valleys offer few opportunities for effective concealment, and it seems highly probable that their present populations represent a reoccupation sub-sequent to the Navaho return from Fort Sumner in 1868.

EUROPEAN PENETRATION

The first European penetration of the northwestern Navaho area is as obscure as the earliest Navaho penetration. An unknown Spaniard has left an inscription—now illegible—and the date "1661 A. Dn." (cf. Van Valkenburgh, 1941, p. 78) upon the wall of In-scription House ruin in Navajo Canyon, one of the most remote corners of the entire region. Four decades of search have failed to uncover the circumstances of this early exploration. Subsequent to it there is no indication of Spanish entry in the region for 115 years. The date of the inscription coincides with a time when a Franciscan mission was maintained among the Hopi at Awatovi, and it can only be conjectured that some adventurous member of its staff went wandering northward, perhaps guided by Hopi. Inscrip-tion House is about three days' hard ride from Awatovi.

The visit of Escalante and Dominguez in 1776 has already been mentioned. Crossing the Colorado just below Navajo Mountain, they turned southward across the Kaibito Plateau and thence eastward, skirting the base of Black Mesa, to Oraibi. Sporadic Spanish exploration followed Escalante and Dominguez, but to the end of Spanish and Mexican rule in 1848 the region north of the Hopi remained virtual terra incognita. The most enigmatic record of Spanish or Mexican exploration that remains is a reference to a trading expedition which left Abiquiu on March 13, 1813, visited the Salt Lake area, turned southward, and returned via Escalante's crossing on the Colorado to Abiquiu on July 12. At the "Crossing of the Fathers" they found a native trader waiting "as was his custom." (See Corbett, 1952, p. 155.)

THE AMERICAN PERIOD

American exploration of the northwestern Navaho country did not get under way until some 10 years after the United States acquired the territory by the Mexican Cession of 1848. In the fall of 1858 the great Mormon pioneer Jacob Hamblin made the first of many crossings into the "Indian Country," reaching the Hopi villages via the Crossing of the Fathers and pioneering what was later to become the Mormon Road to the Little Colorado settlements. As of 1858 Hamblin and his companions felt that, once across the Colorado River, they were in Navaho country.

In the following winter, Capt. John G. Walker led a regiment of mounted rifles northwest from Fort Defiance to Canyon de Chelly, and thence along the northeastern scarp of Black Mesa to the present site of Kayenta. The group subsequently traversed Marsh Pass into Long House Valley, on the very borders of the modern Shonto community. Their presence here is authenticated by a series of still legible inscriptions upon the walls of Long House ruin, some 15 miles from Shonto. Walker was in all probability the first white man ever to set foot in the Shonto area proper. After leaving Long House Valley his group ascended to the rim of Black Mesa above, and turned eastward across the mesa to Chinle Valley and so back to Fort Defiance (Van Valkenburgh and McPhee, 1938, p. 16).

During the campaign of 1863 a group of Navahos who had been captured on Black Mesa by Navaho scouts were driven into Shonto Canyon itself, preparatory to their march to Fort Defiance. Some Navahos believe that in the following year Carson's own troops were in the canyon (Van Valkenburgh, 1941; p. 145), but there is no authentic record of this. In the same year 1864, however, a heliograph station was established on the summit of Navajo Mountain for the transmission of military information, via a series of relay stations, to Fort Defiance. There are no tales of depredations committed by soldiers around Shonto or Navajo Mountain, and it is certain that no extensive campaign was ever undertaken in the area.

Notwithstanding occasional American military operations during the Civil War era, there is no question that the chief Anglo-American contacts for northwestern Navahos until after the turn of the present century were with the encroaching Mormon population west of the Colorado River. Colonies along Kanab Creek and in House Rock Valley, just over the river, were established in the 1860's. Navahos raided these frontier settlements repeatedly until 1871, when a kind of truce line was established at the river (McClintock, 1921, p. 79). Thereafter they continued to visit them for many years, trading for supplies and especially horses. It is notable that the Navahos from Shonto, Navajo Mountain, and Oljeto continue up to the present day to trade for horses, usually offering rugs in exchange, in the Mormon communities to the north and west.

In 1871 John D. Lee, in his enforced exile from Utah, settled on the Colorado at the mouth of the Paria River, where he had a small ranch and operated sporadically the little ferry which has permanently given his name to the site. Lee's Ferry became an important link in the Mormon Road connecting the Utah settlements with newly founded colonies along the Little Colorado. Lee and his family carried on a considerable Navaho trade during their two years' sojourn at the ferry (see Lee, 1955, vol. 2, pp. 197–262; Van Valkenburgh and McPhee, 1938, pp. 43–44).

In 1873 the ever-present threat of retribution for his complicity in the Mountain Meadows Massacre forced Lee and two of his wives to flee still further into the wilderness, abandoning the river site. In the words of his own journal, "I swam my horse over the foaming Colerado by a skift & bent My way for the Mowencroppa [Moencopi], there to take up My abode with the House of iseral—Mokies, Orabias [Oraibis], Piutes, & NavaJoes" (Lee, 1955, vol. 2, p. 263). The "lost children of Israel" actually awaiting him on the Moencopi were a large encampment of Havasupai.

The Lees located first at Moenave Spring and later near the present site of Tuba City, where a tall, typically Mormon stone homestead still stands beside Moencopi Wash. The long-delayed forces of justice finally overtook John D. Lee in 1875, and he was executed in the following year. Surviving members of the family remained on the Moencopi until after the turn of the century, and were later joined by other Mormon homesteaders. This was the first American settlement within the western Navaho country, and the little community seems to have carried on a thriving trade with both Navahos and Hopis.

Meanwhile, an entirely different species of American colonization was beginning to push westward from the Rio Grande. Rumors of an impending transcontinental railroad aroused a flurry of interest in Northern Arizona, and led indirectly to the establishment, in 1876, of the little town of Flagstaff (see McClintock, 1921, pp. 149–151), far to the southwest of Shonto at the foot of the San Francisco Peaks.

The Atlantic and Pacific Railway (now A.T. & S.F.) actually laid track between the Rio Grande and Flagstaff in 1883, and the line was opened to the Pacific Coast 2 years later. Along its right-of-way developed a string of typical frontier railroad towns; notably Gallup, Holbrook, and Winslow. Both Flagstaff and the railroad were destined to play an important role in the future life of Shonto.

DEVELOPMENT OF THE MODERN COMMUNITY

Coincident with the building of the railroad came official recognition of Indian sovereignty in the western Navaho country. An enormous block of land immediately south of Shonto, and including the area now occupied by the Red Lake and Cow Springs stores, was set aside as Hopi Reservation by executive order at the end of 1882. Two years later Shonto itself, and the region northward to the state line and westward to Kaibito, was added to the reservation originally granted to the Navaho by treaty in 1868. Another executive order added the territory as far west as the Colorado River in 1900. Shortly thereafter the remaining Mormon holdings on Moencopi Wash were bought out, and the site became Tuba City, agency for the newly established Western Navajo Indian Reservation. North of Shonto, the so-called "Paiute Strip" between the Utah-Arizona line and the San Juan River was originally granted to the Navaho before the turn of the century, but later restored to public domain. It was finally returned to the Navaho Reservation by an act of congress in 1934.

TRADING

Systematic American penetration of the Shonto country finally began in the last years of the 19th century, with the tireless explorations of the Wetherill family. John and Louisa Wetherill established themselves at Kayenta in 1909, after a brief sojourn at Oljeto, and their Tyende (later Kayenta) Trading Post became one of the most celebrated outposts in the Southwest. The Wetherill brothers had pretty well completed their reconnaissance of the territory north and west of Kayenta by 1910, and had discovered most of the principal features of the region. As of 1910 a passable wagon road already extended from Kayenta via Marsh Pass and Klethla Valley to Tuba City, and there can be no doubt that Navahos from the Shonto area traded extensively at Kayenta until 1915.

Shonto Trading Post, like so many other stores in the same region, began as an outpost of the Kayenta store. John Wetherill, in the course of his repeated expeditions west of Marsh Pass, had found a concentrated Navaho settlement farming the permanently watered floor of Shonto Canyon, a "lush meadow with many small lakes" (Van Valkenburgh, 1941, p. 145). In 1915 he and Joe Lee (a descendant of John D.) brought over a wagonload of supplies and a tent, and set up the first Shonto Trading Post. The enterprise continued intermittently for several years under hired operators, and was eventually sold out to Harry Rorick, who built the present store buildings. At that time the only access by wagon was up Shonto Canyon from its mouth, through a series of deep sand drifts. The little post was entirely isolated during the winter months. During the 1920's, however, a primitive road was hacked out of the steep west canyon wall, allowing wagon trade with the populous area to the west as far as Cow Springs Canyon. The east canyon wall, giving access to Long House Valley, Marsh Pass and Tsegi, was not breached by auto road until 1935.

In the years following the establishment of Shonto, various other trading enterprises came into the northwestern Navaho country. Red Lake and Cow Springs stores were opened southwest of Shonto, the latter operating as an outpost of the former. Oljeto was reactivated about 1920. Ben Wetherill ran a small outpost on Navajo Mountain in 1928, but the present Inscription House and Navajo Mountain stores did not come into operation until the Rainbow Plateau was finally made accessible by auto road in 1934. The little Tsegi Trading Post in Marsh Pass was opened immediately after World War II by an enterprising Navaho, former employee of Shonto Trading Post, underwritten by a loan from the Navaho tribe.

TOURIST DEVELOPMENT

Navajo National Monument, consisting of four small reservations enclosing the principal cliff dwellings of Tsegi and Navajo Canyons, was created by executive order in 1907. The Wetherills at Kayenta built up a lively tourist business guiding visitors to these ruins, originally discovered by them, as well as to the Rainbow natural bridge, which John Wetherill and Byron Cummings had discovered in 1909. By 1915 the Wetherills had added an extensive guest ranch to their trading enterprise. Development by the U.S. National Park Service was not undertaken until 20 years later, when a passable auto road was constructed from the Tuba City-Kayenta highway in Klethla Valley to the rim of Tsegi Canyon just above Betatakin ruin. At that time a permanent national monument headquarters with the usual camping facilities was established at the end of the road. Betatakin, as the settlement is commonly called, has since been the home of a permanent Anglo custodian and two seasonal Navaho employees. In recent years Navajo National Monument has drawn nearly 2,000 visitors annually.

Also during the early 1930's, a new auto road was constructed from the lower end of Klethla Valley, near Cow Springs, northward to the foot of Navajo Mountain. This road afforded good access for the first time to Rainbow natural bridge, a national monument since 1910, and to Inscription House ruin in Navajo Canyon. To accommodate anticipated tourist travel, the Richardson family, traders at Kaibito, built guest lodges at the head of the Rainbow Bridge trail on the south slope of Navajo Mountain, and at the head of the Inscription House trail. The Rainbow Lodge burned out in 1951, and overland trips to Rainbow Bridge have since been operated by Navajo Mountain Trading Post, on the east slope of the mountain. Since the inauguration of summer boat trips on the San Juan River, Rainbow Bridge National Monument has been drawing several hundred visitors a year. The national monument, having no staff of its own, is under the jurisdiction of the superintendent at Betatakin.

Anticipated tourist travel at Inscription House never materialized, but the original lodge survives in the form of the present Inscription House Trading Post. Guest facilities have not been maintained for many years.

GOVERNMENT DEVELOPMENT

The first school ever operated for western Navahos was a tiny day school in Blue Canyon, some 20 miles south of Red Lake. Its foundations are still visible at the site, which is now almost inaccessible. It began operation in 1895 and was abandoned in 1904, when the present Tuba City boarding school was opened (Van Valkenburgh, 1941 p. 13).

The Western Navaho Indian Reservation was formally constituted in 1906, with Tuba City as its agency. Two years earlier the large Tuba City boarding school—still extant—had been opened to Navaho and Hopi children from the first to the sixth grades. Establishment of the Tuba City agency brought the usual additional institutions: a court of Indian offenses and jail staffed by a couple of Indian police, a tiny and underequipped hospital, a "Government farmer" or extension agent, a small group of administrative and clerical offices, and the inevitable mission.

For nearly '30 years after 1906, Tuba City presented the typical sleepy appearance of Indian agencies throughout the West, with its dusty, tree-lined streets running between rows of barrackslike stone dormitories and school buildings. Developments on the western Navaho outside Tuba City itself were few and far between. It was the "agency era" in Indian administration, and Indians who had any business with the White man were expected to find their way to the agency as best they could.

The comfortable guardianship which inaugurated this era in Navaho administration become increasingly uncomfortable as the years went by, and flocks and population multiplied out of all anticipated proportion. Finally, in the early 1930's, the era came to an abrupt end with the coming of the Collier administration and the "Indian New Deal." The five independent Navaho reservations were con-

solidated under a single agency at Window Rock, and Tuba City
was relegated to a sub-agency role, though it continued for many years
to have the only boarding school and hospital in the western Navaho
country. During this period a concerted effort was made to carry
modern American institutions far beyond the agency, into the midst
of the Navaho people themselves.

From 1934 until the beginning of World War II, the Shonto
country was alive with developmental activity. A whole series
of new roads and truck trails were laid out, opening up previously inaccessible areas such as Navajo Mountain. During the same
years, the present U.S. Highway 89 was paved between Flagstaff and
Salt Lake City, and the great Navajo Bridge at Marble Canyon was
constructed, giving the northwestern Navaho country new accessibility
from the outside world.

A new approach to Shonto from the southwest was built, coming
across the lower Shonto Plateau from the vicinity of Cow Springs. A
second road was blasted out of the east canyon wall at Shonto with
branches leading to Betatakin and to Klethla Valley, giving direct
wagon access to Shonto from the east for the first time. A truck
trail was laid out from a point south of Shonto westward across Cow
Springs Canyon and the head of Navajo Canyon to Kaibito, and a
direct route from Shonto to Navajo Mountain was developed. The
formerly isolated communities of the plateau became interaccessible
by wagon and truck for the first time. During the same period a mag-
neto telephone system was installed, connecting most of the trading
posts and newly completed schools of the region with each other and
with Tuba City and Flagstaff. Until its replacement in 1955, this
party line was believed to be the longest in America, with 41 sub-
scribers and over 700 miles of wire in a single circuit.

Soil and water developments were also instituted. Deep wells were
put down north and south of Shonto, with the conventional wind-
driven pumps and ample storage tanks. Innumerable check dams
were built in the canyons, along with stock tanks on the mesas above.
Springs in Shonto Canyon were cleaned out, and the surface drainage
confined by planting the canyon floor with cottonwoods. Small irriga-
tion systems both upstream and downstream from Shonto store were
operated.

The most lasting development of the Collier era was the local school
program. A day school at Shonto, consisting of four connected pairs
of hoganlike stone structures, with a staff of two White teachers, was
opened in 1935. It had a capacity of 70 pupils, and ran through the
first three grades. A bus was run daily east and west of the canyon;
children received their noon meal at the school. A smaller hogantype
school was opened at Navajo Mountain in the same year, and other

day schools of more conventional construction were built at Kaibito and Kayenta. In addition a large outpatient clinic was instituted at Kayenta.

Perhaps the least important aspect of the Collier regime from the standpoint of lasting effect, and yet the one which is destined to live longest in the consciousness of Navahos, was the celebrated stock reduction program. Navaho livestock holdings were reduced in toto from some 1,250,000 sheep units to slightly less than half that figure. The program made heavy inroads in the Shonto area as elsewhere, and aroused bitter opposition on all sides; yet the drastic livestock cutback of the 1930's has been almost totally offset in the intervening 20 years as a result of subsequent failure to enforce capacities. It is possible that the number of livestock grazed in the Shonto area today actually exceeds the number in 1936. Nevertheless, John Collier remains the modern Navaho culture-villain at Shonto as throughout the reservation; "the man who took away our sheep." In 20 years, he and the livestock program associated with his regime have supplanted Kit Carson and the "long walk" as symbols of Navaho resentment, and the military period of the 1860's has faded into the quaint unreality of folktale.

To implement and perpetuate stock reduction, land administration on the Navaho Reservation was decentralized to a degree never previously attempted. In 1937 the reservation was divided into 18 land-management districts, each with a resident supervisor. The latter had general jurisdiction over all livestock and agricultural operation within his area, and was further intended to act as an intermediary between local Navahos and the administration higher up. District supervisors, even more than schoolteachers, became the first line of contact between Navahos and the Indian Bureau. Shonto was selected as the "capital" of Land Management District 2, which included also Navajo Mountain, Paiute Mesa, Inscription House, Klethla Valley, and a considerable portion of Black Mesa. A district supervisor was resident at Shonto School from 1935 until 1949.

World War II brought much of the activity of the early Collier regime to a halt. Curtailment of funds prevented further extension of soil and moisture developments, and many projects had to be abandoned for lack of personnel. Automotive equipment had always suffered unduly on the rough Navaho roads, and when adequate maintenance and replacement became impossible, day school operation could not be continued. Several day schools closed down altogether, and the remainder were converted to boarding schools by the hasty addition of quonset-hut dormitories and expanded kitchen facilities. Shonto School was so converted early in the war, and remains to this day a boarding school. Converted day schools of this type are now

officially termed community schools. World War II forced the closing
of the Kayenta clinic, which has never resumed operation.

Indian reservations throughout the United States were essentially
under caretaker administration during much of the war, as the focus
of National interest and effort shifted elsewhere. The number of
Government personnel on the Navaho Reservation was cut back approximately 50 percent, to a sort of skeleton crew. An immediate
result was that the hard-fought battle to maintain range capacities
could not be sustained, and livestock remultiplied throughout the
western part of the reservation. This was particularly true in more
inaccessible areas, including Shonto.

The gradual reversal of Collier's decentralizing policies which was
necessitated by the war, has, in general, continued in the post-war
period. Day school operation has never been resumed; some of the
schools which were shut down have not reopened; and there has
been no expansion of the community school program. Immediate
post-war emphasis was on getting Navaho children into existing
Indian school facilities off the reservation, where more than half
the children from Shonto are still sent. Later came a program of
large, new, concentrated boarding schools within the reservation. One
of the first of these was opened at Kaibito in 1952; another has recently been opened at Kayenta. A step in the opposite direction is
seen in the trailer day schools recently established in several smaller
communities, including both Red Lake and Cow Springs.

Medical facilities remain centralized. The Kayenta clinic has never
been reopened, but the old Tuba City hospital was replaced by a
completely new and much larger unit in 1954.

On the administrative level, the 18 prewar land management districts were consolidated into 8 in 1949, and the resident district supervisor was removed from Shonto to Kayenta. A further withdrawal
occurred in 1954, when all land and resource management was concentrated in six sub-agencies, more or less paralleling the old five-
reservation structure of 1904–36. Tuba City is once again the chief
administrative center for the Shonto area.

Concurrent with recentralization of Indian Bureau operations has
been the growth and ramification of activities of the Navaho tribe.
It is expedient to consider this phenomenon under the general heading of Government Operations, since few Shonto residents make a
consistent distinction between Tribal and Federal Government.

The first Navaho Tribal Council was constituted in 1924, but it
had little real authority until after World War II, and in any case
western Navaho participation was nominal at best. Few people at
Shonto can recall who represented them at Window Rock in the
prewar years; indeed, many are surprised to learn that there was a

tribal council prior to 1940. As of 1956, however, there is a general awareness of some, at least, of the activities of tribal government, and an interest in tribal politics on the local level. Tribal Council constituencies exist in each of the trading communities of the Shonto Plateau.

More important locally than tribal councilmen are the members of the District Grazing Committee, an independent functionary of the Navaho tribe which is responsible directly to its chairman and Advisory (i.e., executive) Committee. Grazing committees took over the regulation of range operations and livestock capacities when Indian Bureau district supervisors were withdrawn in 1949. The committee for District 2 is composed of one member each from Long House Valley, Klethla Valley, and Navajo Mountain. Its membership and authority are well known throughout the Shonto community.

A significant consequence of tribal activity thus far, so far as Shonto is concerned, has been an increase in law enforcement. For many years the only police anywhere in the western Navaho region were at Tuba City itself, and they ventured into the hinterlands only upon receipt of sworn complaints. It was a famous observation for years that the Tuba City jail was never locked unless it was unoccupied—to prevent theft of bedding.

The Navaho tribe assumed responsibility for law and order in 1948, and since that time the police force on western Navaho has been doubled (to 12, for an estimated population of 8,000). Patrolmen are now stationed at Kaibito and Kayenta, as well as at Tuba City. One patrolman from Kaibito spends one day a week at Shonto, from 9:00 a.m. until 6:00 p.m. Federal and Arizona State Indian liquor laws were repealed between 1952 and 1954, but the Navaho tribe still maintains strict prohibition within the reservation, and the police are occupied largely in dealing with liquor cases.

The State government of Arizona has never had direct jurisdiction over the Navaho Reservation, but it has nevertheless been important indirectly to the Shonto community since 1948. In that year Indians were made eligible for the first time for Public Assistance in the State of Arizona, and an enormous Navaho caseload was added to the State welfare rolls. The combination of Old Age Assistance, Aid to the Blind, and Aid to Dependent Children now contributes nearly 10 percent of the total income of the Shonto community (see "Welfare," pp. 136–137). Indians remain ineligible for General Assistance from the State; it is administered on the Navaho Reservation directly by the Indian Bureau.

MISSIONS

Prior to 1954 missionary activity had never been significant in the Shonto Plateau region. The first mission anywhere in the area was maintained at the little Mormon colony which preceded Tuba City, for the benefit of the neighboring Hopi colony of Moencopi. The Hopi village remains Mormonized to this day and has its own L.D.S. church, but the original mission went out of existence along with the Mormon settlement. It was replaced by a small Presbyterian mission, consisting of a chapel and social room, when Tuba City became the Western Navaho Agency in 1906. The latter survives to the present day, and is staffed by a single pastor and his family. In the 1920's a similar Presbyterian establishment was set up at Kayenta.

Until 5 years ago these remained the only missionary activities among the northwestern Navaho. A subsidiary of the Kayenta mission, with its own resident pastor, was set up at Oljeto in 1952, on deeded land donated by the trader. Two years later the Navaho tribe lifted many restrictions on missionary activity, and a flood of semi-itinerant missionaries entered the reservation. Missionaries who are so far without permanent establishments are now resident at Navajo Mountain, Kaibito, and Shonto. The Shonto missionary arrived early in 1955, representing the Assembly of God sect, and set up a house trailer adjacent to the Shonto trading post and school premises, where he and his family now reside. Services are held 4 days a week at various Navaho residences.

THE OUTSIDE WORLD

The Santa Fe Railroad brought permanent American settlement and a measure of prosperity to northern Arizona in the 1880's, though the region remains to the present day one of the least developed areas in the United States. An additional boost was given in later years by U.S. Highway 66, paralleling the railroad. The highway was paved during the 1930's, and in that decade became perhaps the most celebrated tourist route in the United States, giving access to the West Coast by way of the Indian Country and the Grand Canyon. By 1940, tourist business was the largest single industry in northern Arizona, and was especially important to Flagstaff, with its favored location at the junction of U.S. 89. Flagstaff was, in addition, a lumbering and cattle center with a population of about 7,000; Winslow was a roundhouse town of about 4,000; Holbrook was a somewhat smaller livestock and agricultural center, and Gallup was the center of a coal-mining area serving the railroad, with about the same population as Flagstaff. These, together with the little Mormon communities farther north, which are virtually unchanged since the turn of the century, represented most of the outside world to prewar Navahos.

The world beyond Tuba City was remote and unimportant to Shonto prior to World War II. With development projects everywhere and stock reduction in progress, the community's attention was focused upon itself and not upon the distant and incomprehensible

White man's domain. One or two men from Shonto worked for brief periods in Flagstaff and Winslow, and several went shopping in Flagstaff from time to time, but as of 1941 less than half the members of the community had ever been away from the reservation.

The Navaho Reservation, Shonto included, woke up fast when the great conflict started. Selective service took 3,500 Navahos into the armed forces, primarily from the better-educated eastern portions of the reservation. Far more important still, the war brought labor recruiters into every part of the Navaho country for the first time. Prior to 1940, Navahos had been regarded as a significant labor force only in localized agricultural areas; the great majority of Shonto men had never held a paying job, except perhaps for a few days or weeks on a local construction project.

The beginning of World War II created an immediate shortage of unskilled labor, especially in sections of the United States less favored by wartime economy. Industries in the upper Southwest abruptly became aware of the huge and virtually untapped Navaho labor pool, as ammunition depots sprang up near Gallup and Flagstaff, and the overtaxed railroads were unable to secure way labor. By 1943 recruiters were in every part of the reservation, assisted by traders, and any able-bodied Navaho, regardless of education, could have his pick of steady, well-paid jobs, with housing and free transportation thrown in.

Within 3 years, the economy of much of the Navaho country was revolutionized. Before the war it is doubtful whether wage work ever contributed more than 30 percent of Navaho income, and wage work other than Government employment on the reservation certainly contributed no more than 10 percent (cf. Kluckhohn and Leighton, 1946 p. 20). Home industry was far and away the most significant source of Navaho livelihood. By contrast, at no time since World War II has wage work contributed less than 50 percent of Navaho income, as ammunition plants and railroads have continued to rely on Navaho labor. Native industry as of 1956 has diminished to a supplementary role, in terms of its actual contribution to livelihood.

The situation at Shonto is characteristic of northwestern Navaho generally. Before World War II not more than six men in the community had ever earned wages except on temporary Government projects, and none had served in the armed forces. At the end of the war only two men had been in the army, but at least 50 out of a total labor force of around 70 had been employed either in the Navajo Ordnance Depot near Flagstaff or on the Santa Fe Railroad. Many also engaged in seasonal agricultural work in Utah and Idaho.

Wartime conditions brought other interesting changes in Navaho life. Acceptance of American jobs, and life outside the reservation, resulted in acceptance of a number of American values. Resistance to schooling and to modern medicine lessened enormously, and schools and hospitals which were once half empty have been filled to and often beyond capacity in recent years. At the same time, a new class of leaders emerged in Navaho society: up-to-date men who knew their way around in the White world.

The small numbers of truck owners—passenger cars are virtually nonexistent in the Navaho country—on the reservation had always been in an economically favored position because of bootlegging opportunities. After the beginning of the war, some of them suddenly discovered a lucrative new field in wildcat labor contracting, transportation, and even pirating. After World War II, at least 100 individuals, in all parts of the reservation, were engaged in this type of enterprise, in addition to desultory bootlegging. Such activities have diminished in recent years along with the demand for agricultural labor, but in their day they enabled several up-to-date Navahos to acquire power and influence in their communities, and these men now form one of the most significant elements in the Navaho Tribal Council.

The end of the war saw a sharp decline in demand for ammunition handlers, and agriculture has subsequently shifted to a reliance on other labor sources; but as of 1955 Navahos continue as the primary track labor force on the Santa Fe, Union Pacific, and D. & R.G.W. Railroads. Shonto community in 1955 obtained fully half of its total income directly and indirectly from the Santa Fe Railroad (see "Railroad Income," pp. 133–134). In addition, improved roads and the increasing number of pickup trucks in the community have made Flagstaff immeasurably more accessible than before the war, and nearly all Shonto families go to town at least twice a year. In a normal year the community is virtually deserted over the Fourth of July, date of the annual Flagstaff All-Indian Pow-Wow (a celebration closely akin to the better-known Gallup Ceremonial). As of 1956 the life and economy of Shonto are heavily geared to, and dependent upon, the outside world.

MINING

There has been a certain amount of mineral interest in the northwestern Navaho country since before the turn of the century, but little development up to the present time. Prior to its inclusion in the Navaho Reservation in 1934, there was sporadic prospecting along the "Paiute Strip," between Navajo Mountain and Oljeto, and a small gold deposit was actually worked for a time. Ledges of medium-grade copper were also discovered in the area. A small, independently owned copper mine upon patented land west of Kaibito has been in operation for many years. Low-grade coal deposits on Black

Mesa were remarked on by Captain Walker in 1859 (Van Valkenburgh and McPhee, 1938, p. 16), and they have been exploited in
the past 20 years by enterprising Navaho families from Kayenta and
Cow Springs, the product being sold to local schools and trading
posts.

It is uranium, however, that has given the whole San Juan Basin
new economic significance, and the part which it may play in the
future life of Shonto remains to be determined. The year 1956 finds
the community once again undergoing a process of economic transition. Wage work opportunities off the reservation are declining.
Participation in seasonal agricultural work has almost ceased, and
there are warnings of an impending curtailment in the demand for
railroad way labor. In such circumstances interest focuses increasingly upon the possible future economic development of the reservation itself.

Uranium developments in the Navaho country have so far been
mostly north and east of Kayenta, where several paying mines are
now in operation. As of 1955 they were providing a source of steady
employment for over 100 families in the surrounding area. No Navahos from the Shonto region are employed in them, and up to the
present there has been a marked tendency on the part of Monument
Valley Navahos to resent the intrusion of outsiders into the mining
industry in their area.

Significant uranium deposits have yet to be discovered west of
Marsh Pass, despite sporadic prospecting. Nevertheless, the Rare
Metals Corporation of America, a recently formed subsidiary of the
farflung El Paso Natural Gas Co., has obtained a permit to prospect
throughout the far western portion of the Navaho Reservation and has
already constructed a complete ore reduction plant, along with permanent housing for some two dozen families, along the road from Tuba
City to Red Lake. Prospecting continues in the Shonto area and on
Black Mesa, and there is at least some possibility that a local mining
industry may in the future be as important to Shonto as it now is to
Monument Valley and Dennehotso.

SHONTO IN 1955

Modern Shonto community has a surface area of approximately 230
square miles, equal to 147,200 acres. Navaho population at the end
of 1955 numbered 568 individuals, belonging to 100 households and
38 residence groups (see "Social Structure," pp. 54–65). Population
density averaged 2.47 persons per square mile. Dividing the total
area by the number of households included, the average land area per
household was 2.30 square miles or 1.472 acres. Average area per
residence group was 6.05 square miles, equal to 3,874 acres.

Settlement in different parts of the community was uneven in density, as indicated in map 3. Heaviest population was found in the lower altitudes, averaging nearly four persons per square mile in the long-settled region southwest of the trading post. The recently occupied higher area north of the store averaged only slightly more than one inhabitant per square mile.

Distribution of Shonto's Navaho population in 1955 by age and sex is shown in table 1.

TABLE 1.—*Distribution of Shonto population in 1955 by age and sex*

Age group	Males		Females		Total	
	Number	*Percent*	*Number*	*Percent*	*Number*	*Percent*
15 and under	140	24.6	149	26.3	289	50.9
16–25	54	9.5	59	10.4	113	19.9
26–35	30	5.3	28	4.9	58	10.2
36–45	21	3.7	26	4.6	47	8.3
46–55	14	2.5	12	2.1	26	4.6
56–65	8	1.4	7	1.2	15	2.6
65 and over	11	1.9	9	1.6	20	3.5
Total	278	48.9	290	51.1	568	100.0

In addition to its Navaho residents, Shonto in 1955 had a White population of 10: the writer and his wife at Shonto Trading Post; 2 unmarried women teachers at Shonto Community School; the missionary, his wife, and 1 child at their nearby location; and the superintendent, his wife, and 1 child at Betatakin, 10 miles away.

From Shonto Trading Post it is 18 miles (by truck only) to Inscription House, the closest trading post outside the community; 29 miles to the nearest post office at Red Lake (P.O. Tonalea); 34 miles to Kayenta and the nearest police patrol, permanent mission, large boarding school and guest facilities; 54 miles to the administrative center at Tuba City with its hospital, court, jail, and other facilities; 56 miles to the Hopi Village of Moencopi; 67 miles to the nearest paved highway, U.S. 89; and 132 miles to Flagstaff, the nearest town and off-reservation shopping center for Shonto Navahos.

NAVAHO LIFE

It might be said that the fabric of modern Navaho life is woven of a series of distinct threads, sometimes blending, sometimes contrasting, representing culture elements of diverse origins. The individual threads often do not vary much as between one Navaho community and another; where present at all they are likely to be found in readily recognizable form. What distinguishes different communities is not the character of these threads so much as the pattern into which they are woven. No two communities have ever faced quite the same range of external contacts in time and space; consequently no two have, perhaps, come to quite the same terms with the world around them.

Until recently it was the usual practice of anthropologists to follow up different culture threads individually; the result is an enormous body of literature upon specific aspects of Navaho life—especially in its aboriginal forms—which is applicable to Shonto with little modification. The underlying warp of uniquely Navaho traditions and institutions upon which the pattern of Shonto's daily life is woven has been isolated and elaborately described in the numerous works of Matthews, Haile, Hill, Reichard, Kluckhohn, and a host of others. To these works the reader is referred for relevant information which will not be repeated or restated in the present instance except where it is significantly augmented or controverted by data from Shonto.

However, the fabric of Shonto's life in 1956 includes a series of threads which are not of native origin. The particular complex of adjustments—the pattern of native and alien threads—which is unique to Shonto remains to be described here. Integrative studies in other Navaho communities, nearly all resulting from recent researches by Kluckhohn and his associates, furnish an initial guide to Shonto, but there are consistent and significant differences, as will be indicated.

SOCIAL STRUCTURE

The divisions of modern Shonto society are distinctly Navaho in origin and form, showing little or no modification as a result of Anglo-American influence. They are effectively described by Reichard (1928), Kluckhohn and Leighton (1946, pp. 54–69), and Vogt (1951, pp. 16–17). The social structure is formed of a series of basic functional units as well as other groupings that are essentially historical in derivation, and whose functional significance is incidental or vestigial. In the former category are households and residence groups; in the latter, resident lineages or "outfits." Clans, the only nonterritorial units of Shonto society, belong to some extent in both categories.

Economic functioning of social units is the subject of extended discussion in succeeding pages ("Economic Structure and Function," pp. 97–109); consideration here will be limited to definition and description. For this reason descriptive terms are substituted for the analytic designations employed by Kluckhohn and Leighton (1946, pp. 54–69) and their successors.

HOUSEHOLDS

The household corresponds to the "biological family" of Kluckhohn and Leighton (1946, pp. 54–56; see also Reichard, 1928, pp. 51–57 and Roberts, 1951). A household is defined here as a group of people who regularly eat together and share food resources in common, thus constituting a minimum subsistence unit. Seventy-five percent of Shonto households may further be distinguished by the fact that they inhabit a single dwelling. The remaining 25 percent of households involve either plural marriages or very large numbers of children, or both. In all such cases one or more additional dwellings, smaller and without housekeeping facilities, will be found in close proximity to the original.

Shonto's 1955 population of 568 Navaho individuals included 279 adults and 289 minor children, residing in 100 households. Mean household composition is therefore 2.79 adults and 2.89 children, or 5.68 total individuals. Frequency distribution of households by size is shown in table 2.

TABLE 2.—*Frequency distribution of Shonto households according to number of members*

Number of households	Members per household	Number of households	Members per household
1	1	12	8
14	2	6	9
17	3	5	10
13	4	3	11
5	5	1	12
10	6	2	13
10	7	1	14

Mean: 5.68   Median: 5.50   Modes: 3, 8

All Shonto households are comprised basically of nuclear families or remnants thereof. Frequency distribution of households according to family structure is indicated in table 3.

Table 3 offers an essentially historical classification of Shonto households. It does not, moreover, take into account minor extensions by adoption which may occur within households (cf. Kluckhohn and Leighton, 1946, p. 56; Roberts, 1951, p. 10). Incidence of such extensions at Shonto is shown in table 4.

Table 5 offers a purely functional analysis of Shonto households, incorporating the data from tables 3 and 4.

TABLE 3.—*Family structure of Shonto households*

Structural type	Number of households
Single marriage:	
Simple nuclear family	63
Nuclear family with stepchildren	6
3-generation: nuclear with children of divorced or deceased daughter included	3
Split: husband normally absent	4
Remnant: husband deceased or divorced	4
Remnant: wife deceased	1
Remnant: sole survivor	5
Plural marriage:	
Husband, two wives (sisters) and children	5
Husband, two wives (mother-daughter), children and stepchildren	2
Remnant: one or more wives deceased, one survives	5
Split: husband has two wives in separate households (one not in Shonto community)	1
No marriage:	
Woman and illegitimate children	1
Total	100

TABLE 4.—*Family extensions within Shonto households*

Extension	Number of households
Maternal grandchild adopted	6
Paternal grandchild adopted	4
Other related child or children adopted	9
Elderly female relative incorporated	2
Total	21

TABLE 5.—*Functional analysis of Shonto households*

Household composition	Number of households
1 adult male, 2 adult females plus children	9
1 adult male, 1 adult female plus children	66
1 adult male, 1 adult female without children	11
1 adult male plus children	1
1 adult male without children	1
2 adult females plus children	1
1 adult female plus children	11
Total	100

Table 5 reveals definite functional consistencies in Shonto households. Seventy-five percent of households correspond to the nuclear norm, singular or plural. Twelve households lack adult male members, 2 lack adult females, and 12 lack children.

Of the 12 households lacking adult male members, 4 involve split nuclear families, the husband being permanently employed outside the community and returning only for short periods each year. In any given year from 30 to 50 additional households may be in the same category for brief periods, while the men are away working on the railroad (see "Railroad Work," pp. 129–133). All such families are dependent upon economic support from the absent male, who is therefore functionally a member of the household. Among the 8 remaining households which lack an adult male member at any time, 6 are dependent upon State welfare assistance, as are also the 2 households lacking adult females. All but one of the adult women involved are over 50—presumably too old to remarry.

The nine households having two adult female members include seven plural marriages and two cases where an elderly relative, the last survivor of a former household, has been adopted. One such case involves the husband's paternal aunt; the other the wife's paternal great-aunt. These are the only cases of adult extensions in Shonto households.

In the two households lacking adult females, both men are commonly suspected of witchcraft. One of them lives in total isolation, constituting a household, and also a residence group unto himself. Both are supported by Old Age Assistance from the State welfare department.

Of 12 households containing no children, 8 are those of young couples married within the past 2 years. Three others are situated in residence groups where they are attended by young children from nearby households most of the time. Several older people are provided with children in their households by outright adoption of grandchildren, either paternal or maternal. Two Shonto couples who never had children currently have adopted grandnephews and nieces living with them, in default of grandchildren. A couple of informants have stated that grandparents may assert a definite claim upon the services of the fourth or any subsequent child of either a son or a daughter, if they have no remaining children of their own.

Shonto households, in sum, show a strong tendency toward a simple nuclear norm which is maintained by remarriage and adoption when it is not maintained by nature. Plural marriages, when included within a single household, are included within the norm. Only 12 households actually deviate from it, by virtue of lacking either children, existing or potential, or an adult male or female member. It is significant that no less than 10 of these are dependent upon public welfare assistance.

RESIDENCE GROUPS

Shonto's 100 households cluster in 38 clearly defined territorial units, called residence groups in the present study and corresponding to the "extended family" of Kluckhohn and Leighton (1946, pp. 56–58; see also Landgraf, 1954, p. 83 and Vogt, 1951, p. 16). Territorial distribution of both households and residence groups is shown in map 3. A residence group comprises one or more closely related households living in close proximity (within "shouting distance" according to Kluckhohn and Leighton) and sharing certain basic resources in common, as detailed in "Economic Structure and Function," pp. 97–109.

Residence groups at Shonto include from one to six households each, as shown in table 6.

TABLE 6.—*Frequency distribution of Shonto residence groups according to number of member households*

Number of residence groups	Number of member households	Number of residence groups	Number of member households
7	1	5	4
10	2	0	5
15	3	1	6

Mean: 2.63   Median: 2.63   Mode: 3

Of the seven single households which comprise residence groups unto themselves, five are those of very large wealthy families having children of marriageable age. Three have, in fact, been recently established by moving the household a couple of miles from the residence group to which it formerly belonged. The presumption is that

TABLE 7.—*Frequency distribution of Shonto residence groups according to number of individual members*

Number of residence groups	Number of members	Number of residence groups	Number of members
1	1	5	16
1	2	0	17
0	3	2	18
0	4	2	19
0	5	3	20
1	6	0	21
1	7	0	22
0	8	1	23
2	9	0	24
3	10	0	25
4	11	1	26
3	12	0	27
2	13	0	28
3	14	1	29
2	15		

Mean: 14.7   Median: 14.3   Modes: 11, 16

new households will be attached to all of them within a year or two. Current individual membership within these five households is respectively 7, 10, 10, 13 and 14; or far above the Shonto mean of 5.68. The remaining two single-household residence groups are the isolated abodes of persons believed to be witches.

The single residence group comprised of six households appears to be aberrant, and could possibly be classed as two residence groups of three households each. The group as a whole is divided between two separate residence areas throughout the year, but the member households as between one and the other seem to be interchangeable, and from an economic standpoint a single unit is indicated.

Range of size for residence groups in terms of individual members is shown in table 7.

The two residence groups which include only one and two members, respectively, are, again, those of Shonto's "witches." It is clear that the normal range of residence group membership is from 9 to 20 individuals.

The kinship structure of residence groups, like that of households, is essentially nuclear. Table 8 shows the kinship structure of Shonto residence groups.

Adoptions long before marriage account for the presence of married nephews and nieces in two of three residence groups. For practical purposes 28 of Shonto's 31 multihousehold residence groups are of nuclear derivation.

The relative unimportance of sex as a determinant of residence (see below) makes it difficult to identify a modal pattern among nuclear-derived residence groups; among those containing more than one household 19 include both matrilocal and patrilocal residences, 8 are purely matrilocal and 3 are purely patrilocal. Nine residence groups include the households of both married sons and married daughters,

TABLE 8.—*Residence group structure at Shonto*

Structure	Number of residence groups
Nuclear derivation:	
1 Generation: households of siblings	2
2 Generations: parents and married children	17
3 Generations: parents, married children, and married grandchildren	6
3 Generation remnant: grandparents and grandchildren; middle generation deceased	1
Extended derivation:	
Parents, married children, and married niece	1
Uncle-aunt and married nephews and nieces	2
Uncertain, apparently affinal relationship	1
Isolate: 1 household	7
Not kin-determined (Shonto School)	1
Total	38

one other has a married daughter and married grandson, and still another consists of the households of married siblings of both sexes. Twelve residence groups have married daughters only, and four have married sons only.

Three households reside permanently at Shonto School, maintaining no resources elsewhere save for unfurnished hogans for occasional visiting in the residence groups of parents. Additional employees of the school are participating members of households which reside elsewhere, and return to these on days off and during the summer. Employment and residence at the school are not in theory determined by kinship; nevertheless, the school's three permanent households are, in fact, closely related (sister, brother, and female parallel cousin) and function as a distinct residence group. The significance of this situation is discussed later (see "Control of Resources," pp. 98–103).

RESIDENT LINEAGES

Kluckhohn and Leighton (1946, p. 62) and their associates (e.g., Vogt, 1951, p. 16; Landgraf, 1954, pp. 83–84) have repeatedly spoken of certain social units more extended than the residence group, which they term "outfits." Their choice of designations is, however, misleading; traders and other Anglos on the scene habitually use "outfit" as synonymous with residence group. The groups to which Kluckhohn and Leighton refer undoubtedly correspond to what are identified as resident lineages at Shonto. It is hoped that a brief discussion here may help to clarify their function and significance in other Navaho communities as well.

Resident lineages do not belong in the same structural category as households and residence groups, in that they are not a priori functional units. They are, rather, essentially historical divisions which because of the social and historical traditions of Navaho land tenure (see "Control of Resources," pp. 98–103) may retain a certain amount of functional significance as land-use communities (cf. Kimball and Provinse, 1942, p. 20; Thompson, 1950, pp. 144–145). In general, however, they do not manifest any recognizable internal structure of authority, and residence group membership does not a priori determine interaction within a resident lineage. Consequently, resident lineage membership, unlike household and residence group membership, cannot be determined by inspection and without reference to genealogies.

The entire territory of Shonto community is divided among 12 resident lineages, each including one or more residence groups, as shown in map 3. These can be further reduced to three or possibly four original population elements (see "Navaho Settlement," pp. 37–39). Each resident lineage has developed through the multiplication and expansion of an original preempting family within the community, such that each has its own distinct, contiguous territory. The incidental consequence of this historical development is that resident lineages tend to fulfill within themselves both of the two principal conditions necessary to Navaho social interaction: geographic and consanguinal proximity. A high degree of internal interaction inevitably results. It is not, however, structurally dictated as is the case in households and residence groups. Indeed, overt hostility is sometimes found to exist between residence groups in the same resident lineage, such that neither will assume any economic or social responsibility for the other.

In Shonto community, membership in resident lineages is shown in table 9.

The basic structure of resident lineages differs little from that of households and residence groups; all normally develop from the multiplication of an original nuclear family. Shonto's resident lineages may include the households of siblings of either sex plus their married children and grandchildren of either sex. Lineage No. 1, the largest in the community, includes the households of one female and two male siblings in the oldest generation; four females and three males in the first descending generation; and four females and one male in the second descending generation. Lineage No. 7 includes households of one surviving female and two surviving male siblings in the oldest generation; three females and eight males in

TABLE 9.—*Household and residence group composition of resident lineages at Shonto (cf. map 1)*

Resident lineage No.	Number of residence groups	Number of households	Resident lineage No.	Number of residence groups	Number of households
(1)	7	15	(8)	1	2
(2)	6	17	(9)	2	9
(3)	2	5	(10)	1	4
(4)	1	4	(11)	1	2
(5)	2	7	(12)	2	3
(6)	3	11	(?)	2	2
(7)	7	16	(School)	1	3

the first descending generation, and two females in the second descending generation. Five resident lineages are seen to be identical with residence groups.

CLANS

Navaho clans have been studied exhaustively by Reichard (1928), and their function and significance in modern Navaho life have been set forth by Kluckhohn and Leighton (1946, pp. 63–65) in terms which perfectly characterize Shonto. Like resident lineages, Shonto's clans are of much more historical than functional significance. Their uneven distribution among the various lineages sheds a certain amount of additional light upon the sources of original settlement in the Shonto area.

Virtually the sole surviving function of the clan is in the limitation of marriage choices; clan exogamy at Shonto remains universal. On the positive side, however, no pattern of clan preference in marriage is discernible. The frequency of marriage between different pairs of clans is proportional throughout to the numerical strength of the clans themselves. Beyond limiting marriage choice, clan affiliation serves only to establish certain special etiquette patterns as between members, especially if they happen to be strangers. The relations and reciprocal behavior established are essentially similar to those which ensue when two Anglo-American namesakes meet by chance, and probably have no more functional significance. Economic and social responsibility for clan brothers and sisters are definitely things of the past at Shonto (cf. Kluckhohn and Leighton, 1946, p. 65). It is readily observable that interaction between households and residence groups is determined by blood relationship without reference to clan.

More than any other factor, it is probably the lack of a clear-cut residence tradition (see below) which has in the long run robbed Shonto's clans of most of their functional significance. The result of this situation is that clans cut completely across territorial lines, and cannot be correlated with any of the regular functional units of Shonto society.

Members of at least 13 clans are resident at Shonto today, as shown in table 10.

Only the first six clans in the list, plus kinłichi'ini, were present in the Shonto area two generations ago. The clan inventory is extremely limited as compared with other Navaho communities (cf. Carr, Spencer, and Woolley, 1939; Kluckhohn and Leighton, 1946, p. 64). In addition to those represented in the community, only 14 additional clans are recognized by some Shonto informants. Many of the clans given separate designation by Reichard (1928, pp. 11–13) are believed to be not merely linked but identical. In particular, all of the clans

TABLE 10.—*Clan membership at Shonto* (*numbers in parenthesis correspond to Reichard, 1928, pp. 11–13*)

Clan name and No.	Translated name	Number of members
Lok'adine (8)	Reed	158
Todichi'ini (29)	Bitter water	118
Tlizitani (14)	Many goats	77
Ashihini (32)	Salt	74
Tabaxa (36)	Shore	49
Tachi'ini (20)	Red streak	28
Adoots'osni (44)	Narrow canyon	18
Bitani (9)	Folded arms	10
Deschi'ini (19)	Red rock bend	6
Xonagha (3)	He walks around	2
Kintichi'ini (15)	Red house	1
Tsinajini (17)	Black rock	1
Xashgha'atso (16)	Much yucca	1
Unknown or uncertain		25
Total		568

of supposed eastern Pueblo origin are believed at Shonto to be of Zuni origin, and the same as the Salt clan. Zuni may well be the only eastern Pueblo known to many older people at Shonto. Tachi'ini, a numerous clan throughout the reservation, is locally supposed to be of Ute origin.

Lok'adine, the most numerous single group at Shonto, can properly be considered a local clan. Probably 90 percent of its membership is found within the Shonto, Inscription House, Cow Springs, and Black Mesa communities. In other parts of the reservation it is commonly thought of as a variant of the much larger xoghatani (Many houses) clan, but this relationship is not recognized at Shonto, although lok'adine is universally conceded to be of Hopi origin. It may be of interest that all of Shonto's pottery and basketry makers are members of this one clan.

MARRIAGE

Marriages at Shonto give an impression of far greater stability than might have been anticipated (cf. Reichard, 1928, pp. 58–73). However, figures on divorce may be inadequate. Leighton and Kluckhohn (1948, p. 83) observed at Ramah that about 50 percent of Navaho divorces occur within the first year of marriage and 83 percent within the first 2 years—in other words, before there are children. After a few years it is usually difficult to find any trace of such marriages without exhaustive research. A similar situation may possibly obtain at Shonto, although only one young and childless couple has been divorced in the past 4 years.

Figures at hand would indicate that of 201 individuals in the community who have been married at one time or another, 153 remain with their original spouses. Another 15 who are currently divorced, widowed, or widowered were married once only. Thirty-three persons (not including men with plural wives) are definitely known to have been married more than once.

Seven of 88 marriages now in force at Shonto are plural. The total number of currently married persons is therefore 183, including 88 men and 95 women. In addition, one Shonto man supports two unrelated wives in separate establishments, one of which is located nearly 40 miles from Shonto. It is said that his two wives have never seen each other. The practice of having unrelated wives in widely separated households is definitely disapproved by the community, including the older wife, although in former times it was apparently not uncommon (cf. Kluckhohn and Leighton, 1946, p. 55; Reichard, 1928, p. 60).

At the present time no Shonto man has more than two wives. Five men have plural wives who are sisters, and two are married to mother-daughter pairs. One of the former five recently attempted to acquire a third sister as a wife, but was forestalled by the Shonto school-teachers, who shipped the prospective bride (age 13) off to boarding school. Shonto men sometimes boast of exercising sexual rights upon unmarried sisters of their wives, an opportunity which is frequently afforded in cases of matrilocal residence. It has been suggested by two informants that this is a common reason for plural marriages; that they are, in effect, "shotgun" propositions resulting from careless exercise of extramarital sexual rights. Certainly, the traditional wealth sanction for plural marriage (cf. Kluckhohn and Leighton, 1946, p. 55) is lacking at Shonto; the community's polygynous households as a group are not richer but distinctly poorer than the community average (see table 17, p. 112). Informants' suggestions about a certain factor of involuntariness may be corroborated by the fact that six of seven plural marriages are matrilocal.

Seven Shonto men who are currently monogamous or unmarried formerly had plural wives. In all cases the wives were sisters. Two men had three wives, and one claims to have had four. Incidence of plural marriage is probably declining. Nevertheless, three such marriages have been effected within the past 5 years, in spite of a Navaho tribal regulation which has forbidden plural marriages since 1948.

RESIDENCE

Shonto contrasts sharply with repeated statements by anthropologists (e.g., Reichard, 1928, pp. 69–70; Kluckhohn and Leighton, 1946, p. 55; Landgraf, 1954, p. 82) concerning the predominance of Navaho matrilocalism. Of the 100 households extant in 1955, 52 were matrilocal, 42 were patrilocal, 3 were uncertain, and 3 (at the school) were neolocal. It has already been remarked that 19 of 31 residence groups involving more than one household included both matrilocal and patri-

TABLE 11.—*Residence affiliations of Shonto households*

Number of years household established	Number matrilocal residences	Number patrilocal residences	Number neolocal residences[1]	?	Total
20+	18	21	0	2	41
10–20	15	11	1	1	28
0–10	19	10	2	0	31
Total	52	42	3	3	100

[1] Shonto School.

local units, while only 8 were purely matrilocal, 3 were purely patrilocal, and 1 was neolocal.

True neolocal residence, in the sense of preempting unoccupied and neutral territory, does not occur except in the case of the school. The structure of land tenure (see pp. 97–109) is such that any new household must inevitably be either matrilocal or patrilocal with respect to resident lineage. Nowadays, new households are also always established initially within existing residence groups, either of the husband's or wife's parents. Later, as the household expands, it may in some circumstances be moved 2 or 3 miles away to form the nucleus of a new residence group (cf. above).

Residence affiliations of Shonto households of different ages is shown in table 11.

Table 11 suggests the emergence of a matrilocal tradition in the present generation. Seven of the eight most recent marriages at Shonto have, in fact, established matrilocal residence.

Variation in residence tradition occurs spacially as well as temporally. Table 12 gives the distribution of matrilocal and patrilocal residences as among the population elements occupying the southeastern, southwestern, and northern portions of the community respectively (see map 3).

The preponderance of patrilocal residence, not only in older households but also in the most recently and sparsely settled portion of Shonto community, points strongly to a historical factor. In view of the traditional Navaho pattern of masculine authority in economic

TABLE 12.—*Residence affiliations of Shonto households in different population groups*[1]

Number of years household established	SE Group		SW Group		N Group	
	Matrilocal residence	Patrilocal residence	Matrilocal residence	Patrilocal residence	Matrilocal residence	Patrilocal residence
20+	13	8	2	7	4	5
10–20	9	5	5	3	1	3
0–10	9	5	6	1	3	5
Total	31	18	13	11	8	13

[1] Excluding uncertain and neolocal residence.

matters it is not unreasonable to suppose that a high percentage of households established in newly colonized territory would be patrilocal, while later generations, under more settled conditions, would witness a return to traditional matrilocalism. Shonto's marked divergence from the matrilocal norm may well reflect the fact that it is up to now the only recently settled Navaho community to be studied.

SOCIAL AND POLITICAL AUTHORITY

Shonto society manifests two distinct power structures which are unrelated. In all relations within the community, leadership follows traditional lines independent of formal recognition (cf. Kluckhohn and Leighton, 1946, pp. 69–73; Hill, 1940 a). Relations with the outside world, including "government," both tribal and Federal, are the responsibility of the tribal councilman and grazing committee. These latter functionaries are themselves "government," and derive their authority entirely from external sources.

The structure of authority in native Navaho society is for the most part implicit in the kinship structure of household and residence groups. The father is at least nominally the head of the household, and the father in the oldest household, provided he has not reached senility, is nominal headman in the residence group. At Shonto these individuals exercise a very real measure of authority in determining activities of the group as a whole. When younger men reject a railroad employment call, the most common reason given is "my father (or father-in-law) told me to stay home." Cases of the reverse, where fathers have ordered their sons in no uncertain terms to go to work, are also common. Many of the sons are themselves heads of households, yet they regularly defer to the dominant authority in matters affecting the economy of the whole residence group (see "Economic Structure and Function," pp. 97–109). Residence group headmen nearly always decide on whether or not to hold a sing for any member of the group, and undertake most of the preparation and arrangements if one is to be held. The decision when to move from summer to winter quarters and vice versa is also principally theirs.

Navaho society has probably never had significant functional units more extended than the residence group, and patterns of more extended authority are difficult to identify. Hill (1940 a) notes that in former times there were, at least in some areas, certain formally invested leaders termed nat'ani (literally, "folded arms"). Communities commonly had two nat'anis, one of whom was a war leader only, while the other exercised leadership in everyday affairs. The actual extent of authority enjoyed by these individuals, either territorial or social, is not certain.

The role if not the office of "peace nat'ani" clearly survives at Shonto, embodied in the community's most active singer. While it is doubtful if this individual has ever received any kind of formal investiture, he plays a part closely analogous to that described by Hill (1940 a). He is quite frequently required to arbitrate disputes between families and to decide upon ritual matters, and he seldom fails to address public gatherings (especially at ceremonials) with a sermon on morality, obedience, or adherence to the good ways of doing things. He attends nearly all the major ceremonials in neighboring communities as well, and commonly delivers sermons on these occasions. In the course of his rather frequent trips to Shonto store he is nearly always asked for advice in family and ritual matters by other persons who happen to be present in the store, and is sometimes heard admonishing the younger generation for its unheeding ways.

No comparable degree of native authority is exercised by any other individual in the community. There is, in fact, a very marked differentiation between the "nat'ani" and the remainder of Shonto's singers, all of whom occupy distinctly low status (see below). The "nat'ani" is a man of 58, lacking any formal education and speaking no English. He is said to have a ritual repertory far more extensive than that of any other singer in the community, and is certainly infinitely the most popular. He is only moderately well-to-do in goods and livestock, and, unlike three other singers, has only one wife.

Most Shonto Navahos recognize two not very distinct external sources of authority: waashindoon (Washington) and tseghahodzani (Window Rock). To these might possibly be added hozdo'i ("the hot place;" i.e., Phoenix), seen as the source of welfare checks and license plates. Waashindoon is employed as a sort of generic term for the Bureau of Indian Affairs, and tseghahodzani similarly for the Navaho tribe (official designation for the tribal organization). The community does not, however, distinguish clearly between the two; they are separate but related forces imposing essentially the same authority. The two terms are, in fact, interchangeable in many contexts; e.g., waashindoon binaltsos or tseghahodzani binaltsos for livestock permit. As a general rule, either term translates simply as "government."

Few Shonto residents identify themselves or their interests with Window Rock. The community has little or no sense of participation in self-government, but sees Window Rock as a group of Navahos employed by and serving the interests of Washington. Thus, although Federal and State Indian liquor laws have been repealed, and prohibition is now imposed by tribal edict only, White people continue to bear the brunt of resentment for the supposed injustice of the measure. Window Rock is assumed to be enforcing prohibition on behalf of Washington. Similarly, the transfer of grazing control from the Bureau of Indian Affairs to the grazing committees of the Navaho tribe has not noticeably abated animosity toward "Anglos" for setting limits on livestock holdings.

Shonto elects a tribal councilman, representing the whole community, every 4 years. Tribal elections are seen as, and in fact essentially are, competitions for well-paid "government" jobs. Both Shonto candidates in the most recent election readily admitted to overriding financial motivations. The councilman's function, as he and the community see it, is not to represent Shonto at the seat of government (he has never made a speech in the council assembly), but to represent government at Shonto. He attends council meetings at Window Rock four times a year, usually lasting from 1 to 2 weeks each, and brings back information on recent Government activities and programs which is disseminated through public meetings at Shonto, held on an average of once a month.

In addition to the tribal councilman, tribal government is represented in the community by the three members of the district grazing committee. This body, like the tribal councilman, is elected every 4 years. It has jurisdiction over range management and livestock capacities throughout District 2, including several other communities besides Shonto. At the present time none of its members is a Shonto resident. The district grazing committee acts as an independent functionary of the Navaho tribe, responsible directly to its chairman and Advisory (i.e., executive) Committee. It passes out information and regulations through periodic public meetings which are normally held in conjunction with those of the tribal councilman.

Shonto's tribal councilman is one of the community's most aberrant personalities. To the White outsider he appears as a typically conservative western Navaho, 63 years of age, long-haired, and unable to speak English. His experience with the outside world and its ways derives principally from a period of 18 months' servitude in the Federal penitentiary at Leavenworth, Kans. Whatever his education in prison may have been, he has a reputation far beyond the borders of the community for his ingenuity and energy in devising ways of acquiring money and goods. In addition to his tribal council activities, he has at the present time a concession from the National Park Service to run pack-trips to the more remote cliff dwellings in Tsegi Canyon and he is one of the community's largest manufacturers of home-brew liquor ("tulapai"). He is said to have Shonto's greatest accumulation of jewelry and other material goods, most of which has been taken as security against cash loans. He has picked up additional income in recent years by marching in costume in the Gallup Ceremonial parade, and by appearing as an extra in several movies made in the vicinity.

In spite of his wealth, the councilman occupies low status in the community, and is a common object of ridicule. This is certainly due in part to the fact that he has never had any children, although he has by his own count been married many times, and once he had four wives at once. At the present time he has two wives, one of whom lives at Shonto and the other far in the interior of Black Mesa. The community's disapproval of this arrangement has already been noted. The councilman's apparent sterility remains a cause of anxiety to him; probably once a month he asks the trader to get him some White man's medicine to make him have children. As a start in this direction, he has been taking large quantities of vitamin pills for years. Other derogatory remarks commonly heard concerning the tribal councilman take note of his acquisitiveness and supposed avarice.

Shonto Navahos, like other Navahos, tend to share with their Pueblo neighbors a distrust of any ambition to power (cf. Benedict, 1934, pp. 91–92). This is particularly true in the case of tribal council service, which is usually believed to consist in the long run of serving White interests as against Navaho interests. While few Shonto people disapprove of Government service in any capacity if the economic reward is sufficient, they often do not feel obligated to respect or even to obey the authority implicit therein.

The differentiation between Shonto's internally derived and externally imposed structure of authority is thus total. The tribal councilman is in effect a Government agent who, with the grazing committee, has inherited almost intact the role of the old district supervisor (see "Government Development," pp. 44–48). He is a man of low status who plays no part in the internal relations of the community. He never intervenes in Navaho disputes, seldom attends sings (he has never sponsored one), and takes no part in community activities.

The nat'ani, on the other hand, has no voice in Shonto's relations with the outside world. While he is frequently in attendance at public meetings held by the councilman, he never under any circumstances speaks to them, nor takes any part other than that of spectator.

LAW AND ORDER

The situation of Shonto with respect to law presents inevitable parallels with the political situation (see above). In each case the community recognizes the authority of dual sets of sanctions: the one traditional and internally derived, the other alien and externally imposed. Two important distinctions may be made in the case of the legal systems, however. First, unlike the two political systems, both legal codes govern essentially the same field of relations. Second, the agents of Tribal (i.e., American-inspired) Law are not normally present within the community, so that its operation is not automatic. These two factors together have led to a rather different type of adjustment between the two legal systems than has taken place in the case of political systems.

Navaho common law (see Van Valkenburgh, 1936, 1937, 1938; Hill, 1940 a; Kluckhohn and Leighton, 1946, pp. 70–75) is not much concerned with crimes, or public wrongs. In the absence of an organized body politic, nearly all offenses are treated as private wrongs or torts, subject to private retribution according to established procedures. As a general rule, restitution or economic compensation is sought first; failing these, force sanctions may be resorted to, commonly in the form of a severe beating administered by the injured party and/or his relatives.

Navaho Tribal Law, by contrast, is closely patterned after Anglo-American models, and thus comprehends a variety of both civil and criminal actions. In theory it does not countenance private retribution of any sort in criminal cases, nor the application of force in civil cases.

The absence of resident police at Shonto, however, results in a wide gap between the theory and practice of Tribal Law. Since the Navaho police are not permitted to make arrests except in the presence either of direct evidence of guilt or a sworn complaint, spontaneous arrests have in practice been confined exclusively to cases of drunken and disorderly behavior observed in the course of occasional police visits to the community. For all other actions, police intervention must be deliberately invoked by individual initiative: summoning of the police by telephone and, upon their arrival, swearing a complaint.

In these circumstances it is not surprising that the majority of Shonto Navahos tend to think of liquor violations as criminal actions but of all other offenses as essentially civil, since in these latter cases the law appears in the role of intermediary rather than initiator. The overall effect of tribal law, in fact, is simply to provide Shonto with an additional set of retributive sanctions which may be invoked at will whenever native sanctions fail to provide satisfaction. Both Tribal Law and Navaho common law are in practice optional and dependent upon individual initiative for their operation. Neither is in any sense conceived as impartial and immutable. To Shonto's people it is the function of law to be partial to injured parties—to offer them retaliatory weapons.

Tribal law is seldom readily available, however. Individuals must find their way to the trading post to use the telephone, and perhaps half of the time the call to Tuba City jail goes unanswered. On other occasions no patrolmen are available to make the 55-mile trip to Shonto. Nearer police at Kayenta have no jurisdiction in District 2. If police from Tuba City are summoned, the plaintiff must wait from 2 to 3 hours for their arrival, and be on hand to present his complaint.

The result is that in nearly all cases, Shonto resorts initially to native legal sanctions. Beatings arising out of supposed theft or nonpayment of debt occur four or five times a year, and generally go unchallenged in the community. Only in prolonged or severe cases is the law at Tuba City likely to be invoked.

Occasionally the differential nature of tribal law and of Navaho common law has worked to produce a legal stalemate. A guilty party who refuses to make restitution, when threatened with a beating according to accepted tradition, may retaliate by threatening to invoke the police on his behalf. Such a threat may or may not be sufficient to forestall the beating; in the past it has been effective in a few cases. Within the writer's cognizance one case of manslaughter, one of attempted murder, one of assault and battery, and several thefts have come to legal impasses more or less of the nature of the case given above, and have gone unpunished except in the sanctions of public opinion. In the cases of theft these have not been particularly effective, but the one man who committed manslaughter (by administering a severe beating to his pregnant wife) aroused such general animosity that he was forced to remove himself entirely from his mother's residence group and make his abode in the interior of Black Mesa.

RELIGION AND RITUAL

Shonto's religious life stands almost alone among the complex cross-currents of modern Navaho life in being hardly altered by Anglo-American influence. In intensity and form the community's religion hews closely to those traditional patterns which have been studied and described in elaborate detail by a host of anthropologists (see especially Reichard, 1950; Kluckhohn and Wyman, 1940; Kluckhohn, 1938; Kluckhohn and Leighton, 1946, pp. 121–181).

No data on ceremonial participation comparable to that collected by Kluckhohn (1938) at Ramah has been assembled for Shonto. Kluckhohn estimates that Ramah men spend from one-fourth to one-third of their waking hours in overt ritual activity, and women from one-fifth to one-sixth of their hours (Kluckhohn, 1938, p. 364). The estimate is in all probability valid for Shonto today.

Major ritual occasions of the year are the great "public" ceremonies, involving participation or at least attendance by members of nearly every household in the community. In nearly all cases these take the form of 3-day Enemy Way rituals (see Haile, 1938 a, b; McAllester, 1954) during the spring, summer and fall; and 5- (rarely 9-) day Night Way ceremonies (see Matthews, 1902) during the winter. In colloquial English the two rituals are invariably termed "squaw dances" and "yeibicheis" by both Navahos and Anglos.

At least five Enemy Ways and one Night Way were performed wholly or partially within Shonto community in 1955. Probably twice as many more took place in neighboring communities and were attended by large numbers of Shonto people. All such occasions aroused excitement throughout the community; they were commonly the sole subject of conversation in the trading post for 3 or 4 days in advance. More than 30 Shonto residents attended one Enemy Way at Kaibito (41 miles away), and two truckloads went to one at Denne-hotso (64 miles).

Minor rituals involving more limited participation are far more frequent than the "public" ceremonies. From the standpoint of the trading post the best index of their frequency is the sale of baskets and printed cotton cloth—indispensable paraphernalia which are always presented to the singer in part payment for his services. Sales of these items suggest that minor ritual performances take place as often as twice a week in the winter and summer, and once a week in the spring and fall. Blessing Way (see Kluckhohn and Leighton, 1946, pp. 149–150) is undoubtedly the most frequent of all lesser rituals; the more so since it is commonly performed before the departure and upon the return of school children and railroad workers.

Shonto's population includes at least five regular ritual practitioners, and two apprentices. In all probability the community "nat'ani" is the only full-fledged singer, as distinguished from curer (cf. Leighton and Leighton, 1944, p. 28), in the group. He is far and away the most popular practitioner, and is probably active on an average of 2 or 3 days out of every week—about the same as the most active singers at Ramah (cf. Kluckhohn, 1938, p. 362). At least three very old men were formerly respected singers, but with approaching senility, they have retired from practice. The community's two apprentices are both sons of singers, and normally work only in collaboration with their fathers.

Currently active ritual practitioners other than the "nat'ani" occupy, without exception, distinctly low status at Shonto. For this reason it is assumed that they are curers (a distinction originally noted by Morgan, 1936) rather than singers. None of these individuals approach the frequency of practice enjoyed by the "nat'ani," nor do they conduct major ceremonies. Two of them are forced to supplement their income by annual railroad work, another is supported by his wife's weaving, and all derive additional support from the manufacture and sale of home-brew liquor, commonly known as tulapai (though not the same as the Apache article—see "Tulapai Making," p. 126). The curers are common objects of ridicule both because of their poverty and because of their heavy drinking and disorderly behavior.

It is not known when or why the making of tulapai became associated with the ritual practitioner's profession, but the pattern is constant throughout most of the northwestern Navaho country.

Singers and curers do not by any means enjoy a monopoly in the tulapai trade, but they are nearly always among its principal practitioners. There is not, on the other hand, any evidence of formal introduction of tulapai into ritual itself; drunkenness at ceremonies, although common, is usually confined to the younger male spectators (see below), and is often roundly condemned by practitioners. Tulapai, however, undoubtedly helps to give Shonto's curers a bad name. The community does not by any means disapprove of tulapai-making itself; but it distinctly condemns disorderly and violent behavior resulting from excessive use thereof.

No data are at hand regarding diagnosticians (cf. Leighton and Leighton, 1944, pp. 28–29; Morgan, 1931) at Shonto; it is not certain that any individual in the community follows this profession.

Witchcraft (see Kluckhohn, 1944) appears, on the basis of direct observation, to play a much more overt role in the life of Shonto than has been observed in eastern Navaho communities (cf. Kluckhohn, 1944, p. 35). Not only is indicative behavior such as the careful concealment of hair and fingernail cuttings (cf. Kluckhohn, 1944, pp. 31–35) manifest in individuals of all ages and both sexes, but the actual social and physical avoidance of a few persons (see "Social Structure," above) reaches extreme proportions. Shonto's most commonly suspected witches are a brother and sister, both over 70 years of age, and another oldster of 75. Two of these have seen their own married daughters deliberately move away from the residence group after several years' residence, leaving the household of the "witch" in isolation. Two daughters of another, although unmarried, have moved a couple of miles away and no longer have anything to do with the old man.

Arrival of one of the "witches" at Shonto Trading Post is a common signal for the departure of most of the other customers, or at least for their removal to the far end of the counter. An atmosphere of tense restraint, which is in marked contrast to the usual highjinks of trading, prevails while these individuals are doing their shopping. Their departure is marked by general relaxation which is nearly always accompanied by boisterous mocking. The trading post's Navaho hired man, although the son of one of the "witches" and maternal nephew of another, seldom fails to find business in the warehouse or yard while they are in the store.

One Shonto "witch," a man of 83, was severely beaten by a much younger man in the spring of 1955, and suffered several fractured ribs. In characteristic Shonto fashion (see "Law and Order," above), he took no formal legal action at first, but attempted to secure a cash settlement. The community's sympathies were distinctly against him, however, and the settlement was not forthcoming. He then retaliated, some 6 weeks after the attack, by filing assault and battery charges. After 5 months' additional delay, his assailant was arrested and sentenced to a fine of $120 or 60 days in the Fort Defiance jail. The man was unable to pay the fine and was forthwith jailed, but after a couple of weeks Shonto's tribal councilman, himself son-in-law of the injured "witch," arrived at Fort Defiance with funds sufficient to procure the prisoner's release.

Up to the present time the role of Christianity at Shonto has been negligible. Prior to 1955 there was never any concerted missionary activity within effective reach of the community, with the result that Shonto was undoubtedly one of the few areas on the Navaho Reservation which boasted not a single professing convert to Christianity. One man had been "converted," to the extent of renouncing all former beliefs, at least twice by visiting missionaries for whom he acted as interpreter, but in each case he had relapsed. In actuality he maintained two wives throughout, and was a common object of derision for his reputed laziness and drunkenness.

Because of lack of missionary contact, Shonto has yet to witness anything comparable to the wholesale religious changes observed at Ramah (see Rapoport, 1954). On the other hand, the characteristic "eclectic interest in other systems dealing with the supernatural" (ibid., p. 6) is manifest; Shonto Navahos undoubtedly have complete faith in the existence of a Christian God and the ability of White people to obtain benefits from Him. Nearly everyone at Shonto knows a few of the elementary features of Christianity: the deities God and Christ; the other worlds above and below where deities and ghosts dwell (cf. Reichard, 1949); the major ceremonies of Christmas and Thanksgiving ("little Christmas" in Navaho), and the custom of ritual abstention from productive activity on Sunday. Owing to boarding-school education the Christmas story has taken a place in the regular folklore of the community. On one occasion when Shonto school had been decorated for a Christmas party, the accidental omission of any lambs from a representation of the manger scene at Bethlehem drew vociferous protest from several adults present.

A missionary representing the Assembly of God sect was active in the community from February 1955 until the summer of 1956. His efforts were hampered by lack of permanent establishment as well as by his unfamiliarity with Navaho language and society, and he aroused comparatively little interest. Two formal conversions were made; both individuals being employed by the missionary as interpreters. One of these was the same man who had been converted twice previously. In 1956, as a result of adverse recommendation by one of the grazing committee members, the missionary was denied a building permit by the Navaho tribe. He has since departed from Shonto.

MEDICINE

In 1955, Shonto people relied almost equally upon native medical practice, and upon modern American medicine, as represented by the Tuba City Hospital. Maternity cases, injuries, and all other emergency conditions nearly always went to the hospital initially; often to be followed up later by native ritual treatment. Infectious diseases, and especially nonpainful conditions, were regularly submitted to sings first, and only went to the hospital if the latter proved ineffective, or upon recommendation of the singer.

Admission records at Tuba City Hospital, which are incomplete, show that at least one-half of Shonto's adults have been treated there since 1950. Patients came about equally from both sexes, and proportionately from all age groups. Among the patients were all but one of Shonto's regular singers. Obstetrical cases accounted for the largest number of admissions, with injuries second. Voluntary entries for treatment of disease, including tuberculosis, were rare.

Acceptance of American medicine has not resulted in any proportionate decline in the frequency of Navaho sings at Shonto. In actuality the two types of medical practice are not in effective competition. It is very probable that Navaho "medicine" has never been regarded as particularly effective in treating the types of conditions which are now submitted to hospital treatment, and that singers themselves are glad to be freed of responsibility for them.

Repeated statements by anthropologists to the effect that the focus of Navaho religion is upon the curing of disease (cf. Luomala, 1938, p. 92; Leighton and Leighton, 1944, pp. 24–26; Kluckhohn and Leighton, 1946, pp. 164–167; Rapoport, 1954, p. 44) are not literally true. Kluckhohn and Leighton (1946, pp. 121–181), in particular, have shown that Navaho ritual practice serves to rectify disharmonious relations with the supernatural of every sort, of which conditions that we term "disease" are only one manifestation. Consequently, even the full acceptance of American medicine for disease and injury conditions would leave a large residue of nonmedical cases to the care of the singer.

An adjustment more or less of this sort is manifest at Shonto. White medicine has replaced or, more often, supplemented Navaho practice in the areas where the latter was always weakest, with the full approval of singers themselves. In addition, the fairly extensive native materia medica (see Leighton and Leighton, 1944, p. 62; Kluckhohn and Leighton, 1946, p. 164) has been largely supplanted by patent remedies of all sorts bought from the trading post. Aspirin and Alka-Seltzer, in particular, are universal panaceas; many adults take them every morning as preventives. Liniments and poultices made from chewing tobacco are also widely applied.

Some Shonto Navahos have, at the same time, a genuine sense of the real psychotherapeutic value of native Navaho medicine (see Leighton and Leighton, 1944, pp. 24–39; Kluckhohn and Leighton, 1946, pp. 164–167), and the singer's practice persists accordingly. "The hospital can cure your body and the singer can cure your mind" is a response heard from several younger Shonto residents, and is an attitude which Public Health Service doctors themselves are now beginning to foster.

EDUCATION

No aspect of encroaching Anglo-American culture has had a more profound effect on Shonto's life in recent years than the advent of all-but-universal schooling for Navaho children. As of 1955 less than one-third of Shonto adults had ever been to school, and average length of attendance for those who had been to school was about 2 years. School experience had little or no overt effect upon the subsequent lives of these individuals; they had almost without exception reverted to the ways of their uneducated neighbors.

Only within the past 2 years have school facilities been made available to all Navaho children (cf. Officer, 1956, pp. 58–73). In 1955 all Shonto children between the ages of 6 and 10, and most others up to age 16, were in school. All pupils attended Shonto Community School for the first 2 years, after which they were promoted to one of several off-reservation schools in Oklahoma, New Mexico, Arizona, Utah, Nevada, California, and Oregon.

Educational developments have come so recently and so rapidly that their ultimate effect upon the life of the community is not yet determinable. It is impossible to say how long children now in school are likely to remain, or what they will do when their schooling is completed. At the present time some 50 Shonto children are enrolled in Shonto school; some 90 are in the higher grades in various off-reservation schools; and about 10 are in high school. Among a handful of students who have already completed off-reservation schooling, none has yet returned to the community.

Shonto parents have voiced little or no objection to the new school program, and several have encouraged their educated children to accept permanent employment off the reservation. Several families, however, have attempted to retain one school-age child at home to help look after the household.

RECREATION AND PLAY

Aside from simple visiting and gossiping, which take place at all hours and in all places, ceremonial occasions continue to present the principal recreational opportunities for Shonto Navahos (cf. Kluck-

hohn and Leighton, 1946, pp. 51–54). Games and other organized
recreational activities of Anglo-American origin have not taken hold
in the community. Most Navaho men know how to play a peculiar
variety of Mexican rummy, but occasions for play are few, and Shonto
Trading Post did not sell a deck of cards in 1955. Contests are
limited to impromptu horse races and roping sessions, and occasional
shotputting with a heavy stone by young men who have been to
off-reservation school.

Drinking is undoubtedly the principal diversion which Shonto
Navahos have borrowed from their White neighbors. Use of alcoholic
beverages, both imported and domestic, is widespread in the community, and drinking appears at the present time to be gaining acceptance as a social institution.

Excessive drinking is largely confined to the younger men, and
it is on most occasions considered as antisocial behavior. Probably
no individual fault is more frequently cited than drunkenness. For
this reason men seldom indulge heavily at home; as a general rule,
a group of young men will meet at Shonto store and go off up the
canyon to engage in a drinking bout. Sings, meetings, and other
public gatherings are also common occasions for excessive drinking,
although it is regularly disparaged by the "nat'ani."

While drunken behavior is strongly disapproved, "orderly" drinking seems to find wide acceptance. About three-fourths of Shonto
men are believed to use alcoholic beverages from time to time, along
with a lesser but considerable number of women. It is said that moderate or at least self-controlled drinking is a fairly common family diversion, although groups seldom get together for the express purpose
of drinking. No disapproval is expressed with regard to drinking by
either sex so long as it does not result in disorderly behavior or
interfere with performance of necessary duties.

Illicit sex is another popular Shonto diversion. Actual frequency
of occurrence is, needless to say, impossible to determine. Some older
men have had intercourse with nearly every woman in the community,
to hear them tell it. Boasting of extramarital adventures, especially
to the trader, with whom a kind of patterned teasing relationship
exists, is universal among men.

Shonto has one acknowledged professional prostitute, but it is
assumed by most men that every woman has her price. Illicit sex
is a diversion that can be had by anyone for the money; the necessity
of paying in all cases is a condition which Shonto's men take entirely
for granted (cf. Hill, 1943, p. 26; Roberts, 1951, pp. 68–70).

It is not uncommon for Shonto men to tease their wives by hinting
at their sex relations with other women. Especially frequent is the
practice of making invidious comparisons between Navaho women

and the Negro prostitutes to whom railroad workers have frequent recourse, Negro women being held up as a kind of standard of sexual desirability. Negroes are seldom thought of in any other context at Shonto, and any mention of them is almost invariably an occasion for humor.

Shonto's one professional prostitute occupies a universally recognized status as such in the community, and openly solicits in and around the trading post (contrast Bailey, 1950, p. 101). She is a woman of 44 who has never borne children, and the daughter of Navajo Mountain's most respected singer. Her husband, who abets her activities to some extent as procurer, is reputed to be impotent and is a universal object of derision.

MATERIAL CULTURE

Shonto's material culture is fundamentally American of 50 to 100 years ago, with a few more up-to-date introductions, one or two peculiarly Navaho adaptations (e.g., the hogan) and a handful of native survivals. (For a detailed inventory of modern Navaho material culture see Roberts, 1951, pp. 15–24; also Kluckhohn and Leighton, 1946, pp. 26–32.) The Navaho community is entirely without electricity, gas, and plumbing, and largely without automobiles; its material development in general is consistent with these conditions.

SHELTER

With two exceptions, all Shonto dwellings are hogans of one type or another (see Mindeleff, 1898; Page, 1937). About three-fourths of the hogans are of the "beehive" type, with vertical lower walls formed by a circle of upright posts, surmounted by a hemispherical cribbed roof, and the whole normally covered with earth. The related hexagonal or octagonal hogan (see Page, 1937, pls. V, VI) with lower walls formed by horizontal logs is found nowhere in the Shonto area. Beehive hogans vary from 15 to nearly 30 feet in diameter, and from 7 to 12 feet in height.

Nearly all remaining hogans are of the supposedly older conical or "forked-stick" type (see Page, 1937, pls. I–IV). These are commonly somewhat smaller in size, averaging 7 to 8 feet in height and 14 to 16 feet in diameter. Cribbed huts, similar to the beehive hogan but much smaller and lacking the vertical lower walls, are used for storage and as auxiliary residences for second wives or older boys. A few older persons, lacking resources to handle heavy timbers, also live in cribbed huts. These are considered unsatisfactory, however, and are often objects of derision.

One man, an employee of Shonto Trading Post, has built a square cabin of upright posts surmounted by a pitched plank roof. Another very wealthy individual, formerly employed at the school, has a square house of cinder block, with four windows and a flat roof supported on vigas. Both these structures have dirt floors.

All Shonto dwellings have hinged plank doors, which are invariably locked when the structure is uninhabited. Other modern innovations in hogan construction are the introduction of roofing paper between earth covering and underlying logs, and the common use of concrete for chinking.

Choice of hogan type seems to be dictated largely by the practical availability of timber, with the beehive type of structure preferred. In addition to hogans for each household, every residence group has at least one ramada, one sweat house, and one corral.

HOUSEHOLD EQUIPMENT

The following items are universal in Shonto households:

> Stove with pipe
> Iron skillet and dutch oven
> Enamelware kettles, coffee pots, breadpans, pudding pans, plates, and cups
> Butcher knife, roasting fork, stirring spoons, can opener
> Water drum or kegs
> Washtub
> Galvanized buckets and dipper
> 1-gallon can for coal oil
> Coal oil lantern
> Flashlight
> Broom, miscellaneous rags, copper scrubbers
> Scissors, needles, thread
> Bedding of old Pendleton blankets, cheap blankets, quilts, and sheepskins
> Wooden crates for storing cooking equipment
> Cheap metal suitcases for clothing and bedding

Common but not universal are table knives, forks, and spoons, food grinders, shredders, and a few other "modern" conveniences for food preparation. Nearly all households containing younger persons have a watch or clock, a calendar, and pencils, writing paper, and envelopes. The one mechanical device which is all but universal is the treadle sewing machine.

Probably half of the stoves in Shonto community are made from end sections of 20-gallon oil drums. The remainder are small wood ranges bought at the trading post. Three families have large enamelstand wood ranges with double burning chambers. Wood is the universal fuel, though a few families who are willing to pay for it also burn coal in the winter. Fires are always started with coal oil bought at the trading post; it is one of the indispensables of modern Navaho life.

Furniture other than stoves is rare. Perhaps two dozen households have homemade tables. Still less common are store-bought chairs or homemade benches. Eight or ten families have rollaway beds and mattresses. Two households have gasoline-powered washing machines, and about a dozen have Coleman lanterns.

TOOLS AND AGRICULTURAL EQUIPMENT

Axes, shovels, hoes, picks, hand saws, claw hammers, and pliers are found in just about every household, and every Navaho man carries a pocket knife. In addition, every residence group has at least one team plow, sledge hammer, and buck saw. Most households have a .22 rifle, but larger bores are not used. Wrenches, screwdrivers, hacksaws, chisels, and the like are rare, and specialized tools virtually nonexistent. There is always plenty of rope and baling wire around for repairs.

TRANSPORTATION

Most households have a wagon and chain harness, and there is at least one in every residence group. In 1955 there were only 13 Navaho-owned motor vehicles in the community: 7 express-body pickups, 4 stake-body pickups, and 2 sedans. Motor vehicles were owned in 9 of the 38 Shonto residence groups. The broken terrain in the Shonto region is not well adapted to either wagon or automobile traffic, and the horse remains the principal means of travel. Every adult owns or has the regular use of a horse or, in a few instances, a mule or burro, along with saddle, bridle, and latigo.

DRESS AND ORNAMENTATION

The appearance of modern Navahos has been photographed innumerable times, and is described by Kluckhohn and Leighton (1946, p. 44). As of the present time, the basic male wardrobe consists entirely of ready-made American articles, as follows:

Shorts
T-shirt
Low socks
High-top work shoes
Levi's
Cotton work shirt (everyday wear)
"Western" type dress shirt (dress occasions)
Levi jacket
Straw hat or cap (summer)
Felt hat (winter and dress occasions)
Pendleton blanket (dress occasions)

It is unusual for a man to have more than one of each of these items; normally an article is worn until it wears out, and then replaced. Common but not universal additional articles are leather jackets, work gloves, belts, and neckerchiefs (for headbands, normally worn only by persons with long hair). A few young men wear oxfords rather than work shoes, and engineer boots are common in the winter. The so-called "cowboy" boot is practically unknown at Shonto, and the store does not carry them.

Hats, along with hair style (see below), are considered an infallible index of acculturation among Shonto men. Long-haired and uneducated men wear the so-called "Indian hat," with unformed crown and brim (resulting from the fact that all hats formerly came from the factory unblocked, and Indians did not know that they were supposed to be shaped by the purchaser). Younger men wear the "bat-wing" hat with wide, curling brim, and shaped crown, often found in lurid colors. The bat-wing hat is thought of by both traders and older Navahos as the trademark of the idle younger generation; hence the common expression "bat-wing bums."

Basic female wardrobe remains extremely conservative, showing modern American influence only in the footgear. It consists only of shoes, socks, full skirts, blouses, and Pendleton blanket. The wearing of undergarments of any kind is practically unknown. Four adult women (three of them employed at the school) regularly wear ready-made American dresses, except on ceremonial occasions. All other women wear homemade Navaho costume at all times.

Footgear is to women what hats and hair styles are to men. Older and uneducated women wear high-top "squaw" shoes and long cotton hose; younger and educated women wear saddle shoes and bobby sox. Women normally have only one pair of shoes and stockings. Nearly all women, however, have at least two and more often three or more skirts and blouses, of which the newest are reserved for dress occasions. Skirts are made of from 8 to 12 yards of sateen, sometimes moderately decorated with rickrack or bias tape. A few wealthy women have dress skirts of satin or taffeta.

Blouses are made from a 2½-yard piece of plush or, occasionally, velvet. Initially they are heavily adorned with rickrack, bias tape, silver ornaments, and coins. When new, both blouses and skirts are worn only on dress occasions, such as sings and trips to Flagstaff. Later, when new outfits are made, the older garments are used for everyday wear. At such times the ornamentation is usually ripped off to be used on the new outfit; consequently little or no ornamentation is seen on Navaho women in everyday dress. Most Navaho women make new outfits about twice a year, with the income from wool and lamb sales. However, additional new outfits are often made in anticipation of major ceremonies, and it is not uncommon for some well-to-do women to have new clothes as often as four times a year. The recognized way for any man to appease an angry wife is to buy her the material for a new blouse and skirt. A study of credit books over several months' time indicates that Shonto women regularly spend over twice as much on their clothes as do their menfolk, and that in some households the bill for women's clothing runs as high as 30 percent of total income. It is certain that sewing has taken the place of weaving as the principal avocational activity of many Shonto women.

Shonto women, unlike men, commonly carry Pendleton blankets on all occasions. Consequently, most women have a new "dress" Pendleton and an older everyday Pendleton. Additional common but not universal articles are readymade jackets, cotton mittens, and head scarves.

The dress of boys and of girls not in school is usually an exact miniature of their parents'. Girls in school are required to wear readymade clothes much the same as those of White schoolgirls. Children's garments in all sizes from one year up are bought at the trading post.

Most personal ornamentation consists of "Navaho" silver jewelry, of which every adult has a considerable supply. Such jewelry was formerly made in the community, but nearly all newer pieces are of Zuni manufacture, bought in the trading post. Small bracelets, rings, turquoise beads, as well as various blouse ornaments are universal, and are worn on nearly all occasions. Concho belts, silver ("squash blossom") beads, and large bracelets are less common, although most households have at least one of each. These items are worn only on special dress occasions—the large quantities of heavy jewelry usually seen in photographs of Navahos is a sure indication that the scene has been artificially posed.

Hair styles deserve mention in connection with ornamentation, since they are often used as an index of acculturation by outsiders. All but three of Shonto's women wear the traditional hairknot, two of the exceptions being school employees. Hairknots are also universal among very young girls. Older girls who are in boarding school are sometimes required to cut their hair, and many of these feature bobs or permanent waves when they return to Shonto in the summer. If they return to the community permanently, however, they are almost certain to revert to the traditional fashion.

The wearing of long hair in a hairknot was universal among Shonto men a generation ago. At the present time it survives primarily among the older and uneducated men. Among adult men the community has 58 long-haired and 80 short-haired men. Forty out of 54 men over the age of 35 wear long hair, whereas among 84 men between 16 and 35, only 18 have long hair. Short hair is nearly always a sign of boarding-school education, since schoolboys are required to cut their hair. Once cut, very few return to the hairknot. Only three such reversions have taken place at Shonto in recent years. In each case the individual was deliberately symbolizing a return to Navaho ways.

COOKING AND HOUSEKEEPING

Little survives of the aboriginal Navaho diet. As of 1955 all Shonto families were heavily dependent upon the store for both staples and processed foods (cf. Bailey, 1940). The modern basic diet includes mutton, potatoes, fry-bread, canned fruits, coffee, tea, and candy.

All of these items may be expected at every meal when a family is in affluent circumstances. A variety of canned and prepared foods may be added less frequently. In harder times, canned meats, especially corned mutton, take the place of fresh mutton, and soda crackers sometimes replace fry-bread. Other items, except coffee, may be omitted entirely in dire circumstances.

Shonto's dietary ideal would probably be attained if each family could butcher every 2 weeks. In practice, most families average about once a month. Nevertheless, judged by hide sales at Shonto Trading Post, the community's dietary standard of living is one of the highest on the Navaho Reservation. Shonto store is said to handle a heavier volume of hides than its three nearest competitors combined, amounting to an average of 2,000 a year.

Mutton is usually boiled in a stew with potatoes and corn; only the ribs, head, and feet are roasted, always immediately after butchering. Potatoes are frequently fried, along with onions, in deep shortening (animal fat is not saved). Fry-bread (recipe in Bailey, 1940, p. 282) resembles the Mexican sopapilla, and is made from coarse bleached flour, baking powder and salt.

A peculiarity of the Shonto diet is the fact that it is virtually salt-free. No salt whatever is normally used in the preparation of meat and potatoes, and only a minimal quantity in fry-bread. Navaho salt consumption is nearly all for hide curing.

Native industry contributes mutton to the basic diet at all times of the year, as well as considerable quantities of corn in the summer and fall. Small numbers of squash and melons and a few peaches are also grown. For other food items Shonto's inhabitants rely on the trading post.

Common housekeeping equipment includes brooms, dishpans, and wash tubs. Most hogans are kept pretty well swept out. Homemade brushes of stiff grass are used for sweeping up ashes. Dishes are washed in a pan of hot water with commercial soap or detergent powder, and are dried with a rag without rinsing. Skillets are usually scrubbed out with ashes. Clothes are washed in a tub of hot water with commercial soap, but are not normally scrubbed, as washboards are few. Yucca-root suds are used only in washing hair.

ARTS AND CRAFTS

Native craft enterprise continues to be important to Shonto's women. Craftwork has some economic value (see pp. 124–125), since with the partial exception of baskets and saddle blankets all products are made for sale to the trading post. The number and variety of items produced, however, is out of all proportion to their economic significance. It is apparent that craft practice among women retains a high degree of prestige value as well as furnishing avocational interest.

All but about half a dozen of Shonto's married women weave. Shonto weaving in general is noted more for quantity than for quality; over 90 percent of woven products are saddle blankets of simple banded design and coarse weave. Most of the rugs are only slightly larger than saddle blankets, and are not much different in design. The weaving of large rugs of good quality is confined to five closely related women in a single lineage, and to one other woman. The community has taken no interest either in the recently fashionable vegetable dyes or in the bright aniline hues characteristic of earlier Navaho weaving; natural blacks, browns, grays and white, plus aniline red, are virtually the sole colors found in Shonto weaving. Rug-and-saddle-blanket production averages around 100, or one per household, each month.

Craft production by women does not stop with weaving. Shonto is believed by dealers to stand apart from all other Navaho communities in the quantity of its minor craft production, including pottery, basketry, pitched water baskets ("pitch bottles"), and woven cotton sashes similar to those made by the Hopi and the Zuni. (For artistic and technological details see Amsden, 1934; Reichard, 1936; Hill, 1937; Stewart, 1938; Tschopik, 1941, 1942.) Also seen from time to time are such near-extinct woven items as twilled and two-faced saddle blankets (cf. Amsden, 1934, pp. 52–57) and old-fashioned woven women's dresses.

Craft activity other than the weaving of plain saddle blankets is uneven and unpredictable in occurrence, suggesting that it is often a matter of fad. The summer of 1955 brought an unexpected proliferation of double-faced saddle blankets as well as cotton sashes; none of these items had appeared in the trading post for over 2 years previously. The store bought no more than three pitch bottles in the whole of 1954 and 1955; in the first 3 months of 1956 nearly 50 of these items came across the counter. No pottery was made for sale between 1952 and April of 1956, when three women brought in a total of 21 vessels within a single week. Basketry, essential to nearly all ceremonial occasions, is made somewhat more consistently. About half a dozen Shonto women make perhaps two baskets a year each.

By contrast to women's crafts, the manufactures which were formerly carried on by males are all but extinct. No silversmithing has been practiced for at least 10 years, although several men claim to have done silverwork earlier. Most older men can make moccasins and other leather items, but do so only very occasionally, for their own and their families' use. Knitting is confined to a few very old men.

As might be expected, the implements employed in craftwork are largely of native manufacture, perpetuating traditional forms. These, along with ceremonial paraphernalia, are the only significant native survivals in modern Navaho material culture. With the single exception of commercial tow cards, which are universal, all implements used in the weaving process are just about indistinguishable from prehistoric forms. They include wooden battens, heddle and shed rods, and combs. Wooden awls are used in the manufacture of baskets and moccasins as well as in weaving.

DAILY LIFE

Shonto's Navahos of all ages continue to pass most of their lives within the limited realm of their own household and residence group. Active men alternate periods of 2 to 3 months' employment on the railroad with much longer stretches during which they seldom leave home. Simple subsistence activities involving the provision and preparation of food, water and wood, as well as sheepherding and farming, occupy most of the waking hours every day of a majority of families. Such activities usually involve nearly every day some interaction with other households in the same residence group, but interaction beyond the residence group is much less frequent. Women find occasional relaxation during the day in weaving and sewing; men in visiting and gossiping.

Trading at the store provides the most frequent occasion for travel and visiting beyond the residence group. Frequency of visits to the store varies enormously, depending principally on how far away the family lives and what their transportation resources are. Most households manage a visit of the entire family to the trading post and school about once a week. Such visits usually involve a great deal of gossip and exchange of news around the store, visits to children at the school (seldom neglected), and opportunities for drinking sessions (see above) for the younger men.

Public meetings and major ceremonials are the great events of the year and are usually attended by members from every residence group, and from nearly every household. They might be called the high points in the social calendar.

THE LIFE CYCLE

BIRTH

Obstetrical reliance upon the Tuba City Hospital is all but universal. All 11 children born into Shonto families in 1955 were delivered at the hospital. However, only two mothers had had prenatal examinations or had contacted the hospital at any time during pregnancy; prenatal care instead follows closely traditional Navaho practice (see Bailey, 1950).

Postnatal confinement at the hospital averages 4 or 5 days. At the time the patient is discharged the Tuba City medical authorities try to insist on at least one later examination, but with indifferent success. Return to the hogan involves return to traditional postnatal observances for both mother and child (see Reichard, 1928, pp. 134–135; Leighton and Kluckhohn, 1948, pp. 18–31; Bailey, 1950, pp. 50–73).

INFANCY

Use of the cradleboard remains universal. The period between birth and the age of 5 or 6 years is, in fact, the only phase of modern Navaho individual development which remains almost entirely uninfluenced by encroaching White culture. Time-honored practices in child care, nursing, weaning, and education are followed throughout (see Leighton and Kluckhohn, 1948, pp. 18–43; Bailey, 1950, pp. 74–84).

Universal during the preschool years is the learning of the Navaho language. English is never spoken between Navahos at Shonto, and no child has ever been brought up to speak it by his parents. With the acquisition of Navaho speech, comes the beginning of enculturation into traditional ways and beliefs. In this process the traditionally important role of elders (cf. Leighton and Kluckhohn, 1948, pp. 39–43) is considerably enhanced today by the fact that the fathers of young children are frequently absent on railroad jobs and that parents commonly leave children in the care of grandparents while they go to sings or to Flagstaff.

COMMUNITY SCHOOL

One of the major crises of early life is encountered at age 5, when Shonto's children become eligible for school (cf. Leighton and Kluckhohn, 1948, pp. 63–68). It has been noted above that until recently very few Shonto residents ever went to school, but that at the present time education is universal for children between the ages of 6 and 10, and for most of those up to 16. Some children start school at 5, but a considerable number are obliged to wait until a year later because of lack of space.

All of Shonto's children attend Shonto Community School for their first 2 years. Here they are under the supervision of two white teachers during classroom hours, and of five Navaho assistants and dormitory attendants at other times. Classes are held during most of the morning and afternoon of every day except Sunday. Use of the Navaho language is theoretically prohibited on the school grounds at all times, but the prohibition is entirely unenforceable in practice. The casual visitor is sure to hear a great deal more Navaho than English, not only among children, but between children and Navaho employees of the school.

Children are housed and fed at the school continuously from mid-September until mid-May. During this time they are not permitted under any circumstances to visit their homes. Nevertheless, every year a number of parents come to the school and take their children out on the occasion of major ceremonials or if someone in the household is ill and the child's attendance is desired. On such occasions it is usually necessary for the teachers to go in person to fetch the child back.

The frequency with which schoolchildren see their parents and families depends largely upon how far from the school the latter live. Parents and other near kin seldom pay a visit to the trading post without dropping in at the school to see their children. Some children see parents and relatives nearly every day; most see them at least once a week. Railroad signup day (for unemployment compensation—see "Railroad Work," pp. 129–133) brings all of the able-bodied men in the community to Shonto Trading Post every Thursday during the winter and much of the spring. Signup day is normally "family day," when the whole household comes down, and is the recognized occasion for visiting schoolchildren. Visits are always accompanied by small gifts of candy and toys, which are especially lavish if the father happens to get drunk—another regular Thursday institution. Some parents take their children out of school and bring them up to the store to buy clothing, candy, and other items.

BOARDING SCHOOL

After completing the 2-year curriculum at Shonto School, the community's children today are promoted without exception to any of a series of off-reservation boarding schools in seven States (see Officer, 1956, p. 60). Some of these institutions run as high as the eighth grade; others continue through high school. They differ from Shonto Community School in being considerably larger and more institutional in nature; in having fewer or, in some cases, no Navaho assistants, so that English becomes the regular language of communication; and in bringing together children from many different areas, and sometimes from different tribes.

Boarding-school children do not see their parents at any time during the school year, though they write and receive letters frequently. The occasion of their return for summer vacation is one of Shonto's great annual events, with representatives from nearly every household on hand at the school to meet the buses.

It has already been stated that the extreme recency of school development for Shonto's children makes it impossible to identify any trend in educational experience and its subsequent effects. At the present time only seven individuals have completed off-reservation schooling; two of these are currently in the armed forces and five are employed in off-reservation communities. Whether or not they will ever return to Shonto remains to be seen.

All girls continue to undergo the traditional Navaho ritual at puberty (see Reichard, 1928, pp. 135–139; Leighton and Kluckhohn, 1948, pp. 76–77; Bailey, 1950, pp. 7–8). If first menses occur while they are away at school, as is frequently the case nowadays, the ceremony is likely to be performed immediately upon their return the following summer.

LATER ADOLESCENCE

A generation ago there was no such thing as an identifiable period of adolescence in the life of Shonto Navahos; today, it is a distinct though unrecognized status, particularly for males. Changing economic patterns have left a kind of socioeconomic vacuum in the period of the late teens, after a man has completed school and achieved Navaho adulthood, but before he has any effective earning power. The Santa Fe Railway, which formerly recruited track labor at age 18, has recently raised the minimum age requirement to 21, and virtually no other employment opportunities exist within the community. Since the recognized socioeconomic status of younger men is as wage earners (see "Economic Structure and Function," pp. 97–109), the teen agers are left out of the picture entirely. They have little or nothing to do, and usually lack economic resources to marry (see below).

Casual visitors are nearly always struck by the number of teenage boys who are to be found sitting or standing around in and near the trading post. Lacking any definite social role, they occupy themselves as best they can with such diversions as they can find. It is not surprising that excessive use of intoxicants, often accompanied by disorderly and violent behavior, is more common in this age group than in all other age brackets combined. Many Shonto Navahos have expressed concern over the growing adolescent problem in recent years, and requests for information about jobs for teenagers are frequent. Irresponsible and especially irreverent adolescent behavior, such as drinking at sings, are frequently disparaged by the Shonto "nat'ani."

MILITARY SERVICE

Shonto is theoretically under the jurisdiction of the selective service board in Flagstaff. In practice, however, the board takes no interest in the community, and Shonto men simply do not register for the draft unless they happen to become eligible while away in school and working on the railroad. In 1955 nearly one-third of the men in the community were theoretically subject to registration, and no less than 37 were actually eligible for induction (18–26), but only five of these were registered. Two men were in the Armed Forces at the time, and four had served previously.

MARRIAGE

A generation ago Shonto men normally married at about 17, and women about 14 (cf. Reichard, 1928, pp. 139–141; Leighton and Kluckhohn, 1948, pp. 78–79). At the present time, as a result of changing educational and economic conditions, the average ages for both sexes are at least 3 years higher. Ages at marriage for eight Shonto couples married since 1953 were 23:18, 23:18, 21:18, 20:21, 20:19, 20:17, 20:17, and 18:15. The community has over 15 unmarried men and 5 unmarried women between the ages of 20 and 25.

Marriage at Shonto remains unaffected by tribal law or American sanctions regarding minimum age and number of spouses. The simple Navaho wedding ceremony (see Reichard, 1928, pp. 139–141; Leighton and Kluckhohn, 1948, pp. 81–82) is performed for all marriages, and suffices for most couples. Not more than a dozen have obtained legal marriage certificates from the Tuba City court. In 1955 one Shonto man was married (at Inscription House) with the Shonto missionary in attendance, and underwent the Christian service in addition to the regular Navaho ritual. No other Shonto Navahos have had the Christian service.

Divorce, like marriage, is accomplished according to simple tradition (see Leighton and Kluckhohn, 1948, pp. 83–86) and without recourse to tribal law. Only one woman is known to have a court-order divorce. However, if a woman with children wishes to apply for Aid to Dependent Children benefits from the State department of public welfare, she must file non-support charges against her former husband in the Tuba City court. Such indictment is, in practice, no more than a matter of form; there is no record of the court's attempting to force a former husband to provide support.

EMPLOYMENT

Shonto men become eligible for railroad employment at age 21, and thereby achieve economic adulthood. For the next 20 years at least, their principal economic status is as wage earners; they are expected to provide some cash support to the residence group (see "Economic Structure and Function," pp. 97–109) every year. Once a seniority rating is achieved, any man can count on a seasonal railroad job every year until he is 50. Very few men answer the call every year, especially in later life, but all average at least 3 years out of 4.

Half a dozen Shonto men have managed to secure permanent Indian Bureau or off-reservation jobs upon reaching 21. In the past 10 years only one man has passed his 21st birthday without applying for and securing either a permanent or a railroad job.

MIDDLE AGE

Late maturity brings the highest prestige and authority in Navaho life (see Leighton and Kluckhohn, 1948, p. 89). Men retire from seasonal wage work between 45 and 50, and thereafter occupy themselves at home, often with directing the affairs of the residence group, arranging marriages for their children, and so on. Maximum age limit for railroad work is 50 years. Until 1955 the age limit was 55, and two individuals, by dint of falsified records, managed to work seasonally until they were past 60.

OLD AGE

Men and women become eligible for Old Age Assistance from the State Department of Public Welfare at age 65. In future years a large number of Shonto's railroad workers and their families will undoubtedly qualify also for Old Age and Survivors' insurance benefits from the Federal Social Security Administration, although no one is currently receiving such benefits. At any rate nearly all of the middle-aged people in the community now look forward confidently to regular welfare checks to support them in their old age. Economic eligibility will be established in due time by an official transfer of livestock, permits, and other deductible assets into the names of their children. Two or three farsighted elders have managed to effect such transfer in advance of the 2-year period prescribed by law, and so have become eligible for benefits immediately upon reaching 65. Most elders, however, are resigned to waiting out the prescribed period—during which they are supposed to be supported by income accruing from the property transfer—before becoming eligible.

Of Shonto's 20 residents who are over 65 years of age, all but 6 are receiving either Old Age Assistance or General Assistance. Four of the six who do not receive benefits have applied for them; three are now waiting out property-transfer penalties and will become eligible in 1 or 2 years.

The advent of welfare assistance has provided valuable social and economic security to Shonto's old-timers. Elderly persons, as well as handicapped persons, with their steady monthly income, are today likely to be an economic asset rather than a handicap to the household and residence group. While the aged continue to be feared as witches, most of them can count on being reasonably well looked after in their unproductive final years (contrast Leighton and Kluckhohn, 1948, pp. 89–90) and perhaps to being adopted into the household of a married son when their own households are grown and gone.

DEATH

Shonto community buries its own dead with customary Navaho dispatch (see Reichard, 1928, pp. 141–143; Leighton and Kluckhohn, 1948, pp. 91–93) and without White interference. Although the trader was once called upon regularly to build coffins and inter the dead, this practice has not been followed in recent years. As of the present time the community has not turned to other White sources for aid. No medical examinations have ever been held or death certificates issued for Shonto's dead.

Fear of death and avoidance of the dead remain universal, showing no abatement as a result of American teachings. In line with Navaho practice everywhere, whenever possible, dying persons are carried outside the hogan, to forestall the necessity of abandonment. Nevertheless, the community is dotted with remains of abandoned hogans, whose history and dangers are known to everyone, from nonagenarians to young children.

ACCULTURATION

The foregoing pages have been occupied with an attempt to define the modal patterns of adjustment which have taken place between the native traditions of Shonto and the impinging Anglo-American influences to which the community is subject. Cross-cultural adjustment, however, is in the last analysis an individual matter. While the influence of Navaho tradition at the present time remains more or less constant for all of Shonto's inhabitants, contacts with and adjustments to Anglo-American culture vary enormously from individual to individual.

At one extreme are a handful of elders of both sexes who had never seen a White person until adolescence or early maturity, and who have to this day never been beyond Tuba City or Kayenta. Their experience with non-Navaho influence hardly extends beyond those elements of material culture, politics, law, medicine, and the like which have been mentioned as forming a constant part of the Shonto fabric. These people have no firsthand experience with the outside world, and only a very limited sense of its effect upon themselves. They derive their knowledge of it from the numerous tales told by their younger neighbors which have become an accepted part of the folklore of the community.

At the opposite pole are a few younger people who, in addition to prolonged boarding-school attendance, have lived for periods of years outside the reservation. These individuals speak English fluently, read not only upon necessity but to some extent for pleasure, and have at least a limited sense of participation in a larger social fabric than the purely Navaho one.

The vast majority of Shonto's inhabitants fall somewhere between these two extremes in the acculturation continuum. Until recently a majority of acculturative influences have not been constant in the community; consequently modal patterns are difficult to define.

In his study of Ramah veterans, Vogt (1951, pp. 90–94) has observed that differential patterns of adjustment to white culture are in part conditioned by the family context within which the individual receives his socialization. He noted in particular a significant correlation between acceptance of white values and the absence of dominant elders from the residence group during the years of enculturation. Except in the case of the school group, where its effects are notable, this particular variable is hardly operative at Shonto. All of the community's other residence groups remain under the dominance of older and uneducated people. The context of socialization is therefore more or less constant for all individuals.

The sources of differential acculturation levels must therefore be sought in external influences. At Ramah, Vogt (1951, pp. 94–98) identified three such influences: boarding school experiences, wage work experiences, and service experiences. Only the first of these has widespread significance at Shonto. Military experience is numerically unimportant, involving only six individuals, two of whom are in the Armed Forces at the present time. Wage work, while experienced by more than half of Shonto's men, is confined to a type of employment which offers contact only with a very limited and largely esoteric segment of the outside world. The social context of railroad work is, in fact, almost entirely Navaho (see "Navaho Economics," below). Railroad workers thus acquire only a tourist's familiarity with the White man's country, and almost none with his culture.

Shonto's inhabitants become acculturated, in the sense of acquiring Anglo-American values, mostly through school experience. Inevitably, there is a very high correlation between acceptance of such values and the ability to speak English—a situation also encountered by Vogt (1951, p. 87) at Ramah. The correlation, besides pointing up the superordinate role of boarding schools in value change, suggests also that most Anglo-American values are not understandable in the Navaho linguistic context—that knowledge of English is necessary for their acceptance.

As a key to degrees of acculturation, table 13 rates Shonto's adult inhabitants of both sexes and in various age groups on the basis of their command of the English language.

The categories of English speakers set up in table 13 can be correlated in a general way with Vogt's (1951, pp. 88–89) "stages" in value change as observed at Ramah. These were: (1) (minimal White contact), no acculturation; (2) (increased contact), imitative adoption of selected White values; (3) (prolonged contact), inter-

TABLE 13.—*Command of English among Shonto adults*

Age group	Sex	Number of individuals in category—					Total
		1	2	3	4	?	
16–25	M	14	19	12	9		54
	F	6	11	4	35	3	59
26–35	M	3	9	12	6		30
	F	2	2	5	19		28
36–45	M	1	5	9	6		21
	F	4	6	6	10		26
46–55	M		3	3	8		14
	F			1	11		12
56–65	M			2	6		8
	F				7		7
66 and over	M				11		11
	F				9		9
Totals		30	55	54	137	3	279

1=Good English; read and write.
2=Limited practical English; illiterate.
3=Minimal English, suitable only for trading.
4=No English.

nalization of adopted values; and (4) (total value change), loss of corresponding native values.

Types of White contacts are not specified in Vogt's scheme. These, inevitably, determine the particular White values which are likely to be adopted. Shonto has had only one constant contact—the trader—through much of its history, with the result that certain White economic values are nearly universal. Other values correlate much more closely with command of English; both, in most cases, reflecting boarding-school experience.

Shonto's non-English speakers with few exceptions belong in Vogt's stage 1, having undergone little or no value change. The same is true to a slightly lesser extent of the minimal English speakers, most of whom received their only education at Shonto school.

The group of everyday English speakers (category 2) have largely attained Vogt's stage 2. Some imitative adoption is seen in dress and appearance (short vs. long hair and bat-wing vs. "Indian" hats for men; saddle shoes and bobby sox vs. high tops and long hose for women); in the seeming time-consciousness noted by Vogt (1951, p. 89), and in an expressed regard for the authority of tribal law and government which is seldom manifest in practice.

Shonto's small literate group (category 1) has clearly internalized many values with regard to cleanliness, health, dress, and comfort. None of these, however, has genuinely achieved the final stage where Navaho values are lost. There is no escape from Navaho culture at Shonto; it dominates the life of every individual in the community. The whole process of acculturation at Shonto has been one of augmentation rather than replacement (see below).

The overall contrast between Shonto and Ramah is clearly marked in terms of stages of acculturation. Vogt (1951, p. 89) notes that a number of Ramah residents have achieved the final stage of value change (stage 4), while no one in the community remains in stage 1. The situation at Shonto is reversed; almost exactly 50 percent of adults remain in stage 1, and none has reached the final stage.

On the basis of their ability to speak English, a number of specific qualities and responses can in general be predicted for Shonto's Navahos:

Minimal or no English: Long hair for men, conservative dress for both sexes; no furniture, appliances, or automobile; heavy ritual participation with occasional sponsorship; recourse to white medicine and law only in extreme emergencies or as last resort; respect for "nat'ani's" authority; no interest in tribal government; dependence upon trader for all dealings with outside world.

Everyday English: Occasional furniture and automobiles; heavy ritual participation with occasional sponsorship; initial recourse to either Navaho or White medicine or law, depending upon situation; respect for "nat'ani" as well as consciousness of authority of tribal government; direct dealings with outside world as well as through trader.

Good English: Modern dress in some cases; furniture and automobiles in all cases; moderate ritual participation but sponsorship rare; initial recourse to White medicine and law in most cases, with secondary reliance on Navaho practices; outspoken criticism of tribal government but little interest in "nat'ani;" dealings with trader confined to purely commercial.

SUMMARY

The cultural design at Shonto is not greatly different from that of neighboring Navajo Mountain, which was described by Leighton and Kluckhohn (1948, p. 139) as "harmony in the backwoods." Both communities are set sharply apart from more easterly Navaho groups (cf. Leighton and Kluckhohn, 1948, pp. 122-145) by a relative lack of culture conflict.

In the long run, it is White contacts which spell the difference between one Navaho community and another. Both Shonto and Navajo Mountain have had only two constant contacts; the trading post and the school. The latter in each case is barely 20 years old, and until recently has affected only a limited number of families in the community. The trading post, on its part, acts more often to reduce and forestall culture conflict than to augment it, as will be shown in subsequent pages. All other Anglo-American institutions— legal, administrative, medical, religious—stop short of the community's boundaries. Their operation is not automatically imposed, but may be invoked by the community itself.

Key to the relatively harmonious cultural adjustment of Shonto and nearly all of its neighbors is the fact that the operation of alien institutions is fundamentally optional, subject to the will of the Navaho people themselves. The whole complex of operations and associated beliefs which is represented at Tuba City, Flagstaff, Window Rock, and Washington constitutes a kind of cultural backstop, upon which the community can fall back when native institutions break down or fail to provide satisfaction.

The result is that the process of acculturation at Shonto has been largely one of cultural addition without loss. White institutions provide situational alternatives to native patterns, without displacing them. In some cases, as medicine, their role has become almost entirely complementary. In other cases, notably with regard to law, a situational conflict may occur. Nowhere, however, is conflict structurally inherent.

The situation herein indicated is not likely to obtain beyond the present generation. More than any other factor, it has been lack of schooling which has not only minimized value change but has insured the constancy of native tradition throughout the community. In the individual life cycle, a thorough Navaho enculturation preceded any significant contact with alien institutions. Within the past 5 years this condition has been altered for the first time. As of 1956, all of Shonto's children are being systematically exposed to Anglo-American culture from the age of 6 onward; at the same time they are being removed from their homes and their native social context during those years which were traditionally most important in Navaho enculturation (cf. Leighton and Kluckhohn, 1948, pp. 44-75). Shonto is thus likely to see more culture change in the next generation than has taken place in the preceding century.

NAVAHO ECONOMICS

Shonto's present-day economic life bears little resemblance to anything described in the literature of anthropology (e.g. Kluckhohn and Leighton, 1946, pp. 19-26; Kelly, 1953, pp. 89-92). As in other areas of life (see "Summary," pp. 93-94), the community has adapted new and alien sources of livelihood to a traditional social and cultural context. Again the process of acculturation has been one of augmentation more than of replacement, although the extent of Anglo-American influence in economic life exceeds that in any other sphere of activity. Native subsistence and craft enterprises survive, overshadowed in monetary reward by more modern pursuits and yet dominant in the community's economic scheme (see below). The result is a distinctive balance among native enterprise, wage work, and unearned benefits, all of which play an integral part in the livelihood of nearly every Shonto residence group (see table 18).

ECONOMIC RESOURCES

Shonto today depends directly upon the outside world for about 80 percent of its total income (see table 21). To a very large extent, therefore, the community is no longer in control of its own productive resources. As a consequence, the activities upon which Shonto's inhabitants depend for their livelihood must be recognized as falling into two distinct classes; those which are controlled within the community, and those which are not subject to Navaho control.

UNCONTROLLED RESOURCES

Off-reservation sources of income, whether wages or unearned benefits, are structural features of the modern American economy rather than the native Navaho economy, and they are governed by modern American economic concepts. Access to jobs is determined by impersonal standards of qualification, either physical or educational. Eligibility for welfare assistance is established by a combination of physical and economic conditions, again entirely impartial. Since these criteria of productive potential apply impartially to all Navahos regardless of kinship status and group membership, they are beyond the control of Navahos themselves. In particular, railroad wages, railroad unemployment compensation, and relief, which in combination contribute 60 percent of community income, are resources upon which Shonto depends for its livelihood but which it does not control.

CONTROLLED RESOURCES

Control of economic resources is exerted through institutions of property or proprietary right. All resources within Shonto community, including jobs, come under such control in one way or another (see "Control of Resources," below). Consequently, controlled resources are synonymous with local resources in Shonto's economy.

Property concepts under Navaho common law show interesting parallels with and at the same time a marked divergence from Anglo-Saxon common law. The latter, a product of the feudal age, is based on the concept of land as the fundamental economic resource of human society (cf. Powell, 1949, p. 364). Anglo-Saxon law thus made, and makes, a fundamental distinction between land, or real estate, and all other categories of property, which are classed as personal estate (see Black, 1951, p. 1430; also Powell, 1949, pp. 363–364).

Real estate is set apart from personal estate in being subject to a complex series of special restrictions upon the right of exploitation and alienation which, in sum, recognize the vested interest of larger social units in the basic resource upon which all depend, regardless of ownership. The result is a variety of categories of ownership or control (fees) which apply only to real estate (cf. Black, 1951, p. 1383).

Personal estate, comprising property other than land and thus not considered essential to the common welfare, is always owned in the equivalent of fee simple. In nearly all cases it is subject to free individual rights of exploitation and alienation (Black, 1951, p. 1382).

Categories closely parallel to real estate and personal estate are found in Navaho common law as well as in Anglo-Saxon. The means of subsistence—sheep-raising and farming—in general are to Navaho society what land was to medieval England (cf. Powell, 1949, pp. 43–44), and these are set apart as a group from personal property in terms of restrictions upon ownership.

Restricted property, in Navaho common law, includes all resources connected with land and subsistence livelihood. It is the equivalent of real property in Anglo-Saxon common law. In this category are land, livestock, hogans, wagons, and even local jobs, which are considered as one of the resources of the land (see "Resident Lineages," below). Land control always involves control of all resources thereon (with one or two minor exceptions—cf. Hill, 1938, p. 23), thus including jobs as well as water, timber, and feed.

Basically, Navaho restricted property is subject to the ultimate control of residence groups and resident lineages despite the fact that formal ownership is often found in the name of individuals. An ultimate vested interest (cf. Black, 1951, p. 1735) of the residence group is recognized throughout. Categories of control to which real estate is subject within the structure of Navaho society are indicated in table 14, page 102.

Restricted property is subject to special restrictions upon inheritance, setting it clearly apart from personal estate. Regardless of kinship of clan status (see below), it is ultimately alienable only within the residence group. Hence it is essentially entailed estate (held in fee tail—see Black, 1951, p. 742), with the residence group comprising the unit of entailment.

Personal property, as in Anglo-Saxon law, is not subject to comparable restrictions upon exploitation and alienation. Such property is both owned and ultimately controlled in the name of individuals. Insofar as it comprises elements not considered essential to the common welfare, personal property is equivalent to esoteric property. Included in this category are strictly personal material possessions such as clothing, jewelry, and bedding; horses and their trappings; and many esoteric skills and bodies of knowledge which may be turned to economic account (see Reichard, 1928, p. 89; Kluckhohn and Leighton, 1946, p. 60).

Not all personal estate is classifiable as productive or capital resources. However, three special categories of personal property do play an important part in Shonto economy: trucks, esoteric skills, and jewelry. Ownership and exploitation of trucks seems to be analogous to that of horses (see table 14), and in clear contrast to that of wagons. Shonto's situation of isolation from the outside world and at the same time dependence upon it gives the community's handful of truck owners numerous opportunities which are of considerable economic significance (see "Native Commercial and Professional Enterprise," below).

Esoteric professional and craft skills are the principal resources of a few households, and contribute to a lesser extent to the livelihood of many others. Included are singing and curing skills, the knowledge of tulapai making, and all commercial craft practices—weaving, pottery and basketry making, and the like. (See "Crafts" and "Native Commercial and Professional Enterprise," below).

Silver jewelry, of which nearly every Shonto adult has at least one or two pieces, plays a special part in the community's economy. To a very large extent, it is Shonto's only liquid capital. It can be pawned (for merchandise only in most cases) at the trading post at any time, and can serve to some extent as a basis for credit in default of all other resources. Because of the extreme seasonal fluctuation and general uncertainty of Shonto's productive economy (see "The Economic Cycle," below), capitalization is essential to the community's livelihood; many households find it necessary to "dip into their capital" (by pawning their jewelry) for parts of every year.

Although holdings in jewelry may serve as collective capital for households and even residence groups, all pieces remain distinctly personal property—owned, controlled, and potentially exploitable individually and for the benefit of individuals only. Shonto's capital organization thus does not entirely correspond to its productive organization. Status of jewelry and other personal estate under Navaho common law is shown in table 14.

Inheritance of personal estate differs sharply from that of restricted estate. In the first place it is more or less freely disposable by the owner without reference to household and residence group. Traditional inheritance, however, is within the owner's clan, again without reference to territorial social units (see Reichard, 1928, p. 94). Probably for this reason all native professional and craft activities in Shonto community appear to be strongly concentrated in certain clans rather than in geographical areas. Particularly interesting is the case of pottery and basketry making, both of which are practiced only by the members of the Lok'adine clan (see "Clans," pp. 61–62).

In sum, Shonto's economic resources are basically productive rather than capital resources. Holdings in the latter category are confined to limited amounts of jewelry. In this sense the community's economy remains a subsistence economy.

ECONOMIC STRUCTURE AND FUNCTION

Modern Shonto community depends upon the outside world for nearly 80 percent of its total annual income (see table 21). Sources of livelihood upon which the community relies today are not much different from those of White settlements in the same region. The special character of Shonto's economy, setting it clearly apart from that of non-Indian populations, lies principally in its institutions of distribution rather than of production.

Heavy reliance upon uncontrolled productive resources (see above), limited capital resources, and an essentially seasonal economy (see "The Economic Cycle," below) all conspire to produce a situation of highly irregular income production both in time and space. At the same time the sedentary life of the community creates consumption demands which fluctuate little from year's end to year's end. Hence, uneven production both seasonally and as between different social units has to be reconciled with consumption needs which are more or less constant in both respects.

Discrepancies between production and consumption are compensated for by a special set of distributional institutions which are essential and integral to modern Navaho livelihood, and at the same time give it its unique quality. Variable productive capacity among social units is compensated for by a complex series of controls upon native productive resources and, intimately associated with them, a regular pattern of functional interdependence among both individuals and households. Variable production in time is compensated for by capital and, to a much greater extent, credit. All of these institutions are fundamental features of Shonto's annual economy.

CONTROL OF RESOURCES

As mentioned above ("Economic Resources"), modern Shonto community relies for its livelihood largely upon resources which are beyond its own control. All local sources of income are, however, under the community's control in one way or another. Types of controls vary distinctly as between restricted property and personal property (see above), and to a lesser extent as between types of property in each category. The structure of economic control by social units, for both restricted and personal estate, is schematized in table 14.

Within the framework of Navaho common law and tradition it is possible to recognize at least six distinct categories of functional control to which resources are potentially subject. Theoretical imposition of Navaho tribal law has added two additional categories (see table 14). None of these controls are necessarily mutually exclusive. They are, rather, exerted differentially by Shonto's four functional economic units: resident lineages, residence groups, household, and individuals (see "Social Structure," pp. 54–65).

Legal ownership, under Navaho tribal law, is always vested either in individuals or in the entire tribe as a collective body. All land, with the natural resources thereon, is tribal property—essentially Navaho public domain. This particular phase of tribal law is largely consonant with traditional beliefs, and has not been a source of conflict at Shonto.

Like the Anglo-American law after which it is patterned, Navaho tribal law classes as personal estate all resources other than land, and recognizes no superordinate rights as devolving upon them (cf. Black, 1951, p. 1382). Disparity between this and traditional Navaho practice has in recent years led to profound conflict in many Navaho communities (see Reichard, 1928, pp. 92–95; Van Valkenburgh, 1937; Kluckhohn and Leighton, 1946, pp. 60–61). Shonto, however, has largely escaped this situation. The functional status of tribal law in the community (see "Law and Order," pp. 68–70) is such that it seldom governs property ownership, and conflicts of interest are, at the present time, theoretical and potential rather than actual. Few Shonto individuals have any real concept of their rights under tribal law.

Legal control, under tribal law, is a function of legal ownership unless contractually delegated. In practice the latter circumstance is found only in connection with certain farmlands, which are a part of Navaho public domain but are formally assigned to users (without fee), the tribe retaining rights of ultimate adjudication but not of eminent domain (cf. Black, 1951, p. 616).

The role of tribal law in sanctioning control of Shonto's farmlands varies principally according to the land involved. A consistent distinction can be made between primary and supplementary farmlands in the community. Primary farmlands are those around which the community has been oriented since its beginnings, and which largely determine its pattern of settlement today (see "Agriculture," p. 123). These are the valuable, irrigated or irrigable lands located chiefly in Shonto and Cow Springs Canyons.

Supplementary farms are small, unirrigated clearings developed subsequent to settlement and located on any convenient piece of ground close to the group residence. These are always well within the territory controlled by the group. As often as not, they are squash and melon patches rather than cornfields, although plenty of corn is also grown in them.

Perhaps because they have always and traditionally been a source of conflict under Navaho common law (cf. Reichard, 1928, p. 92; Van Valkenburgh, 1937; Hill, 1938, pp. 22–23), modern Shonto community has turned readily to tribal law to sanction its control of primary agricultural land. Nearly all users of the bottom lands have obtained legal assignments to their holdings. The practice has not put an end to conflict, however, since in the absence of law enforcement any Shonto resident can legitimately choose to ignore tribal law and invoke custom sanctions instead. There was a fight over a cornfield

in Shonto Canyon early in 1955, resulting in a severe beating of one
of the parties involved—the assignee. In this particular case the
community's sympathies were distinctly with the other party, who
was attempting to establish a preemptive claim upon unused land.
A former Chief of Law and Order on the Navaho Reservation (1935–
42) has informed the writer that disputes over cornfield tenure were
the principal source of civil disorder with which he was asked to deal
during his period in office.

Supplementary fields are not involved in such conflict. They are
clearly under the control of specific residence groups, and are considered as "belonging" to them. Consequently formal assignments
to them are not obtained.

Traditional ownership, like legal ownership, is largely in the name
of individuals. The title thus conferred is, however, always a restricted one in the case of real estate, since it is subordinate to use-
rights and vested interests (see below).

Land is not owned according to Navaho tradition (see Reichard,
1928, p. 93; Hill, 1937, pp. 21–22); it is subject to use-rights and
vested interest but remains, in fee, public domain. With the exception of hogans all other resources, real and personal, are thought of
as owned by individuals (cf. Kluckhohn and Leighton, 1946, p. 59;
Van Valkenburgh, 1937). In terms of formal ownership, hogans
are said to belong to the residence group (however they are sometimes said to belong to the residence group headman, irrespective
of occupancy).

Use-right, with respect to all restricted estate, is a far more significant control sanction than formal ownership. It is the primary
control to which real estate is continuously subject. By contrast,
personal estate is never encumbered by use-rights.

Use-right (see Reichard, 1928, p. 91; Hill, 1938, pp. 21–23; Kluckhohn and Leighton, 1946, pp. 59–61) is always a function of membership in one or another of Shonto's socioeconomic units (see "Economic
Interdependence," below). All members of the group enjoy equal
use-rights to whatever productive resources it controls, individually
or collectively. Since membership itself rests on more than one basis,
however, it is possible technically to distinguish between different
categories of use-right.

Those members of a residence group whose membership is hereditary (i.e. the wife and children in a matrilocal household, or the
husband in a patrilocal household) may be said to enjoy a hereditary use-right upon its resources. Those whose membership is established by marriage into the group enjoy a use-right which is a function
of the marriage contract—in other words a contractual use-right.
Where hereditary use-right is a birth-right, contractual use-right is

a marriage-right. The latter, consequently, is valid only so long as the marriage contract is in force.

In the case of land, inherited use-right rests with the resident lineage rather than with residence groups. Ultimate control of territory is, in fact, the sole economic function of Shonto's resident lineages (see "Economic Interdependence," below). Within the resident lineage territory, utilization of land by member residence groups is a matter for adjustment between interested parties, on the basis of need. In practice the grazing territories utilized by different groups are constantly fluctuating with the increase or decline of individual flocks. Consequently residence group use-rights to land are neither hereditary nor contractual; they are simply established ad hoc— hence may be termed established use-rights. In the case of farms, established use-right may be in the name of residence groups or, in some cases, individual households.

Control of livestock (other than horses) by residence groups also comes more or less under the heading of established use-right. While livestock are owned in the name of individuals, subject to contractual rights in the household, they are in practice usually operated on a communal basis by the whole residence group. Through such operational participation, all households establish some claim upon the products of slaughter, regardless of ownership.

The structure of use-rights as exerted by socioeconomic units is shown in table 14. Of particular interest here is the status of wage opportunities in Shonto community. Regardless of the will of White employers, all such jobs are under the effective control of one or another resident lineage. Attempts to secure employment by non-members are overtly treated as acts of trespass, punishable as such.

Sanctions against trespass are only a part of the set of sanctions by which control is established. Once an intruder has actually secured employment, or such a situation is anticipated, members of the threatened lineage will commonly furnish the employer with a steady stream of adverse reports on the work and character of the intruder. Especially effective are accusations of drunkenness and undependability. Other employees will also frequently refuse to cooperate with the intruder.

Among the employees of Shonto school (all of whom are closely related) the ultimate and completely effective device for disposing of intruders has been to provide them with ample liquor, with the assurance that drinking during off-duty hours was tolerated by the school's White teachers because they did it themselves. When a vacancy occurred at the school in 1955, three successive incumbents were discharged in less than 5 months for drinking on the school grounds. In each case it was reported that liquor had been furnished by the school's other employees. The teachers were well aware of the situation, but had no power to control it. Their fourth choice for the job was a member of the controlling lineage, who had been recommended in the first instance by the school's other employees. At the present time he has held the job successfully for over a year.

All seasonal and temporary jobs at Navajo National Monument have similarly been monopolized by the lineage upon whose territory the monument is situated. Seasonal sheepherding and wool jobs at Shonto Trading Post, as well as the one permanent helper's job there, have been under the domination of a third lineage. The proprietary interest which is overtly expressed in these circumstances suggests strongly that jobs are classed among the productive resources involved in land tenure, and subject to the same controls.

Vested interest (cf. Black, 1951, p. 1735) is the ultimate category of control to which Shonto's subsistence resources are subject. It does not imply regular exploitative rights, but functions simply to set limits upon alienation in the common interest. The exercise of vested interest serves to define the highest levels of Shonto's economic organization. With regard to land and land resources (including jobs) it rests in resident lineages; for all other restricted property it is exerted by the residence group.

Units of operation, in Shonto's subsistence economy, are nearly always equivalent to units of exploitative control. Where control is fundamentally a matter of use-right rather than ownership, it is often in the long run simply established ad hoc. The close correspondence between units of operation and units of control through use-right is indicated in table 14.

TABLE 14.—*Navaho ownership and control of economic resources*

Resource	Legal owner-ship [1]	Legal control [1]	Traditional ownership	Inherited use-right	Contractual use-right	Established use-right	Vested interest	Unit of operation
Restricted property:								
Range land [2]	(PD)	(PD)	(PD)	RL		RG	RL	RG
Farm land	(PD)	Ind. (2)	(PD)	RL		RG, HH	RL	RG
Livestock	Ind. (1)	Ind. (1)	Ind.		HH	RG	RG	RG
Hogans			HH	RG	Ind.	HH		RG	HH
Wagons	Ind.	Ind.	Ind.		HH		RG	HH, RG
Local jobs		(3)		RL		Ind.	RL	Ind.
Personal property:								
Trucks and horses	Ind.	Ind.	Ind.				HH	Ind.
Skills [3]			Ind.					Ind.
Jewelry	Ind.	Ind.	Ind.					Ind.

Ind.=Individual
HH=Household
RG=Residence group
RL=Resident lineage
(PD)=Public domain
[1] By tribal law.
[2] Including resources thereon.
[3] Singing, weaving, tulapai making, etc.

(1)=Permit holder
(2)=Assignee
(3)=Employer

ECONOMIC INTERDEPENDENCE

Shonto's complex structure of economic control of productive resources is not in itself sufficient to insure an equitable distribution of income. As stated previously, the community today is largely dependent upon uncontrolled resources for its livelihood. Thus, in default of controls at the level of production, wage income is subject instead to a similar set of controls at the level of distribution. As in the case of productive controls, the overall effect is to solidify the threefold structure of individual, household, and residence group which is basic to Shonto's economic operations.

One of the most distinctive features of Navaho social and economic organization is its threefold character, representing three fairly distinct levels of economic organization in contrast to the two levels (individual and household) of modern American society. While the basic division of labor in both societies is within the household, in Navaho society there is frequently a further division of labor as between households in the same residence group. Households and residence groups are clearly distinguishable as minimum and maximum subsistence units, respectively, whereas in American society the household alone normally functions as both. The structure of economic interdependence among the units of Shonto society is schematized in table 15.

Resident lineages (see pp. 59–61) actually correspond to the highest level of economic organization in Shonto community. They are not, however, functional units either of production or of consumption.

TABLE 15.—*Navaho economic interdependence—Units of production and consumption*

Source of income	Form of income	Control of resource [1]	Marketing unit	Unit of production	Basic unit of consumption	Secondary unit of consumption
Controlled resources:						
Restricted property:						
Agriculture	Prod.	RG		RG	RG	
Livestock—home consumption	Prod.	RG		RG	RG	
Livestock—sales [2]	{Mdse. {Cash	}Ind. [3]	HH, Ind.	RG	HH	RG
Personal property:						
Esoteric skills	{Mdse. {Cash	}Ind.		Ind.	Ind., HH	HH, RG
Crafts	Mdse.	Ind.	Ind.	Ind.	Ind.	HH
Pawn	Mdse.	Ind.	Ind.		Ind.	HH
Uncontrolled resources:						
Wage income	Cash			Ind.	HH	RG
Unemployment comp	Cash			Ind.	HH	RG
Welfare	Cash			Ind.[4]	HH	RG

[1] See table 14.
[2] Including wool sales.
[3] While ultimate control of livestock rests with residence group, individual owner has equal authority over sales.
[4] Application is made and eligibility established on individual basis, but income is intended for support of entire household and is dependent on size of household.

Organized exploitative activity among their member groups, as observed elsewhere by Kimball and Provinse (1942, pp. 22–23; see also Thompson, 1950, pp. 144–145), is rarely seen at Shonto.

Resident lineages are simply land-use communities (cf. Thompson, 1950, p. 144; Kluckhohn and Leighton, 1946, p. 63) wherein a group of related residence groups retain a common vested interest in a specific and contiguous range area which all occupy. Vested interest extends to all resources of the land occupied, including job opportunities. As earlier stated, land tenure by resident lineages is ultimately a matter of inherited preemptory right stemming directly from historical conditions involved in the original settlement of the community. No formal organization or communal activity is implied.

Residence groups are the regular maximum subsistence units of Shonto society (see "Residence Groups," pp. 57–59). Although Navaho households are ideally self-supporting (see Kluckhohn and Leighton, 1946, p. 54), they are not always so in practice. Specialization in productive activity as well as differential productive capacity often results in considerable income discrepancies among households in the same residence group. These discrepancies are compensated for by a regular pattern of interdependence among households.

In all activities connected with the exploitation of native subsistence resources the residence group normally functions as a single unit of production and consumption (see table 14). Livestock, although individually owned, are nearly always herded and corralled together in a single band as a cooperative enterprise of the entire group (cf. Kluckhohn and Leighton, 1946, p. 51). Both the labor of herding and the products of slaughter are likely to be shared among all participating households, the actual owning household being entitled to the choicest parts of the animal. By tradition the hide goes to the individual owner of the slaughtered animal.

Cornfields, although assigned by law to an individual holder (normally the residence group headman), are likewise commonly operated as a joint enterprise of the entire group, with all households entitled to a share in the harvest. Even where the residence group controls more than one field, as is true in a few cases (see table 17), there is seldom a clearcut division of labor or reward among households.

Wagons, although individually owned, likewise function for the benefit of the entire group in most cases. As shown in table 17, there is seldom more than one wagon to a residence group. Horses and trucks do not fall in the same category; they are strictly personal estate.

Where Navaho households are ideally self-supporting, residence groups are necessarily so—hence their classification as maximum subsistence units. They are, in fact, organized economic units subject to the superordinate authority of a headman (cf. Thompson, 1950, p. 44). Organization of productive activity goes far beyond the communal operation of native subsistence resources. Many modern Shonto residence groups show a consistent division of labor among member households. The group is almost certain to be dominated by an older but still physically vigorous man, whose household is in effect the central household of the group. This household will function to manage and regulate the affairs of the entire group, and will have special responsibility for the pursuance of native subsistence activities.

There is seldom more than one such household in a residence group. All other households in the group are likely to be either a generation older, hence beyond the status of active productivity and authority (cf. Leighton and Kluckhohn, 1948, pp. 89–91), or else one or two generations younger. All such households function essentially as subsidiary households to the central one. Among the younger households, it is the principal economic function of the men to work for wages, and thus augment the group's subsistence resources with cash income from both wages and unemployment compensation. Participation in wage work at any given time is likely to be decided by the residence group headman to a greater extent than by the individual actually involved—at any rate he usually has the final say in the matter.

Older or handicapped households are nowadays expected to play their part in the group economy by getting on relief and thus providing a limited but absolutely dependable year-round income. The advent of Navaho eligibility for welfare assistance has, probably for the first time, enabled every household in the community to occupy some productive role, regardless of resources. Thus, no household today is necessarily entirely dependent upon any other.

All income except from joint subsistence activities is first and foremost the property of the household in which it was earned. Unlike households, the residence group cannot exert an a priori claim upon income. In time of need, however, any household can claim assistance from any other. The function of the residence group as a unit of consumption is therefore a secondary one, always potential but not automatically operative (see table 15).

In practice, specialization of productive activity commonly results in considerable disparities in income among member households at different times of the year (see "The Economic Cycle," p. 141), and a regular pattern of interdependence is likely to develop. During the winter and spring an entire residence group may be forced to subsist largely on unemployment compensation drawn in one or two households. "Indebtedness" which thus accrues is compensated for at the time of wool sales, when the creditor household may be given quantities of fleeces to sell in its own name. Similarly, in the fall, households which have supported the group through their railroad earnings are given a number of lambs to sell in their own name. When all other resources fail, an entire residence group may even live on one member's relief check for brief periods. Similar compensation is made in due time to these individuals. One index of such regular interdependence is the fact that 81 Shonto households had some income from lamb and wool sales in 1955, although only 55 officially own livestock (cf. tables 17 and 19).

The overall structure of residence groups is in many respects analogous, at a higher level or organization, to that of households. There is a consistent, if not formalized, division of labor along age lines (but none, of course, by sex), in which one member is dominant and the others subsidiary. Since most Shonto residence groups are no more than households extended by the marriage of grown children, it is hardly surprising that the relations which unite the member households are not much different from those which formerly united them when they were members of the same household. The overall economic function of the residence group may perhaps be summed up by saying that each member household has a duty to produce what it can, and each has a right to consume what it needs. This relationship is expressed schematically in table 15.

Households have been mentioned as Shonto's minimum subsistence units. Their organization is in many ways analogous to that of residence groups, but is more formal and rigid in every respect. This applies especially to the division of labor, which at the household level is made on the basis of both age and sex, and is formalized to the degree of almost total differentiation (cf. Kluckhohn and Leighton, 1946, pp. 50–51). Fundamentally, it is the duty of the male spouse to provide support for the entire household. He alone is responsible for the production of capital income; the economic roles of wife and children are confined to the subsistence level, and in any case are essentially ancillary. (For a detailed study of household economic function see Roberts, 1951, pp. 28–37.)

As a result of rigid division of labor, economic interdependence within households is an a priori matter instead of a situational and discontinuous matter as in the case of residence groups. Households are Shonto's basic units of consumption for nearly all cash income, as residence groups are for home produce (see Kluckhohn and Leighton, 1946, pp. 54–55; Landgraf, 1954, pp. 82–83). The household has a collective prima facie claim upon all income earned by the male spouse.

Households, like residence groups, also exert situational secondary claims. In time of need any income earned by any member of the group is certain to be claimed collectively by the group. This applies to categories which are normally regarded as personal income, such as the craft earnings of women (see below). A man's obligation to support his household is such that in default of other resources he may even be required to pawn his own jewelry in behalf of the group collectively.

In Shonto's economy, households are units of consumption rather than of production. The latter is either an individual matter or, in the case of subsistence activities, is integrated with the activity of the whole residence group.

Individuals function as primary units of production in Shonto's modern economy, with its heavy dependence upon uncontrolled resources. Their role as primary units of consumption is on the other hand distinctly limited, being confined to a few classes of income which accrue from the exploitation of purely personal resources (see "Control of Resources," above). In this category are the craft earnings of women, which, not being a part of the regular subsistence complex, are often treated as a sort of windfall. While many Shonto women in practice contribute their rug money (actually merchandise) to the support of their households, they are apparently not obligated to do so, and a few always spend it entirely on themselves. The status of weaving income as a private resource is indicated in the fact that craft production is never a basis for credit.

To the extent that they are received in goods rather than in cash, singers' earnings are also individual property. They are, however, subject in all cases to claim by the household if needed for its support. A final category of basically personal income is that derived from the pawning of jewelry, which is always personally owned.

The individual's role in the overall economic scheme is ultimately a matter of membership in larger units of production and consumption, which itself is a function of residence. Every individual is by birth a resident, and hence a participating member, of a given household and residence group. At the time of marriage, residence for members of either sex may or may not change, depending upon the terms of the individual marriage contract involved. The contracting families are likely to come to whatever arrangement seems most economically advantageous to both, without too much regard for sex-oriented tradition.

Where residence is transferred as a condition of marriage, the exolocal partner acquires contractual rights and a specific role within the new residence group which in practice are in no way different from those of hereditary members. They are, however, always conditional to the marriage contract itself, and thus are subject to termination, in contrast to birthrights which are inalienable.

For Shonto's present-day socioeconomic system no more fundamental principle of participation can be delineated. The common characterization of Navaho society as overwhelmingly matrilocal, in which a basic distinction is made as between hereditary female "ownership" and contractual male use-right (cf. Reichard, 1928, pp. 91–92; Thompson, 1950, pp. 143–145) is probably an oversimplification in any case, and cannot be applied to modern Shonto. It is residence and not sex which per se determines economic participation. Residence itself may or may not be determined on the basis of sex, but such determination is never automatic; it is always subject to contractual adjudication.

CREDIT

Credit extended by the trading post is as much an integral part of Shonto's modern-day economic life as is household interdependence. It is the ultimate institution which frees the community's living standards from the vicissitudes of a seasonal economy (see "The Economic Cycle," p. 141), as household interdependence frees them from discrepancies in productive capacity. Eighty-six of Shonto's 100 households regularly draw credit at the trading post during part or all of every year. This figure refers only to "book credit" (see "Types of Trade," pp. 186–201), which is drawn by and in the name of households. If individual credit against pawn is added, members of every household in Shonto community drew credit in some amount at Shonto Trading Post in 1955.

It is estimated that Shonto community annually spends between 40 and 50 percent of its income before it is earned. Of income which actually reaches the community (i.e., excluding wages of railroad and other off-reservation workers which are spent while on the job), as much as 67 percent is likely to be owed in advance. Particularly during the winter months, the entire community lives largely on credit. Since Shonto Trading Post normally extends credit only in the form of merchandise, and also pays for native products wholly or partially in merchandise, it follows that cash transaction is not a major feature of Shonto's economy.

Capital plays only a limited role in the credit structure. Insofar as jewelry is always pawned with the full intention of redeeming it, and is in fact redeemed in well over 99 percent of instances, the community lives on its future earnings rather than on its principal. This consideration is inherent in the trading post's credit policy, wherein credit limits are determined on the basis of anticipated future earnings rather than by the value of the collateral (see "Types of Trade," pp. 186–201). The special function of pawn is primarily to raise strictly individual income which is unencumbered by household claims. At most it may also serve as a basis for very limited credit in emergencies, when no other resources are at hand or anticipated.

Credit is allowed to all Shonto households (or, in a few cases, individuals) excepting one or two which are considered unreliable, against all predictable income. Chiefly involved are wool, lambs, paychecks, and benefit checks. Credit limits vary according to the predictability of the income from the trading post's point of view—meaning both the total amount of income expected and the success with which it can be collected. In the latter connection any income in the form of checks is considered as much better security than cash income, since checks are mailed through the trading post and will inevitably have to be cashed there. (A general discussion of credit policy at Shonto Trading Post is included in pp. 188–199.) The overall structure of Shonto's dependence upon cash, credit and merchandise transactions is indicated in table 16.

Nearly all Shonto credit is officially accounted in the name of households. Individuals within the same household have separate accounts (other than pawn) in only three cases. Except in instances of specific instruction to the contrary, which are rare, all members of a household including children are permitted to draw against the common account. Many households have standing permission, recognized by the trading post, to draw against the accounts of other households in the same residence group; in emergencies some such arrangement is nearly always made (cf. Kluckhohn and Leighton, 1946, p. 57). The "debts" thus incurred are regularly adjusted at the time of lamb and wool sales, when income from a single sale is frequently applied on more than one account.

SOURCES OF LIVELIHOOD

The sources and extent of Shonto's income in 1955 are shown in table 21. Distribution of income from various sources within households and residence groups is indicated in table 18, and averaged in table 22. The most immediately notable feature of the whole economic

TABLE 16.—*Structure of cash, merchandise, and credit transactions at Shonto Trading Post*

Source of income	Form of income	Normally drawn on credit	Normally unencumbered	Season of credit [1]	Season of earnings [1]
		Percent	*Percent*		
Wool sales	{½ cash ½ mdse}	67	33	Dec.–May	Apr.–June.
Lamb sales	{½ cash ½ mdse}	50	50	June–Sept.	Sept.
Crafts	Mdse	None	100	None	All year.
Miscellaneous native enterprise.	Various	None	100	None	Do.
Local jobs	Checks	50–90	10–50	All year	Do.
RR jobs	do	25	75	May–Sept.	May–Sept.
Unemployment compensation.	do	90	10	Dec.–Apr.	Dec.–Apr.
Other off-reservation jobs.	Cash, checks	None	100	None	Variable.
Welfare	Checks	99	1	All year	All year.

[1] See Charts A and B.

complex is the fact that railroad employment directly and indirectly contributes just over half of the community's entire annual income, or more than four times as much as any other single source of livelihood.

In the curious complex of modern Navaho economics, this does not mean that Shonto's energies are oriented chiefly toward railroad work, or even that the community regards railroad work as its main source of subsistence. The psychological value, which means in general the prestige value, of different productive pursuits hews closely to established tradition, and often bears little resemblance to their actual economic return. In its own eyes, Shonto is undoubtedly a largely self-sufficient subsistence community, which voluntarily supplements its income and achieves a higher material standard of living through seasonal wage work.

In Shonto's scheme of things traditional economic pursuits—subsistence agriculture and livestock, and the practice of esoteric skills—come first, forming the necessary subsistence base of nearly every household and residence group irrespective of their monetary value (cf. Kluckhohn and Leighton, 1946, p. 20; Roessel, 1951, pp. 68, 90). The role of wage work is subsidiary and supplementary. It is seldom allowed to interfere with more traditional pursuits and is not in itself considered a satisfactory substitute for them by most of Shonto's inhabitants. In other words, in Shonto's present-day economy a clear-cut distinction can be drawn between basic and supplementary economic activities. The former, consisting of those traditional pursuits which were once the community's entire economic base, have served to establish a traditional standard of living which still dominates economic thinking. The latter, consisting of economic opportunities brought about by contact with White culture and society, serve in large measure to establish the community's actual day-to-day level of living.

An index of the predominance of basic over supplementary pursuits is the fact that Shonto's Navahos undoubtedly continue to conceive of all economic life in seasonal and cyclic terms (see "The Economic Cycle," p. 141). Hence, while native resources are exploited to full practical potential, Shonto's wage earnings consistently fall far short even of their immediate potential. Railroad work for nearly all men is limited to seasonal extra-gang employment (see p. 114), although numerous permanent section gang opportunities are available every year. It is virtually impossible to recruit any number of men for any wage work during the seasons of planting, shearing, harvesting, or lamb sales. At other seasons there is consistent emphasis on short-term employment, and a high turnover in permanent jobs.

LIVESTOCK

Livestock raising is second only to farming (see pp. 123–124) as the most basic and necessary, in native terms, of all Shonto's productive activties (see Hill, 1938, p. 18; Kluckhohn and Leighton, 1946, p. 20; Roessel, 1951, pp. 72, 95). It is the one and only source of fresh mutton, an absolute necessity according to Navaho ideals, and, hence, even such high-prestige activities as the practice of native crafts and professional skills are secondary to it. All Shonto residence groups except that at the school have some livestock. Distribution of animals (in terms of formal ownership) among Shonto households and residence groups is shown in table 17. Average and total holdings are shown in table 19.

The best recent discussion of Navaho livestock practice in general is that of Landgraf (1954, pp. 60–64) at Ramah. His description applies to Shonto, with little modification.

Sheep are owned in all but one of Shonto's 38 residence groups. Formal ownership is by individuals, often involving several members of a single household (cf. Kluckhohn and Leighton, 1946, p. 59). However, actual sheep operation is usually undertaken as a joint operation of the whole residence group. The average band comes to about 100 head (see table 19). Herding is traditionally the job of children between the ages of 6 and 12 years (cf. Leighton and Kluckhohn, 1948, pp. 57–58), but in the present day, when nearly all children of those ages are in school, it is likely to be done by older children and even, in a few cases, by adults. Flocks are herded during the daylight hours only, and are normally corralled at the residence group center for at least 12 hours out of 24 (cf. Kluckhohn and Leighton, 1946, p. 30). Herding follows a very limited itinerary, usually within 2 miles of the hogan, as dictated by limited range holdings and water sources (see map 1). There is seldom any significant variation in the daily grazing itinerary (see Franciscan Fathers, 1910, p. 257).

Shonto's sheep practice is essentially sedentary; it is a type of practice normally adapted to pasturage rather than range conditions. As map 1 clearly shows, the Navahos' celebrated seasonal migration with their flocks seldom amounts to more than "moving onto the back 40." Of 38 Shonto residence groups, 15 have only one residence which is occupied throughout the year. Sixteen groups have two residences, 6 have three residences, and 1 has four. In all but half a dozen cases summer and winter hogans are located upon a single contiguous range area, and, in fact, average less than 2 miles apart.

TABLE 17.—*Economic resources of Shonto households and residence groups*

Residence group No.	Household No.	Number of members	Number of hogans	Transportation [1]	Livestock Permit capacity [2]	Sheep	Goats	Cattle	Horses	Cornfields	Weaving	Singing etc.	Misc. native	Railroad	Local [3]	Welfare [4]	Belts	Beads	Bracelets
1	1	3	1		59–6			3	6		X	X					1	1	
	2	7	1	W	45–5	52	6	1	5	X	X	X				TP			2	1
	3	3	1								X	X			X			1		
2	4	10	5	2T	161–6	195	21	10	6	X	X	X	X	X		Sc		1	2	
3	5	2	1																1	1
	6	9	1	W	161–4	128	32		6	X	X	X		X					1	1
	7	3	1								X			X				1	1	
4	8	5	3	W	21–2	60	29		4		X						ADC	1		
	9	6	2	T	115–4	101	4		4	X	X	X		X					2	1
	10	5	2								X	X		X						1
5	11	4	2		131–5	73	27		6	X	X			X					2	2
	12	9	1	W	161–9	66	55		7	X	X	X		X					2	2
	13	8	2								X	X						1	2	
	14	2	1											X				1		
	15	6	1											X						1
	16	4	2								X			X					1	
6	17	3	1														OAA	1		
	18	6	2		30–3	104	22		3	X	X			X					1	1
	19	8	1	W	160–4	83	23	1	5	X	X			X				1		2
	20	3	1															1	1	
7	21	9	2	W	192–8	241	15		8	X	X			X				1		
	22	2	2																	1
8	23	8	1	W	161–5	85	35		5	X	X		X	X				1		
	24	4	1								X				X				1	1
9	25	9	2	W	80–4	71	11	4	4	X	X			X				1		
	26	8	2		161–6	106	36	3	5	X				X					1	
	27	9	2								X			X			ADC			
10	28	2	1		101–6	47	13		6					X			OAA			1
	29	4	1								X			X				1	1	
	30	11	1	W	100–6	42	12		5	X	X			X				1		
	31	2	1								X			X						
11	32	7	3	W	30–3	40	12	2	4	X	X	X		X				2	1	
	33	4	3								X										1
12	34	2	2	W	161–6	96	3	4	9	X		X	X			NM			3	
	35	7	2	T	10–2	21	13	1	3	X	X		X		NM					2
13	36	8	3	W	107–3	44	25	14	4	X	X				NM		1	1	
	37	2	1								X			X						1
14	38	5	3	W	10–2				2		X									1
	39	2	2							X	X	X								1	
	40	8	2	W	181–4	55	11	8	11		X	X		X			1		2
15	41	14	3		161–6	83	45	9	7	X	X			X	NM		2		
16	42	9	1	W	120–4	68	39		6	X	X			X	NM		1		
	43	3	1											X						
	44	4	1										X					1		
17	45	10	2									X	X		NM	ADC				1
	46	6	2	W	73–3	19	7		4	X	X			X			2		
	47	4	2		20–0									X					
18	48	2	2		160–6	118	23			X							2 OAA			
	49	7	1		86–3	29	7	3	4	X				X					
	50	7	2	W	112–4	141	33		7					X					
	51	3	1											X				1	
19	52	12	2	W	124–4	66	27	2	5	X				X		ADC	1	1	
	53	4	2	T							X			X				1	1
	54	2	1																	

See footnotes at end of table.

TABLE 17.—*Economic resources of Shonto households and residence groups*—Con.

Residence group No.	Household No.	Number of members	Number of hogans	Transportation [1]	Livestock — Permit capacity [2]	Sheep	Goats	Cattle	Horses	Cornfields	Skills — Weaving	Singing etc.	Misc. native	Jobs — Railroad	Local [3]	Welfare [4]	Pawn [5] — Belts	Beads	Bracelets
20	55	3	1	---	---	56	14	---	4	X	X	X	---	---	---	---	1	---	---
	56	7	2	W	---	---	---	---	---	X	X	X	---	---	---	---	1	---	1
	57	5	2	---	25-2	9	6	---	3	X	X	---	---	X	---	---	1	---	---
21	58	4	2	---	20-3	2	4	---	3	---	X	---	---	---	---	GA	1	1	1
	59	6	2	W	52-4	11	6	---	5	---	X	---	---	X	---	ADC	1	---	---
	60	11	2	W	100-5	31	22	---	5	X	X	---	---	X	---	---	1	1	---
	61	2	1	---	---	---	---	---	---	---	---	---	---	---	---	---	---	---	1
22	62	3	1	---	49-6	10	4	---	7	---	---	---	---	---	---	OAA	---	1	---
	63	10	1	---	48-3	17	9	---	4	X	X	---	X	X	---	---	---	1	2
	64	3	1	---	---	---	---	---	---	---	---	---	---	---	---	ADC	---	---	---
23	65	2	1	---	42-3	22	17	---	2	---	X	---	---	---	---	---	---	---	---
24	66	10	2	W	30-3	16	7	---	3	X	---	---	---	X	TP	---	1	3	1
	67	2	1	---	---	---	---	---	---	---	X	---	---	X	---	---	---	---	1
25	68	7	1	W	77-3	45	19	---	3	X	X	X	---	X	---	---	2	1	1
	69	7	1	---	---	11	9	---	2	---	---	---	---	X	---	---	---	2	---
26	70	6	1	W	161-6	55	21	9	6	X	---	---	---	X	---	---	---	1	1
27	71	8	1	W	80-5	35	14	---	3	X	---	---	---	X	TP	---	1	2	---
	72	3	1	---	---	---	---	---	---	---	---	---	---	X	---	---	---	1	1
28	73	13	1	T	85-2	31	34	---	6	X	X	---	---	X	---	---	1	---	1
	74	8	4	W	62-3	21	12	---	3	X	X	---	---	---	Sc	OAA	---	1	---
	75	2	4	T	161-6	79	10	---	8	X	X	---	---	X	---	---	---	1	---
	76	6	4	---	---	---	---	---	---	---	---	X	---	X	---	---	---	---	---
29	77	4	2	W	50-2	52	37	---	3	X	---	---	---	X	TP	---	---	1	2
	78	4	1	---	50-2	46	9	---	1	---	X	---	---	X	---	---	---	1	1
	79	8	2	---	30-3	18	3	---	2	---	X	---	---	X	---	---	---	2	1
30	80	4	3	---	161-5	108	16	---	5	X	X	---	---	---	---	---	2	---	---
	81	5	3	T	---	---	---	---	---	---	---	---	---	X	---	---	---	---	1
	82	4	3	T	---	---	---	---	---	---	---	---	---	X	---	---	---	---	1
31	83	7	2	W	186-7	210	210	10	5	X	---	---	---	---	---	---	1	---	1
	84	6	2	---	30-0	---	---	6	4	---	---	---	---	X	---	---	1	---	2
	85	3	2	---	---	---	---	---	---	---	---	---	---	X	---	---	---	---	1
32	86	10	2	W	35-4	11	13	2	6	X	---	---	---	---	---	ADC	---	---	---
33	87	3	2	---	10-2	16	8	---	5	---	---	---	---	---	---	OAA	---	---	---
	88	8	2	T	---	---	---	---	---	---	X	---	---	X	---	---	---	---	---
34	89	3	1	---	161-5	62	26	13	5	X	---	---	---	X	---	---	---	1	---
	90	11	1	W	30-3	---	---	---	3	X	X	---	---	X	---	---	1	---	---
	91	6	1	---	---	---	---	---	---	---	X	---	---	X	---	---	---	2	2
35	92	8	2	W	100-0	165	6	1	9	X	---	---	---	X	---	GA	---	1	1
	93	1	1	---	---	---	---	---	---	---	---	---	---	---	---	OAA	---	---	---
36	94	3	1	---	161-9	96	21	14	7	X	---	---	---	---	---	---	---	---	---
	95	3	1	W	---	---	---	---	---	---	---	---	---	X	---	---	---	---	---
37	96	13	2	---	---	---	---	---	---	X	---	X	---	---	---	---	1	1	1
	97	2	1	---	50-6	25	7	---	6	---	---	---	---	---	---	2 OAA	---	---	---
Sc	98	7	1	T	10-2	---	---	---	1	---	---	---	---	Sc	---	---	---	---	---
	99	3	1	T	---	---	---	---	---	---	---	---	---	Sc	---	---	---	---	---
	100	8	1	---	---	---	---	---	---	---	---	---	---	Sc	---	---	---	1	---

[1] W=wagon, T=truck.
[2] First figure is unit capacity; second is limit in horses.
[3] TP=trading post; NM=National Monument; Sc=school.
[4] For explanation of symbols, see "Welfare," below.
[5] Items worth over $25 only.

TABLE 18.—*Distribution of income in Shonto households and residence groups*

[All figures to nearest dollar]

Residence group No.	Household No.	Number of members	Local Wool sales	Local Lamb sales	Local Crafts	Local Miscellaneous native	Local Local payrolls	Railroad Wages	Railroad Unemployment compensation	Miscellaneous Other off-reservation wages	Miscellaneous Other	Welfare	Home consumption [1]	Totals [2]
1	1	3	----	$8	$200	$100	------				------		------	$308
	2	7	$205	39	150	------	$1,350				$180		------	1,924
	3	3	------	------	------	------	------				500		------	500
Total		13	205	47	350	100	1,350				680		$240	2,972
2	4	10	484	538	175	300	3,750						582	5,829
3	5	2	60	115	------	------	------						------	175
	6	9	291	320	150	------	165	$1,926	$540				------	3,392
	7	3	202	99	20	------	180	2,000					------	2,501
Total		14	553	534	170		345	3,926	540				506	6,574
4	8	5	------	------	50			------				$1,210	------	1,260
	9	6	88	151	25			3,500					------	3,764
	10	5	75	157	25			3,500					------	3,757
Total		16	163	308	100			7,000				1,210	877	9,658
5	11	4	------	------	50	------		------					------	50
	12	9	70	63	70	------		526	480				------	1,209
	13	8	145	191	150	300		------					------	786
	14	2	------	------	------	------		700	480				------	1,180
	15	6	------	------	------	------		------	600				------	600
	16	4	------	------	------	------		3,366					------	3,366
Total		33	215	254	270	300		4,592	1,560				689	7,880
6	17	3	------	------	------			------				420	------	420
	18	6	177	------	35			2,049	200				------	2,461
	19	8	70	78	50			800	540				------	1,538
	20	3	185	98	20			------					------	303
Total		20	432	176	105			2,849	740			420	946	5,668
7	21	9	501	804	20			1,600	700				------	3,625
	22	2	------	------	------			200	300				------	500
Total		11	501	804	20			1,800	1,000				1,086	5,211
8	23	8	175	64	50	------	100	400	200				------	989
	24	4	10	21	40	------	------	2,656					------	2,727
Total		12	185	85	90		100	3,056	200				554	4,270
9	25	9	86	37	40			424	210				------	797
	26	8	10	23	10			400	200				------	643
	27	9	------	------	35			------	600			312	------	947
Total		26	96	60	85			824	1,010			312	1,124	3,511
10	28	2	35	69	------			2,000	------		476		------	2,580
	29	4	------	------	20			671	480				------	1,171
	30	11	70	------	10			1,257	600				------	1,937
	31	2	------	------	90			------	250				------	340
Total		19	105	159	30			3,928	1,330		476		544	6,572
11	32	7	35	38	20	250	------	584	350				------	1,277
	33	4	------	------	30	------	------	592	480				------	1,102
Total		11	35	38	50	250	------	1,176	830				88	2,467
12	34	2	324	------	------	600	------	------		450			------	1,374
	35	7	90	------	35	100	1,931	------		500			------	2,656
Total		9	414	------	35	700	1,931	------		950			547	4,577

See footnotes at end of table.

TABLE 18.—*Distribution of income in Shonto households and residence groups—* Continued

[All figures to nearest dollar]

Residence group No.	Household No.	Number of members	Local Wool sales	Local Lamb sales	Local Crafts	Local Miscellaneous native	Local payrolls	Railroad Wages	Railroad Unemployment compensation	Misc. Other off-reservation wages	Misc. Other	Welfare	Home consumption [1]	Totals [2]
13	36	8	$53	$26	$60	------	$2,073							$2,212
	37	2	------	------	------	------	------	$2,000						2,000
Total___		10	53	26	60	------	2,073	2,000					$240	4,452
14	38	5	------	------	40	$600	------							600
	39	2	35	24	40	450	------	118	$400					1,067
	40	8	84	92	40	75	------	341	------					632
Total___		15	119	116	80	1,125		459	400				411	2,710
15	41	14	107	243	75	------	509		480				516	1,930
16	42	9	88	193	20	------		965	400					1,666
	43	3	------	------	------	------		------	------	$2,000				2,000
	44	4	------	------	------	500		------	200					700
Total___		16	88	193	20	500		965	600	2,000			212	4,578
17	45	10	------	------	------	200	176					$1,080		1,456
	46	6	------	------	------	------		200						200
	47	4	41	56	25	------		436	400					958
Total___		20	41	56	25	200	176	636	400			1,080	98	2,712
18	48	2	------	------	------	------						804		804
	49	7	------	------	------	------								
	50	7	170	139	20	------		1,949	175					2,453
	51	3	247	149	------	------		2,500	------					2,896
Total___		19	417	288	20			4,449	175			804	825	6,978
19	52	12	10	21	------	------		412				1,728		2,171
	53	4	------	------	25	------		2,054	200					2,279
	54	2	------	------	------	------		------	------					------
Total___		18	10	21	25			2,466	200			1,728	364	4,814
20	55	3	101	133	50	500		------	500					1,284
	56	7	106	154	40	100		761	100					1,261
	57	5	50	108	20	------		930	------					1,108
Total___		15	257	395	110	600		1,691	600				580	4,233
21	58	4	------	------	60	------		------	------			852		912
	59	6	25	46	300	------		1,155	150			732		2,408
	60	11	70	------	15	------		1,000	------	600		------		1,685
	61	2	------	------	------	------		------	------					
Total___		23	95	46	375	------		2,155	150	600		1,584	412	5,417
22	62	3	------	------	------	------						355		355
	63	10	------	------	40	------	100		400					540
	64	3	------	------	------	------						927		927
Total___		16	------	------	40	------	100		400			1,282	288	2,110
23	65	2	10	19	30	------							119	178
24	66	10	25	------	------	------	320	1,797	600					2,742
	67	2	------	------	10	------		721	480					1,211
Total___		12	25	------	10	------	320	2,518	1,080				126	4,079
25	68	7	87	23	40	150		624	480					1,404
	69	7	------	40	30	------		991	300					1,361
Total___		14	87	63	70	150		1,615	780				288	3,053

See footnotes at end of table.

TABLE 18.—*Distribution of income in Shonto households and residence groups—*
Continued

[All figures to nearest dollar]

Residence group No.	Household No.	Number of members	Local					Railroad		Miscellaneous		Welfare	Home consumption [1]	Totals [2]
			Wool sales	Lamb sales	Crafts	Miscellaneous native	Local payrolls	Wages	Unemployment compensation	Other off-reservation wages	Other			
26	70	6	$91	------	------	------	------	$2,667	$450	------	------	------	$269	$3,477
27	71	8	35	$89	------	------	$95	1,080	300	------	------	------	------	1,599
	72	3	------	------	------	------	------	------	------	------	------	------	------	------
Total___		11	35	89	------	------	95	1,080	300	------	------	------	136	1,735
28	73	13	53	34	------	------	------	401	400	------	------	------	------	888
	74	8	10	21	$35	------	1,075	400	100	------	$516	------	------	2,157
	75	2	200	54	------	------	------	700	------	------	------	------	------	954
	76	6	77	93	55	------	------	2,937	------	------	------	------	------	3,162
Total___		29	340	202	90	------	1,075	4,438	500	------	------	516	1,043	8,204
29	77	4	13	43	------	------	170	------	300	------	------	------	------	526
	78	4	26	80	35	------	------	1,275	300	------	------	------	------	1,716
	79	8	20	36	------	------	------	800	400	------	------	------	------	1,256
Total___		16	59	159	35	------	170	2,075	1,000	------	------	------	687	4,185
30	80	4	88	60	40	------	------	------	------	------	------	------	------	188
	81	5	10	24	------	------	------	700	450	------	------	------	------	1,184
	82	4	20	34	------	------	------	2,000	------	------	------	------	------	2,054
Total___		13	118	118	40	------	------	2,700	450	------	------	------	411	3,837
31	83	7	182	356	------	------	------	400	------	------	------	------	------	938
	84	6	35	72	------	------	------	2,000	------	------	------	------	------	2,107
	85	3	------	------	------	------	------	500	200	------	------	------	------	700
Total___		16	217	428	------	------	------	2,900	200	------	------	------	649	4,394
32	86	10	------	------	------	------	------	------	------	------	------	1,558	117	1,675
33	87	3	------	------	------	------	------	500	------	------	------	612	------	1,112
	88	8	193	151	------	------	------	821	540	------	------	------	------	1,705
Total___		11	193	151	------	------	------	1,321	540	------	------	612	10	2,827
34	89	3	------	------	------	------	------	------	------	------	------	------	------	------
	90	11	35	17	50	------	------	790	540	------	------	------	------	1,432
	91	6	------	------	50	------	------	688	480	------	------	------	------	1,218
Total___		20	35	17	100	------	------	1,478	1,020	------	------	------	345	2,995
35	92	8	176	246	------	------	------	200	------	------	------	360	------	982
	93	1	------	------	------	------	------	------	------	------	------	732	------	732
Total___		9	176	246	------	------	------	200	------	------	------	1,092	687	2,401
36	94	3	119	294	------	------	------	------	------	------	------	------	------	413
	95	3	------	------	------	------	------	400	400	$200	------	------	------	1,000
Total___		6	119	294	------	------	------	400	400	200	------	------	468	1,881
37	96	13	66	53	------	$300	------	------	------	------	------	------	------	419
	97	2	------	------	------	------	------	------	------	------	------	924	------	924
Total___		15	66	53	------	300	------	------	------	------	------	924	155	1,498
Sc	98	7	------	------	------	------	1,500	600	------	------	------	------	------	2,100
	99	3	------	------	------	------	3,360	------	------	$5,000	------	------	------	8,360
	100	8	25	54	------	------	3,470	------	------	------	------	------	------	3,549
Total___		18	25	54	------	------	8,330	600	------	------	5,000	------	------	14,009

[1] Figures computed for whole residence groups only.
[2] Total income of residence group equals sum of household totals plus home consumption income figure.

TABLE 19.—*Shonto livestock holdings in 1955*

	Number	Number of HH owning	Percentage owning	Avg. HH holding	Max. HH holding	Number of RG owning	Percentage owning	Avg. RG holding	Max. RG holding	G.U.[1] per hd.	Total G.U.[1]
Number of grazing permits__	58	58	58	1	1	38	100	1.5	3	_____	_____
Permitted capacity, all livestock_____	5,250	58	58	90.5	192	38	100	138.2	358	_____	5,250
Actual holdings:											
Sheep_____	3,494	53	53	65.9	241	37	97	94.4	288	1	3,494
Goats_____	1,150	54	54	21.3	210	37	97	31.1	210	1	1,150
Cattle_____	120	21	21	5.7	14	17	45	7.1	16	4	480
Horses [2]_____	280	58	58	4.8	11	38	100	7.4	17	5	1,400

1955 stocking_____ 6,524 G.U.[1]
Total permitted capacity_____ 5,250 G.U.
Excess livestock_____ 1,274 G.U.

[1] Grazing unit.   HH=Household.
[2] Including mules and burros.   RG=Residence group.

Extended seasonal migration was undoubtedly a much more prominent feature of Shonto life a generation or two ago, before the land became crowded, and resources scarce. As of the present time the summer and winter hogans of nearly every group are oriented around the same water source.

Summer hogans are said to be "farming hogans"; they are always located with primary consideration for a nearby area of alluvial soil which can be cultivated (see Franciscan Fathers, 1910, p. 329; Kluckhohn and Leighton, 1946, p. 7), and are occupied during the farming months (see table 24). As shown in map 1, they are heavily concentrated along Shonto and Cow Springs canyons and in the floor of Klethla Valley. Winter hogans are nearly always located upon higher ground, with a better regard for the availability of wood (cf. Franciscan Fathers, 1910, p. 329; Kluckhohn and Leighton, 1946, p. 8). Since the same water source must normally be used throughout the year, seasonal migration in general involves little modification in the grazing itinerary.

The annual round of sheep-raising activity is outlined in table 24. A few of Shonto's older families never segregate or castrate bucks, and are likely to have lambs born at odd times all during the winter. A great majority of groups, however, do segregate their bucks or at least equip them with aprons. Two buck pastures were originally provided for the community's use by the Bureau of Indian Affairs; their upkeep is now the community's own responsibility, under the general supervision of the District Grazing Committee.

Bucks are united with the flocks in late fall (contrast Landgraf, 1954, p. 62), and lambing begins in February. Shonto's annual lamb drop averages a little under 70 percent (i.e., 0.7 per ewe). Lambing season is one of the busiest periods in the livestock year, requiring extensive supplementary feeding of milk for 1 to 2 months, depending on weather conditions. Shearing, another busy season, begins in April and lasts until early June. Shearing practice has been considerably modernized in recent years. Commercial shears are used by all families, and animals are usually sheared on a canvas or woolsack. Under constant encouragement from the trading post, most families today tie their fleeces individually and pack them in standard woolsacks ($2\frac{1}{2} \times 8$ ft. flat). Fleece ties and woolsacks are provided by the trading post without charge.

At a community meeting in 1955, Shonto voted to disinfect its sheep by spraying rather than dipping. (The Indian Service dipping tank, whose upkeep was the community's responsibility, had fallen into disrepair.) A spraying outfit under the supervision of the grazing committee was stationed at Shonto Trading Post for 2 days in July, and a charge of 2 cents a head was levied for spraying. Only about a quarter of Shonto's sheep and goats were brought in for spraying.

In 1952, an African sheep disease, familiarly known as "bluetongue," was found to be present in Navaho flocks. Since that time, annual inoculation has in theory been mandatory as a condition to sale of lambs. An inoculating unit spent 2 days in the community in July 1955, but less than 10 percent of Shonto's sheep were submitted. The compulsory regulation was not enforced, and lamb sales were not affected.

Lamb sales, which take place annually during the fall, are subject to scheduling by the Navaho Tribal Council. In recent years they have always been set during the last 10 days of September. Animals at this time are from 6 to 9 months old. Shonto families seldom sell ewe lambs. Sale of buck lambs is likely to vary from 50 percent to nearly 100 percent from year to year, depending on the price offered at the trading post. All sales take place on the trading post scales, the animals being herded or, in some cases, trucked in.

Slaughtering takes place at all times of the year, averaging perhaps once every 3 weeks in most residence groups (see "Cooking and Housekeeping," pp. 81–82). Heaviest mutton consumption occurs during midsummer, before lamb sales eliminate the opportunity to replace slaughtered animals. Some part of a slaughtered animal usually goes to every household in the residence group.

Goats are present in all flocks of sheep, in the average proportion of one goat to three sheep (see table 19). To a large extent they take the place of wethers. Goat herding practice corresponds to sheepherding practice in all respects, with the addition that goats are regularly milked by many families. They are less frequently slaughtered than sheep despite the fact that the animals themselves have no com-

mercial value. The proportion of goat hides handled at Shonto
Trading Post is about one in six. Goats are kept principally for milk
and for mohair, which always brings a higher price per pound
(although a much lighter clip) than wool.

Cattle are owned in 17 of Shonto's 38 residence groups (table 19),
the average holding being 7.1 head and the largest 16 head. In recent
years cattle have contributed almost nothing to the community's livelihood except through the occasional slaughter of a calf for home consumption. As a result of a complete lack of market, Shonto Trading
Post has not bought cattle since 1953.

Because all range land is unfenced, cattle are usually run into the
larger canyons or the rough "breaks" adjacent to them, to prevent
excessive straying. Animals are rounded up once a year for branding
at Shonto community center. They are seldom looked after at any
other time of year, and for practical purposes are completely wild.
The community does not have a bull pasture, and segregation is largely
a hit-or-miss affair of herding bulls into a separate area from the rest
of the stock.

Horses are the basic and universal means of transportation, and are
also kept to a large extent for prestige, constituting one of Shonto's
most conspicuous wealth items (cf. Reichard, 1928, p. 89; Hobson,
1954, p. 8). Every Shonto residence group has horses, the average
holding being 7.4 head (table 19) and the largest 17 head. Mules
and burros are rare. Horses furnish the basis for considerable native
commerce among Shonto families.

Shonto's present-day livestock practice has undergone relatively
little change since the turn of the century, and continues to be criti-
cized by Whites as uneconomical and inefficient (cf. Franciscan
Fathers, 1910, p. 257; Kluckhohn and Leighton, 1946, p. 31; Landgraf, 1954, pp. 61–63). Nearly all of the alleged defects are directly
attributable to the entirely sedentary character of Navaho sheep-
raising, which itself is a function of its secondary position to farming
in the economic scheme.

Efforts by the Bureau of Indian Affairs and latterly by the District
Grazing Committee to control grazing and to improve stock and
yield have had very little effect at Shonto. As is indicated in table 19,
the community's current stocking is nearly 25 percent in excess of
permitted capacity, mostly due to excessive numbers of horses and
goats. As has been stated previously ("Social and Political Authority," pp. 65–68), the District Grazing Community has inherited most
of the role, including the inherent unpopularity, of the Indian Bureau's livestock program, and it meets with consistent lack of cooperation from other Navahos. The fact that two of the committee
members are themselves known to have holdings in excess of their per-

mitted limits is a source of resentment and lack of respect for the committee's authority.

The livestock committee's inability to enlist the support of Shonto is seen not only in its lack of effective control over range capacities, but also in the very low response to spraying and inoculation programs (see above). Efforts to improve the breed of sheep have met with equal failure (cf. Landgraf, 1954, p. 62). Until 1952 the Bureau of Indian Affairs maintained two thoroughbred Rambouillet bucks in the Shonto pastures, but the community made little use of them. In 1954 Shonto turned down the Grazing Committee's offer of another Rambouillet buck for community use.

LIVESTOCK INCOME

In 1955 Shonto derived $27,090, or one-sixth of its total income, from native livestock. Slightly over half the total was accounted for by home consumption of meat, hides, wool and the like; the remainder resulted from sale of lambs and wool to the trading post (table 21).

Wool sales take place annually throughout the shearing period from mid-April to mid-June. All sheep except very young lambs and all Angora (white) goats are sheared. Five to ten fleeces (equal to an average 10 percent of the total clip) are likely to be set aside to meet the needs of future weaving, and the remainder are sold. Wool is segregated as between standard fleeces, tags (short, dirty wool from the animal's underside), black wool, and mohair, and it is sacked accordingly.

In 1955, 59 Shonto households in 36 residence groups sold a combined total of 18,746 pounds of wool for an income of $6,171. The average sale was 521 pounds per participating residence group and 318 pounds per household. Average earnings are shown in table 22. Prices per pound at the trading post were 50 cents for mohair, 35 cents for standard fleeces, and 15 cents for tags and black wool. Mohair constituted about 5 percent of all sales, tags about 2 percent, and black wool less than 1 percent; a high proportion of the last was reserved for weaving. Average fleece weight was just under 5 pounds for wool (see Hulsizer, 1940, pp. 151–152) and about 3 pounds for mohair.

Trading-post prices for wool were comparable to free market value at the time. However, the ultimate price of Navaho wool in 1955 was supported at 52 cents a pound by the U.S. Commodity Credit Corp. Every Shonto family producing more than 100 pounds of wool was thus entitled to an additional "incentive payment" of 17 cents for each pound sold. This income, in the form of checks drawn directly upon the U.S. Treasury, was not received in the community until late in

1956, and is not included in the 1955 income figures. In future years wool incentive payments, based on the previous year's clip, will undoubtedly become a regular and anticipated feature of Shonto's annual income, so long as the present marketing act stays in effect.

With one or two exceptions, all Shonto families which regularly market as much as one sack (equal to 200 to 250 pounds) of wool are entitled to credit against it at the trading post. Wool credit is normally extended beginning in December, and continuing until the time of sale, when the account is collected. Credit limits are established on the basis of the family's past record of sales and the anticipated market price for the coming year. Consistently, about two-thirds of Shonto's total wool income is drawn in credit prior to the time of wool sales (see table 16). In other words, about $4,000 of the community's total of $6,171 from wool sales in 1955 was simply applied on account. "Surplus" income, over and above that owed on account, is paid out at the trading post at the time of sales. According to standard trading-post policy throughout the region, not more than 50 percent of such income is receivable in cash; the remainder must be taken out in trade. (A general discussion of trading post policies in regard to commodity exchange is included in "Retail Trade.") In these circumstances families which receive extensive surplus wool income will sometimes establish a due account at the store, which is traded out within one or two months at the most.

Shonto's annual volume of wool sales is little affected by fluctuating market prices. Opportunities for home consumption of wool are restricted to weaving, which has an inherently limited potential since it is necessarily a sparetime activity (see "Crafts," p. 124). An increase in weaving activity corresponding to low market prices for raw wool (cf. Amsden, 1934, p. 235) has not been observed at Shonto. For the most part, the community's households are forced to dispose of their wool for whatever it will bring. For this reason it is considered an exceptionally suitable basis for credit at the trading post. Wool prices in recent years have fluctuated from a high of 80 cents a pound in 1950 to a low of 25 cents in 1956, but there has been no corresponding decline in Shonto's wool production.

Lamb sales, subject to scheduling by the Navaho tribe, usually take place in the last 10 days of September. Lambs to be sold, nearly always bucks, are taken from the flocks and herded or trucked to the store for weighing and transaction. Unlike wool, lambs are likely to be divided among household members prior to the time of sale, and thus sold in the name of individuals rather than of the whole household. Shonto Trading Post buys all lambs, male and female, at a uniform price per pound. The store does not buy mature sheep.

In 1955 Shonto Trading Post bought 632 lambs from 55 households in 34 residence groups.[6]   Total earning from lamb sales was $6,280, or about equal to that from wool sales. Distribution of lamb income among households and residence groups is shown in table 18; average earnings per participating unit are indicated in table 22. In terms of animals, the average lamb sale was 18.6 head per residence group and 11.5 head per household; the total number sold constituted just under 30 percent of the community's total holdings in lambs.

Lamb sales, unlike wool sales, are considerably affected by market fluctuation, since range capacities are not enforced, and in any case the community has ample capacity for home consumption. In recent years they have varied from an estimated 25 percent to an estimated 50 percent of the total drop, as the market price has fluctuated from a high of 30 cents a pound in 1951 to a low of 11½ cents in 1953. The 1955 price was 15 cents per pound. Since the average weight was 67 pounds at the time of sale, lambs were worth an average of exactly $10 apiece.

Because of fluctuating sales, credit against lambs is somewhat more restricted than wool credit. Accounts receivable usually claim about half the income from lamb sales, the remainder being distributed in the same "50–50" form as is surplus wool income.

Hides are always sold for cash at the trading post. By tradition the hide always goes to the owner of the slaughtered animal, who is entitled to dispose of it as he sees fit, and without any obligation to others. In practice, hide money, which seldom comes to more than a dollar at a time, is commonly treated as a sort of windfall and spent entirely on minor luxuries such as candy and soda pop. Annual volume of sale by Shonto families is about 1,000 hides, worth a little over $750 altogether. Hide income has not been figured separately in tables 18, 21, and 22, but is applied instead as a correcting factor in computing home consumption of livestock products (see below).

Home consumption of livestock products, chiefly meat, in 1955 is calculated at $14,639, or slightly over half the total of Shonto's livestock income for the year. The figure is an arbitrary one, computed by allowing 1955 market value at average weight for all lambs not sold, on the assumption that holdings in breeding stock will not be increased significantly. Dead losses are assumed to be compensated by consumption of goats, which have no market value, and by sale of hides (see above). Since home consumption is normally a collective matter, average income can be computed for residence groups only (table 22).

---

[6] The lone wool-producing residence group which did not also sell lambs was that of Shonto's tribal councilman. The latter, having numerous other sources of cash income, prefers by his own admission to enlarge his holdings, already well in excess of his permitted capacity, and to eat plenty of mutton during the winter.

AGRICULTURE

The practical contribution of farming to Shonto's economy is slight. District 2 has one of the lowest agricultural potentials on the Navaho Reservation (see Young, 1955, p. 123), and neither the topography nor the elevation of most of Shonto community is well suited to farming. The community has a total of about 250 acres of dry farmland and some 30 acres of irrigated land, nearly all of the latter being in Shonto Canyon. About half of this area was actually under cultivation in 1955.

Nonetheless, agriculture remains the most fundamental and necessary of all Navaho subsistence activities (see Kluckhohn and Leighton, 1946, pp. 20–22), taking precedence even over livestock raising. Hill (1938, p. 18) has observed that all Navahos "consider themselves primarily farmers." The uneconomic sedentary character of subsistence livestock practice (see above) is manifestly due to its supplementary adaptation to a farming economy. Not only sheep raising but all other phases of productive activity are subordinate at Shonto to the agricultural cycle (cf. table 24). Railroad workers cannot be recruited in any numbers until plowing and planting are completed, and they generally return from their jobs in time for the harvest.

Availability of farmland more than any other factor determines the location of Shonto's hogans. Range resources, wood, and even water are subsidiary factors. Consequently Shonto's population remains heavily concentrated in the southern and especially the southwestern portion of the community, although far superior range is found at higher elevations north of Shonto Trading Post.

Traditional Navaho agricultural practice, surrounded by ritual observations at every turn, survives almost intact at Shonto (see Hill, 1938, pp. 20–51). A more up-to-date description of Navaho farming, also generally valid for Shonto, is that of Landgraf (1954, pp. 58–60).

All but two of the community's residence groups farm. Primary farmlands (see "Control of Resources," above) are normally assigned in the name of the residence group headman, but are thought of as controlled collectively by the group, and exploited accordingly. In only six cases is there more than one cornfield in a residence group (see table 17). The average holding is about 5 acres; the largest single assignment is 18 acres. In the drought year 1955, the area actually cultivated by each farming group probably averaged no more than 2½ acres. All Shonto fields are fenced.

Corn is Shonto's one major crop. Melons and squashes are found primarily in subsidiary patches near the hogans (see "Control of Resources," above). One man has an irrigated alfalfa field in Shonto Canyon. There are no orchards as such in the entire community, but perhaps a dozen families have three or four peach or apple trees each.

Agricultural income is confined to home consumption of the products raised. Since nearly every residence group has its own farm, there is little opportunity for the sale of produce within the community. Shonto's total 1955 agricultural income is estimated at $2,120, on the basis of a $20 per acre yield (see Young, 1955, p. 121). (Farm income is included with livestock income under the heading "Home Consumption" in table 18). In monetary terms agriculture contributed only 1.3 percent of Shonto's total income in 1955.

HUNTING

Excess numbers of livestock have long since crowded most of the aboriginal game from Shonto's ranges, and with it the traditional and ritual hunting practices which were once important to Navahos (see Hill, 1938, pp. 96–176). Hunting today is largely a matter of shooting predatory coyotes, and its only real economic contribution is an occasional rabbit or prairie dog for the family pot. In many instances it is simply a sport, as among Anglo-Americans (cf. Kluckhohn and Leighton, 1946, p. 31; Landgraf, 1954, p. 57). The .22 rifle, present in nearly all households, is the sole hunting weapon. Organized hunting activity among large groups does not take place, and no household today depends on the products of the chase for any part of its subsistence. Coyotes and bobcats were hunted to some extent for their skins prior to World War II, but in post-war years the market for them has disappeared.

CRAFTS

Weaving and the other craft activities of Shonto's women have, like agriculture, much greater psychological than economic value. Weaving, especially, is part of the traditional complex of daily activities, involving prestige value which alone is apparently sufficient to insure its continuation (see Reichard, 1936). As mentioned previously ("Arts and Crafts," pp. 82–84), weaving, basketry, and pottery manufacture are primarily avocational activities for Shonto women, and their purely economic function is secondary. Amsden (1934, p. 236) once calculated that the weaver's actual monetary return for her efforts came to about 5 cents an hour. (The single rug upon which this calculation was based was valued at $12.00. At modern Shonto prices the same rug would bring only $8.00, reducing the weaver's return to less than 4 cents an hour.)

Weaving is carried on at all times of the year, but is heaviest during mid-summer, when there are few conflicting livestock and farming interests. Since nearly all Navaho looms are outdoors, weaving activity tends to be at least partly a function of warm weather and long daylight hours. Ninety percent of Shonto woven products are single (30 × 30 inch) and double (30 × 60 inch) saddle blankets of plain weave and simple banded design, worth a maximum of $4.00 and $8.00 respectively at Shonto Trading Post. Most of the community's weavers are likely to produce from 6 to 12 such saddle blankets a year. Doubles normally outnumber singles in the proportion of about two to one. Larger rugs, when made, are seldom very much larger than double saddle blankets, and bring an average price of about $14.00. Only six women regularly make large rugs, valued at $50.00 and up. The highest price ever paid for a Shonto rug in the writer's knowledge was $95.00.

Craft activities other than weaving are highly irregular in occurrence and volume (see "Arts and Crafts," pp. 82–84). Baskets and sashes ("squaw belts"), unlike rugs and pots, are made chiefly for consumption within the community rather than for sale to Whites. These items are seldom kept permanently, but are traded about within the community as needed for ritual occasions. In most cases they are bought from the store and then sold back to it. The trading post thus acts only as a sort of clearing house. A stock of from 5 to 10 baskets is usually on hand, of which not more than 1 or 2 are likely to be new or nearly so. The price paid for baskets averages about $5.00 for new specimens and $3.00 for old ones, depending on size and condition. In all, basketry, pottery, and the other minor crafts are believed to contribute less than 5 percent of all craft income.

Shonto's total 1955 craft earnings are estimated at $2,685, equal to only 1.6 percent of all community income for the year. Average and maximum earnings are shown in table 22.

Rug income is essentially supplementary income, and does not figure in Shonto's regular economic complex. No credit is extended against rugs (see table 16), and income therefrom is never claimed in payment of accounts due, no matter how large. By standard trading post policy, rugs are exchanged entirely for merchandise, their assessed value being traded out at the time of exchange.

Although 49 Shonto households received some amount of rug income in 1955, only 2 actually depended upon it as part of their subsistence base. In all other cases it was more in the nature of a windfall, and was often spent as such.

NATIVE COMMERCIAL AND PROFESSIONAL ENTERPRISES

The complex of purely internal enterprises and services cannot be overlooked as forming part of Shonto community's general economic picture (cf. Kluckhohn and Leighton, 1946, p. 37). While Shonto depends heavily on the White man's institutions for its cash and trade income, a few individuals regularly derive a large part of their livelihood directly from other members of the community. The practical extent of such activities is virtually impossible to determine, and calculations of income derived therefrom (tables 18, 21 and 22) are little more than informed guesses. Included are singing, tulapai making, bootlegging prostitution, sporadic trucking operations, money lending, and paid employment for other Navahos. (One member of the District 2 Grazing Committee has over 500 head of sheep, and from time to time employs three Shonto men, relatives of his wife, to herd for him.) Total income from all such sources was estimated at $4,525, or 2.7 percent of all 1955 income in the community. Extent of participation is shown in table 22.

Singing is the chief gainful occupation of three Shonto men, and a regular part-time activity of at least four others (see "Religion and Ritual," pp. 70–74). The community's most active singer is estimated to earn about $600 a year from his ritual performances, averaging no more than $5.00 per night of activity (cf. Kluckhohn, 1938, p. 363). No other singer is believed to earn over $300 a year. These figures do not include the value of free board received while on duty. Singers receive about half their income in cash and the remainder in livestock, jewelry, blankets, cloth, and baskets.

All Shonto singers are also livestock owners on a fairly extensive scale, and actually derive a considerable portion of their income thereby. In all but one case, additional income is secured from tulapai manufacture and sale (see "Religion and Ritual," pp. 70–74, and below).

Tulapai making occupies at least six men in addition to Shonto's singers. Navaho tulapai is made from sugar, sirup, raisins, yeast, and water; it is not the same as the Western Apache beverage of the same name, but is closely similar to the "raisin jack" familiar to many GI's. Tulapai making at Shonto is believed to require special esoteric knowledge; it is therefore a profession, like singing, as well as a trade. The community's chief entrepreneur in this field is said to be the tribal councilman, whose annual income from tulapai has been estimated at $250. Tulapai is commonly made in 10- or 15-gallon kegs, and sells for $3.00 a gallon.

Prostitution is the regular profession of one Shonto woman, whose earnings have been estimated at $350. Her standard charge is said to be $5.00. She does business either at her hogan or outdoors, her husband acting as procurer in some cases. Other women in the community are said to engage in occasional prostitution as the occasion permits (see "Recreation and Play," pp. 75–77), but their earnings in the course of a year are probably insignificant.

Truck owners have multiple opportunities for picking up extra income. Nearly all of them engage to some extent in "taxi" operations, transporting people to sings and to Tuba City and Kayenta at a standard charge of $3.00 a head. Trips to the Tuba City hospital are most frequent in occurrence. Additional earnings are derived from hauling wood, livestock, and household furnishings on occasion.

Truck owners are likewise the community's regular bootleggers, bringing in wine from Flagstaff. Since trucks are always bought on time, they represent an investment which must be exploited in order to pay for themselves. Some traders believe that three-forths of the trucks on the Navaho Reservation are paid for out of their own earnings in bootlegging and "taxi" service.

Money lending is more or less a monopoly of Shonto's tribal councilman, the only member of the community other than school employees who has any amount of accumulated cash (which he keeps in a trunk in his hogan). Jewelry and livestock are taken as collateral. Interest rates are variously described as from 25 to 50 percent. Actual extent of the councilman's money-lending activities and income is unknown.

The total of all native enterprise—livestock, agriculture, craftwork, and miscellaneous professional and commercial activities—added up to 21.9 percent of Shonto's total income in 1955. In other words what was virtually the entire economic base a generation ago (see Luomala, 1938, p. 56) today contributes only slightly more than one-fifth of all Navaho income. The complex of activities involved, however, remains basic in the economic scheme of Navahos themselves (see chart C, p. 148).

LOCAL WAGEWORK

Wage opportunities in Shonto community are few as compared with more developed portions of the Navaho Reservation (see table 27). Regular sources of employment are Shonto School, Shonto Trading Post, and Navajo National Monument. In 1955, 15 men and 2 women were employed within the community, 8 of them on a permanent or seasonal basis and the remainder on temporary jobs. Their total wage earnings were $20,324, equal to 12.3 percent of all Shonto income and more than one-third of all locally derived income (tables 18, 21 and 22). Sources and duration of local wage jobs are shown in chart A, page 142.

Shonto School employs two Navaho men and one woman throughout the year, plus one additional man and one woman throughout the school year (see "Community School," pp. 85–86). These employees serve as interpreters, dormitory supervisors, cooks, and maintenance crew. Most individuals double in two capacities. Qualification for school employment involves exceptional education and a fluent command of English. Average salary of the school's full-time employees is $3,400.

Shonto Trading Post employs one Navaho helper throughout the year, at a salary of $30.00 a week. From 1950 until late in 1956 the job was held continuously by a single individual, a long-haired and non-English-speaker. Shonto Trading Post is believed to be the only store on the entire Navaho Reservation employing a "clerk" who does not speak English.   His duties and role in the trading post are described on pp. 163–164.

During late spring, the store puts on one or two extra Navaho helpers, for a period of from 4 to 6 weeks, to sack wool.   Four or five herders are employed for one month during the fall for the annual lamb drive to the railroad (see "Commodity Exchange," pp. 172–175), receiving $5 a day plus their keep.   Personnel hired during lamb and wool seasons varies considerably from year to year, the only qualification being able-bodiedness.   Older and unacculturated men are preferred as sheepherders.   Very commonly, such temporary employment is reserved, if possible, for persons owing delinquent accounts, as a means of settling them.

Navajo National Monument (Betatakin) employs a seasonal ranger and a seasonal laborer during the tourist season (6–7 months) each year.   Each earns approximately $2,000 during a normal year.   The National Park Service does not have an agreement guaranteeing prior rights to these jobs to Navahos; they are theoretically open to all qualified applicants.   In practice, as might be expected, all seasonal and temporary employees at Betatakin have been Navahos. The two seasonal jobs have been occupied for the past 7 years by the same two individuals.   The ranger, who conducts tourist parties through the Betatakin cliff dwelling, is required to speak fluent English.   Betatakin's regular seasonal laborer does not speak English.

From time to time during the busy season Betatakin hires additional labor, on a day-to-day basis, as needed for special construction and maintenance jobs.   Earnings average $10 a day.   Such employment has in practice been the exclusive prerogative of half a dozen men, all of whom live close to the monument headquarters and are closely related to the two regular seasonal employees (see "Control of Resources," p. 98).

Occasional services to "Anglos" provide Shonto with small amounts of extra income from time to time.   The tribal councilman and three of his kinsmen who regularly assist him are believed to earn about $1,000 annually from guided pack trips to Keet Seel cliff dwelling in Tsegi Canyon.   Such trips are run as a sort of concession from Navajo National Monument, which makes the necessary arrangements on behalf of visitors.   They involve a 22-mile, all-day ride, at a charge of $5.00 per horse plus $10.00 for the guide.

One man regularly cuts and hauls firewood for Shonto Trading Post, earning about $75 a year thereby.   He receives $5.00 (in trade) per cut wagonload.   Another man supplies the store with lawn fertilizer from his corral.   Digging out cars and trucks which are stuck in sand or mud is a common source of pocket money, especially during the summer when both roads to Shonto often become buried under drifting sand.

Locally earned income, from wages and all other sources, accounted for 34.2 percent of Shonto's earnings in 1955 (table 21). For the remaining two-thirds of its livelihood the community depended entirely on the outside world.

RAILROAD WORK

Shonto's overwhelming reliance upon seasonal railroad work, to the virtual exclusion of all other off-reservation employment, is indicated in table 21. The combination of wages and unemployment compensation from the railroad accounted for just over half the community's total income in 1955. Nevertheless, railroad work remains a supplementary activity in Shonto's economic scheme, spelling the difference in actuality as well as in theory between bare subsistence and a comfortable material standard of living.

Railroad work for Navahos means maintenance of way (track) labor. At Shonto in nearly all cases it is a matter of employment in seasonal extra gangs on the A.T. & S.F. Railway.

All major railroads rely chiefly on extra gangs for maintenance of way. (The function of section gangs, which are housed permanently along the right-of-way, is confined to track inspection and small, routine maintenance jobs.) Extra gangs are employed when and where major maintenance or construction is needed; the nature of operating conditions in the West is such that large numbers of them are always on the road every year, primarily during the summer months of good weather.

Extra gangs are recruited annually from a standing labor pool. Employees are shipped at the railroad's expense to an assigned worksite where their gang is in operation. The gang is housed and fed in way cars along the right of way, for which a daily pay deduction of about $2.00 is made. The gang remains in operation usually for 3 or 4 months, or until its assigned project is completed, after which it is dissolved and the men are paid off. The standard work week for extra gangs is 40 hours, at a base pay rate (on the Santa Fe) of $1.54 per hour. Many gangs are called out for emergency right-of-way repairs, however, and in such cases overtime may bring the total week's work to as high as 70 hours. Time-and-a-half is allowed for all overtime work.

In recent years most Shonto men have worked in extra gangs along the isolated desert sections of the Santa Fe Railway, between Kingman, Ariz., and Barstow and Mojave, Calif., where the railroad has undertaken an extensive program of double-tracking and right-of-way realinement. Employment is open to all able-bodied men between the ages of 21 and 50, with no education requirement of any kind. Shonto's men nearly always work in all-Navaho gangs, where Navaho is the only language of communication. Even in mixed gangs Navahos are always grouped in large numbers. However, each year a few men manage to catch on with section gangs, where personnel turnover is always high. In such cases they serve individually, and are required to speak English or Spanish.

The Santa Fe, Union Pacific, and Denver & Rio Grande Western Railroads all rely chiefly on Navahos for way labor. Their needs are supplied through the U.S. Railroad Retirement Board (the oldest of all Federal labor agencies), which regulates railroad employment of every kind. For employment purposes the Navaho Reservation per se is treated as a discrete labor pool, and is under the jurisdiction of special Railroad Retirement Board branch offices in Gallup, N. Mex., and Winslow, Ariz. The reservation has been carteled geographically among the three railroads concerned, labor for each being recruited from a definite area. Shonto and surrounding communities are in the territory allocated to the Santa Fe, under jurisdiction of the Winslow office of the Railroad Retirement Board (familiarly known as the R.R.B.).

Shonto's trader, like nearly all other traders, is officially designated as a Claims Agent for the Railroad Retirement Board. In this role he is the contact agency through which all way labor is recruited from the community. The complicated mechanics of recruitment and employment are generally as follows:

Initially, the railroad notifies the R.R.B. of its impending manpower needs, usually 1 to 2 weeks in advance of actual recruitment. The draft required is then allocated by the board among agencies (i.e., trading posts) under its jurisdiction. In normal practice, 15 men are called from each trading post selected, selection of the trading posts themselves being a matter of rotation. Considerable preference, however, is given to those trading posts which have most successfully filled their quotas in the past.

Men are called from each trading post on the basis of seniority rating, based entirely on earnings during the previous calendar year. When the trading posts and men to be called have been selected, the R.R.B. telephones the trader, giving him the names of men to be contacted. In the event of refusals or failure to contact, additional men are to be contacted, in order of seniority, until either the 15-man quota is filled or a total of 30 men has been contacted. The board also informs the trader of the time and date, usually about 5 days later, when men are to be delivered to the board's office in Winslow.

Thereafter, all responsibility rests with the trader. It is his job to get the word out to the community, secure the necessary quota, and provide or arrange transportation. Recruitment frequently necessitates actually driving around the community from hogan to hogan. Each man, if he accepts the call, is instructed to be at the trading post with his gear on the appointed day. (Railroad workers always take along a small suitcase full of clothing and personal effects.) Shonto Trading Post nearly always transports its own railroad workers to Winslow in the store's stake-body truck. Transportation is paid for on delivery by the R.R.B. at $4.00 a head. After processing in the board's offices, men are shipped out to their jobs on work trains the same night.

Unemployment compensation is a regular concomitant of all railroad work, and accounts to a large extent for Shonto's overwhelming preference for it. The Railroad Retirement Board levies a payroll tax upon all railroads to support its retirement fund, from which unemployment compensation is paid to qualified applicants. The seasonal nature of way maintenance is such that nearly all track laborers are eligible for compensation during part of every year; at Shonto such compensation is an anticipated and necessary part of each year's income.

Any Shonto man who has earned more than $400 (recently raised to $500) during any calendar year is entitled to compensation for every day of unemployment during the following fiscal, or "benefit" year. In other words a man earning $400 in 1954 was entitled to compensation, if unemployed, at any time between July 1, 1955 and June 30, 1956. Benefits are paid at a rate ranging from $3.50 to $8.50 for each day of unemployment, depending on wages earned during the previous calendar year. Total compensation is limited to an amount equal to twice the previous year's wages (recently reduced by half, to an amount equal to wage earnings). In practice, however, at Shonto and throughout the Navaho Reservation, income from unemployment compensation seldom totals more than one-third of railroad wage earnings (see tables 21 and 26). This is due to the fact that work is available—and compensation therefore unavailable—during a large part of the year.

Some time after the beginning of each benefit year (July 1), the Railroad Retirement Board sets an opening date for general eligibility for compensation. This may occur at any time from July until late fall depending upon a sufficient decline in the labor demand. Once eligibility is opened up all of Shonto's railroad workers, subject to certain qualifications, are entitled to continuous compensation until they are called to work, take another job, or exhaust their financial eligibility. Men who leave work voluntarily and not because of job termination are not eligible for compensation until they have been home for 30 days. Likewise, men who refuse a call to work forfeit their eligibility for 30 days. Barring forfeitures of this sort, eligibility continues until manpower demand becomes sufficiently general to justify termination of all benefits, usually in late spring.

Continuing eligibility is established by signing a weekly affidavit expressing willingness to work and unavailability of work. These "claim affidavits" are the responsibility of the trader in his function as claims agent for the Railroad Retirement Board. The mechanics of unemployment compensation at Shonto are generally as follows:

Some time between mid-summer and late fall the Winslow R.R.B. office notifies the trader that general eligibility for benefits will begin on a given date. The trader immediately passes the word on to the community. On the basis of records kept by him he informs each railroad worker if and when he will become eligible.

A given day of the week (always Thursday in recent years) is designated as railroad sign-up day. Each Thursday during the period of eligibility, every railroad worker must come to the store and sign his claim affidavit. In practice it is always filled out in advance by the trader and is merely thumbprinted by the claimant, since few of Shonto's railroad workers can read or write. The trader is required by law to ask each claimant if he is ready and willing to go to work and if he has had opportunities to work every time an affidavit is signed. A negative answer to the first question or a positive one to the second automatically disqualifies the claim, but few traders take the trouble to ask in practice.

The standard affidavit covers a 2-week period, so that each one must be signed twice. When completed, they are mailed to the Winslow office. Checks in compensation for the period claimed in each affidavit are mailed to the claimants every 2 weeks by the R.R.B. regional office in Dallas. Shonto residents in 1955 drew biweekly checks ranging from $42.00 to $78.00, depending upon their daily base-rate as determined from earnings in the previous year.

Throughout the winter the trader keeps track of men returning from railroad jobs, checking as soon as they return to see if and when they will become eligible for benefits, and informing them accordingly. Constant reminders to sign up are issued.

The annual cycle of railroad work and unemployment compensation is outlined in Charts A and B. Although work calls are occasionally received during the winter, in general they do not begin until about April. The store usually receives one order for 15 men in each of April and May. These early orders, conflicting with agricultural and livestock activities (Chart A), are always difficult to fill; usually over half the men called simply refuse work and forfeit their remaining compensation. Benefits are likely to be terminated for all claimants in May or June, as manpower demand becomes general. Throughout June, July, and August, Shonto may get calls for 15 men as often as every two or three weeks. Refusals at this time of year are rare. Many quotas are overfilled, as men who are not called by seniority will choose to ride into Winslow with the crew in the hope of being taken on anyway. By the first of September nearly all the community's railroad men are usually out on the road, though a few of the "early birds" will already have returned.

Shonto's extra gang workers stay on the job for an average 2 to 3 months, depending to a large extent on how early in the year they were called out. Few workers stay on the job until they are terminated; most simply work until they are ready to come home and then quit. There is a general drift back to the community in mid-September, in time for lamb sales; and harvesting in October brings at least 50 percent of workers back each year. Thereafter, remaining men continue to straggle back by two's and three's until the end of the year. Each year, however, a few men manage to pick up section jobs, and may not return to the community for several months. This is especially true of men who answer the infrequent calls in late fall; they are not likely to return to Shonto until planting time the following spring.

General eligibility for unemployment benefits usually opens up in October or November. Not more than a fraction of Shonto's claim load is likely to be eligible initially, as some workers are still on the road and many others will have returned voluntarily less than 30 days previously. The claim load mounts rapidly in November and December. Usually all or nearly all claimants are drawing compensation by the first of the new year, and continue to do so until around the first of April.[7]

RAILROAD INCOME

Railroad wages in 1955 were earned by 61 men out of a total eligible labor force (21–50 years of age) of about 80. The total earning was $67,964, equal to 41.1 percent of Shonto's entire income for the year (table 21). The average earning per individual was $1,114, and the maximum (on a section gang) was about $3,500 (table 22). All but six Shonto residence groups received some railroad income. Distribution of earnings by families is shown in table 18.

Figures shown for railroad income are gross earnings, before deductions for quarters, food, and social security. Federal income tax is not deducted from Navaho railroad worker's pay. Net earnings run about 20 percent less than the figures shown. All of this income is, of course, earned and paid outside the community. It is estimated that about 50 percent of it ultimately reaches Shonto, either sent home in money orders or brought home by the returning workers in the form of cash or merchandise. Nearly all workers send home at least

---

[7] 1955 was an exceptional year in terms of its limited manpower demand. Eligibility for unemployment benefits was never terminated at any time, but ran to the end of the old benefit year on June 30 and began immediately with the new one on July 1, despite the fact that Shonto received four calls during the summer. This situation was not repeated in 1956.

one money order while on the job; those with large families often send them regularly, to a total of as much as $500.

Credit against railroad work is allowed as soon as a job has been secured. Limits are necessarily fairly low, since the trader has no control over railroad pay, and must rely entirely on the goodwill of the individual. Nevertheless the families of many railroad workers live largely on credit against the latter's earnings while they are away. Accounts receivable usually claim about 25 percent of railroad income, or about 50 percent of that which reaches the community. Some workers always send their money orders directly to the trader, for application on account.

Unemployment compensation was drawn by 49 Shonto men (80 percent of the number of wage earners) in 1955, in a total amount of $17,815. The value of such compensation was equal to about one-fourth of railroad wage earnings for the same year, and 10.8 percent of total community income (table 21). The average individual claim came to $364, and the highest was about $700 (table 22).

Every family receiving unemployment compensation drew credit against it. Compensation, like relief, is considered one of the most secure of all credit bases, since it is received in the form of checks mailed through the store (see "Book Credit," pp. 188–195). "Railroad accounts" are always limited to the amount of the biweekly check, and are payable on receipt of the check. It is estimated that such accounts receivable annually claim about 90 percent of Shonto's income from unemployment compensation.

OTHER WAGEWORK

Income from outside wagework other than track labor plays only a small and irregular part in Shonto's economy. It does not fit into any seasonal pattern, and no household regularly and consistently depends on it. Its role is chiefly as a last, emergency stopgap in default of all other resources. Each year a few individuals pick up various jobs in agriculture or defense plants for a period of a few weeks or months, and then return to the community. Ineligibility for railroad work because of disqualification or lack of seniority is the principal condition leading to wagework in other off-reservation industries.

Exclusion of nonrailroad wagework from Shonto's regular economy is a development of the past 4 years. During World War II most of Shonto's men worked at the Navajo Ordnance Depot (outside Flagstaff) rather than on the railroad. Track labor was opened up for the community in 1945, along with a variety of other employment opportunities. Particularly between 1948 and 1952 there was systematic recruiting of agricultural labor in the community, under the direct sponsorship of the Bureau of Indian Affairs. A majority of Shonto families worked at one time or another in the sugar-beet and carrot fields of Utah and Idaho during those years.

In 1952 the recruitment of nonrailroad labor was brought within the operations of the Arizona State Employment Service, and energetic recruiting was halted. The State employment service maintains a field office at Tuba City and posts an occasional clearance order on the Shonto Trading Post bulletin board, but no active recruiting has been carried on in the community. Almost immediately after the cessation of recruiting, Shonto's response to agricultural and all other nonrailroad work dropped to almost nothing, where it remains at the present time. The community in 1955 had no effective contact with the State employment service office, and classification cards were carried on only about half a dozen of its residents.

Neither Shonto nor any of its neighboring communities ever took kindly to seasonal agricultural work. Probably an important factor was that its heaviest manpower demands (in Utah and Idaho) conflicted with the most active period in Shonto's own agricultural cycle. There also persists in the community today a general feeling that the work is overly hard and the reward low—a feeling that is shared by most traders (see pp. 280–281).

In 1955 the total of known income from jobs outside Shonto community, other than railroad jobs, was estimated at no more than $3,750, equal to 2.3 percent of total community income (tables 18, 21). Only 5 men and no women were involved. Included in the total are wages earned by the tribal councilman while in session at Window Rock, by one man as a policeman at Tuba City, by one man from harvesting tomatoes in Utah, and by two men who worked during part of the year as ammunition handlers in California and Arizona defense plants. These figures reflect only employment and income known to the trader. It is possible that a few other individuals may have been employed briefly on the outside, but the total of nonrailroad wage income was almost certainly no higher than $5,000.

MISCELLANEOUS INCOME

Table 18 contains three entries under the heading "other," totaling $5,680 (table 21). Chiefly involved is an insurance settlement of $5,000 paid to one of Shonto School's Navaho employees for the accidental death of her husband. One Shonto man received a regular G.I. allotment check from a son in the Marine Corps, totaling $180 over the year. The remaining $500 represents support received by a Shonto woman from her long-absent husband, who normally does not support her.

WELFARE

Shonto residents are entitled to Public Assistance (Aid to Dependent Children, Aid to the Blind, and Old Age Assistance) from the Arizona State Department of Public Welfare, and to General Assistance (noncategorical aid) from the Bureau of Indian Affairs. Such income has a definite role in the community's economy as the standard and rightful contribution (in Navaho terms) of elderly and disabled households (see "The Life Cycle," pp. 84–90). In effect, it gives every adult in the community at least a potential contributing role in the economy regardless of physical or economic condition. Every Shonto household is thus at least in part economically independent.

Eligibility for public assistance is established on the basis of fixed criteria of age, marital status, medical condition, and financial condition which are uniform for all Arizona residents. Welfare payments are always made to households, the amount depending on the size of the household and the extent of other economic resources. Most Shonto households receive maximum or near maximum support.

Aid to Dependent Children (ADC) is paid to households having dependent children in which the husband is deceased, divorced, or incapacitated. As stated earlier ("Social Structure," pp. 54–65) all but one of Shonto's broken households are support by ADC. The size of many ADC grants nearly doubles during the summer months when children return from school.

Aid to the Blind (AB) is normally paid to needy adults under the age of 65. Blind persons over 65 are transferred to the category of Old Age Assistance. Shonto has two blind women, one of whom draws AB and one OAA.

Old Age Assistance (OAA) is paid to needy persons over the age of 65. Of Shonto's 16 households including persons over 65, 7 receive OAA, 3 others receive ADC or GA, and 6 currently receive no welfare assistance, although 4 of these have applied for it.

General Assistance (GA) has no categorical requirements, but is conceived as emergency assistance to needy persons who are not qualified for public assistance. In practice, it is only paid to persons who have applied for public assistance and have been refused.

Shonto's 1955 welfare income amounted to $13,598, equal to 8.2 percent of all community income. The caseload by categories is shown in table 20.

Welfare income is received in the form of monthly checks. Because it is paid to households with necessarily low mobility and because it is required to be spent exclusively for subsistence needs, welfare is considered the most secure of all credit bases at Shonto Trading Post. As in the case of unemployment compensation, credit limits are equal to the amount of the monthly check, and accounts are payable on receipt of the check. All of Shonto's families on relief live almost

TABLE 20.—*Welfare caseload at Shonto in 1955*

Category	Number of cases	Number of house-holders	Number of residence groups	Income	Percentage of all welfare income
ADC	8	8	8	$7,856	57.8
AB	1	1	1	465	3.4
OAA	8	7	7	3,915	28.8
GA	3	3	3	1,362	10.0
Total	20	19	19	13,598	100.0

exclusively on credit; not more than 1 percent of all welfare income in the community is received in cash over the year (see table 16). Families fear that if they do not spend the total amount of their check each month they are likely to receive a reduction in grant.

SUMMARY AND INTERPRETATION OF INCOME FIGURES

As indicated in table 22, the mean income of all Shonto households in 1955 was $1,656, and the median was $1,406. Mean and median incomes per residence group were $4,357 and $4,083 respectively.

TABLE 21.—*Summary of Shonto Community income, 1955*

I. BY SOURCES

Source of income	Income	Percentage of all income
Local:		
1. Wool sales	$6,171	3.7
2. Lamb sales	6,280	3.8
3. Home consumption, livestock	14,639	8.8
4. Home consumption, agriculture	2,120	1.3
5. Crafts	2,685	1.6
6. Miscellaneous native enterprise	4,525	2.7
7. Local payrolls	20,324	12.3
All local	$56,744	34.2
Railroad:		
8. Wages	67,964	41.1
9. Unemployment compensation	17,815	10.8
All railroad	85,779	51.9
Miscellaneous nonlocal:		
10. Nonrailroad wages	3,750	2.3
11. Other outside income	5,680	3.4
All miscellaneous	9,430	5.7
Welfare:		
12. Welfare (all)	13,598	8.2
Total community income, 1955	165,551	100.0

II. BY ACTIVITIES

Activity	Income	Percentage of all income
A. Native enterprise (1–6)	$36,420	21.9
B. Wage work (7, 8, 10)	92,038	55.7
C. Unearned income (9, 11, 12)	37,093	22.4
Total community income, 1955	165,551	100.0

TABLE 22.—*Shonto income production in 1955—average and maximum earnings per unit*

I. BY SOURCES

	Total income	Unit [1]	Number [2]	Average earning	Maximum earning
1. Wool sales	$6,171	Ind	61	$101	$484
		HH	59	105	501
		RG	36	171	553
2. Lamb sales	6,280	Ind	81	78	804
		HH	55	114	804
		RG	34	185	804
3. Home consumption, livestock	14,639	RG	37	396	1,074
4. Home consumption, agriculture	2,120	RG	36	59	175
5. Crafts	2,685	Ind	54	49	250
		HH	50	54	300
		RG	28	96	375
6. Misc. native enterprise	4,525	Ind	17	266	600
		HH	17	266	600
		RG	17	266	1,125
7. Local payrolls	20,324	Ind	17	1,196	3,600
		HH	16	1,270	3,750
		RG	12	1,694	8,330
8. Railroad wages	67,964	Ind	61	1,114	3,500
		HH	59	1,152	3,500
		RG	30	2,265	7,000
9. Unemployment compensation	17,815	Ind	49	364	600
		HH	44	405	700
		RG	28	636	1,560
10. Nonrailroad wages	3,750	Ind	6	625	2,000
		HH	6	625	2,000
		RG	5	750	2,000
11. Other outside income	5,680	Ind	3	1,893	5,000
		HH	3	1,893	5,000
		RG	2	2,840	5,000
12. Welfare	13,598	Ind	20	680	1,728
		HH	17	800	1,728
		RG	14	971	1,728

II. BY ACTIVITIES

	Total income	Unit	Number	Average earning	Maximum earning
A. Native enterprise	$36,420	Ind	134	$272	$1,192
		HH	83	439	1,477
		RG	38	958	2,563
B. Wagework	92,038	Ind	76	1,211	3,600
		HH	69	1,334	3,750
		RG	35	2,630	8,930
C. Unearned income	37,093	Ind	72	515	1,728
		HH	62	598	1,728
		RG	34	1,091	1,928

III. TOTAL INCOME PRODUCTION, ALL SOURCES

	Total income	Unit	Number	Average earning	Maximum earning
	165,551	Ind	191	841	8,360
		HH	97	1,707	8,360
		RG	38	4,357	14,009

IV. AVERAGE INCOME CONSUMPTION

	Total income	Unit	Number	Average earning	Maximum earning
Mean	165,551	Ind	568	[3] 291	
		HH	100	1,656	
		RG	38	4,357	
Median	165,551	Ind	568	00	
		HH	100	1,406	
		RG	38	4,083	

[1] Ind=Individual, HH=Household, RG=Residence group.
[2] Number of units participating.
[3] Mean per capita income for Shonto community, 1955.

Frequency distribution of 1955 income in Shonto households and residence groups is shown in tables 23 and 24. Because of the high degree of economic interdependence within residence groups, however, individual household income figures are significant primarily as showing the distribution of production in the community. Consumption is reflected much more accurately in the residence group income figures. At the household level the most realistic picture of income distribution is achieved by dividing the income of each residence group by the number of households included therein, and plotting a frequency distribution of these dividends. A column of such "adjusted household incomes" is included in table 25. Entries in this column follow a much more normal and expectable curve than do those in the column of raw household incomes.

The contexts of day-to-day living as between Shonto and off-reservation White communities, even in the same general region, are so completely different that income figures cannot be compared at face value. With one or two exceptions Shonto's Navahos pay no taxes, no utility charges, and no rent or use fees. (School employees are subject to a deduction for quarters, and also pay Federal income tax, as do seasonal employees of Navajo National Monument.) They also receive entirely free all medical and dental service; schooling, board and lodging for all school-age children; and a variety of minor services for which non-Indians regularly have to pay. The combined value of these exemptions is probably equal to at least one-third of Shonto's

TABLE 23.—*Frequency distribution of income in Shonto residence groups*

1955 income	Number RG	1955 income	Number RG	1955 income	Number RG	1955 income	Number RG
$0–$249	1	$2,500–$2,749	2	$4,000–$4,249	3	$5,500–$5,749	1
$1,250–$1,499	1	$2,750–$2,999	3	$4,250–$4,499	3	$5,750–$5,999	1
$1,500–$1,749	2	$3,000–$3,249	1	$4,500–$4,749	2	$6,500–$6,749	2
$1,750–$1,999	2	$3,250–$3,499	1	$4,750–$4,999	1	$6,750–$6,999	1
$2,000–$2,249	1	$3,500–$3,749	2	$5,000–$5,249	0	$7,750–$7,999	1
$2,250–$2,499	2	$3,750–$3,999	1	$5,250–$5,499	2	$8,000–$8,249	1
						$14,000–$14,249	1

TABLE 24.—*Frequency distribution of income in Shonto households* [1]

1955 income	Number HH	1955 income	Number HH	1955 income	Number HH	1955 income	Number HH
$0–$249	5	$1,250–$1,499	8	$2,500–$2,749	4	$3,750–$3,999	2
$250–$499	9	$1,500–$1,749	10	$2,750–$2,999	5	$4,000–$4,249	1
$500–$749	10	$1,750–$1,999	6	$3,000–$3,249	2	$4,250–$4,499	1
$750–$999	9	$2,000–$2,249	6	$3,250–$3,499	2	$4,500–$4,749	1
$1,000–$1,249	12	$2,250–$2,499	4	$3,500–$3,749	1	$5,750–$5,999	1
						$8,250–$8,499	1

[1] Income from home consumption of livestock products prorated among livestock-owning households only (cf. table 18).

TABLE 25.—*Adjusted frequency distribution of income in Shonto households* [1]

1955 income adjusted	Number HH	1955 income adjusted	Number HH	1955 income adjusted	Number HH	1955 income adjusted	Number HH
$0–$249	1	$1,000–$1,249	7	$2,000–$2,249	13	$3,000–$3,249	0
$250–$499	0	$1,250–$1,499	19	$2,250–$2,499	2	$3,250–$3,499	4
$500–$749	5	$1,500–$1,749	25	$2,500–$2,749	2	$4,500–$4,749	3
$750–$999	16	$1,750–$1,999	1	$2,750–$2,999	1	$5,750–$5,999	1

[1] To allow for household interdependence within residence groups, total residence group income is divided by number of member households, such that all households within any group are figured to have the same "adjusted" income. See "Summary and Interpretation of Income Figures."

total income. The community's mean household income should probably be figured at somewhere between $2,000 and $2,500 for comparison with non-Indian communities.

In most respects it is impossible to compare Shonto's standard of living with that of Whites. Items such as basic utilities which most "Anglos" take for granted are not available to Shonto at any price. In consequence, the labor involved in hauling water and cutting and hauling wood throughout the year probably adds up to far more, in equivalent terms, than the utility bills run up by most White people.

While many services are provided to the community free of charge, the cost of others is disproportionately high. Prices at the Trading Post are consistently 10 to 15 percent higher than those in off-reservation towns (see "Markup," p. 182). Most of all the cost of all transportation, if available at all, is excessively high. Lack of transportation resources more than any other factor holds down the community's material standard of living. Trips outside the community, to buy goods at lower prices or to take advantage of services provided without charge, are likely in three cases out of four to cost more than they are worth both in time and in cash. Shonto pays a high price for isolation in this regard.

Navaho and Anglo-American ideal standards of living are not the same in any case. The categories of necessity and luxury vary enormously as between the two groups. Shonto's material standard of living is geared to a subsistence economy (see "The Economic Cycle," p. 141), and even if the ideal is low by White standards, the community's nonmaterial standard of living, especially in terms of time and money spent in ritual activity (cf. Kluckhohn and Leighton, 1946, pp. 159–162), undoubtedly remains high. Beyond the subsistence level the community's income goes immediately into what White people would term luxuries, both material and nonmaterial: luxury dress, luxury ornamentation, luxury foods, and ritual activity.

In the material sphere Shonto's ideal standard of living is derived from and adapted to the community's old base of subsistence activities (see chart C, p. 148). Above all, nothing will ever replace the plentiful mutton which was taken away by stock reduction. At the same time the complex of wage-earning activities which is still considered supplementary (see chart C) has trebled Shonto's income in the past generation. The practical result has been that in many respects the community's day-to-day level of living has actually surpassed its ideal standard of living. Thus cash income from wage activities is often not merely supplementary, but surplus income. Inevitably, it goes to maintain a high level of luxury consumption.

This state of affairs is reinforced by the low level of subsistence consumption which the community is capable of maintaining. The striking discrepancy in Shonto's economic situation is that rapidly expanding sources of income have not been matched by any comparable development of a consumer's market for material goods. Regardless of surplus income, the elements needed to increase material standards of living, notably public utilities of any kind, simply cannot be had at any price. Consequently traditional noneconomic activities and luxury spending continue to absorb Shonto's earnings.

Shonto does not save its money (cf. Roberts, 1951, p. 54). Only two or three employees of the school have either insurance policies or bank accounts in Flagstaff, and only the tribal councilman has any cash on hand in the community (see above). For most Shonto residents, banking is entirely out of the question, the nearest bank being 132 miles away. More important in any event, it is still possessions—"hard goods," "soft goods," and livestock—which bring prestige and have psychological security value (cf. Reichard, 1928, p. 89; Hobson, 1954, p. 25). Finally, Shonto's conception of economic life remains a seasonal one (see below), in which each year is a repetition of the last, and each brings the same chances to make a living as did the last.

THE ECONOMIC CYCLE

The seasonal round of productive activity and income consumption is shown in charts A and B.

To a very large extent, Shonto lives on credit and on railroad unemployment compensation during the winter. Livestock owners draw credit against forthcoming wool sales, and railroad claimants draw against the amount of their biweekly checks. Not more than half a dozen men are likely to be out on the railroad during the winter months. This is the slackest season in the economic year, when only the community's singers and tulapai makers are especially active.

Lambing is the first major operation of the year for most Shonto families (cf. Landgraf, 1954, p. 62), occupying most of February and March. It is closely followed by the beginning of the agricultural year, with plowing and planting in April and May.

Late spring is one of the busiest times in the economic year (cf. Landgraf, 1954, p. 62). All adult members of every family are likely

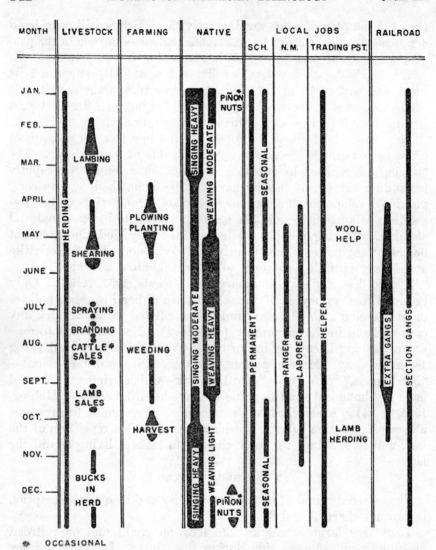

CHART A.—Annual cycle of productive activity at Shonto.

to be kept very busy for nearly 2 months. Shearing and wool sales begin before planting has been completed and continue until the middle of June. Livestock credit accounts are terminated. At the same time the earliest railroad calls are received, and eligibility for unemployment compensation ends for all claimants. Betatakin's two seasonal employees go to work during April and May.

During shearing season Shonto lives largely on surplus income from its wool sales, and immediately thereafter credit against fall lamb sales begins. Railroad workers move out in large numbers throughout the summer, and by August are sending home a significant

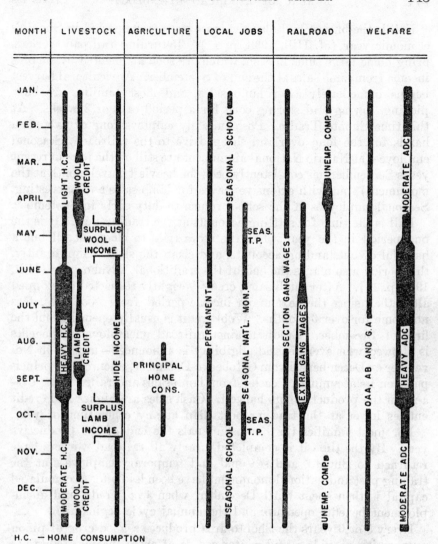

CHART B.—Annual cycle of income consumption at Shonto.

portion of the community's income in money orders. Credit against railroad earnings as well as against lambs supports many families.

Within the community, mid-summer is another relatively idle season. School children of all ages are at home, but most of Shonto's able-bodied men are absent. Sporadic weeding of cornfields is the most frequent activity. Branding, sheep spraying and inoculation are annual summer events, each lasting 1 or 2 days. Shonto School's two seasonal employees are off duty. Of all productive activities, weaving shows the most pronounced increase during the summer months.

Fall is the busiest and also the most prosperous period in Shonto's economic year (cf. Hill, 1938, p. 17). Returning railroad workers bring home large sums in cash, which are soon augmented by surplus income from lamb sales at the end of September. Agricultural harvest begins immediately after lamb sales, and most families are busy picking, drying and storing corn for a period of 2 or 3 weeks. At this time Shonto Trading Post annually employs four or five extra hands for the long overland sheep drive to the railroad. Seasonal employees at Navajo National Monument are still on the job (in recent years September has consistently been the heaviest travel month at the monument), but with extensive leaves for lamb sales and harvesting. Seasonal employees of the school return to duty early in September.

Fall is the time for settling accounts at the trading post. It is the one period in the year when the store tries to close out all but a handful of outstanding accounts, and clean the slate. Significantly, this period also marks the end of the traditional Navaho year (Hill, 1938, p. 15). After lamb sales, credit is tightly restricted or stopped altogether, since the next major income period, from wool sales, does not come for over 6 months. Wool credit is usually opened about the first of December. Credit against railroad unemployment benefits is allowed whenever general eligibility is announced—usually in November or December. From October to December, Shonto lives principally on its accumulated cash—from lamb sales and railroad wages—and on the products of its harvest. Cash sales are higher and credit entries lower at the trading post than at any other time of year.

For most families the harvest signals the end of the productive year. By the time it is completed, nearly all railroad workers have returned to Shonto, and seasonal and temporary employees at the trading post and national monument have been laid off. Accumulated capital is then spent until December, when wool credit and unemployment benefits open up, and the annual cycle begins anew.

Every 5 or 6 years the Shonto area produces a good crop of piñon nuts, which provide a mid-winter source of extra income. Nuts are gathered by the entire community during December and January, and sold to the trading post. In 1954–55 the store bought an incredible total of 107,000 pounds of piñon nuts at 45 cents a pound, for a total investment of nearly $50,000 (cf. Landgraf, 1954, p. 58). About 40 percent of the crop was sold by Shonto families; the remainder was brought in by Navahos from other communities. By contrast, piñon nuts bought in the winter of 1955–56 totaled less than 200 pounds.

Of all Shonto families, the only ones that are in any sense free of the seasonal economic cycle are those 4 having permanent jobs in the community and the 17 which receive regular welfare benefits. Income for these individuals is subject to little fluctuation during the year, and alone among all members of the community they are entitled to uniform credit at all seasons.

Seasonality and cyclic repetition are the essence of Shonto's entire economic life, and continue to dominate the community's economic thinking and values. Wage income is involved no less than native subsistence enterprise. Here lies the fundamental limitation upon Shonto's productive potential and at the same time the source of its social and cultural strength. The seemingly unlimited productive opportunities of modern America have been adapted, almost without exception, to an unyielding economic scheme of things that is as old as mankind (see Herskovits, 1952, pp. 67–87).

SUMMARY

Shonto is not a typical Navaho community in terms of its economy any more than in the other phases of its life (see "Summary," pp. 93–94). Within the Navaho Reservation regional diversification has, in fact, reached its greatest proportions in the field of economics (see Kluckhohn and Leighton, 1946, pp. 32–33; Roessel, 1951, pp. 70–71). Modern communities in different parts of the reservation depend upon various combinations of government and tribal employment, railroad work, defense work, seasonal off-reservation agriculture, construction, and home industry.

Table 26 lists the individual income of the entire Navaho tribe from all sources in 1955. (The figures have been compiled by the Navaho Agency at Window Rock for inclusion in a forthcoming "Navajo Yearbook of Planning in Action—Calendar Year 1955," and are supplied by courtesy of Robert W. Young. They do not include undistributed income accruing to the Navaho Tribe, Inc., and deposited in the tribal treasury. It will be noted that the categories of income included in table 26 do not entirely correspond to those in tables of Shonto income included herein.)

Table 27 compares percentages of total income earned from various sources by Shonto Navahos and by the Navaho tribe as a whole. The table may serve to illustrate the features more or less distinctive of Shonto's economy and that of surrounding communities. Most immediately apparent is the fact that Shonto's heavy reliance upon railroad work is not typical of the reservation in general. While both community and tribe derive roughly half their total income from off-reservation wage work, the ratio of railroad to nonrailroad wages for the whole tribe is about 1:1, whereas at Shonto it is more like 20:1.

TABLE 26.—*Total Navaho individual income, 1955* [1] *(figures courtesy of Robert W. Young)*

Source of income	Income	Percentage of all income
Off-reservation employment:		
1. Railroad wages	$8,005,317	22.2
2. Railroad unemployment compensation	2,668,439	7.5
3. Government defense projects	2,618,394	7.3
4. Seasonal agriculture	3,314,625	9.2
5. Seasonal nonagricultural	3,311,680	9.2
6. Income of self-placed	250,000	.7
All off-reservation	20,168,455	56.1
Reservation resources:		
7. Gallup Area (BIA) payroll	3,476,307	9.7
8. Navaho tribal payroll	1,399,731	3.9
9. Mining	1,772,560	4.9
10. All livestock and agriculture	4,000,000	11.1
All reservation	10,648,598	29.6
Unearned income:		
11. Welfare	2,335,185	6.5
12. Old Age & Survivors' Insurance	256,436	.7
All unearned	2,591,621	7.2
Miscellaneous:		
13. Arts and crafts	2,000,000	5.6
14. All other	530,000	1.5
All miscellaneous	2,530,000	7.1
Total Navaho individual income, 1955	35,978,674	100.0

[1] Figures represent income earned severally by individual Navahos. They do not include undistributed corporate income of The Navaho Tribe, Inc.

Community and tribe both derive a little over 30 percent of their income from local sources. The proportions as between home industry and local wages are reversed, however. Shonto relies more heavily on its native subsistence patterns where Navahos in general rely more heavily on wages. The estimate of $2,000,000 in craft income for the tribe, representing over 5 percent of total earnings, is perhaps too high, as it is over three times the Shonto figure.

In railroad income, the proportion of unemployment compensation to wages is about 1:4 at Shonto as against 1:3 for the entire tribe. Shonto is slightly more dependent on welfare than is the tribe as a whole, however. One of the most potentially significant of all differences between community and tribe is seen in the category of mining income, which contributed nearly 5 percent of all Navaho earnings but not one cent to Shonto.

As in other areas of life (see "Summary,'" pp. 93–94), it is largely differentiation of White contacts which spells the difference in economy between one Navaho community and another. Shonto and its neighbors, isolated and remote from wage work opportunities in general, have direct access through the trader to railroad employment, and rely heavily upon it as a result. Isolation and lack of development in District 2 are further reflected in the low figure for local

TABLE 27.—*Shonto individual income compared with total Navaho individual income, 1955*

I. OVERALL COMPARISON

	Shonto	All Navaho
1955 income	$165,551	$35,978,674
Percentage of all Navaho income	.46	100.00
1955 population	568	[1] 80,000
Percentage of all Navaho population	.71	100.00
Mean per capita income	$291	$450
Mean size of households (number)	5.68	5.60
Number of households	100	14,286
Percentage of all Navaho households	.70	100.00
Mean household income	$1,656	$2,520

II. COMPARISON BY SOURCES

Source of income	Categories included		Percentage of all income	
	Shonto [2]	All Navaho [3]	Shonto	All Navaho
Local:				
All livestock and agriculture	1–4	10	17.6	11.1
All payrolls	7	7–9	12.3	18.5
Crafts	5	13	1.6	5.6
All local			31.5	35.2
Railroad:				
Wages	8	1	41.1	22.2
Unemployment compensation	9	2	10.8	7.5
All railroad			51.9	29.7
Miscellaneous:				
Nonrailroad wages	10	3–6	2.3	26.4
Other	6, 11	14	6.1	2.2
All miscellaneous			8.4	28.6
Welfare	12	11, 12	8.2	7.2
All welfare			8.2	7.2
Total percent			100.0	100.0
Activities:				
Native enterprise	1–6	10, 13, 14	21.9	18.9
Wagework	7, 8, 10	1, 3–9	55.7	66.4
Unearned income	9, 11, 12	2, 11, 12	22.4	14.7
Total percent			100.0	100.0

[1] Estimate by Navaho Tribal Census Office, 1955.
[2] See table 21.
[3] See table 26.

wage income. The correspondingly high income from livestock is to some extent an indication of the grazing committee's failure to enforce capacities.

Mean household income for the Navaho tribe in general has been estimated at over $2,500 (table 27), or nearly $1,000 in excess of the Shonto figure. Some of the income estimates upon which this calculation is based are almost certainly too high, as in the case of crafts noted above. The figure for total agricultural income (including that from livestock) is only slightly lower than estimated income from

POSITION IN CONCENTRIC SEQUENCE INDICATES PREFERENTIAL VALUE
WIDTH OF RING INDICATES PROPORTIONAL ECONOMIC VALUE IN 1955

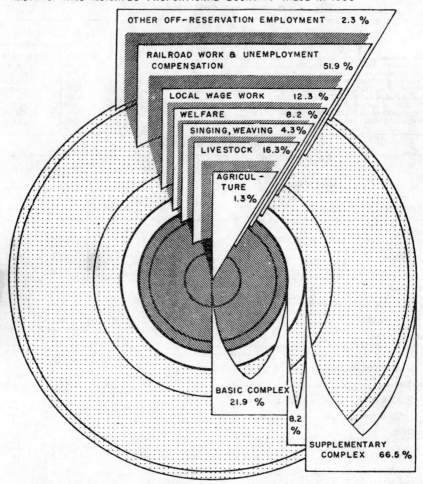

OTHER OFF-RESERVATION EMPLOYMENT   2.3 %

RAILROAD WORK & UNEMPLOYMENT
COMPENSATION   51.9 %

LOCAL WAGE WORK   12.3 %

WELFARE   8.2 %

SINGING, WEAVING   4.3%

LIVESTOCK   16.3%

AGRICUL-
TURE
1.3%

BASIC COMPLEX
21.9 %

8.2
%

SUPPLEMENTARY
COMPLEX   66.5%

PERCENTAGE FIGURES REFER TO TABLE 21.
(3.4 % OF INCOME DERIVED FROM IRREGULAR SOURCES IS NOT SHOWN ABOVE.)

CHART C.—The structure of Shonto's modern economy: preferential vs. economic
value activities.

the same source in 1952 (Young, 1955, p. 113), although both lamb
and wool prices declined markedly in the intervening period. Likewise, the figure for the Bureau of Indian Affairs payroll (item 7,
table 26) probably includes the earnings of non-Navahos as well as
Navahos, since B.I.A. payroll records do not show race or tribe.

Nevertheless, Shonto undoubtedly remains a poor community by
modern Navaho standards. At this stage it is still largely beyond
the reach of recent economic expansion on the Navaho Reservation.

PART 2. THE TRADING POST

BACKGROUND

HISTORY

By all accounts extensive trading with neighboring peoples is a long-established feature of Navaho life. Considerable prehistoric trade is believed to have taken place between Navahos and most of the Rio Grande Pueblos, and in the early historic period occasional commercial relations were also noted with Southern Ute, Hopi, upland Yumans, and various Apache groups (Hill, 1948, p. 374). Regular Navaho trade with Spanish invaders in the Southwest is recorded at the end of the 18th century (Thomas, 1932, pp. 113–114). At a later date the Spanish government of New Mexico forbade Navaho cultivation of tobacco in the hope that the Indians would be forced to buy it from Spanish traders (Van Valkenburgh and McPhee, 1938, p. 7).

Navaho trade with Anglo-Americans began, according to one source (Sanders et al., 1953, p. 232), in the early 1800's. First contacts were sporadic and perhaps often accidental. Formal trading relations were first established with the newly colonized Mormon settlements north and west of the Colorado River in the middle of the 19th century (cf. Van Valkenburgh and McPhee, 1938, p. 43; Hill, 1948, p. 375; Sanders et al., 1953, p. 232). The development of this relationship was largely coincident with the rapid westward expansion of the Navahos occasioned by the Carson campaigns of 1862–63 (see "Navaho Settlement," pp. 37–39).

Prior to the Bosque Redondo exile Navaho trading with all alien groups, Indian and White, was normally conducted by specially organized trading expeditions (see Hill, 1948, pp. 382–384). These were nearly always planned long in advance, and elaborate preparations were made for them. The trading party might be absent for periods up to several weeks. Often trading and preparations for trading were accompanied by a great deal of special ritual (see Hill, 1948).

In the early historic trade complex it was nearly always the Navahos who took the initiative. There is no satisfactory evidence of a reciprocal pattern, wherein members of other tribes visited the Navahos for trading purposes. Apparently not until the middle of the 19th century, when traveling Mormon traders began entering

149

their territory in considerable numbers, were the Navahos ever considered as a substantial or profitable market by their neighbors (cf. Van Valkenburgh and McPhee, 1938, p. 43; Sanders et al., 1953, p. 232).

Buckskins and, especially in the later years, blankets were the major items offered for exchange by Navahos (see especially Hill, 1948, pp. 376–381). In return they received agricultural products from the Pueblos, bolt goods and various articles of European manufacture from the Spaniards, and horses and guns from the Utes and, later, the Mormons. Horses were an especially important item of trade in the last years of the pre-reservation period (cf. Van Valkenburgh and McPhee, 1938, pp. 43–44).

To what extent the Navahos actually became regularly dependent upon their early trade relations is uncertain. Their subsistence agricultural and livestock economy flourished largely unchecked during much of the 19th century, and it seems likely that the items for which they traded were chiefly in the class of luxuries, so that no functional interdependence at the subsistence level developed. However, Dyk's (1938, pp. 49–53) narrative of "Left-Handed" in the early reservation years suggests that there was widespread reliance on trading with the Hopi as a source of food in hard times.

EARLY TRADING POSTS

The period of Navaho military exile at Bosque Redondo, 1864–1868, coupled with the 10-year treaty period which followed, mark a turning point in commercial relations as in many other aspects of Navaho history. During these economically disastrous years a high percentage of families came of necessity to rely for subsistence upon rations issued by the United States Army, first at Fort Sumner and later at Fort Defiance (see Underhill, 1956, pp. 178–180). A process of increasing dependence upon foreign goods and manufactures was set in motion, which has persisted to the present day. In its course the Navahos became increasingly a stable and dependable market, which pioneering American entrepreneurs were quick to exploit.

There is no clear indication today as to when and where the first permanent trading mission to the Navahos was set up. Simpson recorded a White man established at the Zuni village of Pescado and trading with the local Navaho population as early as 1849 (Van Valkenburgh and McPhee, 1938, p. 44). However, it is certain that institutionalized Anglo-Navaho trade within the present reservation area did not develop until some 20 years later.

The trading-post system as it is known today appears to have had its roots in two distinct historical developments (cf. Dyk, 1947, p. 19). In the eastern area, beginning at Fort Defiance, it was a natural and perhaps inevitable outgrowth of the rations system; the first traders were, in fact, army "sutlers" (Underhill, 1956, p. 181). They began by encouraging the Navahos to bring in their surplus wool to trade for extra rations at the ration depot, and ended by quitting Government service to make a full-time specialty of trading for Navaho wool. Neale and Damon operated at Fort Defiance after 1868; in the next 3 years were opened the Dodd (later Keam's) store at Keams Canyon, the Crary store near Ganado, and the Stover & Coddington store at Fort Wingate (Van Valkenburgh and McPhee, 1938, pp. 44–45). All of the individuals involved were former army men or Indian agents.

Farther to the west, trading posts were a direct outgrowth of the earlier, friendly trading relations between Navahos and Mormons beyond the Colorado River. For a long time Navaho-Mormon trade was a sporadic affair, conducted by occasional trading expeditions sent out by both parties. In later years, when Mormon colonization southward from Utah reached the borders and actually penetrated within the Navaho country, permanent trading establishments were set up. The first of these was probably the Lees Ferry enterprise mentioned earlier ("The American Period," pp. 40–42). For a Navaho reminiscence of Lees Ferry in 1876, see Van Valkenburgh and McPhee, 1938, pp. 43–44). It was followed within a year by the store which still operates at Tuba City, and later by another at Bluff City (Dyk, 1947, p. 20).

Throughout its 80-year history, trading on the Navaho Reservation has remained largely in the hands of a few pioneer families, and it is still true in modern times that a majority of traders are descended either from early army men or from Mormon pioneers. Prominent in the former category are, or were, Damons, Days, Hubbells, Parquettes and Shillingburgs. Outstanding Mormon trading families are those of Foutz, Hunt, Kerley, Lee, and McGee. These and a few other "old-line" families still operate about half of all Navaho trading posts.

According to Underhill (1956, pp. 178–179) it was the building of the transcontinental railroad (1882–84) which established the trading post as a permanent fixture on the Navaho Reservation. It assured the territory a steady and unlimited volume of American manufactured goods at moderate freight cost. At the same time Navaho wool and blankets could now be transported economically to Eastern markets. Gallup, railhead of the Santa Fe in 1882, became the great depot from which most of the Navaho country was supplied—as in fact it still is. Such a situation inevitably led to the development of a flourishing wholesale mercantile business specializing in trading-post supply. In later years secondary centers, each with its mercantile house, developed at Flagstaff, also on the Santa Fe, and at Farmington, terminus of the D & RGW narrow gage line originating in Alamosa, Colo.

In 1876 five trading posts were reported to be operating in and around the Navaho Reservations (Sanders et al., 1953, p. 232). By 1890 there were nearly 40 (Underhill, 1956, p. 182), and the number increased steadily until about 1930. At the present time the number of stores on and around the reservation, and devoted chiefly to Navaho trade, is in the neighborhood of 200 (cf. Kluckhohn and Leighton, 1946, p. 38).

Many of the first Navaho trading posts were more or less transient enterprises, changing ownership and location frequently in response to the unstable and undeveloped frontier market. Few of them could boast any installation more permanent than a tent for many years. Frontier trading involved considerable capital risks, but in return offered big, quick profits from a largely untapped consumer market.

In the beginning on-the-spot barter was necessarily the only basis of exchange, as no cash was in circulation and unstable population conditions did not premit credit transactions. Where large commodity exchanges were involved written "due bills" were issued to the Navaho consumer, which might be traded out at any time in succeeding months. Navahos soon learned to counterfeit these (see Van Valkenburgh and McPhee, 1938, p. 45), and a type of trade money or scrip was substituted (cf. Van Valkenburgh and McPhee, 1938, p. 45; Underhill, 1956, p. 183). This historic practice continues to be commemorated in the bewilderingly complex Navaho system of counting money, according to which all amounts under one dollar are expressed as sums of "blues" (10 cents) plus "yellows" (5 cents) plus "reds" (1 cent), regardless of the actual coins involved. (The change-reckoning system is further complicated by surviving vestiges of a still older Spanish system: 25 cents, 50 cents and 75 cents are expressed not as sums of "blues" and "yellows," but as two, four and six *reales* respectively. Likewise 15 cents for some reason remains simply *quince*. For a complete analysis of the system, a thorough control of which is essential to all traders, see Mitchell, n.d., pp. 17–18). Use of trade money has long been outlawed, but it can still be seen at a few of the more isolated stores on the Navaho Reservation.

Wool and blankets were the two commodities which formed the basis of the early Navaho trade, with hides and pelts a distant third. Although blankets had been the chief item of pre-reservation expeditionary trade, it was the addition of enormous quantities of raw wool, most of which had previously gone to waste, which made commerce lucrative in the early reservation period. In 1886 Navaho traders bought a million pounds of it; 4 years later the yield had doubled (Underhill, 1956, p. 181).

In 1890 and increasingly in subsequent years weaving came back into its own as the basis of the Navaho trade. It was during this period that traders began to organize with the idea of deliberately developing a market for Navaho weaving. New methods, designs, and dyes were introduced and virtually forced upon the native weavers; unheard-of prices were offered; and the Navaho blanket, under the careful nurturing of traders, evolved into an ornate, brightly colored rug, slightly suggestive of oriental models for which a large Eastern market existed (see especially Underhill, 1956, pp. 185–190). The period from about 1890 until the beginning of World War I was the heyday of the rug trade, and in many ways marked the climax of the old style barter trading system. Later years saw a steady decline in the quantity market for Navaho rugs, a reemergence of raw wool as the basic trade commodity, and the ever-widening institution of credit as an essential feature of the economy.

Undoubtedly the building of the Santa Fe railroad and subsequent development of trading posts revolutionized Navaho life, as Underhill suggests. The change did not by any means take place overnight, however. So gradual was the evolution toward a market economy, in fact, that it went largely unnoticed by White observers (cf. Underhill, 1956, p.181), and many of its details remain shrouded in uncertainty to the present day.

It is clear from the narratives recorded by Dyk (1938, 1947) that in the early reservation years trading continued to be a sporadic and highly irregular occurrence preserving most of the features of the old expeditionary pattern. When luxury goods were desired, or when it was deemed necessary to supplement existing subsistence resources, a sufficient quantity of wool would be sheared and an expedition to the then remote trading post organized. There is no suggestion of regular or even seasonal dependence upon such trade, and it appears that the families studied by Dyk sometimes went for years without visiting a trading post. In many respects the newly arrived White traders seem to have stepped into the role already occupied by the Hopis, as an optional and, to some degree, an emergency source of trade goods. The family of "Left-Handed" traded about equally with both, under very similar circumstances (see Dyk, 1938).

Apparently between 1870 and the beginning of the present century both the Navahos and the trading posts "settled down." In all probability the two processes contributed to each other. Increasing dependence upon imported manufactured goods, hence upon the trading post, may well have been an important factor in the development of a sedentary Navaho society. At the same time with the growth of a stable and developed consumer market the trading post lost much of its speculative, frontier character. It became a permanent operation geared to a well-defined, protected market, offering moderate but sustained annual profits. Basic to this transformation and indicative of it was the transition from a barter to a commodity credit economy.

Pawn was undoubtedly the earliest basis for Navaho credit, and may possibly go back to the beginnings of the trading post system. "Book" or unsecured credit was in all probability an outgrowth of the rug trade after 1890, and may well have been introduced initially as a device to insure a steady supply of rugs. By 1910 many traders were definitely allowing large accounts against rugs. Decline of the rug market and the substitution of raw wool as the primary commodity after World War I made the Navahos increasingly dependent upon seasonal production, and undoubtedly further solidified the credit system.

Throughout the present century credit operation has become a necessity to the Navaho trader no less than to the Navaho consumer. With increasing development of the Navaho market and the multiplication of trading posts the first concern of the modern trader is to protect rather than to expand his consumer market. Territorial monopoly which was once in itself a satisfactory guarantee of a captive market has been of diminishing value in the days of new roads and automobiles. In general, modern traders have come to rely instead on retail credit saturation to insure market control. In this operation the trader has found a new benefit in territorial monopoly: he is the only merchant close enough to the Navaho market and familiar enough with it to be able to grant credit without security.

Whatever the original motive for introducing credit in the Navaho economy, it was in practice entirely effective. Characteristic Navaho concentration upon immediate conditions and lack of concern for the more distant future provided a climate favorable to unlimited acceptance. By the end of World War I it had become, as it remains, the essential basis of trading-post operation. This development clearly marks the end of the "frontier" period in Navaho trade and probably in Navaho life generally. The trading post had become, as it largely remains, a late version of the old general store which was the cornerstone of the American rural economy throughout the 19th century.

TRADING IN THE NORTHWESTERN NAVAHO AREA

Although Navaho-Mormon trade beyond the Colorado River dates back at least to the middle of the 19th century, permanent trading posts were slow in coming to the northwestern Navaho country. Probably because of the scattered and unstable population conditions, the Mormon colonists in the region never pushed their trading ventures beyond the limits of their own farming settlements. Until well into the present century Tuba City was the only Navaho trading center between the Colorado River and Chinle Valley, and between the San Juan and the Hopi villages. It remained for others to bring trade into the "backwoods" (cf. Leighton and Kluckhohn, 1948, p. 139) of Shonto and neighboring communities.

Three names are inextricably associated with trading in the northwestern Navaho country: those of Wetherill, Richardson, and Babbitt Bros. John and Louisa Wetherill, of the now-celebrated Mancos family (see Gillmor and Wetherill, 1934) have the undivided honor of having pioneered trade in this most remote corner of the reservation. They began operations at Oljeto in 1907 and removed to Kayenta in 1909, where their original business still flourishes and has become the center of a lively community. From Kayenta, John Wetherill and his son Ben established a series of outposts which one by one were sold out and became independent enterprises. Among them were Oljeto, Chilchinbeto, Cow Springs, and Shonto.

While the Wetherills were pioneering trade in the Kayenta region, the Richardson family of Flagstaff moved in farther west during and after World War I. Richardson holdings at one time or another included Cameron, Kaibito, The Gap, Inscription House, Rainbow Lodge, and Shonto (see map 1).

The last and most important entry in the field was that of Babbitt Bros. Trading Co., of Flagstaff. Beginning as livestock growers around the turn of the century, the Babbitt family became engaged in trading for Navaho wool, then entered the wholesale mercantile field in Flagstaff, and have finally ended by operating a string of trading posts on the reservation as well. The Babbit trading empire today is the largest on the reservation, including sole or majority interest in trading posts at Tuba City, Cedar Ridge, Red Lake, Cow Springs, Kayenta, Piñon, Jeddito, and Indian Wells.

Entry of the Babbitt company into the Navaho retail field emphasizes the growing importance of the mercantile wholesaler in 20th-century Navaho trade. This development has been an inevitable outgrowth of the credit system at the retail level. Since most traders have little in the way of capital reserves they have themselves become heavily dependent upon wholesale credit. The measure of Navaho economic dependence upon the trader is commonly, in modern times, the measure of the latter's dependence upon his own suppliers. If the trading post is the only institution able to grant long-term, unsecured credit to the Navaho individual, the off-reservation general wholesale house is equally the only institution able to carry the trading post on the same terms. The modern Navaho market economy is thus underwritten ultimately by the wholesale houses.

In the present century trading throughout the Navaho Reservation has been backed, and hence largely controlled, by three general mercantile houses in Farmington, Gallup, and Flagstaff. These enterprises have always been devoted very largely to serving the Navaho trade, and are closely geared to it. The Babbitt Company is, however, the only one that has ventured into outright ownership of its own retail outlets.

Other important trading interests in the northwestern Navaho country have been those of the Kerley family at Tuba City, Kayenta, Navajo Mountain, and Moenave; and Heflin & Carson at Oljeto, Kayenta, Inscription House, and Shonto.

Commercial enterprise came to the northwestern Navaho country toward the close of the great rug-trading period, and for this reason weaving has never at any time been as important here as in other parts of the reservation. Conspicuously absent are the very large rugs which were once so heavily subsidized, and continue to be made in some quantity, farther east. Shonto Trading Post and all of its neighbors have long since ceased to allow any credit against rugs.

SHONTO TRADING POST

Many details of the early history of Shonto Trading Post are obscure today. The enterprise was founded, on the site which it still occupies, in 1915, by John Wetherill and Joe Lee (Van Valkenburgh, 1941, p. 145. Lee later traded at McElmo Creek and appears occasionally in the narrative of "Old Mexican"—Dyk, 1947). Supplies were brought in by wagon from Kayenta and were sold out of a tent. Water was obtained from the wash and from Shonto Spring, a couple of miles upstream from the store. The enterprise was originally called Shonto Springs Store, a name which still appears on some maps.[8]

Shonto Springs Store continued as a tent operation and an outpost of Kayenta until shortly after World War I, when it was sold to Messrs. Sid Richardson and Tobe Turpen. The new owners built the first permanent building on the site, consisting of the present store, warehouse, and most of the family living quarters (A, C, and D on fig. 1). They also developed a well and pumphouse (F) at the store site, and put up an overnight hogan (P) for transient Navahos.[9]

Early in the 1920's Richardson & Turpen in turn sold out to Babbitt Bros., who were then just beginning to enter the trading field on a large scale. The company operated Shonto for several years, making no significant additions to the plant or methods of operation. Wool and, to a lesser extent, rugs, with heavy emphasis on credit, continued to be the basis of trade throughout their tenure. In 1930, Babbitt's sold the store to Mr. and Mrs. Harry Rorick for $10,000 in cash.

---

[8] Many years later the name was changed briefly to Betatakin Trading Post, also seen on some maps today, and finally to Shonto Trading Post. The name Shonto, which translates roughly as "spring in the sunshine," is rather common on the reservation. At least two other trading posts go by the same designation in Navaho, though both of these go by the English name of Sunshine Trading Post.

[9] Popular accounts of trading post life and times during this period may be found in Coolidge, 1925; Faunce, 1934; Gillmor and Wetherill, 1934; and Schmedding, 1951. All of these are written by or about traders and give a good general impression of the physical conditions under which they worked.

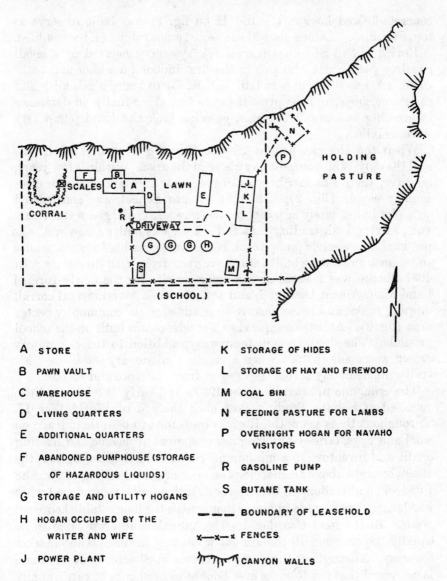

FIGURE 1.—Shonto Trading Post grounds.

The new owners made many changes in the trading post, and brought the physical plant more or less to its present state of development. Like many other traders at that time they anticipated a heavy influx of tourist travel following the construction of new roads in the early 1930's and hoped to set up a guest lodge in emulation of the success of the Wetherills at Kayenta. For this purpose a row of concrete-floored hogans (G and H on fig. 1) was built to serve as tourist cabins.   Later a pair of connected stone cabins (E) was added. Rorick put in Shonto's first electric system, generated by a small gasoline plant.   He also put in the first indoor plumbing and bathroom.   A line of sheds was built (J, K, L) to house blacksmith and carpenter shops, and the premises were fenced.   Finally, in deference to growing automobile travel, a gasoline tank and hand pump (R) were installed.

When the Roricks bought Shonto Trading Post in 1930 it was still the only White outpost anywhere in the area.   Within a few years, however, their site in Shonto Canyon grew into an extensive community center (fig. 2).   In 1934 Shonto School was constructed on a plot immediately adjacent to the store.   An enlarged water reservoir, serving both trading post and school, was built; a new well was put in and an electric pump installed.   Roads passable for automobiles and school buses were built into the canyon from both directions.   In 1937 Shonto was selected as headquarters site for the newly formed Land Management District 2, and at that time a governmental corral, dipping tanks, and horse pasture were added to the community center area (fig. 2).   A district supervisor's residence was built on the school grounds.   The final, though temporary, addition to the community center was made in 1955 when a resident missionary established his trailer immediately across the canyon from the store and school.

The economic upheavals of the 1930's and early 1940's were little reflected at Shonto Trading Post until the end of World War II. Throughout these years the Roricks continued to base their trade on wool and rugs, largely ignoring newer sources of income and holding credit and inventory to a minimum.   Stock reduction throughout the 1930's brought about an enormous amount of forced selling of Navaho livestock, and traders all over the reservation quickly developed what was largely a new trade in lambs to augment the long established wool trade.   In the next two decades the annual lamb crop came to be equally important with the annual wool crop in the Navaho market economy.   Throughout their 15-year tenure at Shonto, however, there is no record that the Roricks ever bought either lambs or cattle at any time.

Shonto's trade was for a time considerably augmented by the numerous local construction projects of the mid 1930's, but the stimulus was a temporary one.   The store's owners did not make any effort to build up payroll credit accounts from the school or national monument.   In later years Rorick was a partial invalid and could not move around readily.   In these circumstances the business sank to near-marginal proportions, with minimum inventory and depending

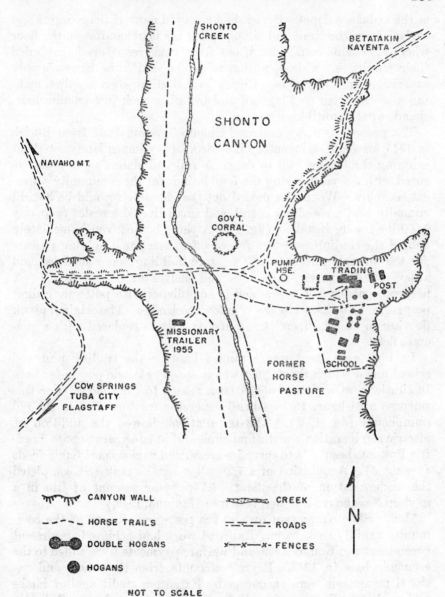

SHONTO
CREEK

BETATAKIN
KAYENTA

SHONTO
CANYON

NAVAHO MT.

GOV'T.
CORRAL

PUMP
HSE.   TRADING
                POST

MISSIONARY
TRAILER
1955

FORMER   SCHOOL
HORSE
PASTURE

COW SPRINGS
TUBA CITY
FLAGSTAFF

꿈꿈꿈 CANYON WALL   CREEK

- - - - HORSE TRAILS   ROADS

DOUBLE HOGANS   x—x—x- FENCES

HOGANS

N

NOT TO SCALE

FIGURE 2.—Shonto community center.

on hand-to-mouth supply. While railroad labor was booming in other parts of the reservation, Rorick did not apply for a claims agency, and Shonto's able-bodied men were forced to find their own jobs, mostly at the Navajo Ordnance Depot near Flagstaff.

At the time when Shonto was bought by its present owners the business was still dependent chiefly on wool and rugs, plus whatever surplus cash was brought or sent home from time to time by workers at the ordnance depot. Rorick had removed most of the counters and shelves from the store and simply piled his merchandise on the floor where his clients could pick it out for themselves where he recorded their purchases. This operation might be said to be Shonto's only experiment in self-service. Rorick hauled all his own supplies, making a weekly trip to Flagstaff and bringing back just enough merchandise to last until his next trip.

The present owners purchased Shonto Trading Post from Rorick in 1945 for $45,000, inventory included. They immediately set about bringing the business up to date. A railroad claims agency was secured within a year, laying the foundations for the community's present economy. Word was passed out that livestock would be bought annually, and a weighing corral, and small livestock scales (capacity 2,000 lbs.) were installed (fig. 1). A short box canyon immediately behind the trading post was fenced off to serve as a holding pasture for the animals purchased. The store building was remodeled and a new set of counters, showcases, and shelves added (see fig. 3). A fireproof pawn vault was added in compliance with postwar trading post regulations issued by the Window Rock office. The original plank flooring in the "bullpen" (customer area) was replaced with a concrete floor.

In 1949 a contract was arranged between the trading post and school under which the former was to supply electric power for both institutions, at a charge of $30.00 a month to the school. For this purpose a 24-hour, 15 kw. diesel generator was installed in the old pumphouse (fig. 1, J). The installation allowed the addition of electric refrigeration for the first time, and in late years Shonto Trading Post has been able to carry ice cream and various perishable foods (see fig. 3). Acquisition of a 750-gallon butane tank (S) completed the modernization of the plant. (A popular account of life in a modern Navaho trading post is that of Hannum, 1946.)

Under Shonto's present owners the postwar economy of the community rapidly took form. Railroad work had achieved its present preeminent position by 1950, and welfare payments were added to the economic base in 1948. Payroll accounts from the school and national monument were encouraged. Extensive credit against lambs and wool, as well as against relief, unemployment, and payroll checks, became an integral part of store operation.

In spite of mounting profits and cash volume, later postwar years in some ways were difficult for all traders. With one or two exceptions their stores had been built, without any kind of formal contract, upon tribal land held in trust by the United States. Throughout their long history the legal status of trading posts had never been clearly defined. In 1949 the Navaho Tribe, through its attorneys, sought to establish a right of accession upon the store buildings and all fixed assets. The claim if allowed would have permitted out-right confiscation. The long dispute which followed resulted chiefly from the fact that tribal claim would, in the traders' view, destroy the investment value of their properties, many of which had recently been bought for prices in excess of $50,000. Negotiations between the Navaho Tribe and the United Indian Traders' Association were car-ried on for several years, during which time there was a high turn-over in store ownership throughout the reservation. Of the 10 major trading posts nearest to Shonto, 7 changed hands between 1949 and 1954.

A settlement between traders and tribe was ultimately reached in 1954. The traders' proprietary claim upon buildings and fixed assets was surrendered in exchange for a 25-year transferable and renewable lease, and the traders' sole proprietary interest in the business was recognized. An annual lease rental of 1½ percent of gross volume was agreed upon. Inevitably this addition to operating costs has been passed along to the Navaho consumer through higher markups.

THE TRADING POST TODAY

Modern Shonto Trading Post occupies a 2½-acre leasehold on its original site on the floor of Shonto Canyon (figs. 1, 2). The store is licensed to operate (under $50,000 bond) annually by the Bureau of Indian Affairs, and is subject to the terms of its 25-year lease from the Navaho tribe. Through its owner it has membership in the United Indian Traders' Association.

PLANT

Business is still conducted in the original store building (fig. 1, A) erected shortly after World War I. In its physical layout Shonto remains a typical trading post of an earlier day: a long, low, stone building with a single door and a few small, heavily barred windows, and capped by a slightly pitched roof. Like many neighboring trad-ing posts it gives the initial impression of a large shed. The building is constructed entirely of local red sandstone laid up with adobe mortar and is quite obviously the work of untrained local builders. Woodwork inside and out is unfinished, and some of it is rough-hewn.

Interior dimensions of the store itself (see fig. 3) are about 25 by 45 feet. Inside walls are plastered and painted. The dim light ad-mitted by five small windows is augmented by half a dozen 150-watt electric bulbs hanging from the ceiling.[10] An interior ceiling of fiberboard was added to Shonto Trading Post in 1954. It has an aver-

---

[10] Because of the necessity of keeping a constant minimum load upon the 24-hour gen-erator, most light bulbs at the store, as well as at the school, are kept burning at all times, so that the visitor entering Shonto Canyon even in the early hours of the morning is likely to get the impression that he is approaching a sizable settlement.

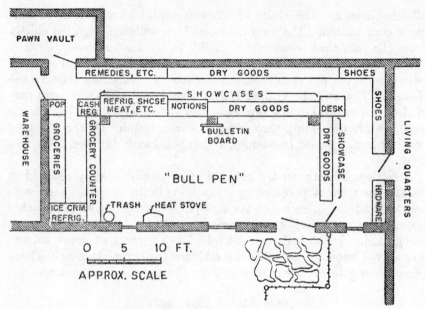

FIGURE 3.—Shonto store layout.

age height above the floor of 11 feet. The cantilevered roof is partially supported by three interior posts (fig. 3).

Interior layout of the store is shown in figure 3. Three of the room's four walls are covered with stock shelves from floor to ceiling, and are paralleled by counters and/or showcases. In addition most of the larger hardware stock and harness equipment is suspended from nails in the ceiling. Very large items of hardware and furniture, such as stoves, rollaway beds, and water drums are likely to be set out on the bullpen floor at the foot of the wall. Shonto Trading Post, like most of its neighbors, always has a cluttered appearance, giving the impression that every available inch of space has been utilized for merchandise display and storage. Wagons, wagon parts, and plows are kept in the yard behind the store.

Extra stocks are stored in the warehouse room adjacent to the store (fig. 1, C). Because of limited space here additional merchandise stocks must usually be kept in the series of hogans (G) which were built originally as tourist cabins. (One hogan, H, served as quarters for the writer and his wife in 1955–56.) Hazardous liquids are stored in the old pumphouse (F).

Thanks to its abortive history as a tourist lodge Shonto is unusually well equipped with living quarters. The original family quarters (D), adjoining the store, are now used only by the owner and his family on their infrequent visits to Shonto (see below). Two stone cabins (E) and one hogan (H) serve as quarters for the resident

White trader and for traveling salesmen and other occasional overnight visitors.

Other structures on the trading post premises include a series of
log sheds (J, K, L) used for storage of wood, hay, and hides and
housing the power plant; the original overnight hogan for Navaho
visitors (P) ; and the weighing corral and scales.

EQUIPMENT AND UTILITIES

Shonto generates all its own electric power, and also supplies the
school (see above). Water is pumped from a nearby Government
well (ca. 15 feet deep) into a reservoir above, which serves both store
and school. Because the reservoir holds only about 30 hours' supply,
it is necessary to pump water for 3 to 4 hours every day. Under the
original agreement both reservoir and electric pump were installed
by the Bureau of Indian Affairs, but are operated and serviced by the
trading post. Both the water and sewage systems of the store are
tied into those of the school.

A 750-gallon butane tank is leased from a Flagstaff gas supply
company. It must be replenished about every 4 months. Butane is
used only in the main kitchen range and in a heating stove in the
store (fig. 3). All heat in the living quarters, including water heating, is obtained from wood and coal stoves and a fireplace. Cut firewood is regularly supplied at $5.00 a wagonload by a local Navaho.
Coal is delivered from a small Navaho-operated coal mine on Black
Mesa at $20.00 a ton.

Rolling stock belonging to the trading post consists of a 1½-ton
stake-body truck for occasional hauling of supplies and a ½-ton
pickup for local runabout work.

STAFF

The full staff of Shonto Trading Post consists of the owner and
his wife, a resident White trader and his wife, and one Navaho
helper.

Shonto's owner, who also has interests in neighboring trading posts,
serves chiefly as absentee business manager of the enterprise. As a
general rule he spends no more than 1 or 2 days a week on the
premises, and is often absent for several weeks at a time. Nevertheless he retains nearly all executive authority in his own hands. He
handles most wholesale and commodity transactions, accounting, and
finance. All relations between the store and outside institutions
such as the wholesale house, the bank, and the Bureau of Internal
Revenue are entirely his responsibility. He also retains for himself
the position of claims agent for the Railroad Retirement Board,
necessitating his presence at the store on every Thursday during the
"benefit year" (see "Railroad Work," pp. 129–133).

The resident trader is in full charge of all on-the-spot operations involved in the store and plant. To a large extent he combines the roles of retail manager, credit manager, clerk, day bookkeeper, and maintenance man. His regular duties include opening and closing the store, handling all retail transactions except some cash sales, keeping daysheets for accounting purposes, fill-in merchandise ordering, arranging for supplies of gasoline, diesel fuel (for the generator) and oil, butane, coal and wood, and keeping up the premises and equipment. In the last analysis, the resident trader is simply a general storekeeper; all his other duties are ancillary in character. The position has been filled by no less than 11 individuals since Shonto was bought by its present owners in 1945. It was occupied by the writer during most of the time when the present study was made (see "Introduction," pp. 12–14).

Although nearly all trading posts employ one or more Navaho helpers, Shonto is believed to be the only store on the reservation which regularly employs a helper who does not speak English. As a result his role is considerably more limited than that of native clerks in other stores. Like most Navahos, he can and does read numbers and hence is able to make cash sales, having acquired considerable adeptness in operating the cash register. He cannot, of course, handle any recorded transactions. Aside from sales clerking he serves as warehouseman, stocker, gardener, and general handyman. He spends most of his time moving merchandise in and out of the warehouse, stocking shelves, making gasoline deliveries (a job which is considered onerous, since Shonto has only a gravity pump), janitoring, watering lawns, and doing odd jobs on the premises. Building and stoking fires is one of his most constant jobs throughout the winter months. His work routine throughout the day is under the supervision of the resident trader.

Shonto Trading Post is always compelled to put on additional Navaho help at peak seasons. One or two wool sackers and sorters are needed in April and May, and several herders are required for the fall lamb drive to the railroad. Sometimes extra clerical help, either Navaho or White, is hired for a few hours or days under extreme rush conditions, as during lamb season.

BUSINESS OPERATION

Shonto Trading Post is open for business every day of the week except Sunday, and including holidays, throughout the year. Business hours vary seasonally and to some extent according to demand. Usual hours are from about 7:30 a.m. until 6:00 p.m. during the summer and from 8:30 a.m. until 5:00 p.m. in winter. However, it is common practice to reopen the store for late customers up to 7:30 or 8:00 p.m., and to open on Sundays to accommodate clients who have traveled a long distance to trade.[11] During wool and lamb seasons the store frequently remains open until far into the night, and on Sundays as well.

Shonto's entire operation is geared to its Navaho clientele, which accounts for over 99 percent of the total annual volume of business. White trade, either from transients or from neighbors at the school and national monument, is considered incidental, and no real attempt is made to attract it. There is, in fact, a common tendency for traders to say that tourist trade is "a nuisance" (see "Clientele," pp. 184–186).

About 65 percent of Shonto's annual trade comes from the 100 families which are considered in the present study as comprising the Shonto community. The remaining 35 percent of trade comes from occasional, and in some cases regular, visits by Navahos from other communities. Because Shonto often pays higher prices for lambs and wool than do its neighbors (see "Commodity Exchange," pp. 172–175), it receives a disproportionately high percentage of the livestock trade from Districts 1 and 2. Numerous families from Cow Springs, Kaibito, Navajo Mountain, and especially Black Mesa carry regular livestock accounts at Shonto.

The gross sales volume of all trading posts is subject to considerable annual variation, owing largely to fluctuating commodity prices and an uneven market for Navaho labor. Shonto's gross varies between normal limits of about $120,000 and $150,000 a year. Net profit (owner's salary not deducted) averages between 10 and 15 percent of gross, or between extreme limits of about $12,000 and $22,000 annually. In 1955 the store's present owners refused an offer of $65,000 for Shonto Trading Post.

WHITE SOCIETY AT SHONTO

Shonto Trading Post is one of three White institutions permanently established in the community, the others being the neighboring school and the national monument headquarters 10 miles away. The missionary establishment across the canyon from the store and school temporarily added a fourth institution in 1955. In that year the adult White population of Shonto community numbered eight persons; one married couple each at the store, mission and national monument, and two women teachers at the school.

A distinct social barrier separates White society from Navaho society at Shonto. Relations between the two groups, though seemingly personal in many respects (see pp. 287–290), are confined to institutional contexts in which a role distinction is maintained at all times. Notably absent is any pattern of personal hospitality as between

---

[11] These privileges are never extended to White tourists unless they indicate a strong interest in buying rugs.

Shonto Navahos and local Whites. A White person visits a Navaho camp only upon specific business and without advance notice. While there, he is almost never invited inside the hogan or offered food, and conversation is confined entirely to the matter in hand. This pattern is in marked contrast to that experienced by tourists and other casual White visitors, who often enjoy Navaho hospitality quite readily.

A similarly institutionalized relationship exists when local Navahos visit the store, school, or monument headquarters. Dealings with Whites are supposed to take place in the store or office buildings, and living quarters are distinctly off limits. Trading-post customers who are compelled to stay overnight do not share the trader's table and are not invited to use the guest quarters; they use the overnight hogan at the back of the premises (see fig. 1) and are given the necessary supplies to prepare their own meals. The national monument also has an overnight hogan for Navaho visitors. Educated Navahos from outside the community who are Government or tribal employees, however, are not subject to the same social distinction: they are always received on the same basis as White visitors.

Although Shonto's non-Navaho residents are set clearly apart in the social order of the community, they do not in themselves constitute any sort of cohesive social unit. Casual visitors are nearly always surprised at the very low degree of social interaction between trading post, school, and national monument headquarters.

The simplest explanation is that for its White residents Shonto is not a community but a job. Shonto is not "home" to any of them, but simply a place where they work. Their personal ties of kinship, property, or long residence are with other communities away from the reservation.[12] Like most other White people on the reservation, Shonto's traders, teachers, and monument employees rely for their social life chiefly on regular trips to town and occasional vacations at their family homes. Hence, paradoxically, the very isolation of Shonto militates against a close-knit White society.

The situation results also from purely physical factors. Because of the nature of their jobs it is seldom possible for any of Shonto's White residents to leave their premises for any length of time. There is, moreover, a consistently high turnover in all three jobs. Since World War II, Shonto has had four national monument superintendents, four sets of schoolteachers, and at least 11 resident traders (see "Staff," above).

Shonto's White society is, then, fluid and loose-knit. Social relations between store, school, and monument employees are not by any means structurally inherent, but depend to a very large extent on the

---

[12] While some traders undoubtedly do consider their stores as their home, Shonto's owner maintains family residences both in Flagstaff and Farmington, and regards Shonto strictly as a business property.

personalities involved. Some traders at Shonto have maintained no social relations of any kind with either the school or Betatakin. In 1955, however, fairly frequent reciprocal visiting and dining relations exsited between the national monument people and both the school-teachers and the traders. These groups exchanged dinners about every 2 weeks. Much less frequent visiting relations existed between the traders and the teachers, and at no time did all three groups get together for a purely social occasion. Fairly frequent visiting relationships also existed between all three groups and the traders at Red Lake, and between the traders at Shonto and those at Inscription House (who are the father- and mother-in-law of Shonto's owner).

It is notable that there is associated with each of the three White institutions in Shonto community a distinctive social life of its own. The schoolteachers are regularly visited by various Bureau of Indian Affairs officials—particularly the building- and utility-maintenance crew from Tuba City. Navajo National Monument receives a steady stream of tourists throughout the summer, many of whom are annual visitors and have become personally acquainted with the superintendent and his family. The latter are, in fact, the only Shonto residents who extend hospitality to tourists.

Shonto Trading Post has perhaps the most extensive home social life of all. The store is visited throughout the year by a succession of salesmen, truckers, hide and rug buyers, and government and tribal officials of all sorts. Hospitality is extended to all of these as a matter of course and policy, and several of them have made Shonto a regular overnight stop for years. The result is that throughout the year the trader has dinner and overnight guests on an average of once or twice a week.

TRADING POST ECONOMICS

In most respects the modern Navaho trading post is not, as it has sometimes been called, a "remaining example of frontier commerce" (Kluckhohn and Leighton, 1946, p. 41). Purely as a retail operation it belongs properly to the general store era, which followed the trading-post period in American retail development and was particularly characteristic of much of the 19th century (cf. Nystrom, 1930, p. 70). In its physical plant, its systems of transaction and accounting, and many other aspects of operation the Navaho trading post of today is inescapably reminiscent of the old rural general store (see especially Atherton, 1939, and Carson, 1954).

In other respects, however, the trading post of today has no historical precedent. While its consumer market remains characteristic of an earlier era, the wholesale markets in which inventories must be purchased and commodities exchanged have undergone sweeping changes in the present century. In tying the semisubsistence economy of the Navahos to the modern United States mercantile economy the trading post is thus in the position of bridging a 100-year gap in economic development. The result, at the wholesale level, is a complex and sometimes makeshift system of commercial and financial relationships very different from those of the old general store (cf. Carson, 1954, pp. 135–190; Atherton, 1939, pp. 47–82).

The trading post, moreover, has been undergoing a period of transition reflecting that of its consumer market. The store, together with its customers is becoming "acculturated," and the process in both cases is replete with uncertainties. Increasing volume of cash and short-term retail transactions is lessening the store's historic dependence on long-term wholesale credit (cf. Nystrom, 1930, p. 81), but at the same time undermining its competitive position in the consumer market (see "Market Control," p. 169). Emergence of a cash-based economy has the further effect of forcing the trader increasingly to seek special markets for that part of his income which is still received in the form of commodities—markets which are no longer related to direct channels of supply and finance.

Finally, the Indian trade has always involved inherent risks both at the retail and wholesale levels which are almost without precedent in American business practice. Because of their special legal status the assets of Navahos and other reservation Indians are not subject to lien or attachment of any kind, so that the trader, unlike the general storekeeper, cannot deal in notes or crop mortgages, and has no legal recourse of any kind in case of default. Except in the case of pawn, trading post accounts receivable are entirely unsecured.

The wholesale merchant who supplies and often finances the trader inevitably absorbs much of the same risk, for the trader himself has little or nothing to offer as credit security. His land, buildings, and fixed assets belong legally to the Navaho tribe (see "Shonto Trading Post," pp. 157–161), and his accounts receivable are largely unsecured. The result is that the wholesaler must for the most part carry the trader on the same terms as the latter carries the Navaho consumer. Under these circumstances ultimate control of the Navaho trade in the present century has passed very largely into the hands of a small group of general wholesale houses in off-reservation towns whose operation is especially adapted to the Navaho trade and capitalized accordingly. These "mercantilers," as they are commonly called, are in every case branches of larger and more diversified wholesale organizations and thus infinitely better able to absorb the risks of the Indian trade than is the retail trader. In nearly every respect, both financial and commercial, they stand in the same relation to the trader as the latter in turn stands to the Navaho consumer.

The modern Navaho trade thus manifests a dual structure of institutions performing closely comparable functions at the wholesale and retail levels; each equally indispensable to the total economy. This relationship is beginning to change with the increasing circulation of cash in the Navaho market, but it is still largely true in 1957 that a group of less than half a dozen mercantile houses ultimately supplies the credit which underwrites the Navaho economy.

THE CONSUMER MARKET

MARKET CHARACTERISTICS

The productive economy of Shonto community has been described in detail above (pp. 94–148). In many respects it is classifiable as a "colonial" economy, intermediate between commodity barter and a pure cash economy (cf. Foulke, 1941, pp. 25–46). Similar market conditions a century and more ago gave rise to the country general store (ibid.,1941, pp. 52–54), and many of its aspects are faithfully preserved by the trading post. The basis of transaction is the exchange of both cash and locally produced commodities primarily for necessities of food, clothing, shelter, and transportation. Commodities are exchanged at equivalent cash valuation according to a fixed price system. In this respect the Navaho trading post of today differs sharply from the true frontier trading post which served a wide-open and almost moneyless market (see especially Carson, 1954, pp. 20–42).

Modern Navahos constitute a consumer market which might be termed underdeveloped, but which is decidedly not undeveloped. As consumers, no less than as producers, they are in a colonial stage of evolution, depending on trade to supplement a subsistence economy. This is the consumer market for which modern trading posts compete.

MARKET CONTROL

The competitive position of Shonto and nearly all other trading posts, like that of the old general store, is based on territorial monopoly. The trading post has a recognized local clientele for which it is the only convenient commercial enterprise, and which affords a protected consumer market. In the face of increasing competition from off-reservation towns and the large number of trading posts now operating, the first concern of every modern trader is to retain and protect, rather than to expand, this market.

By general agreement trading posts do not, in theory, compete with one another. It is a commonly expressed sentiment that there are enough Indians to go around if everyone will confine himself to his local clientele and hold the prevailing price line. Again in theory, all traders are united against the ever-increasing threat of off-reservation competition. In practice it is chiefly territorial monopoly rather than collusion which tends to minimize competition, for attempts to draw trade away from neighboring stores are not infrequent. Shonto Trading Post has had considerable success in drawing trade from stores farther west by offering more liberal credit terms, higher prices for lambs and wool, and by a double-price system whereby outsiders buy flour and coffee at lower prices than do Shonto residents. These practices are condemned by other traders, but are common enough in all parts of the reservation.

If reservation trading posts offer comparatively little competition to one another, the same is not true of off-reservation retail merchants. Lower freight rates, high turnover, and straight cash operation allow the latter to offer prices consistently at least 15 percent lower than those found on the reservation (cf. Kluckhohn and Leighton, 1946, p. 39), and create a very real competition for the increasing Navaho cash dollar. To meet this competitive threat many traders have sought to minimize expendable cash by the technique of credit saturation. At Shonto, credit terms and limits have been made consistently more liberal in recent years with the idea of getting most of the community's income spent before it is earned. If the trader is no longer the only merchant in contact with his particular consumer market, he is still the only one close enough to it to be able to grant unsecured credit. Thus traders have, in a sense, found a new way to exploit territorial monopoly so as to minimize traffic with rival merchants.

CAPITAL AND FINANCE

CAPITALIZATION

Although small retail business is traditionally undercapitalized (Kaplan, 1948, p. 136; Comish, 1946, p. 326), probably no enterprise in modern America operates with less capital investment and smaller reserves than the Navaho trading post. Buildings, land, and fixed assets belong legally to the Navaho tribe, so that the trader has in actuality no equity save in the value of his leasehold. As a result trading posts have extremely low investment value, and seldom can be sold for more than three or four times their annual net earnings.

Low investment value has an inevitable effect upon operating reserves. In order to protect themselves personally most trading post owners annually draw out nearly all net earnings in the form of salary and distributed profit, leaving a bare minimum of funds tied up in store accounts. Shonto's operating reserves often amount to no more than a few hundred dollars. The result, year in and year out, is an overwhelming dependence on mercantile credit.

FINANCE

Small businesses in general find bank financing difficult to obtain (see Kaplan, 1948, p. 136), and for traders with their negligible assets and unsecured accounts it is entirely unavailable. The trader, like his retail clientele, requires long-term credit without security to operate throughout the year. Such credit is available only from the mercantilers of Flagstaff, Gallup, and Farmington; these institutions provide not only the mercantile credit necessary to operate, but also in many cases funds for improvement or expansion, and not infrequently carry trading posts through bad years. They are unquestionably the financial backbone of the Navaho trade.

The credit status of the trading post once depended directly upon recorded and/or anticipated commodity trade, and rugs, wool, and lambs went directly to the mercantile house in payment of account. One trader of nearly 40 years' experience remarked, "We never used to keep any kind of books. We took our wool and our rugs to the 'merc' once a year, and they weighed them up and told us if we made a profit or took a loss for the year." The trader of that era was in a position of financial dependence exactly comparable to that of the individual Navaho today.[13]

The flow of retail goods to the Navaho consumer, however, is no longer paid for entirely by an equal flow of commodities to the mercantiler. The credit status of the modern trading post is considerably more complex. Livestock trade still necessitates and at the same time furnishes a basis for mercantile credit, but rug and other craft trade has declined to such an extent that these items are no longer even convertible at the wholesale house. Cash volume, on the other hand, not only furnishes a basis for additional credit at the wholesale house, but also to some extent enables the modern trader to deal with specialty wholesalers on short terms, and even in some cases to buy for cash. It has become a regular practice to make monthly payments even on long-term accounts, thereby considerably reducing the amount of interest paid annually.

While wholesale trade has tended more and more toward a cash basis, retail Navaho trade, particularly in the western Navaho area, continues to be based on multiple media of exchange, with the result that the burden of commodity transaction falls increasingly onto the trader. The general mercantilers no longer handle even lambs and wool in direct payment of account; instead they act as commission agents in contracting the sale of these products directly from trader to feeder or wool house, receiving whatever is due them out of the proceeds of the sale. Rugs, piñon nuts and other commodities must

---

[13] The regular relationship of the general merchandise wholesaler to the rural general store is discussed in Beckman and Engle, 1951, pp. 201–202.

usually be sold for cash to occasional buyers who are entirely outside the structure of supply and finance, and turnover is often slow. In a few cases they can be substituted for cash, on the same terms, in dealing with certain suppliers (see below), but they are never a basis for credit.

COMMODITY EXCHANGE

The variety and diversity of products still accepted by the modern Navaho trading post in lieu of cash undoubtedly exceeds that found in any other retail business. Regular media of exchange include lambs, wool, hides, rugs, and a variety of other native crafts, and, in favored years, pinyon nuts. Each of these items plays a specific part in the overall operation of the trading post, and each must be sold or traded in its own special market. Circulation of commodities as between Shonto Trading Post and its various buyers and suppliers is shown schematically in chart D.

Lambs and wool are sold to feeders and/or commodity houses either directly by the trader, or, much more commonly, through the agency of one or another of the wholesale mercantile houses. The mercantilers perform this service in view of their vested interest in the outcome of the sale (see above), and as a result usually maintain close contacts with commodity markets.

High costs of handling and transportation are an inevitable disadvantage of the commodity trade. Shonto's lambs, when buying is complete, must be trailed overland some 135 miles to weighing and shipping pens on the Santa Fe Railway near Winslow, where actual sale to feeders takes place. The process involves not only considerable labor costs, but also unavoidable dead losses and in some cases a weight loss as well. Wool is trucked at the trader's expense to any of various warehouses off the reservation, where the buyer or his representative takes possession.

Rugs, once the cornerstone of the Navaho trade (see "Early Trading Posts," pp. 150–154), now move in the weakest and most uncertain of all Navaho commodity markets, and are generally considered an unavoidable nuisance by traders in the Shonto area. The great majority are actually saddle blankets of medium to poor quality, and turnover averages less than 10 percent in most months. For the most part they are sold by mail order, in lots of from 50 to 200 at a time, to curio dealers on the East and West Coasts. Because of the accidental circumstances that Shonto's bulk gasoline supplier is also engaged in an extensive retail curio trade, rugs are sometimes substituted for cash in paying the gasoline bill. A few rugs are sold directly to

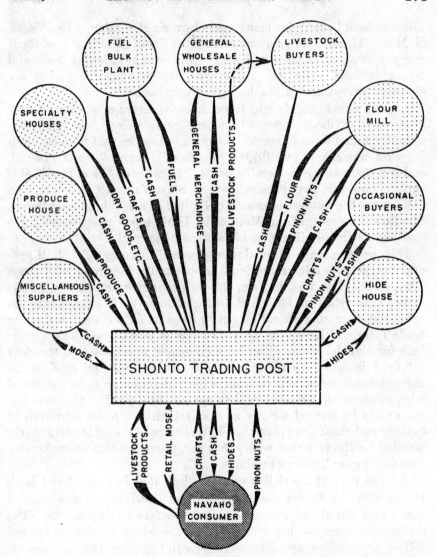

CHART D.—Circulation of cash, commodities, and merchandise at wholesale and retail levels at Shonto Trading Post.

tourists who visit the trading post during the summer months. Most minor crafts must also be sold in this way, since little market for Navaho pottery, pitch bottles, and the like exists outside the reservation.

Hides find a steady market—sufficiently so that most traders pay cash for them as an act of good will, since their total annual value is negligible. The entire output of hides from the Navaho Reservation has been bought for many years by a single dealer in Las Vegas, N. Mex. The dealer's representative visits Shonto Trading Post about every 3 months; he sorts and weighs the accumulation of sheep and goat skins and writes out a check for the amount due. They are shipped by truck and rail to the buyer's warehouse.[14]

A good piñon crop is said to occur on an average of every 6 or 7 years in the Shonto area. In recent years piñon nuts have consistently found a ready market, so much so that in 1954 Shonto Trading Post was able to buy 107,000 pounds of them at 45 cents a pound, and sell them at a considerable profit. Because of the unpredictable supply, however, they do not figure in Shonto's credit structure. In "off" years the harvest is generally limited to a few hundred pounds. Shonto's flour supplier in Monticello, Utah, sometimes accepts these small quantities of piñon nuts in payment of account.

The two-way trade in goods and commodities once offered all general storekeepers a lucrative double opportunity for profit (cf. Carson 1954, p. 23). It was, in fact, the lure of quick commodity profits rather than retail profits which brought many early traders into the field, and a number were thought to have made fortunes in the rug trade (Underhill, 1956, p. 183). In recent years, nevertheless, markets for Navaho commodities have become so uncertain that the risks involved in handling them usually outweigh potential profits. In these circumstances modern traders tend increasingly to be concerned with minimizing risk rather than maximizing profit. Commodities are apt to be treated strictly as cash substitutes, to be converted as quickly and cheaply as possible. This change of policy is particularly attested by the fact that with a few exceptions traders no longer pay cash for rugs or livestock products.

A large part of the risk is usually eliminated from wool and lamb transactions by future contracting. A contract to sell a stipulated quota at a stipulated price is concluded before buying begins. The trader can then set his buying price according to the contracted selling price, allowing sufficient differential to cover the very considerable costs of handling and transportation. To the extent that this practice eliminates the trader's risk it also eliminates any opportunity for extra profit, since it will normally be necessary to pay the highest feasible price in order to be sure of filling the contracted quota. The most extreme competition to be found among Navaho traders is often for lambs and wool when future contracts have been made, with the

---

[14] The hide buyer has stated that in the course of a year more hides are bought from Shonto Trading Post than from any other two stores on the Navaho Reservation—a significant indication of the high volume of home consumption of mutton which is maintained in this area. (See "Cooking and Housekeeping," pp. 81–82.)

result that operating margins are sometimes shaved to the bone. In general they average about 5 percent.

A few Navaho traders still attempt to speculate, particularly in wool, when the market shows signs of advancing. "Making a killing" in wool is still perhaps the trader's dream, but it has seldom been possible in the face of a generally declining market, and the attempt more often than not has been disastrous. A sudden decline in the wool market in 1952 bankrupted several trading posts, and cost Shonto's owner over $20,000.

Very slow turnover in rugs and other crafts results in consistently high markups in these items, and it is traditional to get as much as the traffic will bear out of them. Saddle blankets normally bring between 10 and 20 percent; larger rugs may be marked up as much as 50 percent.

Because of the inevitable markups necessary to cover costs of handling commodities, most Navahos undoubtedly believe that traders make a profit on them as producers as well as consumers (cf. Rapoport, 1954, p. 7). There can be no doubt, moreover, that such was and often still is the ideal of traders themselves. Nevertheless the average trader's commodity transactions today are unlikely to do more than pay their own way, and may even bring a loss as compared to cash transactions. Hence the often stated axiom of the modern Navaho trade that expected profit must be based entirely on retail markup.

SUPPLY

So long as it continued to produce chiefly commodities rather than cash, the Navaho wholesale market remained almost exclusively under the control of the handful of general mercantilers who were equipped to underwrite the commodity trade with long-term credit. These houses, in Flagstaff, Winslow, Gallup, and Farmington, had divided up the entire reservation territory in a sort of cartel system, so that each served an exclusive territory, and competition was virtually absent.

Increasing wage work and the circulation of large amounts of cash on the reservation in recent years have had the effect of opening up the Navaho wholesale market, freeing traders from total dependence on the general mercantilers and attracting new and specialized wholesale enterprises to the territory. Today more than 20 wholsale houses make regular sales calls at trading posts throughout the reservation, and as many more sell the territory by mail. Included are specialty dry goods and novelty houses, pharmaceutical manufacturers, curio dealers, produce and feed dealers, coffee brokers, and even a mail-order grocery house, in addition to the general merchandise wholesalers.

GENERAL MERCANTILE HOUSES

Persistence of an essentially seasonal Navaho economy (see "The Economic Cycle," pp. 141–145) makes inevitable a continued heavy dependence on the general mercantilers who have traditionally dominated the Navaho trade. Throughout the Navaho Reservation they probably retain two-thirds of the total annual wholesale trade at the present time. At Shonto their long credit terms are necessary to underwrite not only the livestock trade, but much of the trade based on railroad earnings as well.

The general mercantilers remain the only wholesale enterprises which make regular deliveries throughout the Navaho Reservation, employing their own vehicles. A salesman from each house calls on every trading post in his territory once every 2 weeks. Delivery is normally made in the following week. In a region where regular freight service of any kind is nonexistent and where mail is undependable, this service alone guarantees a large share of the Navaho market. Mail comes to the northwestern Navaho area only twice a week, and must be picked up from a point 30 miles from Shonto store.

Shonto Trading Post consistently does some 75 percent of its total wholesale business with a single general mercantile house in Farmington, N. Mex., some 200 miles to the east. Regular biweekly sales calls and deliveries are made, as noted above. The store buys all of its hardware, nearly all of its groceries, and the bulk of its other stock from this single source, where a year-round running account is carried. Occasional fill-in orders are given to the mercantile house in Flagstaff, which also sells the Shonto territory. Like most traders, however, Shonto's owner prefers to ally himself to a single wholesale house as a means of assuring continued credit and financial backing. This attitude is naturally encouraged by the wholesale house itself.

OTHER WHOLESALERS

The volume of Shonto's trade with wholesalers other than the general mercantile house is limited by the store's cash receipts, since such trade is commonly on straight cash or, at most, 30-day terms. A few items, nevertheless, have always been supplied by specialized wholesalers. Flour is purchased exclusively from a small mill in Monticello, Utah, which is devoted exclusively to the Indian trade. This enterprise, like the mercantilers, makes deliveries direct to trading posts, and also offers long terms of account. Piñon nuts have sometimes been accepted in lieu of cash in payment of account.

Gasoline and other fuels and lubricants are supplied by a bulk plant at Cameron, Ariz., some 75 miles southwest of Shonto. Rugs are sometimes used in payment of account here, since the Cameron operation includes a lively summer tourist trade. Produce is ordered chiefly from a Flagstaff concern. During the summer months private truckers often deliver melons and feed directly to the reservation.

Several single-line wholesalers make periodic sales calls at Shonto and other trading posts. Among them are dry goods houses in Phoenix and Albuquerque, remedy manufacturers in Oklahoma and Michigan, and several dealers in silver jewelry and curios. The latter exchange Zuni-made jewelry, for sale to Navahos, for rugs and cash. In addition mail-order business is conducted with a dry goods house and a saddle and harness manufacturer in Denver, and with a wholesale coffee house in St. Louis.

RETAIL POLICY

It has been stated earlier ("Material Culture," pp. 77–81) that modern Navaho material culture is basically American of 50 to 100 years ago. The same statement necessarily characterizes the inventory of the Navaho trading post, which in this respect remains a picture of the old country general store. Every kind of merchandise which the community might possibly demand is stocked, as is required by the store's monopoly position. The number and diversity of products sold rivals that found in a modern supermarket. Table 28 presents a classified inventory of products normally stocked at Shonto Trading Post.

TABLE 28.—*Classified inventory of Shonto Trading Post*

GROCERIES

Staples:		
Bleached wheat flour	Shortening	Dry yeast
Baking powder	Canned milk	Potatoes
Sugar	Coffee	Onions
Salt	Tea	
Canned foods:		
Meats:		
Corned mutton	Spaghetti and meat balls	Vienna sausage
Chopped beef	Chili con carne	Sardines
Beef stew	Tamales	
Vegetables:		
Corn	Beans	Green beans
Fruits:		
Peaches	Plums	Fruit cocktail
Pears	Tomatoes	
Juices:		
Pineapple juice	Tomato juice	Orange juice
Soups		
Packaged preparations:		
Whole wheat flour	Dry cereals	Spaghetti
Cornmeal	Powdered milk	Rice
Oatmeal	Kool-Aid	Raisins
Baked goods:		
Soda crackers	Graham crackers	Cookies
Sweets:		
Jams	Mixed candy	Soda pop
Peanut butter	Candy bars	Cocoa
Sirup	Crackerjack	
Condiments etc.:		
Pepper	Pickles	Catsup
Green chili	Salad dressing	Tomato sauce
Fresh foods and perishables:		
Mutton (occasional)	Cabbage (seasonal)	Carrots
Salt pork	Watermelon (seasonal)	Eggs
Bologna	Apples (seasonal)	Cheese
Oleomargarine	Oranges	Ice Cream

TABLE 28.—*Classified inventory of Shonto Trading Post*—Continued

GROCERIES—Continued

Household needs:
　Cleansing agents:

Powdered soaps	Scouring powder	Scrubbers
Bar soaps	Bleaches	Brooms

　Miscellaneous:

Matches	Toilet tissue	Kleenex

DRUGS AND SUNDRIES

Remedies and treatments:

Analgesics	Digestive remedies	Cough drops
Aspirin	Eye drops	Cough syrup
Liniments	Ear drops	Adhesive tape
Ointments	Toothache remedies	Gauze
Salves	Laxatives	Band-Aids
Disinfectants		Kotex

Cosmetics, etc.:

Cold cream	Hair oil	Baby oil
Rouge	Toothpaste	Baby lotion
Lipstick		Baby powder

Grooming aids:

Combs	Bobby pins	Tooth brushes
Hair brushes	Pocket mirrors	Shoe polish
Hair clippers		

Stationery:

Writing tablets	Ball-point pens	Postage stamps
Envelopes	Pencils	

Tobacco:

Cigarettes	Rolling tobacco	Chewing plug
Pipe tobacco	Cigarette papers	Snuff

DRY GOODS

Yard Goods:

Satin	Taffeta	Flannel
Crepeback satin	Sateen	Muslin
Velvet	Cambric	Oilcloth
Plush	Cotton print	

Readymade garments:
　Infants':

Diapers	Baby pants	Baby shirts

　Children's:

Underwear	Cotton shirts	Belts
T-shirts	Denim overalls	Caps
Socks	Denim jackets	Hats
Cotton dresses	Lined jackets	

　Ladies':

Pants	Cotton dresses	Cotton hose
Bras	Cotton blouses	Bobby sox
Slips	Cotton skirts	Mittens
Scarves	Denim overalls	

　Men's:

Long underwear	Levi's	Leather belts
Shorts	Work shirts	Leather gloves
Undershirts	"Western" shirts	Straw hats
Socks	Denim jackets	"Western" hats
Boot socks	Leatherette jackets	

　Miscellaneous:

Pendleton blankets	Quilts	Towels
Cotton blankets	Dishcloths	Wash cloths

Footwear

Children's low shoes	Ladies' oxfords	Men's oxfords
Children's high shoes	"Squaw" shoes	Men's work shoes
		Engineer boots

Sewing and weaving needs:

Thread	Needles	Sheep shears
Rickrack	Straight pins	Tow cards
Bias tape	Safety pins	Wool dyes
Buttons	Scissors	Fabric dyes
Yarn		

Notions:

Side combs	Costume jewelry	Film
Barrettes	Shoe laces	

TABLE 28.—*Classified inventory of Shonto Trading Post*—Continued

HARDWARE

Housewares:
Enamel:
Plates	Cups	Dippers
Bowls	Coffee pots	Dishpans
Pudding pans	Tea kettles	Pails

Sheet iron and zinc:
| Fry pans | Buckets | Wash tubs |
| Bread pans | | |

Cast iron:
| Skillets | Dutch ovens | Grinders |
| Griddles | | |

Utensils:
Butcher knives	Cake turners	Table knives
Roasting forks	Spatulas	Table forks
Stirring spoons	Shredders	Table spoons
Ladles	Peelers	

Miscellaneous:
Gasoline lanterns	Flashlight batteries	Grills
Kerosene lanterns	Kerosene cans	Nursing bottles
Lantern parts	Washboards	Nipples
Flashlights	Scrub brushes	Soft rope

Hand tools and implements:
Shovels	Pliers	Hacksaws
Axes and handles	Screwdrivers	Saws
Picks and handles	End wrenches	Pocket knives
Hoes and handles	Hammers	Rifles
Mattocks	Files	Ammunition

Building supplies, etc.:
Lumber (occasional)	Nails	Hinges and hasps
Roofing paper	Screws	Bolts
Cement	Staples	Padlocks
Paint	Carriage bolts	Barbed wire

Auto supplies:
Tires	Batteries	Antifreeze
Tubes	Fan belts	Stop-leak
Tire patches	Spark plugs	Brake fluid
Tire pumps	Grease guns	Solder

FURNITURE, APPLIANCES, ETC.

Cast iron stoves	Mattresses	Tents
Cabinet stoves	Card tables	Water drums
Sewing machines	Folding chairs	Water kegs
Hand washers	Wooden chairs	Water bags
Rollaway beds	Radios and batteries	

HARNESSWARE AND LIVESTOCK EQUIPMENT

Riding gear:
Saddles	Latigo ties	Latigos
Saddle pads	Bridles	Neatsfoot oil
Stirrups	Reins	Saddle soap
Cinches	Bits	Horseshoes
Buckles		Horseshoe nails

Team equipment:
Collars	Chain harness	Singletrees
Collar pads	Trace chains	Doubletrees
Hames	Team bridles	Yokes
Hame buckles	Team reins	Harness straps
		Plows & handles

Running gear:
Team wagons	Wheels	Axle nuts
Wagon trees	Axles	Carriage bolts
Wagon tongues	Boxings	Seats

Livestock equipment, etc.:
Sheep paint	Tow cards	Lamb nipples
Shears	Wool sacks	Ecthyma vaccine
Bells and collars	Fleece ties	Steel traps

FUELS AND LUBRICANTS

Leaded gasoline	Motor oil	Chassis grease
White gasoline	Gear oil	Axle grease
Kerosene	Machine oil	

TABLE 28.—*Classified inventory of Shonto Trading Post*—Continued

FEED

| Baled hay | Oats | Stock salt |

NATIVE CRAFTS

| Rugs
Saddle blankets
Cotton sashes | Baskets
Pitched bottles | Pottery
Silver jewelry |

INVENTORY CONTROL

Lack of operating capital, limited warehouse space, and extreme diversity of products handled, all conspire to dictate a policy of extremely limited inventory for the modern trading post. Such a practice is of course an outgrowth of regular biweekly supply, and is in marked contrast to the practice necessarily followed in the days of infrequent and uncertain transportation (cf. Carson, 1954, pp. 150–151; Atherton, 1939, p. 40). Shonto Trading Post is so committed to hand-to-mouth buying that the store seldom carries more than 2 or 3 weeks' supply of most items—often just enough to last until the next order can be delivered. Even where volume discounts or special buys are available it is unusual if more than a few month's supply of any item is laid in. Shonto's owner has stated that it should ideally be possible to hold retail inventory to $5,000, although in practice it is commonly nearer to $10,000.

Extremely limited inventories, particularly in groceries, necessitate careful attention to ordering. Even so, modern Navaho trading posts are famous among their clientele for being out of several items at one time. This condition is a source of considerable customer ill will, and, according to some Navahos, is a prime reason for shopping in town rather than patronizing the trading post.

It is generally believed by traders, at least on the western portions of the Navaho Reservation, that Indians are not quality conscious. This belief is strongly reflected in trading-post inventories, where it is standard policy to carry only the cheapest brands in any line. Suppliers of the Navaho trade do a lively business in seconds and economy lines, particularly in groceries and dry goods. Trading posts are almost never found to carry more than one brand of any item on display at the same time. The one-brand policy is due in part to considerations of inventory control, and partly also to the common feeling that competing brands confuse the Navaho customer and slow down trading.

SALES PROMOTION

A trader of long experience on the Navaho Reservation has stated to the writer: "What it takes to run one of these places is a credit

manager, not a salesman." The statement accurately reflects the view
of most traders to the effect that, thanks to a protected consumer
market, sales take care of themselves. Whatever income is received
in the community will inevitably come to the trading post, so that
the trader's principal concern is not to promote the outflow of goods
to the highest level which can be sustained, but rather to hold it down
to that level through credit restriction.

Trading posts have never found it necessary to advertise, partly
because of their protected position and partly because their clientele
has been largely illiterate in any case. The recent widespread introduction of battery-powered radios is beginning to alter the picture, as
off-reservation merchants increasingly bid for the Navaho trade with
commercials and whole programs in the Navaho language. Traders
so far have done little or nothing to retaliate, but continue to count
on receiving their share of the Navaho trade without any special
inducement.

The one consistent principle of trading-post sales promotion is
"they won't buy what they can't see." Like its cousin the rural general store, the average trading post presents an indescribably cluttered appearance (cf. Carson, 1954, p. 14; Nystrom, 1930, p. 81), with
every available inch of wall and ceiling space, and often a good deal
of floor space as well, devoted to merchandise displays. This is in
general the nearest approach to sight display that is made, or that
is considered necessary. The store may not present an appearance
conducive to brisk transactions, but at least every type of merchandise carried is in sight. Shonto Trading Post often has as much as
75 percent of its total stock actually on display within the store.

Modern trading posts generally follow a uniform one-price policy,
in marked contrast to general stores of a century ago (Carson, 1954,
p. 93). The use of leaders and discounts is rare. Shonto Trading
Post, however, employs both devices to a limited extent for the
purpose of attracting Navaho trade from outside the community.
Flour and shoes are the store's perennial leaders, and are sold at
prices substantially below those offered by neighboring trading
posts. Flour prices are believed to be especially important because
flour is still the largest selling single item, in terms of total volume,
in the northwestern Navaho country. On this one item Shonto continues to follow a multiple-price policy, offering one price on credit,
a reduced price for cash, and, where feasible, a specially reduced
price to persons from outside the community. Volume discounts
of 5 percent or so are occasionally offered on such staples as coffee
and sugar to speed sales during lamb and wool seasons.

MARKUP

It is a basic principle of modern Navaho trade that profit must be based entirely on retail markup, since the commodity trade has become more hazardous than profitable (see "Commodity Exchange," above). Markups, moreover, are consistently high; often double those of off-reservation merchants (cf. Kluckhohn and Leighton, 1946, p. 39). Partly they reflect high freight rates, low turnover, and generally inefficient business methods (see Nystrom, 1930, p. 82; Dolva and Beckley, 1950, p. 118). Most of all, however, they are a consequence of long-term credit operation, and result from the high interest rate (normally 8 percent) which the trading post must pay on its long-term mercantile accounts. The Navaho consumer thus pays interest indirectly on his own credit accounts.

In the early years of Navaho trading, markups were limited to 25 percent by government decree (Underhill, 1956, p. 182). In the present day a 25 percent markup is considered inadequate even for groceries (cf. Carson, 1954, pp. 93–94). Shonto's grocery markup consistently averages 35 percent, while other average markups are 75 percent in dry goods, 100 percent in hardware, and 100 to 200 percent and even higher in remedies. (Such large profit margins are traditional in the pharmaceutical line, and are sustained by manufacturers' fair trade prices in many cases.)

A distinctive feature of trading-post price policy is that all prices are set at multiples of 5 cents, so that the trade can if necessary be conducted without the use of pennies. Such a practice undoubtedly originated in the days of scrip money (see "Early Trading Posts," pp. 150–154) when 1-cent scrip was dispensed with as a nuisance. It survives in modern times partly because older Navahos still consider pennies a nuisance, and partly because the old system greatly simplifies mental arithmetic for both customer and clerk.

BOOKKEEPING

Until as recently as a generation ago most traders kept no records at all other than those of accounts receivable (see "Finance," pp. 171–172). The trader was content to feed and support himself and family with merchandise from the store, and to find out from his mercantile creditors once a year how much he had made or lost for the year. Such other records as were kept were likely to be in the form of mnemonic devices which reflected the trader's individuality and ingenuity rather than any system. The walls and counters of many trading posts today still exhibit quantities of undecipherable inscriptions and hieroglyphics, commemorating long-forgotten transactions.

Recent developments, including the proliferation of suppliers, the advent of short-term credit and net cash terms, and the necessity of paying regular taxes and lease fees, have conspired to demand somewhat more systematic accounting. Traders have tended to accept this change grudingly at best, and the accounting methods which they have been driven to adopt are still those of the 19th century (see Carson, 1954). Keeping the books, such as they are, is likely to be regarded as a headache which in theory should be unnecessary. It is probably still true that most traders most of the time have only a very vague idea as to whether they are making or losing money, and how much.

The basic "books" of the modern trading post are the same as those of the general merchant of the last century (Carson, 1954) : a cash book to keep track of the amount of money actually on the premises, a ledger in which debit and credit accounts are laboriously posted from month to month, and a day sheet on which each day's transactions are faithfully recorded. In the latter case it is no longer necessary to enter cash sales, since the cash register tape nowadays records and sums these automatically.

Keeping these few books is still part of the nightly routine for every trader. The modern store's accounting does not end here, however. Day sheets and other books, together with receipts, invoices, canceled checks, and all records are turned over to an accounting firm nowadays, and it is the latter rather than the trader which actually keeps track of the business. The demands of modern business accounting are for the most part beyond the experience of traders even today, and it is probable that few of them could operate without the assistance of accounting firms.

THE BUSINESS CYCLE

It is inevitable that seasonality and cyclic repetition characterize the economy of the trading post no less than that of the Navaho community which it serves (see "The Economic Cycle," pp. 141–145). Since both live largely from hand to mouth, the condition of the one necessarily reflects that of the other, and the trader's wholesale accounts payable mirror his retail accounts receivable. The sketch of the annual economy of Shonto community given in an earlier chapter (pp. 94–148) may therefore serve equally well to describe the annual economy of Shonto Trading Post. When Navahos are making money the store is making money; similarly when Navahos are living on credit the store is living on credit.

Figures compiled in 1954 indicate that Shonto Trading Post actually shows an operating profit only during the 6 months from May to October. During this period nearly 75 percent of the store's total annual gross is received. From November to April, costs and accounts receivable consistently exceed receipts from all sources.

Above and beyond the repetitive annual cycle, trading posts are highly sensitive to the larger cycles of inflation and depression which affect retail trade everywhere. The number of variables affecting the trader's profit is especially high, since fluctuating costs, commodity prices, and labor demand all play a significant part in determining both volume and profit. Since 1950 the annual gross of Shonto Trading Post has fluctuated between limits of approximately $100,000 and $150,000, while the net has varied from a profit of $20,000 to a loss of nearly $10,000. The Navaho trade in general continues to justify its long-standing reputation as a "boom-and-bust" proposition.

RETAIL TRADE

The character of any retail business is determined to a large extent by its clientele. It is in this regard that Navaho trading posts are most clearly set off from other mercantile enterprises in modern America. Relations between the trader and his customer are those between persons of distinct culture and members of entirely separate societies. The trading post remains, therefore, a cross-cultural and also what might be called a cross-societal institution.

In the early days of trading, when the Navaho economy was still largely self-sufficient, the cross-cultural nature of trading probably worked as much to the advantage of the Navaho as to that of the trader. The latter at that time had no effective means of controlling his consumer market either individually or collectively, and sometimes took a beating in consequence (see, e.g., Coolidge and Coolidge, 1930, p. 67; Dyk, 1938, passim; Underhill, 1956, p. 183). Increasing economic dependence on American society, however, was and is tantamount to increasing economic dependence on the trader specifically. As a result, today's traders exercise a control over their clientele which is measured by the latter's reliance not merely on them, but on the whole social and economic structure which they represent. It is doubtful if an equal commercial advantage was ever enjoyed by any other merchant in American history. This advantage is strongly reflected in the retail methods and customer relations of the modern trading post.

CLIENTELE

The term Trading Post as employed throughout the present work refers to retail general stores serving a largely or exclusively Navaho clientele, and operating accordingly. A distinction must be maintained (and is insisted on by traders themselves) between these enterprises and off-reservation retail curio stores dealing in Indian and pseudo-Indian crafts. The latter commonly designate themselves "trading posts" because of the fancied picturesque connotations of the term; but they are, of course, straight cash operations serving a strictly White clientele.

By contrast, Navaho trading posts traditionally do not rely on White trade for any part of their income. For the most part they do not even sell post cards and souvenirs. This is particularly true in remote areas such as Shonto, where White trade has little or no potential. Shonto Trading Post makes no effort to attract the trade of the local school teachers and National Monument personnel, nor does it attempt to attract tourists from the latter area. A small volume of trade is actually received from both sources, but it is regarded as entirely incidental.

During the month of April 1956, an accurate record was kept of daily adult clientele at Shonto Trading Post. Since Navahos are apt to do their shopping piecemeal throughout the better part of a day (see "Shopping Habits," pp. 204–210), figures were compiled by counting each individual customer once a day. The information thus assembled, summarizing Shonto's clientele in terms of race and community of residence, is set forth in table 29. (See also table 36.)

As indicated in table 29, not quite three-quarters of Shonto's trade throughout the month of April 1956, came from the local Navaho community. Navahos from neighboring communities accounted for another 15 percent, while the total of all Whites and non-Navahos accounted for less than 10 percent of Shonto's customers.

Except in the case of Whites, the figures in table 29 reflect fairly accurately the sources of trading post income. In actual dollar volume Shonto community is estimated to contribute between 70 and 75 percent of the trade at Shonto Trading Post, with Navahos from other communities accounting for nearly all of the remainder. The

TABLE 29.—*Summary of Shonto Trading Post clientele,*[1] *April 1956*

Clientele	Number	Percentage of all clientele
Navahos (by community of residence):		
Shonto	822	73.9
Cow Springs	41	3.6
Inscription House	29	2.6
Tsegi	27	2.4
Navajo Mountain	20	1.8
Kayenta	16	1.4
Black Mesa	13	1.2
Kaibito	5	.5
Oljeto	3	.3
All others	33	2.9
Total Navahos	1,009	90.6
Other Indians	12	1.1
Whites:		
Missionaries	17	1.5
School teachers	15	1.4
National Monument personnel	14	1.3
All others (tourists, etc.)	45	4.1
Total Whites	91	8.3
Total Clientele	1,112	100.0

[1] Each individual client counted once per day.

latter figure measures the trader's success in luring livestock trade away from his competitors in recent years (see "Sales Promotion," pp. 180–182).

Shonto community is thus the basic market on which Shonto Trading Post depends for its livelihood, augmented where possible by "quality trade" from other Navaho areas. In spite of the growing competition from town merchants the store still expects to receive annually at least 90 percent of the trade of the local Navahos—all of it that does not go to Flagstaff.

Less than 1 percent of Shonto's retail gross actually results from White trade. The rather high percentage of White clientele recorded in table 29, and fairly typical of spring and summer months, results largely from noncommercial interests. Local White residents (see "White Society at Shonto," pp. 165–167) visit the store two or three times a week to deliver or receive mail, while tourists come in primarily to see what the inside of a trading post looks like.

TYPES OF TRADE

The Navaho trade at Shonto and most other trading posts falls into four distinct categories: cash sales, "book" (unsecured) credit, pawn (secured credit), and direct commodity exchange (see Sanders et al., 1953, p. 233). Each is governed by its own set of special trading procedures, many of which are peculiar to the Navaho trade. Approximate distribution of Shonto's total gross volume in terms of these categories is shown in table 30. (For accurate percentage figures for one month see table 31.)

Table 31 presents a detailed record of total trade volume throughout the month of March 1954, broken down according to the same categories listed in table 30. It is notable here that the relative percentages of trade in the different categories hold fairly constant from week to week despite a considerable fluctuation in the total volume of trade. The slightly high percentage of "book" credit transactions shown in table 31 is normal for winter months, when cash income is at a minimum (see "The Economic Cycle," pp. 141–145).

TABLE 30.—*Distribution of total Shonto Trading Post sales by categories of trade*

Type of trade	Percentage of annual sales
"Book" credit	40
Cash sales	30
Pawn	20
Direct exchange	10
Total	100

TABLE 31.—*Daily volume of cash, credit, and direct trade transactions, Shonto Trading Post, March 1954*

Date and day	Cash sales	Book credit sales	Pawn credit sales	Direct trade	Total
March:					
1. Mon	$111.35	$52.85	$93.35	$63.00	$320.55
2. Tue	34.83	50.90	113.45	13.50	212.68
3. Wed	62.42	119.75	11.15	14.50	207.82
4. Thur.[1]	197.98	251.59	39.61	14.60	503.78
5. Fri	25.11	155.45	10.00	31.00	221.56
6. Sat	58.81	88.75	7.70	21.50	176.76
8. Mon	17.80	5.50	69.10	6.20	98.60
9. Tue	62.98	36.55	85.95	5.25	190.73
10. Wed	24.95	42.44	20.00	_____	87.39
11. Thur.[1]	167.10	117.36	66.55	63.50	414.51
12. Fri	73.36	55.69	9.75	46.00	184.80
13. Sat	90.75	138.58	49.10	27.75	306.18
15. Mon	71.50	156.97	88.40	23.50	340.37
16. Tue	87.40	336.58	38.45	9.70	472.13
17. Wed	37.16	108.65	_____	7.25	153.06
18. Thur.[1]	162.63	242.05	110.70	59.15	574.53
19. Fri	99.23	93.27	51.22	57.75	301.47
20. Sat	44.64	112.75	21.50	25.25	204.14
22. Mon	22.14	48.05	8.00	_____	78.19
23. Tue	35.55	134.43	36.60	22.45	229.03
24. Wed	26.93	85.70	_____	36.00	148.63
25. Thur.[1]	141.08	381.81	154.90	51.70	729.49
26. Fri	21.65	106.80	15.10	33.25	176.80
27. Sat	61.45	158.30	88.15	21.60	329.50
29. Mon	125.65	97.45	38.30	37.00	298.40
30. Tue	45.00	52.90	29.30	10.15	137.35
31. Wed	35.65	176.65	45.27	58.00	315.57
Total	1,945.10	3,407.77	1,301.60	759.55	7,414.02
Percentage of all trade	26.2	46.0	17.6	10.2	100.0

[1] Railroad signup days.

CASH SALES

In spite of a marked increase since World War II, cash sales at Shonto Trading Post still account for less than one-third of the store's total volume. Such cash transactions as do take place are primarily with persons from outside Shonto community (see "Clientele," pp. 184–186) and, secondarily, intermittent and incidental purchases by local Navahos.

Low volume of cash sales within the community is in a sense deliberate. It is an inevitable byproduct of the store's policy of credit saturation as a technique of market protection (see "Market Control," pp. 169–170). The total amount of cash actually circulating in the community is kept to a minimum by allowing advance credit against all predictable earnings (cf. Kluckhohn and Leighton, 1946, p. 39). Ideally, it is thought that a really alert and experienced trader should be able to estimate community earnings with such accuracy as to be able to tie up 75 percent of them in advance credit. Uncertainties in commodity prices as well as in the labor market seldom permit such close calculation, but it is true that credit saturation holds down Shonto's cash on hand to a fraction of its potential.

Such income as gets through to Shonto Navahos in cash is likely to be saved for use in purely native commerce (see "Native Commercial and Professional Enterprise," pp. 125–127) and for shopping trips to Flagstaff, in neither of which is credit allowed. In their dealings with Shonto Trading Post, on the other hand, local people are usually quite content to stretch their credit as far as it will go (see below). When they spend cash it is likely to be chiefly for fill-in and impulse purchases, and for gasoline, which is sold only for cash.

BOOK CREDIT

"Book credit" is the term commonly applied to all unsecured accounts, records of which are kept in conventional retail salesbooks. The designation serves to differentiate these from pawn (i.e., secured) accounts which are recorded only on tags attached to the collateral.

Book credit, like cash sales, is a fairly recent phenomenon in the Navaho trade, which probably accounts for the reasonably systematic way in which accounts are recorded. Early stores necessarily required collateral against any and all credit (see Franciscan Fathers, 1910, p. 493). The development of unsecured credit in later years has been a measure of increased stability in Navaho society and economy, together with increased dependence on the trader. In the long run these conditions have proved to afford better credit insurance than any collateral.

Shonto Trading Post allows book credit against nearly all predictable income received in Shonto community, and up to the expected limits of the income itself. Chiefly included are livestock production (lambs and wool), wage earnings, and unemployment and relief checks. The number and value of all outstanding book accounts at Shonto Trading Post in February 1954 and in December 1955 are shown in table 32.

Shonto Trading Post classifies all book accounts according to the four categories shown in table 32, keeping them in separate file

TABLE 32.—*Outstanding book accounts at Shonto Trading Post, February 7, 1954, and December 15, 1955*

Type of account [1] (credit basis)	February 7, 1954			December 15, 1955		
	Number accts.	Total value	Avg. value	Number accts.	Total value	Avg. value
Livestock	58	$4,799	$83	47	$3,475	$74
Railroad	31	1,217	39	22	872	40
Relief	26	1,028	40	20	957	48
Local payroll	10	843	84	9	962	107
Total	125	7,887	....	98	6,266	....
Average	...............$63			...............$64		

[1] See below.

compartments. Such classification represents the trader's conception of the family's basic resource. Nevertheless a very large number of families are entitled to credit on more than one basis during some part of the year, and this has to be taken into account.

Livestock credit, against wool sales in the spring and lamb sales in the fall, is granted to every large livestock-owning household in Shonto community, and to some 25 other households from as far away as Kaibito and Navajo Mountain (cf. Luomala, 1938, p. 5). It is the only credit allowed to Navahos from outside the community (see below). Credit limits are based on records of previous sales multiplied by the anticipated lamb or wool price, as the case may be. Wool credit is ordinarily "open" from December to May, and lamb credit from May to September, so that for practical purposes livestock owners can live on credit throughout the year except during the months of October and November (see chart B, p. 143).

In addition to livestock, regular cash income is a basis for credit under certain conditions. As a general rule (followed by all trading posts), it must be received in the form of checks mailed to or in care of the store. It is widely believed by traders that Navahos, although reasonably conscientious in paying their livestock bills, are untrustworthy with cash. "If you don't get your hands on the check first you'll never see it" is the expression used by traders to sum up their credit policy.

The theory underlying check policy is not that the check can be taken away from its intended recipient, but simply that it is necessary for the trader to know when and how much income is received by his creditors, and to let them know that he knows. Few Navahos will refuse to pay on account when they are known to have the wherewithall to do so, for an immediate stoppage of credit will almost inevitably follow such refusal. On the other hand no one can be expected to pay on account if he has no money to do so; hence, traders believe, Navahos are inclined to conceal the fact that they have received money so as to save it for other purposes. The inestimable advantage of a check or money order, from the trader's point of view, is that it will almost certainly have to be negotiated at the trading post, and so come under his cognizance. Checks have the additional advantage that they are usually mailed in readily recognizable envelopes.

In nearly all parts of the reservation Navahos receive their mail in care of the local trading post, since there is no rural free delivery. Many trading posts are also fourth-class post offices. In the Shonto area, however, mail is delivered only to Red Lake (P. O. Tonalea), from whence it must be picked up by Shonto, Cow Springs, Inscription House, Navajo Mountain, and Kaibito for distribution to their local clientele. At the trading post, mail is kept behind the counter and is only delivered to the addressee on demand.   Checks when recognizable are segregated from the regular mail and kept in the pawn vault, alongside the accounts receivable.

Since having such primary access to checks is considered essential as a basis for credit against them, post office and/or mail distribution facilities are said to be worth $10,000 a year or more to any trading post.   Isolated trading posts such as Shonto enjoy such privileges automatically.   In larger settlements such as Kayenta and Tuba City, where more than one store is located, it is invariably the trading post which has the post office that gets all the relief accounts.

Even more important than mail delivery is the Railroad Retirement Claims Agency (see "Railroad Work," pp. 129–133).   Unemployment checks are always addressed to Navaho claimants in care of the store at which they sign up for benefits; hence delivered directly into the hands of the trader.   Throughout the western part of the Navaho Reservation the claims agency is said to be a necessity for any store.   Purely as a basis for credit against unemployment checks, it was worth about $15,000 to Shonto Trading Post in 1955 (see table 21, p. 137).   Shonto's owner in 1956 refused an offer to purchase a store at Piñon, giving as his reason the fact that the store did not include the railroad claims agency.

Book credit against local checks breaks down into three basic classes: credit against unemployment checks, against relief checks, and against paychecks.   The procedures in each case are essentially the same. Anyone receiving regular income by check may draw against it up to the full amount of the check (which is always recorded prominently on the cover of the account book).   All such accounts are payable on receipt of the check; that is, monthly in the case of welfare checks, every 15 days in the case of paychecks, and every 2 weeks in the case of railroad unemployment checks.   Since the amount of all such income is closely predictable, the careful trader can see to it that almost the exact amount of the check is owed on account by the time it arrives.   If this is not accomplished it is an easy matter to "delay the arrival" of the check, by taking it out of the mail and hiding it for a week or two, until the account is more nearly "filled up," as traders say.   This practice has been common among traders in all parts of the reservation.   Because of the infrequency (twice a week in the Shonto area) and uncertainty of mail deliveries it arouses surprisingly little suspicion.   By one device and another Shonto Trading Post usually manages to let no more than 10 percent of unemployment compensation, and scarcely 1 percent of welfare benefits, reach their destined recipients in cash (see table 16, p. 109).

In addition to livestock and check accounts, a few Shonto families have always been allowed unsecured credit against railroad wages. These are the least secured of all Shonto's accounts, since the money is actually earned and paid off the reservation, and must be brought or mailed back. Trading posts in general have demanded pawn as security against any such accounts, and Shonto for the most part follows the same policy. A few individuals, however, have long-standing records of reliability, and the families of these are permitted to draw against their earnings during their absence. Credit is likely to be shut off promptly if a money order is not received during the first 6 or 8 weeks after the individual's employment, and the account must be settled in full immediately upon his return.

Since book credit accounts form the largest single share of Shonto's trade, the trader must indeed be first and foremost a credit manager (see "Sales Promotion," pp. 180–182). Shonto's Navahos live on credit to such an extent that the trader is in effect budget director and financial manager for the whole community (cf. Kluckhohn and Leighton, 1946, p. 39; Sanders et al., 1953, p. 234). Few Navahos keep any sort of accounts of their own. They rely implicitly on the trader to budget them in accordance with their earning capacity, so that their credit resources are never exhausted for any significant length of time (see Kluckhohn and Leighton, 1946, p. 39). If indebtedness accumulates to such an extent that credit must be shut off, it is the trader who is blamed for this bad management. The consensus seems to be that if the trader is going to allow credit at all, it is up to him to manage it properly.

The trader has the same fundamental problems as all other credit managers: first to determine or estimate earnings so as to set credit limits at the highest possible safe figure, and second to collect his accounts. The trader's operation, however, is additionally complicated by his policy of deliberate credit saturation—making sure that capacities are as nearly as possible exhausted without being actually surpassed. Each of these considerations poses a special challenge, and it is largely on the basis of his ability to meet them that the success and capability of the modern trader is measured. Hence the common assertion that good traders are born, not made.

The purely logistic complexities of trading-post operation, such as frequently impress casual visitors, are considered trivial by comparison to successful credit management. As Shonto's owner has been heard to observe, "Anybody can learn to talk 'Navvy' and wait on counter and fix the lights and drive a truck in a few months. But you can't learn to hold them down and say 'no' to them, and that's what a trader's really got to do."

Accurate credit limits depend on careful records and on knowing the clientele thoroughly. In the long run the type of relationship which exists between trader and community (see pp. 214–231) furnishes far better credit information than could any agency. The trader's secondary role as channel of contact between the outside world and the community is in itself an automatic source of information. As interpreter and mail-reader he finds out in advance the amount of welfare grants, allowing him to set up accounts even before the first check has been received. His official records as claims agent for the Railroad Retirement Board allow him to calculate long in advance the amount of unemployment benefits which any claimant will receive. His White neighbors readily furnish him with information regarding the salaries as well as the financial activities of their Navaho employees.

Where income is entirely by check, as in the case of welfare accounts, budgeting and credit limitation are simple matters. Where there is more than one source of income and basis for credit, as is true during some parts of the year for more than half Shonto's households (see table 18, pp. 114–116), the calculations must be compounded accordingly.

No real budgeting is involved in the case of check credit. The account is simply "shut off" short the moment the limit is reached, which may be within an hour of the time it was settled with the last check. The customer will be warned as he approaches his limit, but not stopped. It is felt that no particular hardship results from trading an account up to its limit at a single session, since the period between checks is short and trips to the store are infrequent and often inconvenient in any case.

On livestock accounts, where a term of several months is involved, some attempt is made to hold the creditor down to a more or less fixed proportion of the ultimate limit each month. "Holding down" in such cases amounts in practice only to repeated warnings not to draw too much at one time. If the client is insistent the trader is apt to say "All right—go ahead and trade, but don't blame me when your credit is cut off next month." In a showdown Navaho traders have never forcibly rationed their long-term creditors, so that accounts are never truly shut off until they have reached their ultimate limits.

Securing payment of account is the trader's greatest single challenge. His success as a collector depends in part upon his own abilities and experience. Even more, however, it is measured by the dependence on credit of the community itself; for the threat of withholding future credit is the trader's one consistently effective sanction against default.

Livestock accounts are thought to present no problem. Few Navahos could profit by holding back their wool or buck lambs, and in any case they are easy to keep track of. If for any reason a large livestock account is not settled, the trader may take or send the store's stake-body truck to the debtor's hogan "to inquire what the trouble is." The usual arguments about forfeiture of all future credit are advanced by the trader, and it is hoped that the debtor will take advantage of the extra inducement of free transportation to send in his lambs or wool forthwith. It is then said that such hauling is done only as a personal favor at the urgent request of the Navaho himself. This transparent subterfuge is necessitated by the fact that traders are licensed to do business only and entirely within their own premises.

Unlike livestock products, modern Navahos find plenty of uses for cash other than to pay their bills at the trading post. Hence the special restrictions on credit against cash income and the peculiar treatment of checks (see above). It is the almost universal belief that the only way to collect a relief account or a railroad account is to present the debtor's check in one hand and his account book in the other.

The negotiation of a check on account is ideally, and often in practice, accomplished without any verbal exchange whatever. The trader hands the check to its recipient together with pen or stamp pad; the moment it is signed or thumbprinted he repossesses it and rings up the amount due on account without any consultation with the owner. If the latter desires to use the check for any purposes other than to pay his account in full it is necessary either to snatch it away from the trader and walk out of the store with it, a course of action which automatically results in suspension of all future credit privileges; or else to argue it out with the trader—a stratagem which is seldom if ever successful. In cases where the debtor can plead a legitimate need for cash (e.g. to pay for a trip to the hospital) he will be required first to settle his account with the check in hand, and then to borrow the necessary cash at 10 percent interest against the next check.

Territorial monopoly affords the trader a special advantage in all transactions involving checks. He is almost invariably the only person in the community with sufficient funds to negotiate a check for more than 10 or 15 dollars. He will, of course, refuse to have anything to do with a check except on his own terms. Even if the check's recipient owes nothing on account he may be required to make substantial purchases before it will be cashed. The alternative, for most of Shonto's Navahos, is a journey of 25 miles or more to the next nearest trading post, and here the same requirments are almost sure to be in force.

Underlying all book transactions is the implicit threat of forfeiture of credit unless accounts are paid on the trader's terms. The threat is kept in the community's consciousness at all times by frequent oblique references and erstwhile "kidding," as well as by straightforward and severe warnings to anyone who shows signs of recalcitrance, even as a joke. The importance of credit obligations is one subject upon which the trader permits no levity.

Within Shonto community, which is to say among those families who have no convenient access to any other store, the expressed and implied threat of credit forfeiture is almost entirely effective. The policy of credit saturation thus in itself tends to make credit risks safer. In a normal year and with competent management Shonto's credit losses will average between 1 and 2 percent, which is considerably less than the average credit loss reported to the writer by a group of Tucson retail merchants.

Most traders are convinced that the threat of credit stoppage will continue to carry weight only if it is carried into action promptly and assiduously in any and all cases of default. Because of their presumed example value Shonto Trading Post never discounts delinquent accounts or countenances any manner of compromise, even though a small amount of revenue is probably lost thereby. If credit is stopped absolutely the defaulting household is in most cases quickly forced to bend all its resources toward getting the debt paid off so as to draw more credit. Sometimes a related household in the same residence group will come forward to settle the account. At other times one or more members must immediately go off to work to raise the money (cf. Collier and Collier, 1953, p. 220). If an honest effort is made to settle the account, and if it succeeds, the defaulter is duly rehabilitated with an admonition to use better judgment.

A few other extra-legal sanctions assist the trader in collecting book accounts. Recipients of public assistance are reminded in one way or another that their grants are for groceries and other necessities which are sold at the trading post; and that if they do not spend all of their money as intended the amount of their grant will be reduced. If local payroll accounts show signs of delinquency the trader can and does appeal to the White employers to help him out by having a talk with the individuals involved. Shonto's schoolteachers have been especially cooperative in this regard on a couple of occasions, with the result that the Navaho employees of the school believe that they will lose their jobs if they do not pay their store bills. This belief is ideal from the trader's point of view, although it has no basis in fact.

One of the most powerful sanctions which the trader can bring against many of Shonto's Navahos is the threatened or actual refusal to perform for them the myriad extra-commercial functions for which they normally depend on him, such as writing and reading letters, securing employment, interceding with the law, and the like (see pp. 214–231). Finally, he may threaten to retaliate upon relatives by cutting off the credit of related households and even holding them responsible for the delinquent account. In nearly all cases the latter will deny any responsibility. Such an act of repudiation, however, threatens the security of the defaulting household as a member of the residence group, and as such may possibly be an extra inducement to come to terms.

PAWN

Pawn probably goes back to the beginnings of the Navaho trade (see "Early Trading Posts," pp. 150–154), and was the only basis for credit until well into the present century (cf. Kirk, 1953). As a basis of transaction its antiquity is attested to some extent by the thoroughly haphazard bookkeeping methods employed. Running accounts on pawn are never recorded in conventional salesbooks, but are simply scribbled wherever space allows on the small identification tags attached to the pawned item.

Pawn is still popularly believed to be one of the cornerstones of the Navaho trade, and the pawn racks with their rows of shining silver and turquoise jewelry and whatnot are seen as a necessary and picturesque feature of every trading post (see, e.g., Collier and Collier, 1953, p. 219). Probably few observers are aware that the continued presence of large quantities of pawn at Shonto Trading Post is due more to the Navahos' desire for a safe deposit facility than to the trader's need for collateral. Under present economic conditions much of Shonto's pawn represents superfluous security: the owners would be entitled to the same amount of credit whether they pawned or not. Some accounts (e.g., against relief checks) are today considered so completely secured by their recipients' absolute dependence on credit that the store has actually refused to be bothered with pawn against them when it was offered.[15]

The importance of pawn in the modern Navaho trade has diminished to such an extent that today it covers only about one-third of Shonto's total credit load. At their peak seasons, in April and September, accounts receivable on pawn normally total about $5,000 as against $10,000 or more receivable on book accounts (see table 33, p. 196).[16]

Notwithstanding their low total value, the actual number of pawn accounts at Shonto Trading Post consistently exceeds the number of book accounts; sometimes by a margin as high as two to one. Consequently average indebtedness on any given piece of pawn is extremely low as compared to average indebtedness on book accounts (see table 33, p. 196. This situation points up the distinct and neces-

---

[15] There is, however, an ulterior motive involved here which is typically illustrative of the role of the modern trading post. Assets in jewelry are never reported to the social worker when applying for public assistance. If pawn is accepted from a welfare recipient, the trader is afraid that the social worker on one of his periodic visits may happen to spot it in the vault and conclude that the owner is better off than reported, resulting in a reduction in grant and hence, ultimately, in the trading post's income.

[16] In 1940, according to Kluckhohn and Leighton, pawn accounted for just over half the total outstanding trading-post credit on the Navaho Reservation (Kluckhohn and Leighton, 1946, p. 38).

sary role still played by pawn: it is a source of limited, purely individual credit in contrast to book credit which is drawn by and for whole households (see "Economic Interdependence," pp. 103–108). No one but the owner of the piece is ever allowed to draw credit against pawn except in a few cases where a specific delegation of privilege has been made; and no one but the owner is ever held accountable for the debt. Thus while a whole household shares a single book account, it is not uncommon for several different members to have items in pawn individually at the same time.

Small pawn accounts, i.e., principally those drawn against bracelets and beads, are not based on any specific anticipated earnings. They are backed, rather, by the value of the piece plus the trader's confidence that the owner can surely raise the few dollars involved from some source or other, or at least borrow it, in the next 6 months (see below). The primary function of pawn is thus to provide credit in the absence of other tangible or anticipated resources.

Pawn has a further function, in a few cases, of securing fairly extensive credit against more or less uncertain earnings or uncertain collection thereof. Particularly involved are railroad and other off-reservation wage earnings, and the livestock accounts of families from outside Shonto community. Finally, the trading-post pawn vault offers the safest possible repository for valuable and bulky items of jewelry. This consideration alone is probably responsible for a third of the jewelry in Shonto's vault, since much of it has been voluntarily entered as security against accounts for which no collateral would be required. In this way Shonto community is thought to keep a good 75 percent of its silver belts and other more valuable pieces of jewelry in the trading post vault at all times.

Some recorded pawn holdings at Shonto Trading Post, and total indebtedness thereon, are shown in table 33.

Under tribal trading regulations all pawn accounts run for a legal term of 6 months. No interest may be charged during this period;

TABLE 33.—*Pawn accounts at Shonto Trading Post, Feb. 1954, Sept. 1955, and Dec. 1955*

Pawned items	Feb. 7, 1954			Sept. 15, 1955 [1]			Dec. 15, 1955		
	No. acc.	Total value	Avg. value	No. acc.	Total value	Avg. value	No. acc.	Total value	Avg. value
Belts	54	$1,893	$35	75	$3,131	$42	53	$1,900	$36
Beads	45	647	14	81	1,393	17	61	937	15
Bracelets	55	550	10	84	1,082	12	60	662	11
Other [2]	9	141	16	27	339	13	12	113	9
Total	163	3,231		267	5,945		186	3,612	
Average			20			22			19

[1] Immediately before lamb sales.
[2] Included silver hatbands, bowguards (gatos), brooches, silver-mounted bridles, saddles, and 1 truck.

at its expiration, however, any unredeemed item may be sold by the trader for whatever it will bring.

The pawn policy of Shonto and many other trading posts in actuality bears little relationship to the legal restrictions governing pawn. Bracelets and smaller items are supposed to, and usually do, turn over considerably more frequently than is required by law. Belts and other pieces of high value, on the other hand, are subject to the same terms as book accounts. They are held as security against specific earnings, and are supposed to be paid off whenever such earnings are realized, whether the term be 30 days or 2 years (cf. Coolidge and Coolidge, 1930, p. 68). From the trader's standpoint pawn is "dead" not at the end of 6 months, but whenever the expected term has expired and the owner has given direct or indirect indication that he does not intend to redeem it (see Kirk, 1953, p. 241).

As a matter of general policy, Shonto Trading Post tries to clean the slate on pawn as on all other accounts receivable at the time of wool and especially lamb sales (see "The Economic Cycle," pp. 141–145). A large sign asserting that "ALL PAWN MUST BE TAKEN OUT AT THE TIME OF LAMB SALES OR IT WILL BE SOLD ! !" is prominently displayed in the store for a month or more before buying begins. The threat is largely sheer bluff, since nothing can be sold until it has been in the vault 6 months, but it is believed to scare the creditors into paying up, and is part of the established ritual of trading. In actual fact, about 75 percent of Shonto's pawn does go out during lamb season; much of it, however, simply "turns over." It is paid off and immediately repawned, never even leaving the store building in many cases. It is then legally safe for another 6 months. The quick turnover in pawn is clearly shown in table 33, where a comparison of entries for September and December 1955 indicates that of 267 items in pawn on the former date, 186 or nearly 70 percent were back in the vault 3 months later. Total indebtedness against pawn had climbed back to over 60 percent of its September peak.

Many pieces of heavy jewelry, and particularly large silver belts, are said to "live" in the trading post pawn vault. They are paid off and pawned anew from time to time, but have not been outside the store for many years. Contrary to popular accounts modern trading posts never "loan out" pawn to its owners for special ritual occasions, and no such loan has ever been requested in the writer's experience.

It has been stated that traders will accept in pawn any item which has resale value (Kluckhohn and Leighton, 1946, p. 38). The statement is true of traders in the Gallup area and on the east side of the reservation generally, but it is decidely not true at Shonto or any neighboring trading post. Shonto's pawn policy is based on the belief that dead pawn is bad business and reflects poor management. The criterion of acceptability in pawn is therefore not what it is worth to the trader or any outside market, but what it is worth to the pawner himself. Shonto will not accept in pawn any item which the owner would probably not wish to redeem, even though its resale value were considerably greater than the amount allowed against it. One or two families are actually blacklisted from pawning for any amount because they have taken so long to redeem in the past.

Because it must be of known value to the owner, Shonto's pawn is limited almost exclusively to the traditional silver and turquoise jewelry (cf. table 33). The only other items accepted with any frequency, and only then under special circumstances, are saddles. On one occasion a wagon has been pawned at Shonto, and on one occasion a truck. Blankets, rifles, and other items of doubtful worth, such as are seen in great quantities in the Gallup area, are never accepted at Shonto.

As in the case of book accounts, it is largely left up to the trader to manage pawn credit properly. If it "goes dead" he may be blamed vociferously for allowing too much credit. Hence dead pawn is to be avoided above all else as a source of customer ill will (cf. Coolidge and Coolidge, 1930, p. 68; Collier and Collier, 1953, p. 220).

Pawn credit like book credit requires intimate knowledge of the individual involved, and his past record. Any reasonable piece of native jewelry may be pawned against its face value for 5 or 10 dollars, since such small sums can always be earned in one way or another. Pawning for any larger sum, however, "depends on what the man is worth and not what the piece is worth," as traders say. This policy consistently restricts the credit value of pawned articles to a fraction of their face value, but it insures their redemption by so doing. Silver belts valued at $150.00 have in some cases been held to credit limits of $20.00.

Despite the legal 6 months' limitation on pawn accounts, pawn is never under any circumstances sold until its owners have had a legitimate chance to redeem it. If expected earnings do not materialize or are genuinely needed for some other purpose the trader will hold the piece to give the pawner a chance to raise the sum required later on (cf. Collier and Collier, 1953, p. 220). Men going off to work on the railroad often pawn their belts or beads before they leave, sometimes for nominal sums, as a means of safekeeping. They may be absent for periods of months or even years, but the piece is always held until its owner returns. In this way two belts have been unclaimed in Shonto's pawn vault since 1952, and several have been in between 1 and 2 years. An interest of 10 percent per annum is charged on all such accounts after the first year.

Regardless of age pawned articles are never actually sold off unless and until their owners have refused to redeem them, or have given evidence that they do not intend to do so. Otherwise they are simply reminded on every conceivable opportunity that they have an account to be settled, and the same sort of coercion is brought to bear as in the case of book credit collection (see pp. 188–195). By careful management and adherence to this policy only three pieces of dead pawn were actually sold out of Shonto Trading Post between 1953 and 1956.

DIRECT EXCHANGE

Direct across-the-counter exchange of consumer goods for commodities, once the backbone of the Navaho trade (cf. Amsden, 1934, p. 178), has dwindled to such an extent that it now accounts for only about 10 percent of Shonto's total annual gross (tables 30 and 31).

The commodity trade of Navaho trading posts has been referred to consistently as barter (e.g. Franciscan Fathers, 1910, pp. 489–490; Amsden, 1934, p. 178). In a purely technical sense this designation is correct, but the term often carries connotations which have led to popular misunderstanding of the nature of the exchange involved. To begin with, there is not and has not been for many years any haggling over prices in the Navaho commodity trade. All items are bought by quality and/or quantity according to fixed, pre-announced unit prices. Furthermore, all exchanges are based on cash valuation and not on valuation in equivalent goods, a policy which allows for free price adjustments (see Franciscan Fathers, 1910, p. 490). A double saddle blanket, for example, is not valued at 50 pounds of flour, 10 pounds of sugar, and 2 pounds of coffee (contrast Amsden, 1934, p. 178); it is valued at $8.00, which may be received in any such goods as the seller desires, or applied on account, or both.

Commodities which are bartered (as well as sold in some cases) at Shonto Trading Post are livestock products, native crafts, and piñon nuts (see also "Commodity Exchange," pp. 172–175). Procedures and 1955 prices involved in handling these items are set forth in summary form in table 34.

TABLE 34.—*Systems of direct commodity exchange at Shonto Trading Post*

Commodity	Credit basis	Traded for—	1955 unit price or average price
Wool	Yes	On account: surplus 50–50 [1]	Mohair, $0.35 lb. Clean fleece, $0.25 lb. Black wool and tags, $0.10 lb.
Lambs	Yes	On account: surplus 50–50 [1]	$0.15½
Cattle	No	Merchandise	(Not bought)
Hides	No	Cash	Goats, $0.18 lb. Sheep, $0.16 lb. Clips, $0.05 lb.
Rugs	No	Merchandise	Single saddle blanket, $4.00 Double saddle blanket, $8.00 Rug, $14.00
Minor crafts	No	...do	Squaw belt, $8.00 Basket, $3.50 Pitch bottle and pot, $2.50
Piñon nuts	No	...do	$0.25

[1] I.e., not more than 50 percent in cash, remainder in merchandise.

Lambs and wool between them account for the bulk of Shonto's annual commodity barter. Nevertheless, direct exchange of both these items is strictly secondary to advance credit transactions (see table 16, p. 109) which annually involve at least 50 percent of all lambs and 67 percent of all wool bought. When these commodities are brought to the trading post the proceeds of sale are first and foremost applied on account. Only the "surplus" or unencumbered income from the sale is involved in on-the-post exchange. According to common trading post policy, up to 50 percent of such "surplus" commodity income is receivable in cash on demand, while the remainder must be taken out in trade (contrast Luomala, 1938, p. 5). Lambs and wool are thus actually involved in three types of transaction: credit sales, direct barter, and cash purchase by the trading post.

Cattle, when there was a market for them, were always involved in straight barter. No advance credit was allowed against them, and they were paid for strictly with merchandise. Shonto Trading Post has not bought cattle since 1952.

Shonto and most other trading posts pay straight cash for hides as a goodwill gesture (see "Commodity Exchange," pp. 172–175), since the value of such trade is trivial. Technically, therefore, hides are not bartered, although in practice 90 percent of the money paid for them comes back immediately for small purchases.

Rugs are the most important commodity involved exclusively in barter transactions. Trading posts in the northwestern Navaho country never allow credit against rug production (contrast Kluckhohn and Leighton, 1946, p. 23), and, moreover, pay for them entirely in merchandise. Traders justify this policy with the assertion that there is no profit in rugs themselves (see "Commodity Exchange," pp. 172–175), so that they are worth handling only insofar as they are a means of additional retail profit. In the case of very large rugs of superior quality a fraction of the total price may be paid in cash as a special inducement to make more of the same.

Shonto Trading Post has recently paid set prices of $4.00 and $8.00 for the majority of single and double saddle blankets, respectively. There are no very rigid criteria for pricing larger rugs, where quality is of far more importance than size. Buying rugs is said by some traders to be an art; by others to be a matter of pure intuition. The latter quality has been possessed in varying degrees by traders at Shonto in the past, and rug prices have fluctuated widely and often irrationally as a result. Correct procedure in buying a rug, as practiced by Shonto's owner, is to look it over in silence for a minute or more, without touching it and especially without measuring it. The trader can then come out in a firm voice with the first figure that enters his head, and stick resolutely to it. The trader who examines a proffered rug closely weakens the authority of his judgment, since he is supposed to be able to spot a cotton warp and other defects at a glance.

Minor crafts—sashes, baskets, pitch bottles, and pots—are handled on the same basis as rugs and traded for merchandise only. The same is ordinarily true of piñon nuts, although during the bumper winter of 1954 there was so much competition among traders for the crop that a certain amount of credit was allowed against it in advance.

PATTERNS OF TRADE

The distinctive shopping habits characteristic of Shonto's clientele are to some extent the result of environmental factors: relative inaccessibility of the store for many families, and its old-fashioned layout and limited inventory. In much greater measure, however, they are purely cultural in origin. They are, in fact, peculiarly Navaho buying habits such as may be observed only in a Navaho trading post.

FREQUENCY OF SHOPPING

Some member of every Shonto household gets to the store on an average of at least once a month. This is apparently the minimum frequency of contact needed to sustain the modern Navaho household. While it is predictable that a few households will always fail to appear during any 30-day period, it is equally predictable that these households will turn up during the next period of equal length.

Above the minimum figure maintained by all households, frequency of trading is chiefly a function of distance from the store, and of transportation resources. Variation in frequency is therefore enormous, as might be expected in view of the size of the community. Shonto's nearest Navaho neighbors live within 200 yards of the store, while families in the extreme north end of the community are more than 15 miles away (see map 1). Consequently members of the former are in the store nearly every day, whereas the latter are seldom on hand more than once a week. For families living on the margins of the community trading at Shonto is a full day's activity, since it involves a round trip of 20 to 30 miles by horseback or wagon. Truck owners, of course, can and do visit the store with considerably greater frequency.

Table 35 presents a frequency distribution of Shonto households according to the number of days on which one or more adult members visited Shonto Trading Post during the 4 weeks from April 1 to April 28, 1956.[17]

---

[17] Since the store is open 6 days a week, the total potential number of visits for any household would normally be 24. However, during the period of record it was necessary to close the store unexpectedly for one entire day in order to repair a breakdown in the power plant. The total potential number of visits was therefore 23. (See also table 36.)

TABLE 35.—*Frequency of Trading Post visits by Shonto households, April 1956*
(maximum possible 23)

Number of households	Number T.P. visits each	Number of households	Number T.P. visits each	Number of households	Number T.P. visits each
1	¹ 23	4	12	9	5
1	19	3	11	14	4
1	18	2	10	7	3
3	16	6	9	8	2
2	15	8	8	1	1
1	14	10	7	8	0
4	13	7	6		

```
Total number households_____ 100
Total number of visits to Trading Post_____ ² 674
Mean number of visits_____ 6.74
Median number of visits_____ 5.92
```

¹ Trading post employee.
² Total number of visits registered by households. 822 visits by adult individuals were involved, as shown in table 36.

Table 35 clearly reveals the wide variation in shopping frequency among Shonto households. Sixty-nine percent of families, however, made between two and nine visits to the store during the month of April 1956. Nine percent came in less frequently or not at all, while 22 percent came in more frequently. Insofar as any single modal frequency is indicated, it results from the fact that railroad benefit claimants are required to report to the trading post once a week to sign claim affidavits regardless of how far away they live. The most common number of visits during the 4-week period of April 1956, was thus four (cf. table 36).

The information contained in tables 35 and 36 was recorded in an "average" month—busier than midwinter and midsummer, but considerably quieter than later spring and fall. Average number of visits to the store would accordingly show considerably lower or higher, as the case may be, during these other seasons (see "The Economic Cycle," pp. 141–145). The modal frequency of one visit per week is sustained only during the railroad "benefit year" (see "Railroad Work," pp. 129–133), which begins in November or December and ends in April or May.

Table 36, based on the same records as tables 29 and 35, shows the volume of Shonto's clientele by days during April 1956, together with a record of significant events within and around the community during the same period. This table reveals some additional distinctive features of the Navaho trade which result largely from the cultural character of the clientele. The volume of trade, although fairly constant from week to week, varies enormously from day to day within the week.[18] In April of 1956 the number of daily customers fluctuated

---

[18] The same condition shows up in the records of cash volume made in 1954 and set forth in table 31.

TABLE 36.—*Clientele volume by days, Shonto Trading Post, April 1956*

Date and day	Clientele					Concurrent events
	Shonto Navahos	Other Navahos	Other Indians	Whites	Total	
April:						
2 Mon	36	3		4	43	Mail day.
3 Tue	35	8		4	47	
4 Wed	29	11	1	5	46	
5 Thur	54	15		8	77	Railroad signup day.[1]
6 Fri	19	9		7	35	Mail day.
7 Sat	29	6		2	37	
Total	202	52	1	30	285	
9 Mon	33	11		4	48	Mail day.
10 Tue	43	6	4	2	55	
11 Wed	41	7	3	1	52	
12 Thur	52	11		2	65	RR signup [1]; P.H. nurse at Shonto.[2]
13 Fri	22	3		3	28	Mail day.
14 Sat	34	5		2	41	
Total	225	43	7	14	289	
16 Mon	60	22		5	87	Community meeting at Shonto [3]
17 Tue	26	2		2	30	"Squaw dance" at Kaibito.
18 Wed	20	4		3	27	Do.
19 Thur	50	11		3	64	Railroad signup [1]; heavy snow.
20 Fri	14	4		4	22	Snow, cold; no mail arrival.
21 Sat	39	9		5	53	Mail arrived.
Total	209	52		22	283	
23 Mon	34	5		3	42	Mail day.
24 Tue	37	9	1	9	56	
25 Wed						Store closed.[4]
26 Thur	51	18		5	74	Railroad signup day.[1]
27 Fri	31	2		4	37	Mail day.
28 Sat	33	6	3	4	46	
Total	186	40	4	25	255	
Total for month	822	187	12	91	1,112	

[1] See "Railroad Work " pp. 129–133.
[2] Regular monthly visit announced in advance.
[3] Held by Tribal Councilman; announced in advance.
[4] For emergency repairs to power plant.

from a high of 87 to a low of 22 within the space of 4 days (table 36). The average daily clientele for the month was 48.

As table 36 indicates, trading is closely affected by other activities in and around the community. Those which take place in the vicinity of the store bring a heavy increase in volume of trade, while activities elsewhere have the opposite effect (e.g., the dance at Kaibito). The four railroad signup days (Thursdays) and one meeting day (Monday the 16th) in April, 1956, provided Shonto Trading Post with an aggregate of 367 customers—almost exactly one-third of the total clientele for the month. A similar heavy concentration of trade on railroad days is shown in table 31. During the heavy snows of midwinter, when trade is at its slowest, the trading post may do as much as half its total volume of business on railroad days. Thus, an additional set of records kept during a 2-week period in January 1954, indicates that

Shonto Trading Post did $1,584 out of a total volume of $3,940 trade on the two Thursdays during that period.

If the volume of trade varies from day to day, it remains nearly constant from week to week during any given season (see table 36). Dollar volume is affected by external economic conditions, but actual clientele volume, in the absence of any trading post competition, remains closely predictable.

Table 36 shows a regular pattern of compensation in the volume of Shonto's trade, in that every especially busy day is predictably followed by an especially slack one. So long as signup day remains on Thursday, Shonto's trader can always look forward to a pleasant rest on Friday. Thus while 4 signup days and 1 meeting day in April 1956 produced a third of the month's total of customers, the 5 days which immediately followed these saw less than half that number, accounting for under 15 percent of the month's total.

SHOPPING HABITS

Navaho buying behavior is characterized by deliberation and wariness. This quality has caught the eye even of casual visitors to such an extent that some description of Navaho trading is almost sure to find its way into any account of Navaho life (see, e.g., Amsden, 1934, p. 178; Collier and Collier, 1953, p. 219; Underhill, 1956, pp. 182–185). It may be, as suggested by Kluckhohn and Leighton (1946, p. 79), that some traders in the past have "shamelessly exploited the Indian's ignorance of markets and of simple arithmetic." Modern traders, on the other hand, will attest that it is no easy matter to put anything over on a Navaho; also that Navahos on their part have sometimes shamelessly exploited the trusting disposition and/or lack of judgment of the trader.

In general it is probably safe to say that Navaho trading behavior obeys what Kluckhohn and Leighton (1946, pp. 223–226) have called the basic premises and "formulas for safety" in Navaho life and thought: be wary of non-relatives, and go slow in unfamiliar situations (Kluckhohn and Leighton, 1946, pp. 225–226). For whatever reason, Navahos today approach their dealings with the trader with a caution which seems to suggest distrust, not of him individually, but of the whole trading context. No transaction is allowed to proceed too fast, and there are frequent pauses to take stock of the situation.

The result of Navaho trading attitudes, from the White man's point of view, is that the pace of trading-post commerce is agonizingly slow. If "a mean disposition" (cf. Dolva and Beckley, 1950, p. 117) is the prime requisite of a country storekeeper, patience, along with firmness, is the necessity of the trader. Not uncommonly, he will find at the

end of what has seemed like a particularly busy day that he has in
fact taken in less than a hundred dollars.

Except under very unusual circumstances Shonto's Navahos do not
begin to trade immediately upon entering the store. In most cases
there will be a delay of at least 20 minutes. This behavior is in line
with Navaho tradition, which prescribes a certain amount of initial
indirection in commercial dealings (cf. Hill, 1948). At the same time
it offers the customer an invaluable opportunity to look over the
stock and review his or her mental shopping list.

Shopping begins and ends, for three Shonto residents out of four,
with a bottle of soda pop. It is the one item which is almost sure
to be purchased immediately upon entering the store, regardless of
the season or weather. While it is being consumed the customer is
likely to walk around the "bullpen" (customer area—see fig. 3, p. 162)
greeting and shaking hands with acquaintances. He will then, in
most cases, settle down against a wall or counter for several minutes'
silent inspection of the entire stock on display. Such inspection serves
as a mnemonic device to remind the customer of the things that he
needs, and at the same time allows him to see what new items may
have been laid in.

The decision to begin the day's trading is taken overtly, and is
signaled by the customer's abrupt advance to the grocery counter
(where the trader normally stations himself) and an immediate opening demand, either for credit or for some specific item of merchandise.
If a hide has been brought in it is sure to be slapped on the counter
with a resounding noise to signal that the customer is ready to trade.
Navahos usually, but not always, wait in turn to trade, as
required by the trader. While waiting, they stand against the
walls or near the stove rather than at the counter. It is an unstated
tradition that only the client with whom the trader is actually engaged
is entitled to be at the counter; indeed by the time he has finished
trading, his purchases are likely to cover the entire counter.
The presence of any person at the counter, therefore, is a signal
of his readiness and desire to trade. It sometimes happens that a
customer decides he has waited long enough and advances to the
counter even though the trader is already engaged. In such cases
he is likely to call and signal for attention, even in the face of repeated
demands from the trader to shut up (see "Trader Behavior," pp. 210–
212), until he is obliged. On particular rush days Shonto Trading
Post sometimes even looks like a bargain basement, with clamoring
customers on all counters.

Trading always begins with the sale of a hide or hides, if they have
been brought in. The trader weighs them up and pays out the requisite cash, seldom amounting to as much as a dollar; in 9 cases out of

10 it is immediately spent for soda pop, candy and small notions. The next stop is always the disposal of any rugs which have been brought in. They are assessed and priced, and their allowed value is traded out in merchandise on the spot. Small quantities of wool (i.e., out of season), minor crafts, and piñon nuts, if any, are similarly disposed of in trade. Only when all trade goods have been taken care of, and value received in merchandise, does the serious business of buying on credit begin. For most families this will account for the bulk of the purchases on any given day, including such staples as flour, coffee, and other necessities of the whole household.

Insofar as large cash purchases are made at Shonto Trading Post, they are made either by persons not entitled to credit (i.e., from outside the community in most cases) or by persons whose credit is exhausted. In these cases they take the place of credit buying in the normal sequence of transactions. In some cases a customer's credit will be exhausted in the middle of trading, in which case he may continue to buy for cash if he has any. It is highly unusual for anyone to spend cash as long as he or she can get credit.

If an item is to be pawned, this is nearly always the final order of business, undertaken when trade, book credit and cash transactions are out of the way

It is very rare for an individual or household to carry out more than two or three types of transaction during the course of the same trading session. The entire sequence from hides to pawn as set forth above has never occurred in actual practice. What the sequence represents is a consistent order of preference which is, from the Navaho point of view, entirely logical.

Navahos buy heavily on impulse, so that few of them, as they enter the store, have more than a very general idea of what and how much they are going to buy. Their uncertainty is increased by the fact that they can never be sure exactly what the store will and will not have in stock (see "Inventory Control," p. 180). Since few of Shonto's customers have had any experience with addition beyond one figure, it follows that they usually have even less idea of how much they are going to spend than of how much they are going to buy. The trader who asks a Navaho "how much credit do you want"? is sure to get the answer "I don't know; I'll just have to see."

Fully aware that they are unable to calculate their expenditures in advance, Navahos simply go through their resources in the order of expendability. First hides; then rugs, wool, and the like; then future earnings; then cash on hand; and finally jewelry, which is to say secure capital, are offered as exchange. If trading can be completed and necessary items acquired before the last of these are reached, well and good; but most Navahos come to the trading post prepared to pay cash or to pawn in case their commodities and book credit will

not cover their desired purchases. Traders constantly complain that
Navahos cannot be induced to part with their cash as long as their
credit is "open," and it has become common policy to deny credit to
persons known to have cash on hand. The Navaho attitude, however,
is based on the worldwide principle of "spending money you don't
have rather than money you do have"; and it is further animated by
the need for cash in Flagstaff and in native commerce, where credit
is not allowed.

Just as they follow a fixed order in their spending, most Navahos
follow a closely predictable sequence in their buying. At least 90
percent of shopping expeditions start at the grocery counter and
move in order through drugs, dry goods, and shoes to hardware, thus
more or less following the layout of the store itself (fig. 3, p. 162).
Fuel and feed, which are not kept in sight, are sure to be purchased
at the very last.

Navaho buying follows the same essential logic as spending, and
for the same reason. Since the buyer cannot be sure in advance
how far his resources will go, it is simply a matter of first things
first. Purchases in each department begin with the most essential
items and work down to the most trivial. Hence those items which
constitute staples in the Navaho diet (table 28, pp. 177–180; see also
"Cooking and Housekeeping," pp. 81–82) head the list on nearly every
occasion. A random examination of 100 trade slips in 1955 revealed
that flour was the first entry in 91 cases, while, flour, baking powder,
coffee, sugar and salt appeared among the first 10 items in 83 cases.

The practice of buying in descending order of importance is so well
developed that it results in "counter jumping"—a practice discour-
aged by traders as highly inconvenient. The "counter jumper" moves
from grocery to dry goods to shoe counter making his most important
purchases first, then returns to the various departments for less vital
items. The whole practice of Navaho buying is arranged as a pre-
caution in case funds and/or credit should become exhausted at any
time, insuring that in any such eventuality the most important purchases will always have been consummated.

The Navaho consumer generally takes such pains as he can to keep
track of his resources and credit position during the process of trading, either by counting his money or inquiring his credit standing from
the trader. All transactions involving direct commodity exchange
are recorded on "due bills" whereon the original amount due in trade
is entered at the top, and from which each successive purchase is sub-
tracted in turn (see Underhill, 1956, pp. 182–183). Negotiation
of a due bill is almost a matter of ritual, in which the amount remaining to be traded out must be stated after each selection has been sub-
tracted. The customer will almost never make an additional purchase
until this information has been supplied. A due bill even for so small

an item as a single saddle blanket is likely to be covered on both sides with scribbled subtrahends and remainders by the time it has been settled in full.

Most pawn accounts are handled in the same fashion. On smaller items, which account for a good two-thirds of all Shonto's pawn, it is traditional to trade out the entire amount allowed at the time of pawning. In the case of bracelets and beads this seldom amounts to more than 10 or 15 dollars (cf. table 33). The credit limit allowed is entered at the head of a slip which is then negotiated by item-by-item subtraction exactly as are due bills.

Large and valuable pieces of jewelry, chiefly belts, are sometimes pawned for amounts up to and exceeding $100.00. In all such cases the belt is simply held as collateral against an account which is actually based on earnings and limited accordingly. These larger pawn accounts are thus essentially the same as book accounts in that they are cumulative and/or fluctuating. They are known as "running accounts" or "open accounts" in contrast to accounts on small pawn, which are traded to the limit and thus "closed" at the time of pawning.

Trading on an open pawn account, like trading on a book account, is a matter of simple addition. Even here, however, a belt is likely to be pawned initially for an arbitrary amount selected in advance by the owner. A slip is made out for the desired amount and negotiated by subtraction as in the case of other pawn. In this case the amount allowed represents the owner's desire to limit his indebtedness and not a credit limit set by the trader. It is a source of mystification to traders that Navahos will arbitrarily fix a sum for which to pawn a piece and then will stick to it as though it were a matter of contract, even though they find that they can think of nothing for which to spend the last few dollars. Rather than reduce the original indebtedness decided on they will leave the remainder of their trade slip at the store to be completed on a later occasion. The sum for which nearly all Shonto's belts are initially pawned is $20.00, although in many cases it is increased by additional purchases within a week.

Traders have been known to say that "Navahos are not nearly so afraid of addition as they are of subtraction," meaning that they are less cautious in increasing their debts than in decreasing their credits. It is true that a credit account will often be augmented by $30.00 in less time than it takes to trade out a $3.00 due bill. The observed fact that most people find it much easier to spend money which they do not have than money which is in hand is the basis for the 20th-century installment boom, and the modern Navaho may thus be said to be up to date in this regard.

A Navaho who wishes to trade on a book (or open pawn) account is almost sure to open the negotiation by inquiring the amount of his bill. The trader has only to volunteer an incorrect answer to discover that his questioner already knows the amount as well as he does, since it is customary to keep track of the amount at the end of each buying session. Statement of the account is followed by an additional question: "Can I have some more?" In most cases this query is as superfluous as its predecessor, since customers are informed in no uncertain terms when their credit has been exhausted; both, however, remain part of the established ritual of trading and are encouraged by the trader as expressions of deference.

Buying on credit is the one rapid transaction in the Navaho trade. Since credit limits here are arbitrary and flexible, rather than inexorable as in the case of due bills, Navahos are accustomed to leave them for the trader to worry about. Buying goes on rapidly and with little interruption for mental calculation until either the buyer's wants are satisfied or the trader calls a halt. However, accounts must be totaled at the bottom of each sales slip (i.e., after every 15 items) in order to carry them forward, and it is customary for the customer to inquire the amount of his bill at that time. Only when he knows he is approaching his limit is he likely to keep closer track of his standing.

Some of Shonto's older clients provide an insight into the processes of the early Navaho trade, when nearly all transactions were by due bill (Underhill, 1956, p. 182). Those of them who are on relief tend to treat their accounts as if they were due bills for the amount of the check. In ascertaining their indebtedness they inquire "how much is left?" rather than "how much do I owe?"

The way in which Navahos spend cash exasperates even experienced traders, by their own admission. Every item is requested, received, and paid for individually (see, e.g., Luomala, 1938, p. 5). Moreover, the money is never proffered until the requested article has been placed in the hands of the customer, so that every single cash purchase requires the trader to make a trip from the counter to the shelves, back to the counter, to the cash register, and back to the counter. Traders are fond of complaining that they walk a mile for every cash dollar, and it is probably true that there is more legwork involved in trading with Navahos than in most other retail trade.

As a consequence of Navaho reluctance to part with cash except piecemeal, the average sale recorded by Shonto's cash register is about 35 cents, and not over 10 percent of recorded sales are over a dollar. The length of cash register tapes (up to 15 feet for one day's trade) gives accountants an impression of prosperity which is frequently unwarranted. Shonto's owner has been heard to justify his practice of encouraging credit sales at the expense of cash (i.e., credit saturation) simply on the ground that it speeds up business and cuts down walking so much.

In essence, Navahos handle cash as they trade out a due bill, and for good reason. The first "money" which was introduced in the Navaho trade was scrip. It was issued against rugs and other commodities just as are due bills today, and like them could only be taken out in trade at the store. Since the amount was absolutely limited to the value of the produce sold, Navahos learned to spend it carefully and to keep track of their standing by counting the remainder after each purchase, as they now inquire how much is left on a due bill after each purchase. The attitudes and spending habits thus acquired have carried over from trade money to legal tender (see Franciscan Fathers, 1910, p. 490).

The role of soda pop in the Navaho trade has often been remarked by popular observers. It is the lubricant of Navaho commerce; so much so that its consumption on some occasions has become almost literally a ritual. In this respect its function is closely comparable to that of tea in the Orient, and to some extent of whiskey in the United States. It is nearly always the first and often the last item purchased when trading, and in between times it is consumed from time to time whenever the customer wishes to "take a break" long enough to refresh his memory or to take stock of his financial position. It may be ordered by a customer who is losing an argument with the trader as furnishing a welcome excuse for silence; likewise an individual who wins an argument or makes his point may get a free bottle as a concession of apology from the trader. It is the only currency with which minor services such as helping to load and unload mercantile trucks are rewarded. Finally, it is traditionally and more or less ritually given as a reward for large purchases or paying off large accounts. "Anyone paying his bill in full gets a bottle of pop" is or was standard trading-post policy throughout the length and breadth of the Navaho Reservation.

TRADER BEHAVIOR

The distinctive behavior of the Navaho as a buyer has its complement in equally distinctive behavior of the trader as a seller. The Navaho trade is almost certainly the only retail business in modern America in which, as it is said, "the customer is always wrong." This humorous allegation has its source in the essential truth that the trader is always right. Another expression of the same conception is "You don't have to take any guff off the customers." This is regarded as one of the great compensations of the Navaho trade.

The trader comes by his attitude partly through the inherent advantages of territorial monopoly and a protected market, which make it unnecessary for him to encourage local trade by being extra polite to the customers. A very popular trader's joke, expressing recognition of this state of affairs, is to say "if you don't like it you can go to the store across the street." To an even greater extent, nevertheless, the trader's advantage over his clientele is implicit in the cross-societal nature of the trade itself.

In White retail trade, the clerk or merchant is in most cases at a status disadvantage with respect to his customer, such that deferential behavior is expected of him. In the Navaho trade the opposite is true. Modern American society is the ultimate dominant factor in the Navaho trade, and by virtue of membership in that society the trader enjoys a status advantage over his clientele which is consistently emphasized and exploited. In any major dispute involved in trading he is always right not because of superior individual knowledge or experience, but simply because he is a White man, and trading is a White man's game. It is the customer, not the merchant, who shows deferential behavior.

The trader's status advantage is implicit in every aspect of the Navaho trade. It is often resented but seldom disputed by the clientele.

The conventional, institutionalized patterns of deference which characterize most White retail trade are almost entirely absent from the Navaho trade. Instead, the trader exploits his status advantage in all commercial dealings by maintaining an attitude of detachment and indifference which forces the customer to take the initiative and come to him. It is always up to the customer to open negotiations; traders almost never speak to Navahos until they have been addressed, even if there is no one else in the store. In this way he avoids committing himself to any attitude toward the client until he has heard what is wanted of him.

Throughout the process of trading the trader speaks as little as possible, maintaining an air of aloofness which continually forces the consumer to come to him in the character of a supplicant. If the customer is hesitant he may be admonished to speed it up or make up his mind. If a rival customer demands attention he will almost certainly be told in straightforward terms to shut up and wait his turn. If a requested item is out of stock, the customer will be so informed with no pretense at apology. In a word, the trader treats his Navaho clientele as if they were children, and he and not they knew what was good for them. Hence the saying that "you don't have to take any guff off the customers"; it is the latter, in fact, who have to "take the guff."

White visitors, accustomed to automatic deference from retail clerks, tend to think of traders as sullen, rude and contrary. They are perhaps unaware that the attitudes which thus impress them are deliberately maintained by the trader in order to emphasize his status advantage. In the case of tourists, however, normal reserve in business dealings is augmented by the suspicion that they are probably "Indian lovers" who will go home and vilify the trader. Traders have been subjected to frequent adverse publicity to remind them that in the folklore of 20th-century America the Indian occupies such an exalted place that it is considered unethical to make even an honest living at his expense.

In actuality most traders enjoy White company when they can have it on their own terms—i.e., when they can do most of the talking. As with Navahos, however, they will customarily wait to hear on what terms they are addressed before committing themselves to any attitude toward the speaker. Under these circumstances it is not surprising that non-Indians, who can normally expect a deferential greeting when they enter a retail store, are apt to conclude that they are being deliberately ignored, and walk out of the store. As a rule of thumb, it is believed that tourists must be greeted immediately on entry and must be waited on to the exclusion of other trade within 2 minutes or the potential customers will leave. The cash reward for such deference is usually so small that few traders bother with tourist trade; hence do not sell post cards or souvenirs.

The reputation for contrariness enjoyed by traders is widespread even among their White neighbors. It results to some extent from the characteristically ambivalent attitude toward Navahos which is held by most traders (see pp. 281–287), and is perhaps augmented by the frequent difficulty which the trader has in making himself heard as an expert on Indian affairs. Whatever stereotype of the Indian is presented to him, he is ready to counter it with evidence based on his own experience.

Traders understandably feel themselves to be better qualified than anyone else to characterize the Navaho. At the same time they find today that many of their White visitors have opinions of the Indian's nature which are as stubbornly held as their own. The superiority of their knowledge and experience is therefore established by contradicting whatever idea the visitor has as a matter of principle. If visitors are inclined to disparage or patronize, they are likely to be told that Navahos are ". . . the finest kind of people you'd want to deal with" (Leighton and Leighton, 1944, p. xvii). If, as is infinitely more common in this age, the visitor indulges in a eulogy on the Noble Redskin, he is almost sure to learn that Navahos are lazy, shiftless, and dirty. These conflicting attitudes are not merely expressed; they are actually held side by side by a very large number of traders on the Navaho Reservation.

COMMUNICATION

The principal language in which the Navaho retail trade is conducted is a jargon which traders call "Navaho" (or, more often, "Navvy" for short) and which Navahos call "trader talk." It is a form of speech known and employed almost entirely by traders and

Navahos, and reserved for trading situations. In this regard, as well as in its formal structure, it is a true "trade jargon"; one of several types of pidgins or marginal languages which have been distinguished by linguists (cf. Reinecke, 1938, pp. 109–113). It will be designated here as "Trader Navaho."

As is generally true of trade jargons, Trader Navaho does not present a mixed vocabulary of Navaho and English words (cf. Reinecke, 1938, p. 111). Its lexicon is pure Navaho, and for that reason outsiders and in many cases even traders themselves believe that they are in fact speaking acceptable Navaho. The grammer and syntax of Trader Navaho, however, retain little of the complex and inflexible sequence of morphological elements (cf. Hymes, 1956, pp. 628–632) and none of the minute differentiation of object and process categories (see Hoijer, 1945–49) found in the true Navaho speech. All of the so-called "nouns" and "verbs" of Trader Navaho occur in only a single form, and the syntax is generally reminiscent of English. Trader Navaho is sometimes said to resemble Navaho "baby talk"; to a certain extent it must be learned as a separate idiom by Navahos as well as by traders. It is not surprising, therefore, that the extent to which it is spoken and understood by Shonto Navahos varies greatly, with the result that effectiveness of trader communication as between one client and another varies to the same degree.

Less than half of Shonto's Navaho adults are capable of conducting even the simplest mercantile transaction in English (see table 13, p. 92). Some command of Trader Navaho (which can readily be acquired in 3 or 4 months) is therefore essential to the trader and is one of the qualities which distinguishes him from all his White neighbors. Every trader on the Navaho Reservation has a working knowledge of Trader Navaho; even in eastern districts where most of the Navaho population understands English it remains the basic language of trade and is considered essential to it.

The use of the trade jargon does more for the trader than simply to enable him to communicate with his non-English speaking customers. In a subtle way it also serves to emphasize his superior status with respect to his clientele as a group. For that reason Shonto's trader habitually uses Trader Navaho to address even many of his best educated customers, and is likely to initiate a conversation in English only in cases where he is especially anxious to be understood clearly.[19]

For their part educated Navaho customers commonly try to converse in English and avoid the use of Trader Navaho. An amusing, not to say absurd, result of this linguistic vying is that conver-

---

[19] The identical phenomenon has been observed with regard to the persistence of Pidgin English in Canton and Hong Kong, long after the Chinese servant groups involved had acquired an adequate command of English. (See Reinecke, 1938, pp. 112–113.)

sations can occasionally be overheard in which the Navaho speaks English and the trader replies in "Navaho," as he calls it.

At least 90 percent of all commerce in Shonto Trading Post is conducted in Trader Navaho, largely from necessity but also through the trader's preference. English is largely reserved for White customers, for a few Navahos who occasionally insist on it, and for situations in which clear understanding is essential.

Although traders vary considerably in their command of Trader Navaho (i.e., in the size of the Navaho vocabulary they control), few if any of them are sufficiently proficient to be able to understand true Navaho speech except in the most general way. It is important to note in this regard that the average trader seldom understands much of the conversations going on around him in the store—he understands fully only what is especially addressed to him in the jargon of trade. The level of effective verbal communication between trader and Navaho is therefore generally low, and is largely confined to conventional trading situations. For communication of a more abstract nature the trader, like other White people, is forced to fall back on an interpreter.

COMMUNITY SERVICES

In situations of culture contact, it has been noted that individuals and institutions ". . . may adopt a complex but limited number of roles" which ". . . may be conceptualized as constellations of behavior that are appropriate to particular situations." (Summer Seminar on Acculturation, 1954, p. 981.) This observation is perhaps nowhere better justified than in reference to the modern Navaho trading post.

The primary functions of Shonto Trading Post, which are more or less inherent in its character as a retail business concern, were described in earlier pages (pp. 184–214). Insofar as they are aimed at the common objectives of maximum sales and minimum competition, such functions are little different in principle from those of many another retail enterprise. In the modern Navaho community, however, they constitute only a small part of the total complex of functions performed by the store. Wittingly or unwittingly, every trading post has a much larger part to play in its community than simply that of mercantile agency; it is also the hub of community life and a basic channel of cross-cultural communication. Its special and sometimes unique activities as such will be described in the present section.

A NOTE ON TERMINOLOGY

Anthropologists on the whole have used the term "role" rather indiscriminately and at various levels of abstraction in their analyses of interpersonal and interinstitutional relations. Ralph Linton (1936, p. 114) noted long ago that the term could be applied either in a specific sense (as ". . . the dynamic aspect of status") or in a general sense, so that it is appropriate to speak of an institution as having a series of specific roles and at the same time a single general role which is the sum of the aforesaid. To avoid ambiguity in the present study, the term "role" is reserved exclusively for the latter, general sense. Shonto Trading Post is therefore considered to have only a single role in the Navaho community, the analysis of which will be the subject of Part 3. In the meantime it is necessary to introduce a series of substitute terms for the more specific aspects of role, as implied, for example, in the statement that an agency of culture contact ". . . may adopt a complex but limited number of roles." (Summer Seminar on Acculturation, 1954, p. 981.) Terms employed here, each at a different level of abstraction, will be "charter," "function," and "activity."

CHARTER

The term "charter" may conveniently be used to designate the basic operational sanction or raison d'etre of an institution. It may be said, then, that Shonto Trading Post is chartered as a general retail store; the Tuba City hospital as a facility for in-patient and out-patient medical treatment of Navahos, and so on. Implicit in the concept of charter are specific motivations as well as a series of overt activities. Shonto's character as a business enterprise carries with it the essential motivation of maximum profit, and a series of profit-making activities such as were described in "Retail Trade," pp. 184–214.

It is possible, however, for an institution to serve more than one purpose, and even to serve purposes other than its own. To the same degree, therefore, it is true that an institution may have more than one charter. In such cases the historic original charter, expressing the purpose of the institution itself, may be termed the formal charter, as distinguished from operational charters which have come about through use. The latter do not, therefore, necessarily imply any purpose on the part of the institution itself; they may rather represent the way in which it is wittingly or unwittingly used by those in contact with it for their own purposes.

For purposes of the present study, Shonto Trading Post may be said to have a formal charter as a business enterprise, and operational charters as a community center and as a channel of communication.

FUNCTION

The term "function" is introduced here as more or less equivalent to the more specific connotation of role; that is, to designate ". . . constellations of behavior which are appropriate to particular situations" (Summer Seminar on Acculturation, 1954, p. 981). Function may be said to express the specific expectation of those in contact with a given agency rather than the will of the agency itself. Shonto

Trading Post is considered to have a considerable number of discrete functions in the community, as diagrammed in charts J and K (pp. 249, 251).

ACTIVITY

Activities are the behavioral aspects of function, and, in a much broader sense, the empirical measure of role itself. Every function of the trading post is manifest in certain empirically observable activities, hence "constellations of behavior." The activities of Shonto Trading Post manifesting its function as a sales and credit agency were detailed on pages 184–214. Remaining activities of the trading post will be described below.

TYPES OF FUNCTIONS AND ACTIVITIES

Of the wide variety of functions performed by Shonto Trading Post, only a portion are inherent in its formal charter as a general store. These are the functions which contribute directly to the ultimate profit goal, and are to that extent deliberate, voluntary, and initiated or sustained by the store itself. They may appropriately be termed "charter functions."

There remains a considerable series of functions arising out of the operational charters of the trading post as a community center and a channel of cross-cultural communication (cf. pp. 231–267). Although in actual performance these functions can often be made to serve the interests of the store in one way or another (see pp. 267–297), they are largely initiated by and sustained for the benefit of others. They are therefore designated as "ancillary functions" in distinction to "charter functions." Ancillary functions may be further distinguished as between those which serve primarily the interests of Navahos, and those which are initiated by and for White institutions.

CHARTER FUNCTIONS

Many of the charter functions of Shonto Trading Post were described in "Retail Trade," pp. 184–214; particularly those contributing to the operational objectives of maximum sales and minimum competition. These are functions which in principle are common to many retail businesses. In addition to these, however, the Navaho trading post has indirect but nevertheless significant opportunities, probably unique in retail trade, to increase its profit by increasing the cash income and buying power of its clientele. Such activities constitute a series of what may appropriately be termed charter functions, even though they are not normally associated with trade. In addition to being a mercantile agency, Shonto Trading Post serves its Navaho clientele directly and effectively as an employment agency, a benefit agent, and a bank (cf. Kluckhohn and Leighton, 1946, p. 38; Sanders

CHART E.—Charter functions and activities of Shonto Trading Post[1]

[Officially sanctioned activities in italic]

Formal charter	Objectives	Functions	Activities
Retail Mercantile Enterprise.	Minimum competition..	Territorial Monopoly....	See pp. 167–184.
		Credit Agency..........	See pp. 167–214.
	Maximum sales.........	Credit Agency..........	See pp. 167–214.
		Sales Agency...........	See pp. 167–214.
		Employment Agency....	*Railroad claims agency.*[2]
			Other job references.
			Job information.
			Job advice.
	Maximum consumer buying power.	Benefit Agent..........	*Railroad claims agency.*[2]
			Agent for tribal relief.
			Agent for state welfare.
			Agent for wool bonus.
			Agent for back pay.
			Contact with charities.
		Bank..................	*Savings banking.*[3]
			Budgeting.[3]
			Moneylending.
			Financing.
			Financial advice.

[1] For explanation of categories see "A Note on Terminology," pp. 214–216.
[2] See "Railroad Work," pp. 129–133.
[3] See "Types of Trade," pp. 186–201.

et al., 1953, pp. 233–234). The overall pattern of charter functions and activities is diagrammed in chart E.

EMPLOYMENT AGENCY

No function of Shonto Trading Post is more important to the Navaho community of today than its complex of activities in securing wage employment for its clientele (cf. Collier and Collier, 1953, p. 220). In the case of railroad labor, the trader's activity as recruiter and contractor is given official sanction in his appointment as claims agent for the Railroad Retirement Board. This activity has been described in earlier pages ("Railroad Work," pp. 129–133). It is not by any means the limit of the trader's function as an employment agent. He often refers Navahos to other jobs, particularly at the Navajo Ordnance Depot, and sometimes furnishes them with recommendations. Shonto's trader has also been active in promoting the employment of favored clients in local jobs at Shonto School, Navajo National Monument, and on the Tuba City police force, and has frequently furnished character references.

Shonto Trading Post regularly disseminates job information, partly in its own interest and partly at the behest of potential employers. The Arizona State Employment Service maintains a field office at Tuba City, but its agent has visited Shonto in person only once to the writer's knowledge. As a rule he contacts the trader by telephone, requesting him to circulate information and to post clearance orders on the store bulletin board. On two occasions in 1955 agricultural employers wrote directly to Shonto's trader, requesting his assistance in recruiting labor.

Even when no information is posted or volunteered, Shonto men not uncommonly seek job information and advice from the trading post. The annual cycle of economic activity (see "The Economic Cycle," pp. 141–145) is such that Navaho men sometimes want or need work at times when there are no regular openings; in such cases they are likely to rely on the trader to "find something for them" or at least to stake them to a cash loan sufficient to take them off the reservation in search of a job. (cf. also Collier and Collier, 1953, p. 220.) Acting as employment agent, in sum, is one of the important institutional functions of Shonto Trading Post, and is so recognized by both Navahos and employers.

BENEFIT AGENT

Shonto Trading Post regularly and sometimes officially acts as an intermediary for Navahos in securing other financial benefits as well as jobs (see Luomala, 1938, p. 5; Sanders et al., 1953, p. 234). In this category are the trader's activities as claims agent in securing railroad unemployment compensation for his customers (see "Railroad Work," pp. 129–133). Equally essential, from the point of view of the Navaho community, is the trader's assistance and often initiative in obtaining public welfare benefits for qualified individuals. It was mentioned earlier ("Economic Interdependence," pp. 103–108) that since Public Assistance was first instituted for Navahos in 1948 it has become the recognized and accepted function of elderly persons and households to contribute relief income to the overall welfare of the residence group. Shonto's oldsters, and others qualified for relief, rely very largely on the trader to keep track of their qualifications and to institute application and furnish information in their behalf whenever appropriate. Most correspondence regarding welfare applications or benefits is never seen by the applicant or recipient; it is conducted entirely between the trader and the State Department of Public Welfare. Letters from the welfare department addressed to Shonto individuals are removed from the mail and opened by the trader as a matter of regular policy, and in many cases (i.e., requests for further information) they are answered by him without even consulting the addressee.

The action of many traders in dealing with the State Department of Public Welfare on behalf of their clients is simplified and also given at least covert sanction by the fact that trading posts are the officially designated points where caseworkers make their quarterly direct contacts with welfare recipients. The Nava-Hopi Unit of the welfare department, like many another Government agency, has long since learned that locating and contacting Navahos at home, given the physiography of the Navaho Reservation and the circumstances of Navaho residence and society, is a logistic impossibility. Instead the welfare caseworker appoints a date in advance on which he will be at the trading post, and asks the trader to see that all welfare cases are on hand on that day. In the course of passing the word along to the community, the trader is at the same time in a position to recommend that every other individual who has even a remote chance of securing welfare benefits also be on hand as a new applicant.

Use of trading posts as points of contact with welfare cases has the further advantage in most instances of allowing traders to act as interpreters, and to a certain extent as "prompters," when applicants and recipients are interviewed. It is often true that virtually all of the information upon which case reports are based is supplied either by or through the traders. This relationship prevails throughout the western part of the Navaho Reservation.

There have been numerous other instances in which Shonto's trader has been designated or has chosen to play the part of benefit agent for his clientele. In 1956 the Navaho Tribal Council voted the sum of $1,000 to each council constituency on the reservation, to be distributed equally among households as "emergency drouth relief." Instead of making a cash payment the Tribe chose to have the stipulated sums issued by the local traders in the form of merchandise. For this purpose what were essentially "due bills" were issued (see "Direct Exchange," 199–201), redeemable only in merchandise at the store. Stores were in turn reimbursed by the Navaho Tribe upon submission of the receipted bills.

Shonto Trading Post inaugurated another important benefit activity in 1955 in connection with the "incentive payment" allowed to wool growers by the Commodity Credit Corporation (see "Livestock Income," pp. 120–123). In order to receive this bonus (amounting to 17 cents for every pound sold) it was necessary for wool growers to submit complicated application forms listing, among other things, amounts sold and dates of sale. On his own initiative Shonto's trader carefully recorded this information during wool sales in 1955, and, at the conclusion of sales, filled out application forms and had them signed by each of his wool producing clients. These were then kept at the store ready for submission as soon as the stipulated period expired in 1956.

A frequent benefit activity of Shonto Trading Post, on request, has been writing for back pay owed to Shonto men by various employers. Far and away the most common client for this service is the local tribal councilman. Immediately upon conclusion of every public meeting his first act is to demand that the trader write for him to Window Rock, informing the tribal chairman that he has held a meeting and is therefore entitled to his $20 stipend. Letters have also been written to railroads and to a movie company, requesting back pay. At various times Shonto's trader has also written to the Navaho Tribal Council for emergency relief (no reply), to the Navy Department in regard to a G.I. allotment (eventually granted), and to a private charity (no known reply) at the instigation of Navaho clients.

It was noted earlier that Shonto Trading Post is the principal repository for the community's capital; not only in the form of pawn (cf. Kluckhohn and Leighton, 1946, p. 38; Leighton and Leighton, 1944, p. 19) but also in untraded due bills (see "Pawn" and "Direct Exchange," pp. 195–201). There are seldom any considerable sums of money circulating in the community, but on those occasions when individuals do come into appreciable sums of money they are nearly always banked in the trading-post vault, whence they are apt to be drawn out piecemeal over a period of weeks or months.

Trading posts, however, are much more than merely savings banks. As the only financial institutions of any kind in many communities, they have an equally important function as moneylending and financial agencies (see Coolidge and Coolidge, 1930, p. 68; Luomala, 1938, p. 5). Most traders lend small sums of cash (up to $10 or $15) against pawn quite freely, considering them a fairly secure source of income. Shonto and neighboring trading posts charge a flat 10 percent interest on all such loans—far less than Navahos ordinarily charge one another (cf. Franciscan Fathers, 1910, pp. 492–493). In a few cases where the prospect of repayment is good, far larger loans have been made either in the interest of increased Navaho income or as outright investments. It is regular practice to loan money to reliable wage workers who wish to go in search of jobs on their own, and Shonto men on occasion have borrowed as much as $200 to take them to Los Angeles. In earlier days it was common practice for traders to stake weavers to their materials (see Amsden, 1934, p. 179) and silversmiths to their tools (Kluckhohn and Leighton, 1946, p. 39): a calculated investment in future production and markets.

Nowadays cash loans are occasionally granted to finance potentially profitable enterprises. One Shonto man borrowed $250 to develop an alfalfa farm in the canyon. Shonto's owner even went so far as to put up $5,000 to back the Navaho-operated Tsegi Trading Post, on the theory (which proved to be only partly correct) that the store would pull trade primarily from Kayenta rather than from Shonto.

No description of any Navaho trading post would be complete which included only its directly profit-motivated activities. Shonto and most other trading posts, particularly in more or less remote communities, are important as community centers and as intercultural communication points no less than as mercantile agencies. As

Chart F.—Ancillary functions and activities of Shonto Trading Post[1]

[Officially sanctioned activities in italic.]

Operational charter	Objectives	Functions	Activities
Culture Contact Agency.	(For Navahos)	Information Agency	Interp. of White culture and life. Teaching spec. White practices. *Information on Govt. programs.* Info. on Govt. and Tribal law. *Bulletin board.* News agency.
		Communication Agency.	*Mail distributor.* Public scribe. *Telephone facility.* Direct contact with outside. *Interpreter.*
		Benefit Agent	*Agent for agricultural benefits.* Securing medical benefits. Securing police intervention.
		Protective Agency	*Financial protection.* Protection from govt. programs. Protection from police.
		Community Services	*Miscellaneous direct services.*
		Promotion Agent	*Railroad claims agency. Miscellaneous labor recruiting. Publicity for Govt. programs. Bulletin board announcements.*
		Distributor	*Distribution of seed, etc. Distribution of surplus commodities. Distribution of emergency relief. Dissemination of information.*
	(For Whites)	Communication Agency.	*Direct contact with Navahos.* Interpreter.
Community Center.	(For Navahos)	Community Center	*Official meeting place.* Unofficial meeting place. News agency. Social and recreational center.

[1] For explanation of categories see "A Note on Terminology," pp. 214-216.

such they have, wittingly or unwittingly, many additional functions to perform for their customers. These are undertaken ostensibly in the interest of good will; also, perhaps, from a recognition that there is no one else to perform them.

Most important, from the point of view of the community, is the complex of functions performed by the trading post for or at the instigation of Navahos themselves. In addition to its various charter functions, Shonto Trading Post may be said to serve its clientele as an information agency, a means of communication, a benefit agency, and even in a sense as a protective agency. (See chart F.)

INFORMATION AGENCY

Shonto's trader, like most other traders, is the only White man who is in regular or even frequent contact with most of the Navahos in his community, and the only one to whom many of them ever have access. As such he stands as the representative of, and spokesman for, the White world in general, and is called upon to account for all manner of White behavior and enterprise (cf. the characterizations of Coolidge and Coolidge, 1930, pp. 68–69; Sanders et al., 1953, pp. 233–234). Navahos leafing through copies of Life or The National Geographic Magazine, which they find in the store, constantly question the trader about the things they see depicted there. Older people have frequently manifested the same interest and credulity with regard to science-fiction and horror comic books—their experience with the outside world being insufficient to distinguish fact from fantasy.

Although most Shonto Navahos manifest a lively curiosity about all manner of White behavior, they are naturally interested chiefly in the things which directly affect them. The explanation and interpretation of Government policies and programs is undoubtedly the most frequently sought of all information. Direct contact between Shonto Navahos and Government officials is rare, and the circumstances are in any case seldom conducive to effective communication of ideas (see pp. 256–263). Time after time, the latter function falls to the trader (cf. Coolidge and Coolidge, 1930, p. 69; Luomala, 1938, p. 5).

Another important though unofficial activity of Shonto Trading Post is in apprising its Navaho clientele of the provisions of tribal and White law to which they are theoretically subject (see "Law and Order," pp. 68–70). Except in regard to the prohibition of drinking, few Shonto individuals have any very clear conception of these legal codes and their implications. In the past they have sometimes run afoul of the law without knowing why, and it is commonly believed that the police (particularly the Flagstaff police) have the power to arrest at any time without cause. It is not surprising, therefore, that Shonto people eagerly seek information from the trader about legal and police powers.

Finally, and perhaps most important of all, the great majority of Shonto residents regularly rely on the store as a kind of newspaper (cf. Coolidge and Coolidge, 1930, p. 67) to keep them informed on all manner of significant events, current and future. Jobs, meetings, visits by the public health nurse, signup days, and every kind of activity that may affect the life of the community are announced by and through the trader, and it is universally regarded as his duty to keep the community informed. For this purpose virtually every trading post on the Navaho Reservation maintains a prominent bulletin board,[20] which constitutes the true newspaper of Navaholand (cf. Kluckhohn and Leighton, 1946, p. 38). The importance of Shonto Trading Post as a news agency is especially great, since no newspapers or periodicals of any kind are received by Navahos in the community. The tribal councilman gets a free subscription to Adahooniligii, the monthly Navaho-language newspaper published at Window Rock, but he is not able to read it.

---

[20] In addition to the conventional bulletin board setup, Shonto Trading Post often displays a slate on which what might be called the "headlines" are posted. It is hung up in a prominent place whenever an announcement of special importance to the community is to be made. Sample headlines during April 1956, were: "Next RR signup day Thursday, April 5;" "Public health nurse will be at the school April 12—Thursday;" "Meeting here April 16 about hospitals;" "Relief man from Phoenix will be here May 8— Tuesday;" and "All pawn must be taken out during wool sales or it will be sold!"

COMMUNICATION AGENCY

Shonto Trading Post undertakes a variety of official and unofficial activities as a means of communication between the community and the outside world. It is, to begin with, the regular mail distribution agency for the district, since all Shonto's Navahos receive their letters addressed in care of the store. This gives the trader the advantage of handling the mail (see "Book Credit," pp. 188–195) without the inconvenience and responsibilities of running a post office. The trader picks up the mail from the post office at Red Lake (P.O. Tonalea), 30 miles to the southwest. Mail for Navahos is kept in pigeonholes behind the store counter, and handed out on demand—usually to any member of the addressee's residence group. Outgoing mail is collected at the store and delivered to the post office.

Inseparable from the postal facility is the activity of the trader as a public scribe. During one month (8 mail deliveries) when records were made, 88 Shonto individuals in 61 households received a total of 191 letters and packages—largely from absent schoolchildren (who are required to write home every 2 weeks) and from husbands working on the railroad. Less than a quarter of the recipients were able to read and answer their mail themselves. Not all letters are faithfully answered, but the volume of outgoing mail is about half of that incoming.

The system of writing in the Navaho language promulgated by the Bureau of Indian Affairs (cf. Young and Morgan, 1943; 1946, p. ii; Underhill, 1953, p. 285) in recent years has no adherents at Shonto. All letters written to and by members of the community are in English, even though the senders and recipients usually cannot speak it, let alone read and write it. A heavy burden of translation and of writing therefore falls upon the handful of literates in the community (see "Acculturation," pp. 90–93), including the trader. The latter's services are especially sought in writing and reading "business letters;" i.e., any letters to or from White individuals or agencies.[21]

The importance of Shonto Trading Post as an intermediary in communication is further enhanced by its telephone facility. Given the difficulties and uncertainties of travel on the Navaho Reservation, the importance of the telephone in the modern era can hardly be exaggerated. White individuals and agencies which have never had face-to-face contact have become closely acquainted and worked together for years over the telephone, and even Navahos are coming to rely on it heavily in their dealings with Government agencies at

---

[21] Since Shonto's Navaho residents do little or no reading, even the best educated of them are largely unfamiliar with the formal, written vocabulary and grammar of English, and hence usually unable to cope with letters from Whites. Letters written by Navahos are highly distinctive in this regard, in that they are rendered in vernacular speech, complete with slang expressions and interjections. It is almost possible to hear the speaker's accent in a Navaho letter.

Tuba City, and particularly with the hospital. As an alternative to a 110-mile round trip its advantages are obvious, although Shonto's telephone is out of operation for an average of 1 or 2 days a week due to primitive equipment and faulty installation.

There are two telephones in Shonto community, one at the store and one at the school. The latter is located in the teachers' residence and is for their use only, so that the trading-post telephone is the only set which is practically accessible to Navahos. It is used from time to time to call various Government agencies such as the court and the Soil and Moisture Conservation office, but most of all for inquiries to the Tuba City hospital concerning admissions, condition of patients, and times of discharge. Month in and month out Shonto Trading Post averages at least three such calls a week. A few individuals are willing to talk directly into the set, but the great majority require the trader to speak for them. In spite of the nuisance involved, telephoning is a privilege accorded to all Shonto Navahos for any reasonable purpose.

Finally, Shonto's trader sometimes serves as a face-to-face intermediary between local Navahos and outside agencies. Because of his existing and formalized relationships with his White neighbors and with such institutions as the Railroad Retirement Board and the State Department of Public Welfare, he is occasionally asked to convey information directly to them, or to find out various matters from them. It should be mentioned also that the trader is not infrequently called on to act as an interpreter, as for example in interviews between caseworkers and Navaho welfare claimants (see pp. 218–219).

BENEFIT AGENT

Shonto's trader is called upon by his customers to secure nonfinancial as well as remunerative benefits (cf. "Charter Functions," pp. 216–220) for them. He may even act as an intermediary in their distribution, as was noted earlier in the case of tribal emergency relief (cf. also Coolidge and Coolidge, 1930, pp. 68–69; Sanders et al., 1953, pp. 233–234). In recent years, for example, he has handed out on request seedling fruit and shade trees, alfalfa seed, and rodent poison for the Bureau of Indian Affairs Soil and Moisture Conservation program, and surplus powdered milk (for supplementary lamb feeding) provided by the Department of Agriculture. He has assisted Shonto families in their relations with Government agencies at Tuba City and Kayenta in such matters as borrowing a tractor for plowing, and in securing construction of charcos and check dams on their grazing territories.

Most of all, Shonto's Navahos require the assistance of the trader in securing the benefits of White medicine. It has not been many years since traders or their wives usually had to take critically ill patients to the hospital. Nowadays there are enough Navaho-owned pickups in operation so that this is seldom necessary. However, it is still often up to the trader to arrange transportation to the hospital, and it is almost always necessary for him to put up the $3 required to pay for the trip.[22]

The trader at Shonto usually tries to facilitate the admission of local residents to the hospital by calling in advance to report their impending arrival and condition. He has also, on occasion, arranged to have his Navaho neighbors sent to the medical center at Fort Defiance for eye treatment and glasses, and in one or two instances has spotted active tuberculars and referred them to the hospital for sanatorium treatment.

Among the benefits obtainable through Shonto Trading Post must be included police action, though not protection. As noted earlier ("Law and Order," pp. 68–74) the law enforcement situation on the western Navaho Reservation is such that the action of the police at Shonto can only be punitive rather than protective. Nevertheless police action can be and sometimes is deliberately invoked as a retaliatory measure by Shonto Navahos. In such cases almost without exception they ask the trader to call the police for them and to back up their complaint.

PROTECTIVE AGENCY

In certain respects Shonto Navahos have come to look to the trading post to protect them from external threats (cf. especially Kluckhohn and Leighton, 1946, p. 79). It may be said that insofar as there is potential conflict or disharmony between Navaho traditions and the conditions of White life, it is often up to the trading post to reconcile or to forestall it.

The most immediate and significant protection afforded by nearly any trading post to its Navaho clientele is financial protection against the vicissitudes of a seasonal semisubsistence economy. This activity has been described earlier (see "Credit," pp. 108–109). In a more general sense, however, it is the function of the store to intervene between Navahos and other, sometimes coercive, White agencies.

In a sense, Shonto Trading Post protects its clientele by concealing information about them which is potentially detrimental to their welfare. Examples of this type are numerous. For instance, large flocks of sheep are thought to benefit the trader as much as the Navaho owners, and it is expected that the trader will keep to himself his knowledge that many Shonto flocks are considerably over permitted range capacities (see "Livestock," pp. 111–120). In referring or recommending men for jobs, the trader habitually conceals from prospective employers any information which might be detrimental to employ-

---

[22] The Tuba City hospital ostensibly operates an ambulance, but during 10 years it has never been despatched to Shonto despite two fatal and two near-fatal auto wrecks and several serious riding accidents.

ment, such as police records, previous unsuccessful job experiences, and in some cases even ages. (One Shonto man worked on the railroad until he was 63, and several others have worked into their late 50's, although the official age limit is 50.)

In spite of the normally close relationship and cooperation between store and community school (see "Intracultural Relations at the Contact Level," pp. 253–256), Shonto's trader has been known to conceal from the school teachers his knowledge that certain families had not sent all their children to school. Also, and time after time, the trader keeps to himself his awareness that recipients of public welfare have assets (e.g., jewelry and, in a few cases, livestock) which are not reported to the State Department of Public Welfare. One Shonto household has drawn Aid to Dependent Children (see "Welfare," p. 136) to the extent of nearly $150 a month for several years on the strength of a case report that the husband is over 65 and has no assets, although he is known in the community to be considerably younger, and has over 100 head of sheep and several cattle. The activities of Shonto's trader in these respects can be legitimately summed up by saying that in the interplay of White and Navaho societies he serves him own interest best by keeping his own counsel, and does not feel compelled to volunteer information unless requested to do so. It is a vitally significant feature of the role of the trader that he does not hold himself responsible to any other White agency in dealing with the Navaho (see "Intracultural Relations at the Contact Level," pp. 253–256).

Although Shonto people occasionally ask the trader to call the police in their behalf, much more commonly they expect him to help protect them from the law (cf. Kluckhohn and Leighton, 1946, p. 79). Here again they are able to take advantage of the fact that he does not feel any obligation to uphold or to enforce the law, since that is the charter function of others. Instead he may warn inebriates or wanted persons in advance if he knows that the police are on their way to Shonto, and may help to hustle them off the scene. It is expected that he will not volunteer information about their whereabouts.

An extreme example of this sort of conspiracy occurred in 1955, when a Shonto man was formally charged with assault and battery (for beating a "witch"—see "Religion and Ritual," pp. 70–74). The trader found an off-reservation job for the offender and shipped him out of the community before the Tuba City police were able to take any action; he subsequently replied to police inquiries with the assertion that the individual in question had left the reservation, but that he himself did not know where he had gone. Still later he counseled the fugitive's daughter on several occasions to write to her father and advise him against coming home until the "heat was off," and in this manner actually succeeded in keeping him at liberty for several months.

When Shonto people do get into trouble with the law, it is always expected that the trader will advance the money necessary to pay their bail and/or fines.

GENERAL FACTOTUM

There remains a variety of ancillary activities which are or have been performed by traders in all parts of the reservation in behalf of their Navaho clientele, and which are not readily classifiable in terms of function. Some of them are performed at Navaho instigation, and some on the trader's own initiative. They include direct assistance in such matters as repairing trucks and sewing machines, and in other matters in which a White man's special knowledge or experience may be needed. They include also the trader's action in cooperating with charitable institutions to stage their now-famous "Christmas parties," and the distribution of various gifts. Finally, they include the unofficial function of community historian and the recording of births, marriages, and divorces, not to mention building coffins and burying the dead.[23]

ANCILLARY FUNCTIONS FOR WHITES

The modern Navaho trading post is a two-way channel of communication, and White individuals and agencies as well as Navahos take advantage of its special cross-cultural position. If the ancillary functions of the store in behalf of Whites are secondary to those in behalf of Navahos, it is to some extent because the interests of the store are more clearly allied with those of Navahos than with those of other White institutions. It is also true that a far greater number of Navahos are necessarily concerned with the White world than vice versa. Nevertheless those few Americans and American institutions which are chartered to deal with Navahos regularly make use of the trading post in doing so (see especially Coolidge and Coolidge, 1930, pp. 68–69; Luomala, 1938, p. 5). On behalf of its White neighbors as well as outsiders, Shonto Trading Post sometimes functions as a promoter, a distributor, an agency of communication, and a source of information.

Other White agencies generally recognize that a trading post probably has more influence (see "The Structure of Contact," pp. 231–237) with its clientele than they themselves are likely to have, and are often anxious to make use of this influence by enlisting the store to promote their own programs. Activities of this kind in connection

---

[23] A variety of descriptive accounts will be found to elaborate on these more or less miscellaneous functions of the trading post. Among the best are Coolidge and Coolidge, 1930, pp. 67–69; Luomala, 1938, p. 5; Sanders et al., 1953, pp. 233–234; and Underhill, 1956, pp. 180–195. Somewhat more dramatized are the strictly popular accounts of Gillmor and Wetherill, 1934, passim; Faunce, 1934, pp. 98–148; Hannum, 1946, passim; and Schmedding, 1951, pp. 306–346.

with labor recruiting have already been mentioned (see "Employment Agency," pp. 217–218). In a more general sense it is also true that Government agents frequently ask the trader to speak on behalf of their programs and to explain and publicize them through their day-to-day relations with Navahos. All traders are expected to display miscellaneous health, school, and livestock posters on their bulletin boards, as requested by interested agencies. The Shonto missionary regularly employed the store bulletin board to announce and advertise his own meetings and services.

Its frequent and predictable contact with all or nearly all members of the community (see "Frequency of Shopping," pp. 201–204) makes the Navaho trading post invaluable as a distribution agency. Several activities of Shonto Trading Post as a distributor were mentioned earlier ("Benefit Agent," pp. 224–225), notably the distribution of seedlings and seed for the Indian Bureau, of powdered milk for the Department of Agriculture, and of emergency relief rations for the Navaho tribe. Most of all, outside institutions and especially Government agencies rely on the trader to disseminate information, by word of mouth and through posted notices.

Except in highly formalized situations, Government agencies seldom if ever make use of the mails in communication with Navahos. (It may take a letter up to a week to reach Shonto from Tuba City.) The telephone, as noted earlier, is infinitely more effective. The hospital, court, and other agencies, and even Shonto school, characteristically get in touch with individual Navahos on all occasions by relaying messages through the trader. Even when Government or State officials visit the community in person, they normally come only to Shonto Trading Post and often find it necessary to employ the trader as interpreter.

Most of all, the trader throughout the reservation is generally recognized as the only consistently reliable source of information concerning his district and its inhabitants (see Coolidge and Coolidge, 1930, p. 68, and Luomala, 1938, p. 5). He is widely conceded by his White neighbors to be the only one who really knows his Navahos personally, and as such he is sought out for every kind of detail which may be required by administrative agency. From month to month Shonto Trading Post is called upon, by mail, telephone, and in person, to supply such things as credit references to Flagstaff auto dealers, verification of relief qualifications to the State Department of Public Welfare, job experience records to the Railroad Retirement Board, character references to prospective reservation employers, genealogical data and vital statistics to the school, information on individual whereabouts to the court, and even case histories to the hospital. The trading post, in other words, is the primary source of information on the Navaho community upon which all other agencies depend.

Finally, on the strength of their special position and relationships, traders in general enjoy a reputation as authorities on certain aspects of Navaho life and culture which is seldom challenged by their White neighbors. Their supposed ability to speak the language (cf. "Communication," pp. 212–214) is in itself often enough to inspire awe even among other persons who have regular contact with Navahos (cf. Coolidge and Coolidge, 1930, p. 68; Underhill, 1956, p. 180). Shonto's trader finds himself again and again consulted to interpret Navaho thought and behavior not only by tourists but also occasionally by Government agents. The White world would seem to expect him to speak for the Navaho just as the Navaho expects him to speak for the White world.

COMMUNITY CENTER

Shonto Trading Post has one operational charter and function which is entirely automatic: that of community center. It requires no initiative on the part of the trader, and involves the store as a location rather than as an institution. Nevertheless the importance of this aspect of the trading post has long been recognized, and has been given official sanction in that the same location was chosen for the building of Shonto school and various other Government installations.

Nearly all observers of the Navaho scene (e.g., Coolidge and Coolidge, 1930, p. 68; Kluckhohn and Leighton, 1946, pp. 38–39; McCombe, Vogt, and Kluckhohn, 1951, pp. 21–24; Sanders et al., 1953, p. 234) have been struck by the purely social significance of the trading post in Navaho life—by the amount of visiting, play, drinking, "horsetrading," and otherwise noncommercial Navaho activities which are always and apparently necessarily associated with the store. The basis for this particular trading post function is not far to seek. In modern times the store has supplemented, if not supplanted, one of the important aspects of native ritualism in providing the most common opportunity for Navahos to associate in groups larger than the residence group.

As Kluckhohn and Leighton (1946, pp. 51–52) have observed:

. . . as is natural for isolated people, the greatest pleasure lies in an occasion which brings crowds together; and in all the major recreational activities there are common threads: the exchange of news and gossip, seeing and being seen in one's best finery, laughing and joking with old friends, opportunities for sexual adventures. Drinking must be mentioned as another diversion for an increasing number of Navahos on these occasions. There is also an opportunity at public gatherings for some serious business, for jewelry and other articles are bought and sold, trades of animals or equipment are arranged, and parents can look over prospective mates for their children.

The above was written primarily to describe the great public rituals of Navaho life, but travelers as well as readers of popular accounts will recognize its entire applicability to the social atmosphere of the trading post.

Both Whites and Navahos have long recognized the essential function of the store as a community center and assembly point, and have utilized it accordingly. As noted earlier, the Bureau of Indian Affairs chose a series of sites immediately adjoining the trading post for various of its own installations, and in 1955 the Shonto missionary completed the little settlement. Community meetings, called by the tribal councilman or the grazing committee, are always held under the cottonwood trees on the store grounds. The store is also important as an informal meeting place where individual Navahos often arrange to meet, and sometimes leave messages or money for one another.

Finally, as a community center and as a communicative agency, the trading post and its bulletin board serve as the newspaper of the community (cf. Coolidge and Coolidge, 1930, p. 68).

SUMMARY

The day is long gone when the trading post alone represented the farthest frontier of American life in Navaholand and was its only source of contact with the outside world (see, e.g., Kluckhohn and Leighton, 1946, p. 79; Sanders et al., 1953, p. 233). Modern Shonto Trading Post must share this role with a school and a national monument (also a missionary in 1955) within the community, and with some 40 other contact institutions of all varieties in the general northwestern Navaho area (cf. map 2, p. 31). Nevertheless, in the number and variety of its functions, the predominant position of the trading post as the representative of modern American culture in Shonto community remains largely unchallenged. Perhaps 90 percent of all contact and communication between Navaho and White sociocultural systems still passes through the trading post. It is still largely true, also, that Navahos rely on the store to interpret American culture for them; to forestall their potential conflicts with it; and to guide and advise their dealings with it in every phase of life from recording births to building coffins. The sources as well as the results of this position of paramount "cross-cultural influence" will be the subject of Part 3.

PART 3: THE ROLE OF THE TRADING POST

THE STRUCTURE OF CONTACT

"Retail Trade," pp. 184–214, and "Community Services," pp. 214–230, were concerned with those direct relationships, economic and otherwise, which exist between modern Shonto Trading Post and its Navaho clientele. It remains, in Part 3, to consider the same relationships from a broader point of view, as forming part of the overall pattern of Navaho-White culture contact. The trading post will be examined not as an economic institution, but as one of a number of active agents of modern American culture.

Even within the narrow confines of Shonto community, the trading post must share its role as contact institution with several other White agencies. Alongside it, in 1955, were the community school, the missionary, and Navajo National Monument. To these must be added certain institutions outside the community which have frequent contact with its members: Government offices at Tuba City, Flagstaff businesses, and off-reservation job situations.

In spite of its historical precedence, therefore (see "Development of the Modern Community," pp. 42–52), Shonto Trading Post cannot a priori be considered the primary agent of American culture in the Navaho community. Its special role as such, the implications of which will be considered in "Cross-Cultural Role," pp. 267–297, must be established in contrast to the roles of other contact institutions. It will be necessary, therefore, to analyze the overall contact situation at Shonto in such a way as to differentiate clearly the parts played by the different American institutions involved.

THEORETICAL FOUNDATIONS

THE STRUCTURAL ANALYSIS OF CULTURE CONTACT

Anthropologists over the past quarter century have produced several general outlines for the study of culture contact (e.g., Redfield, Linton, and Herskovits, 1936; Linton, 1940, pp. ix–x; Malinowski, 1945, p. 73; Summer Seminar on Acculturation, 1954). All of them, in one way or another, have taken the position that "contact" cannot be approached as an abstract phenomenon without reference to specific physical and social situations involving contact between specific individuals and/or culture products. "Cultures do not meet, but people who are their carriers do" as the recent report of the Summer Seminar on Acculturation (1954, p. 980) expressed it. Culture contact, therefore, takes place within a social context or system which should be capable of structural-functional analysis on much the same terms as other social systems (cf. Malinowski, 1945, pp. 14–15).

Involved in this approach to culture contact are several implications which are fundamental in the present study. First, it is assumable that individual carriers of the same general culture may vary considerably as to what part of their own culture they know and are capable of transmitting (cf. Summer Seminar on Acculturation, 1954, pp. 980–981). Secondly, the social and physical environment within which carriers of different cultures meet may vary equally. Finally, the character of the contacting individuals, together with the circumstances which surround their contact, will go far toward determining the cultural effects of the contact itself. In sum, the effects of culture contact, both quantitative and qualitative, are determined by variables in the contact situation no less than by the character of the cultures involved.

It may be assumed, on this basis, that the cultural impact of each and any of Shonto's contact institutions upon the Navaho community will depend in considerable measure upon its own special character.

QUALITATIVE VARIABILITY IN CULTURE CONTACT

In its general consideration of intercultural relations, the Summer Seminar on Acculturation (1954, pp. 980–984) noted, as variable factors, "intercultural roles" and "intercultural communication." The former, in particular, comprehends those conditions which may produce qualitative differences in the pattern of contact between two cultures. It was observed that

> As carriers of traditions . . . contacting individuals never know their entire cultures and never convey all they know of them to one another. That part of their cultural inventory which they do transmit is conditioned primarily by their reasons for making the contact, that is, by the cultural concomitants of the role that they assume in dealing with an alien group. [Summer Seminar on Acculturation, 1954, pp. 980–981.]

The general heading "Intercultural Roles" is perhaps sufficient, for purposes of a universal model, to cover the most common qualitative variables in culture contact. In dealing with a specific contact situation, however, it should normally be possible to achieve a much more refined and precise identification of the factors which differentiate contact institutions one from another. In the analysis of culture contact at Shonto which follows, some 20 factors have been identified which are assumed to affect the impact of White agencies upon the Navaho community (see "A Model for the Analysis of Influence at Shonto," pp. 234–237, and table 37, p. 235). A majority of these may be said to influence the nature, rather than the intensity, of culture contact.

QUANTITATIVE VARIABILITY IN CULTURE CONTACT

All models for the structural analysis of culture contact have given some attention to differences in kind of contact resulting from variables in the contact situation. On the other hand, differences in degree of contact have been comparatively ignored. To some extent such differences are subsumed under the heading "Intercultural Communication" in the model formulated by the Summer Seminar (1954, p. 982). It is noted here that

> Intercultural communication may be specifically or diffusely channeled. Specificity in this sense has to do with whether a cross-cultural message appropriately applies to any member or just to certain members of a receiving group. Extremely diffuse are forms of dominance, discrimination, fear, respect, or approbation which uniformly engage most members of one group vis-a-vis the other. [Summer Seminar on Acculturation, 1954, p. 982.]

If culture contact takes place within any sort of normal social system, it is apparent that differences in degree as well as in kind of contact must be comprehended. In purely physical terms, the frequency and duration of direct contact between Shonto institutions and Navaho individuals varies enormously (cf. chart L, p. 258). Moreover, there are considerable variations among them in regard to ability and opportunity to communicate, and in Navaho cultural receptivity. Many of the factors in the contact situation at Shonto, identified in table 37, affect what might be called the intensity of contact, in contrast to the character of contact, between Navahos and Whites.

THE MEASURE OF CULTURE CONTACT

Anthropologists have, in general, directed their attention toward culture contact as one of the obvious causes of culture change (cf. Albrecht, 1946; Adair and Vogt, 1949; Eaton, 1952). The term "culture contact" is itself used as a synonym for "acculturation" by British as well as some American students (e.g., Mair, 1938; Malinowski, 1945; Wilson and Wilson, 1945; Herskovits, 1938). From this approach culture contact is necessarily viewed as a process (cf. Fortes, 1936) which must therefore be studied diachronically (cf. Redfield, Linton, and Herskovits, 1936; Linton, 1940, pp. ix–x; Malinowski, 1945, p. 73; Spindler and Goldschmidt, 1952; Summer Seminar on Acculturation, 1954). The effects of contact over a given length of time are measured in terms of certain kinds and degrees of culture change.

In the case of Shonto, data for such a diachronic approach to culture contact are not available. It should nevertheless be possible, to a certain extent, to assess the effects of contact synchronically. If it can be assumed that the presence of certain factors in the contact situation will, over the years, influence the outcome of culture contact, then it should be equally legitimate to assume that the presence of the same factors at any given moment in culture contact will affect the ways and degrees in which contact institutions may influence behavior at that moment. The social system at Shonto, within which culture contact takes place, carries with it at any given time a power structure and a communication network which enable specific White institutions to influence day-to-day Navaho behavior in specific ways. As noted above, the extent and character of such influence varies widely as between one contact institution and another, depending in large measure on the history and nature of the institution itself.

This synchronic measure of culture contact may appropriately be termed "cross-cultural influence"—a measure of the way in which carriers of one culture may affect the behavior of carriers of another culture at any given time and within a given contact situation. The discussion which occupies the remainder of this section is, then, a comparative analysis of Shonto's contact institutions in terms of their cross-cultural influence.

As a final note, it is necessary to recognize that "cross-cultural influence," as here defined, is not necessarily a capacity to influence behavior so as to produce culture change. It is, rather, a capacity to influence behavior in specific ways under specific circumstances, either in the direction of change or stability. Given the varied motivations of different American contact institutions (cf. Malinowski, 1945, p. 15; Summer Seminar on Acculturation, 1954, p. 981), it should not be surprising to find them, at one time or another, working at cross purposes in a given contact situation. Thus one contact institution may exert its influence to forestall culture change which is sought by another institution. In either case the extent to which an institution may produce or forestall change depends upon its cross-cultural influence.

A MODEL FOR THE ANALYSIS OF INFLUENCE AT SHONTO

The present study of Shonto involves a special problem in the analysis of culture contact, in reducing it to the microcosm of a single community. The totality of influence exerted by White culture on Navaho society at Shonto must be encompassed within the framework of relations between and among a handful of alien institutions and the Navaho community. Under these circumstances the problem cannot be approached in terms of the contact of two organisms; the complex of contact institutions does not add up to any sort of integrated sociocultural whole, so that each must be analyzed separately. Further, since their interests and purposes are not the same, they must be compared in regard to contact, communication, and influence.

For comparative purposes, the major need is to reduce the vague concepts of "intercultural role" and "intercultural communication"

(Summer Seminar on Acculturation, 1954, pp. 980–982) to a set of discrete quantifiable variables. As an initial step, contact institutions can be studied in terms of three sets of relationships: those with their own culture, those with the alien culture, and those with each other. A whole set of refinements can be made in the area of relations with the alien or contacted culture, recognizing the importantce of historical background, extent of contact, role, and capacity to communicate.

The ultimate model which will be used for the analysis of cross-cultural influence at Shonto is set down in full detail in table 37. For the most part it is self-explanatory; in any case its meaning will become clear through application to the case of Shonto in succeeding pages. Its purpose is to examine and evaluate the factors contributing to the cross-cultural influence of each of the contact institutions in Shonto community. For the sake of the present theoretical discussion it is necessary only to review the major orientations of the model and to clarify certain special concepts which are employed in it.

Even Malinowski (1945, p. 73) has admitted that the structural analysis of culture contact must include some consideration of nonlocal factors, and this is the initial point of approach in other study guides (Redfield, Linton, and Herskovits, 1936, pp. 149–150; Linton, 1940, p. ix; Summer Seminar on Acculturation, 1954, pp. 975–980). By studying the history and the general overall pattern of culture contact between any two groups it is possible to make certain hypotheses about the nature of cross-cultural relations which are likely to be true in any given contact situation. What is established thereby is a sort of least common denominator of culture contact without refer-

---

TABLE 37.—*A model for the structural analysis of culture contact at Shonto*

I. Analysis of nonlocal factors:
    A. General history of culture contact (duration, intensity, amicability, coercion, subordination areas and levels of contact, numbers involved).
    B. Current general pattern of contact (areas and levels of contact, numbers involved, dependence or interdependence, subordination, coercion, deference).
    C. Basic direction of cross-cultural influence.
II. Analysis of the local contact situation:
    A. Nonpersonal contacts (printed materials, radio and movies, other products).
    B. Indirect contacts (culture contact through other members of same society).
    C. Institutions of direct culture contact ("contact institutions") (identification, charters, numbers, distribution).
III. Detailed study of specific contact institutions:
    A. Relations within own culture (areas of contact and familiarity, levels of integration, levels of organization, channels of communication).
    B. Relations with each other (community or conflict of interest, coincidence of contact, intercommunication, cooperation or interference).
    C. Cross-cultural relations:
        1. Historical factors (duration of contact, intensity, amicability, initial acceptance of the contact institution).
        2. Factors of access (frequency of contact, numbers involved, extent of contact in terms of age groups, sexes, etc.).
        3. Factors of role (basic charter: commercial, governmental, etc., integration in alien culture, dependence or interdependence, coercive power, primary areas of culture affected).
        4. Factors of communication (personal or instrumental relations, accessibility, privacy, language and depth of communication).
IV. Evaluation of cross-cultural influence:
    A. Definition of common denominator of culture contact.
    B. Comparative analysis of contact institutions (historical factors, factors of access, factors of role, factors of communication).
    C. Summary evaluation based on all factors.

ence to local institutions. Of paramount importance is the recognition
of any pattern of general subordination or even subjugation of one
group to the other (cf. Redfield, Linton, and Herskovits, 1936, p. 150).
Any such condition will tend to produce a more or less unilateral
structure of influence, that is, exerted almost entirely by one culture
group upon the other. As a further corollary, the major contact
institutions are likely to be those of the superordinate society.

The second heading in table 37 refers to the necessity of identifying
the contact institutions in the community as a preliminary to the
study of their influence. It is also necessary to know to what extent
they monopolize culture contact in the community, or to what extent
they are supplemented by indirect and nonpersonal contacts.

The detailed study of contact institutions begins with the consideration of their relations with their own culture. Two important concepts are introduced here: levels of sociocultural integration and
levels of organization. The first of these is adapted from Steward
(1951; 1955, pp. 43–63), who used it as an analytical tool in de-
scribing relations within a single sociocultural system. Whether
the culture which is manifested by any particular contact institution is a purely local or subcultural phenomenon, or whether it is
part of a national cultural synthesis (cf. Steward, 1955, pp. 64–77)
has an important bearing on the role of the contact institution as
originator and/or transmitter. Levels of organization are a necessary dependent of levels of integration. Sociocultural systems are
not necessarily formally organized at the levels at which they are
integrated; however, within the system there is likely to be a hierarchy
of organizational levels (cf. chart J) of which the contact institution
is one. An additional important consideration is the total extent and
the areas (e.g., material culture, economics, religion, etc.) of its own
culture with which the contact institution is familiar and in communication, and thus capable of transmitting (cf. Summer Seminar on
Acculturation, 1954, pp. 980–981).

The relations of contact institutions with each other are an important aspect of culture contact within a restricted locus, and one
which has been largely overlooked in earlier studies of the subject.
If it is recognized that contact institutions are often activated by
very different motives (cf. Summer Seminar on Acculturation, 1954,
p. 981), it should be apparent that they are not likely to present a
solid front of coordinated activity and interest (see, e.g., Kluckhohn
and Leighton, 1946, pp. 77–79). They may not even be in contact
with any of the same areas of their own culture. This has been
historically true of the position of many missionaries among the
various contact institutions on the Navaho Reservation.

Finally, in the analysis of contact institutions, comes the actual
study of "conjunctive," or cross-cultural relations (Summer Seminar

on Acculturation, 1954, p. 980). The two original categories of relations proposed by the Summer Seminar (1954, pp. 980–982)—"intercultural roles" and "intercultural communication"—have been broken down into a score of variables, most of which are at least roughly quantifiable. They are grouped under four major headings as historical factors, factors of access, factors of role, and factors of communication. In a final section, cross-cultural influence is measured in terms of the sum of these factors.

The remainder of "The Structure of Contact" will be devoted to the application of the model set forth above to the actual analysis of cross-cultural influence in Shonto community in 1955.

THE BACKGROUND OF NAVAHO-ANGLO CULTURE CONTACT

As suggested earlier, it is necessary to begin with a consideration of general factors, both temporal and immediate, which contribute to the nature of the localized contact situation at Shonto. The overall history of contacts between Navahos and Whites, and the predominant character of such contacts at all times and places, need to be considered.

HISTORY OF CONTACTS

The post-contact history of the Navaho people and the effects of their intercourse with intruding European culture have been the subjects of an extraordinary number of studies (e.g., Farmer, 1941; Luomala, 1938; Underhill, 1953 and 1956). It is not necessary to repeat this material in any kind of detail here. There are, however, some special features in the background of contact in the far northwestern Navaho area which have affected the nature of cross-cultural relations at Shonto today, and which require special remark.

The recent history of the western Navaho country was set forth in "Background," pp. 30–53, and the development of White contacts was outlined. A summary chronology of the major contact institutions and their duration is presented in chart G, below. The most notable

CHART G.—Chronology of Navaho-White contacts in the western Navaho country

	1870	1880	1890	1900	1910	1920	1930	1940	1950	1955
Mormon settlements	....	....	....	....						
Railroad towns		.....	.....	.....						
B.I.A. Admin. offices					.....	....	....	....	.....	
Res. boarding schools					----	--------	....	....	--------	-----
Reservation hospitals					----	--------	....	....	--------	.....
Res. courts and police					----	--------	....	....	--------	.....
Reservation trad. posts					----	--------	--------	▬▬▬▬	▬▬▬▬	.....
Missions					....	....	....	....	....	.....
Tribal council [1]						---	--------	--------	-----	-----
Community schools								-----	----▬▬	▬▬▬▬
Off-res. schools							....	-----	-----	-----
Railroads									---	-----

.... Infrequent contact for small numbers of Navahos
-------- Infrequent contact for large numbers of Navahos or frequent contact for small numbers of Navahos
▬▬▬▬ Frequent contact for large numbers of Navahos
[1] Considered a White cultural influence; see "The Contact Situation at Shonto."

feature in the history of intercultural relations in the western area is that they do not begin with, and do not include, the military campaigns of 1863–64. The far western regions of the present Navaho Reservation were settled largely if not entirely by people who escaped the Carson roundup and its aftermath (see "Background," pp. 30–53). Navaho-White relations at Shonto and neighboring communities were thus not affected at the outset by any act of overt subjugation as they were in the Fort Defiance area (see, e.g., Van Valkenburgh and McPhee, 1938; Underhill, 1956, pp. 144–163). It was to be nearly 70 years before Shonto residents were subjected to anything like the same sort of compulsions as their eastern neighbors. In the meantime, intercultural relations were intermittently hostile, indifferent, or amicable, but nearly always voluntary on the part of the Navahos.

For western Navahos, face-to-face contact with Anglo-Americans began with the pioneer Mormon colonies west of the Colorado River, and later at Moencopi (see "The American Period," pp. 40–42). Relations here were in the same sort of trading-raiding pattern which had ultimately provoked the Carson campaign in the eastern area, and which was essentially nothing more than a continuation of traditional relationships with the Hopi and other well-to-do enemy peoples (see "Early Trading Posts," pp. 150–154; also Hill, 1948, p. 374). Sporadic raids and "incidents" occurred as late at 1894, resulting in the intervention of Federal authorities at Moencopi (Van Valkenburgh, 1941, p. 164), but no effective punitive action was taken. At no time in the western Navaho country was there any kind of military establishment comparable to those maintained at Fort Defiance, Fort Wingate, and various outposts in the east. Western Navahos, consequently, showed little awareness of the Treaty of 1868 and did not behave like a conquered people.

In theory the subjugation of the western Navaho began in 1906 when they were "reservationized." A good deal of compulsion was exerted in the immediate neighborhood of Tuba City to get the children into school and also, probably, to control the sale of liquor. Shonto and other more remote communities felt few if any effects of the presence of the Tuba City agency for another generation; it was out of the effective reach of administrative agencies until the 1930's.

The real subordination of western Navahos began in the trading posts, and continued steadily throughout the early decades of the 20th century as the people became more and more dependent on the White man's economy and its products (see Underhill, 1956, pp. 177–195). A condition of economic dependence was established which in the long run proved a greater sanction for cultural subordination than even military subjugation. Nevertheless, and in spite of the efforts of the Bureau of Indian Affairs to enforce culture change and of the legal and military sanctions with which they were implemented, western Navaho cultural and social autonomy persisted, at Shonto and elsewhere, until after 1930.

During the 1930's a number of factors conspired to destroy most of what remained of the cultural independence of the western Navaho. The Bureau of Indian Affairs, which up to that time had largely played the part of a remote and ineffective benevolent agency, established its front lines at the community level with a series of vigorous programs designed to make up for lost time in the acculturation of the Navaho. From the standpoint of overall Navaho-White relations and their future, the most important of these by far was the now-famous stock reduction program. The role of the Bureau of Indian Affairs was transformed in short order into that of a coercive agency; and not only stock reduction but all its other programs, including community schools and hospitals, met with massive and articulate resistance.

Stock reduction and its aftermath finally accomplished what Kit Carson and the Treaty of 1868 failed to achieve: the subjugation of the western Navaho to White society, culture, and influence. It is probably true to say that Navaho cultural resistance burned itself out in its unsuccessful efforts to oppose stock reduction. It undoubtedly seemed to many Navahos as if the basis of their independence, both economic and spiritual, had been destroyed (see Spicer, 1952, pp. 197–207). There was thus created, perhaps, an unusually favorable climate for the acceptance of the White man's jobs and ultimately of his other institutions during the war years which immediately followed.

Seemingly paradoxically, acceptance of White culture and influence have been accompanied by attitudes of antagonism which were not felt in the western Navaho country in the days of Navaho cultural autonomy. If stock reduction forced the Navahos (in their own estimation) to change their ways, it created at the same time a general resentment of White people which has never subsided (cf. Spicer, 1952, p. 203). A considerable number of Shonto, Paiute Mesa, and Oljeto Navahos were jailed for their activities in resisting stock reduction. It was the community's first real taste of physical subjugation, and brought home a lasting sense of subordination and a resentment which still underlies most Navaho-White relations today. There is an apparent, and increasingly articulate, sense of oppression which is a product largely of the past 20 years. It is one of the constants of culture contact at Shonto.

Chart G sets forth the main features of a century of Navaho-White contact in the western Navaho country. From it can be derived a suggestion of overall pattern which has been important in shaping intercultural relations today. First of all, a comparison of charts

G and H indicates that the history of culture contacts in the western country has included three major phases. From 1860 until shortly after the turn of the century it was primarily the Navahos who sought contact with the White man, and on the latter's ground. This was in the days of high Navaho mobility (cf. Dyk, 1938, passim) when the Navaho was still perhaps better culturally adapted to his environment than were the embryonic White settlements of the frontier. Navahos traveled frequently and often considerable distances to the early Mormon colonies in the 1860's and 70's (see "The American Period," pp. 40–42; "Early Trading Posts," pp. 150–154). After 1885 these diminished in importance, and were replaced by various trading centers along the newly constructed Santa Fe Railway.

The second phase of western Navaho–White relations occupied roughly the first four decades of the 20th century. It may appropriately be termed the period of White encroachment and Navaho withdrawal. The first significant and continuing contact initiated wholly by White men and for their own purposes began in 1901 with the establishment of the little Blue Canyon school (see "The American Period," pp. 40–42; Van Valkenburgh, 1941, p. 164). It was followed within the decade by the Western Navaho Indian Reservation, the Tuba City agency with its boarding school, hospital, court, and so on, and by the Wetherill trading post at Kayenta. These first penetrations into Navaholand proper signaled the growing intention of the White man to make Navaho affairs his business. They were the first of a continuing series which saw the establishment of some two dozen trading posts and several missions between 1910 and 1925; formation of the Navaho Tribal Council (at White instigation) in 1924; and finally the development of a number of day schools (now "community schools") in the 1930's. Insofar as all of these White efforts were bent, deliberately or unwittingly, toward the cultural subjugation of the Navaho, it might fairly be said that the culminating act of this phase of intercultural relations was stock reduction.

As the White man took over the initiative in culture contact, the Navaho relinquished it. The products of American and European technology as well as many of its concomitant influences were, in a sense, delivered to the Navaho doorstep, so that it was no longer necessary to travel to Lee's Ferry or Kanab or Flagstaff for them. Navaho mobility, an outstanding social feature throughout the preceding century, declined to such an extent that by 1940 only a handful of Shonto people had ever been off the reservation.

The new government agricultural, health, and educational programs of this era met with comparatively little success among the western Navaho. Except in the immediate vicinity of Tuba City they were never backed by any very effective coercive sanctions, and they had little attraction for Navahos on their own merits. Not until the vigorous enforcement of stock reduction toward the end of the 1930's was the presence of Government truly felt at Shonto and neighboring communities.

On the whole, and excepting the field of commercial relations, the cultural effects of Navaho-White contact from 1900 to 1940 were small. They cannot be classified in terms of any of the recognized patterns of response to culture contact (e.g., Redfield, Linton, and Herskovits, 1936, pp. 151–152; Linton, 1940, pp. 501–502; Summer Seminar on Acculturation, 1954, pp. 984–990). Relations during this period can best be described as characterized by White initiative and Navaho rejection in the western Navaho country. The pattern of Navaho rejection was passive and perhaps even unconscious throughout the first three decades, but rose to a peak of conscious and articulate resistance in the face of stock reduction at the end of the period.

The final and current phase in Navaho-White relations began early in the 1940's. As suggested above, it was probably set off by the exhaustion of Navaho cultural resistance at the completion of stock reduction, followed closely by the opening of a wide variety of new economic fields at the outbreak of World War II. As the magnitude of the new opportunity became apparent, Navahos once again took the initiative in leaving the reservation to seek jobs in mines, lumber camps, ammunition depots, and railroad gangs—wherever unskilled labor in large numbers was needed.

The war brought an equally important change in the White approach to intercultural relations. American interest was naturally diverted to more immediate and pressing problems, and the expansionist and to some extent coercive policies of the Bureau of Indian Affairs during the 1930's ran their course or were dropped. There was a general withdrawal of governmental influence and activity accompanying the return of Navaho initiative (see "Government Development," pp. 44–48).

Acceptance of the White man's jobs apparently brought with it rapid acceptance of certain other Anglo-American benefits, notably schools and hospitals. All observers of the Navaho scene are agreed that the war profoundly and permanently altered the nature of Navaho-White relations, but no one is able to fix on any one year as the turning point. Educators and medical officials who believed their stepped-up activity was merely brought on by wartime curtailments of personnel and facilities found at the end of the war that it actually reflected an enormous absolute increase in Navaho reliance on their programs. Schools and hospitals which were half empty in 1941 were full and overflowing 5 years later.

The patterns of Navaho initiative and White withdrawal have largely continued in the years since 1946 (see "Government Development" and "The Outside World," pp. 44–51). Navahos continue to seek and to depend on American-provided jobs, education, and medical facilities. Postwar Indian Bureau programs have shifted away from community service and development, toward long-range economic planning (cf. Krug, 1948), intensified education of the younger generation at off-reservation schools (Officer, 1956, pp. 35–74), and the relocation of small numbers of exceptionally skilled or educated Navahos in off-reservation communities (Kelly, 1953, pp. 98–99). The future effects of these programs throughout the Navaho Reservation are likely to prove incalculable; for the moment, however, they largely bypass the current adult Navaho population.

In sum, the last 15 years of Navaho-White contact have seen the return of initiative to the Navahos, and selected voluntary acceptance of certain White traits and influence. The overall pattern is one of "adaptation" (Redfield, Linton, and Herskovits, 1936, p. 152) or, as it was termed by the most recent Social Science Research Council report, "progressive adjustment" through the process of cultural fusion (Summer Seminar on Acculturation, 1954, pp. 987–988).

One fundamental trend is discernible throughout the history of western Navaho-White contact. As chart H indicates, a clear and profound distinction, both qualitative and quantitative, can be made between commercial and/or economic contacts (chart H: rows 1, 2, 4, 9) and all other contacts (chart H: rows 3, 5–8, 10–12) between the two groups. To begin with, the former are the only contacts which have ever been instituted originally through Navaho initiative (column E). All other contacts and contact institutions have been founded by Whites for their own purposes. Furthermore, commercial-economic contacts have nearly always been friendly from the start (column J), have never involved White coercion (column H), and have affected greater numbers of Navahos (column C) more regularly (column D) than have any others.

Non-commercial contacts have varied considerably in character according to their purpose, but they have all been instituted originally by Whites (column E). Reaction to them has run the gamut from hostile to friendly (column J); in most cases it was initially indifferent at best. Most of these contacts have affected special segments of the community (column C) rather than the whole, and frequency of contact has been extremely variable (column D).

In spite of their basic orientation toward White interests, non-economic contact institutions have exerted comparatively little compulsion except in the single case of stock reduction. Although founded by Whites (column E), the subsequent initative for establishing specific contacts has been left to the Navaho in many cases (column F). In other words, always excepting stock reduction, the overall pattern of such contacts has been permissive and voluntary,

CHART H.—Historical character of western Navaho-White relations

Contact institution	A Years of contact[1]	B Navaho level of contact	C Numbers involved	D Frequency of contact[2]	E Initiator of relationship	F Initiator of individual contact	G Purpose of contact	H White coercion	J Navaho reaction	K Areas of culture affected
Off-reservation:										
1. Mormon settlements	1860–1902	Individuals, Households.	Very small	Sporadic	Navahos	Navahos	Trading, raiding.	None	Hostile to friendly.	Mater. cult.
2. Railroad towns	1885–pres.	Individuals, Households.	Few until recently.	Sporadic	Navahos	Navahos	Trading, work.	None	Indifferent to friendly.	Mater. cult., economics.
3. Boarding schools	1935–pres.	Individuals	Most older children.	Constant exc. summer.	Whites	Whites	Education.	Strong	Indifferent to friendly.	All?[3]
4. Railroads	1942–pres.	Individuals	Most men	Constant in season.	Navahos	Navahos	Work	None	Friendly.	Economics.
Agency level:										
5. Administrative offices	1906–pres.	Individuals, Households.	Very small	Very infrequent.	Whites	Primarily Navahos.	Permits, info., etc.	Little	Hostile to indifferent.	Various.
6. Boarding schools	1906–pres.	Individuals	Many young children.	Constant exc. summer.	Whites	Whites	Education.	Strong	Hostile to indifferent.	Various.
7. Hospitals	1906–pres.	Individuals, Households.	Formerly few; now many.	Sporadic.	Whites	Navahos	Medical treatment.	Formerly consid.	Hostile to friendly.	Medicine.
8. Court and police	1906–pres.	Individuals	Limited no. of men.	Very infrequent.	Whites, Navahos.	Navahos, Whites.	Law enf., retribut.	Strong	Hostile to indifferent.	Common law.
Community level:										
9. Trading posts	1909–pres.	Households, Community.	All households.	Regular	Whites, Navahos.	Navahos	Trading, work, etc.	None	Friendly.	Mater. cult., economics.
10. Missions	1914–pres.	Individuals, Households.	Small	Sporadic	Whites	Primarily Whites.	Proselyt.	None	Largely indifferent.	Religion.
11. Tribal councilmen[4]	1924–pres.	Community	Most men.	Regular	Whites	Councilman	Primarily info.	None	Largely indifferent.	Political organizat.
12. Community schools	1934–pres.	Individuals, Households.	Most young children.	Adults occas.; Children const.	Whites	Whites, Navahos.	Education.	Consid.	Indifferent to friendly.	Education.

1 Cf. chart G.
2 For individuals or groups principally involved.
3 Effects too recent to be measured; see "Points of Contact," below.
4 Considered channel of indirect culture contact.

resulting in a selective adaptation in which White culture and cultural influences often play an optional part (see "Summary," pp. 93–94). As could be predicted from the general history of contact, adoption of White culture traits has gone to its furthest extent in material culture and economics.

THE MODERN PICTURE

The year 1955 found Navaho-White relations in a condition of relative stability which had persisted since the early postwar years. The rapid acceleration of Navaho initiative and acceptance of certain White institutions which marked the most recent phase of intercultural relations (see above) had seemingly run its course, at least in the more isolated western communities. The result was a temporary condition of "stabilized pluralism" (Summer Seminar on Acculturation, 1954, p. 990). The stability is almost certainly destined to be short lived: today's Navaho children are receiving a degree of White-sponsored education undreamed of by their forebears, and the effects are likely to be felt strongly throughout the reservation in a few years.

The foundation of modern Navaho-White relations is the dependent and subordinate position of the former. Socially and legally, this subordination is expressed in the Treaty of 1868 and the Federal Code of Indian Offenses. Its most powerful sanction, however, is the extreme dependence of modern Navahos on the White man's economy, which destroys much of their power of cultural resistance. The symbol of subordination, as always, remains the memory of stock reduction (Spicer, 1952, p. 203).

The White culture which surrounds and impinges on Navaho life is a national culture, integrated at a national level (cf. Steward, 1951); not a regional subculture or a localized complex. The contact institutions which transmit its influence are merely what Steward (e.g., 1955, pp. 68–69) has termed "local aspects of national institutions." It may be said, therefore, that the subordination of modern Navahos to their Anglo-American neighbors is at a national level: 80,000 Navahos subordinate to 160,000,000 Whites.

The sheer overwhelming numerical superiority of Whites—the original and ultimate source of Navaho subjugation—continues to dictate the character of Navaho-White relations. As of 1955 all Navahos had frequent or regular contact with one or more institutions of Anglo culture, while only a fraction of one percent of Anglos had any significant contact with Navaho culture. Navahos of both sexes, all ages, and all interests had to concern themselves with the ways and wishes of their White neighbors; only a handful of Whites in special capacities—commercial administrative, and charitable—had to concern themselves with Navaho life. Most important of all, every

Navaho had to depend on the modern American economy for some or all of his livelihood, while the trader alone among all White men had to depend similarly on the Navahos.

Modern American society is complex and highly organized at every level from the national on down to the individual (cf. chart J). The regular functional units of Navaho society, on the other hand, extend no higher than the level of the residence group (see "Social Structure," pp. 54–65). Furthermore, the institutions of White society are specialized where those of Navaho society are not. It follows from this and from the overall pattern of interest in Navaho-White relations that the constant focal points of culture contact are those institutions of White society which are specifically chartered to deal with Navahos. No single agency of Navaho society maintains an equal constancy or intensity of contact with White life. Accordingly, the pattern of contact, and Navaho participation in it, is determined by White norms.

In spite of increasing initiative, Navaho mobility in the present era remains highly restricted both as to situations and as to numbers involved. At least throughout the western Navaho country, therefore, the loci of culture contact remain very largely within the reservation. A large number of Shonto men engage in off-reservation railroad work every year, but their job situation actually involves a minimum of culture contact (see "Railroad Work," pp. 129–133). The major points of culture contact, as will be shown in the study of Shonto, are a small group of specialized White institutions within and near the Navaho community which are specifically organized to deal with it.

THE BASIC DIRECTION OF INFLUENCE

Throughout their history and presumably their prehistory as well, the Navahos have been known as culture-borrowers rather than donors (cf. Luomala, 1938, pp. 16–17; Underhill, 1956, pp. 3–4). It sometimes appears as if every group with whom they have ever come in contact has left its cultural mark on them, whereas traces of any similar influence exerted by them on their neighbors are few. The same relationship has characterized the contact of Navahos and Anglo-Americans.

Even in a situation of close culture contact within the Navaho country, and where Navahos outnumber Whites by some 50 to 1 as they do at Shonto, evidences of Navaho cultural influences on Whites are few. It is true that most of the contact institutions have been inaugurated for the specific purpose of dealing with Navahos, and hence owe their existence to the existence of Navahos. Nevertheless, they derive their actual character from purely American models and, with the exception of the trading post, show little or no special adaptation to the conditions of Navaho life or culture.

In a word, cross-cultural influence at Shonto is for the most part a one-way affair, deliberately exerted by dominant White society upon subordinate Navaho society for explicit purposes.

THE CONTACT SITUATION AT SHONTO

Alien cultural traits and influences may be transmitted to and within the Navaho community either by alien peoples, by Navahos themselves, or non-socially through the circulation of alien culture products. It is necessary to consider briefly the actual and potential significance of each of these types of stimulus at Shonto.

The circulation and use of American culture products in the Navaho community is, of course, enormous. Navaho dependence on White culture has reached its zenith in the field of material culture (see "Material Culture," pp. 77–81), with almost total replacement of the native complex. "Inert" or non-communicating goods, however, cannot properly be considered as cross-cultural influences in their own right. They are deliberately introduced and circulated by the trading post, so that their use is properly a measure of its influence and not of their own.

There remains, however, a class of White culture products which have a power to communicate and a potential influence quite apart from that of any sponsoring institution or contact agency. These are the media of mass communication (cf. Steward, 1955, p. 76). They may appropriately be regarded as points of potential culture contact in their own right.

Isolation of the community and lack of education of its inhabitants have so far kept the cultural influence of mass communication media down to negligible proportions at Shonto. The community's literacy rate is under 10 percent (see "Acculturation," pp. 90–93), and the circulation of printed matter of any kind is virtually nil. There is not, to the writer's knowledge, a single Shonto Navaho who reads extensively for pleasure. Even the influence of illustrated cowboy magazines on fashions in men's attire, which is readily observable in the eastern Navaho area, has not been repeated in the Shonto area, where there is no circulation of such magazines.

There is a weekly movie at Tuba City, 55 miles away, but Shonto people have never been known to attend it. Most adults in the community have seen one or two or a few of the adult education movies which the Bureau of Indian Affairs occasionally exhibits at the school, but that is the practical extent of Shonto's acquaintance with the cinema. Radio is a recent introduction in the community, concomitant with the inauguration of Navaho-language broadcasts from Flagstaff and Winslow stations. So far it has had no measurable effect. However, radio listening has become a favorite recreation at Shonto as in many other Navaho areas, so that its future potential may be considerable. Television is absent throughout the area, and will have to await the development of an inexpensive battery-powered receiving set.

The influence of Navahos themselves in introducing American culture into the community is difficult to assess. Use of alcoholic beverages may be pointed out as a widespread American-derived trait which has been introduced and spread by Navahos themselves in the face of articulate disapproval by all White contact institutions. On the other hand Navaho drinking is American only in its ultimate inspiration; the actual behavior involved is in sharp contrast to American drinking habits (see "Recreation and Play," pp. 75–77).

On the whole it seems likely that indirect cultural influence, transmitted to the community from outside White institutions through Navahos, plays only a small part in the structure of culture contacts at Shonto. None of the neighboring Navaho communities with which it has frequent contact (see "Geography," pp. 32–33) have gone noticeably further than Shonto itself in the acceptance of White man's ways, so that they do not furnish any sort of example. In sum, virtually all of the cross-cultural influences which are exerted upon Shonto's Navahos are exerted directly by the White contact institutions which they encounter.

The days are long past when Shonto Trading Post was the only White institution in the community and its only effective contact with the outside world. Modern Navahos have a wide variety of potential points of culture contact both within and outside the community. The most important of these are shown on map 2, page 31. Within the actual boundaries of Shonto community were, in 1955, the trading post, the school, a missionary, the tribal councilman, and the Navajo National Monument (see "White Society at Shonto," pp. 165–167). Within 50 miles of the community boundaries were a dozen more trading posts, three missions, three community schools, two trailer schools, and the administrative subagency at Tuba City with its various administrative offices, court, hospital, and boarding school. Beyond, 132 miles to the southwest, lie Flagstaff and the railroad—gateways to the outside world.

For Shonto people most of these institutions are points of culture contact in theory only. For functional reasons as well as considerations of accessibility there is no basis for recourse to them in actual practice. Trading posts, community schools, tribal councilmen and missions are all essentially community-level institutions; few Navahos have any reason to contact other than those in their own area. Even within Shonto community, Navajo National Monument is a facility set up and operated for the benefit of White tourists and has no real contact with or effect on the Navaho population outside of a small number of households which depend on it for employment (see "Local Wage Work" pp. 127–129).

There remain some eight White institutions which are regular and important points of culture contact for Shonto's Navahos of today, and whose function and influence must be examined in detail. In the community proper are the trading post, school, tribal councilman, and missionary. At the Tuba City subagency 55 miles away are the tribal court (and jail) and the large Indian hospital. Finally, beyond the reservation, are the town of Flagstaff and the Santa Fe Railway.

Off-reservation boarding schools are deliberately omitted from the list of important points of contact. Their future significance may very well be greater than that of all other contact institutions combined, but at the present time the whole program is so new that its effects cannot be measured. Shonto school, however, is included on the strength of its frequent direct contact with adults in the community, and hence potential influence on their behavior.

POINTS OF CONTACT

As noted at the beginning of the present discussion, it is necessary to examine the structure and function of contact institutions not only in their cross-cultural roles, but equally in their intracultural orientations and, at the level of contact, their relations with one another. It is impossible for any individual or institution to be familiar with, and therefore capable of transmitting, more than a fraction of any modern national cultural system such as that of the United States (cf. Summer Seminar on Acculturation, 1954, pp. 980–981; also Steward, 1955, pp. 64–77). In a contact situation such as Shonto, therefore, intracultural orientations set the most immediate limitation on the potential cross-cultural influence of any contact institution.

INTRACULTURAL ORIENTATIONS

In spite of distinctive local manifestations, the Anglo-American culture which surrounds and impinges upon modern Navaho life is truly a national culture and part of a national synthesis (see "The Modern Picture," pp. 244–245; also Steward, 1955, pp. 64–77). That is, the external influences to which Shonto is subject—religious, educational, medical, and so on—would be essentially similar were the community located in California, Colorado, or Connecticut. (A single exception may be made in the case of the livestock-agricultural complex, which is genuinely subcultural and integrated at a regional level. See chart J.) As a result, Shonto's contact institutions must be regarded as local aspects of national institutions, according to Steward's (1955, pp. 67–69) model of analysis.

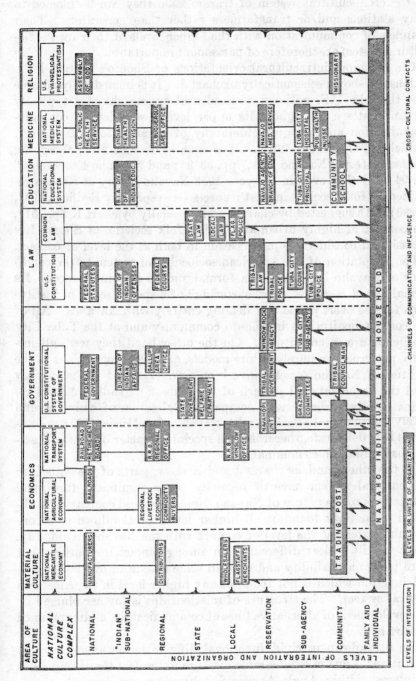

CHART J.—Intracultural orientations of Shonto contact institutions.

In the cross-cultural system of transmission they can be likened to relay stations and/or transformers rather than generators. Their channels of communication with the higher levels of their own sociocultural system are therefore of paramount importance.

The principal intracultural orientations of Shonto's contact institutions are shown schematically in chart J. It is immediately notable here that the U.S. national sociocultural system shows a typically "urban" pattern throughout its upper levels: well-defined compartmentalization and a regular hierarchy of organizational levels (cf. Redfield, 1947; Miner, 1952). It is equally obvious from foregoing discussion (esp. "Navaho Life," pp. 53–94; and "Navaho Economics," pp. 94–148) that even in the year 1955 Navaho society at Shonto remained a "folk" society in most respects (see especially Redfield, 1947, p. 293). As suggested by chart J and especially by chart K (p. 251), the contact of highly urban and highly folk societies at Shonto has necessitated considerable modification in both at the level of contact.

The adaptation of the American sociocultural system to the conditions of Navaho life has both a formal and an informal aspect. Its formal aspect is seen in the "chartering" of a special series of institutions for the overt purpose of dealing entirely with Navahos. All of the contact institutions in Shonto community and at the Tuba City subagency are so constituted. On the other hand they were all initially patterned on purely White models, and overt concessions to the realities of Navaho society have been few. Even at the subagency level the organizational pattern of the Bureau of Indian Affairs remains rigidly "urban," with compartmentalization of activities and purely instrumental relations with Navahos (cf. Miner, 1952). Insofar as it is deliberate, therefore, the special character of contact institutions is pretty much nominal.

On the other hand, as charts J and K show, parts of the American sociocultural system have of necessity made significant functional adaptations to the nature of Navaho life. The rigid compartmentalization of activity found at all higher levels breaks down to a considerable extent at the level of contact with the Navaho community. There is still a clear differentiation among contact institutions, but there is also a flexibility and even to some extent an overlap of role and function which is not found at any higher level in the American cultural system. The structure of relationships is further blurred by the development of alternative lines of communication, as diagrammed in chart K.

The breakdown in rigid functional differentiation among contact institutions is due in considerable measure to the fact that many areas of interest within Anglo-American culture are not formally represented by any contact institution; insofar as there is any contact with them it must be indirect and through roundabout channels, and there

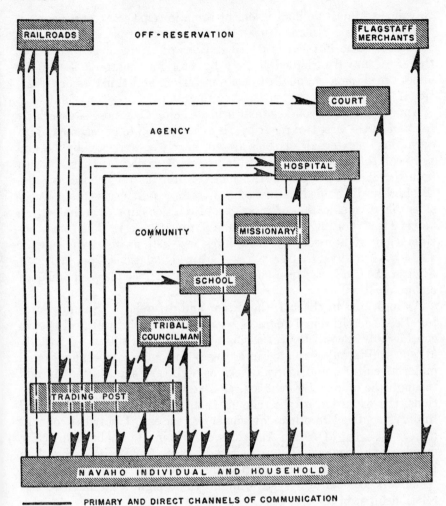

PRIMARY AND DIRECT CHANNELS OF COMMUNICATION

SECONDARY AND ANCILLARY CHANNELS OF COMMUNICATION

USUAL DIRECTION OF COMMUNICATION

CHART K.—Channels and directions of contact between and among Shonto Navahos and contact institutions.

is sometimes little to choose between one and another. Thanks to this set of conditions, the relations of any contact institution within its own sociocultural system are not necessarily dictated and restricted by its "charter" or operational sanction. They may be extended and ramified enormously as a result purely of its effectiveness as a channel of indirect cross-cultural communication.

It is apparent, as diagrammed in charts J and K, that all of the contact institutions within Shonto community have, to varying degrees, a secondary function as channels of communication between

Navahos and outside institutions or even, in some cases, other contact institutions (see "Intracultural Relations at the Contact Level," pp. 253–256). The intracultural orientations of any contact institution, therefore, are determined largely by first its "charter," second its effectiveness as a channel of communication, and third its organizational matrix.

Among Shonto's contact institutions the trading post is especially favored in the first two regards. By comparison to governmental institutions its external relations are not nearly so restricted by fiat and protocol, thus making it accessible to a wide variety of contacts with both Navahos and White institutions. Purely as a business operation the highly diversified nature of the trading post necessitates a considerable diversification of interest and relationships with the outside world (see "Trading Post Economics," pp. 167–184). The same consideration of accessibility to Whites, as well as its frequency of contact with Navahos (see "Cross-Cultural Relations," pp. 256–263) affords the store a paramount position as a secondary channel of communication.

As indicated in chart J, the extent and diversity of Shonto Trading Post's institutional contacts within its own sociocultural system considerably exceeds that of any other contact institution. Virtually all cultural impulses related in any way to commerce, economics and material culture, and many others as well, are transmitted by and through the store. By contrast, as a result of constitutional limitations, the extension of the school's relations beyond their chartered limits is confined to other government agencies. The tribal councilman is an agent of Anglo-American culture insofar as he is an active member of an organization patterned directly after White, rather than Navaho, models. He is not, on the other hand, a member of the Anglo-American sociocultural system, and has no significant institutional relationships within it.

As suggested in charts J and K, the missionary is the most narrowly restricted of all Shonto's contact institutions in his intracultural orientations. His position in this regard results from what might be called the incompleteness of his organizational matrix. The particular area of interest in which he is active is neither integrated nor organized at regional or local levels. Like many missionaries, particularly in this part of the reservation, he comes from outside the Southwest, and is under the special disadvantage of being unfamiliar not only with the institutions of Navaho culture, but also to some extent with the local aspects and agencies of White culture, and with the nature of the adjustment between the two. As a result there is almost no "lateral communication" between him and his superiors and any other institutions affecting or affected by Navaho culture and society (cf. chart J).

INTRACULTURAL RELATIONS AT THE CONTACT LEVEL

The foregoing discussion should make apparent the impossibility of analyzing the contact situation at Shonto in terms of the interaction of two sociocultural wholes. The White individuals who actually reside in the community and are the ultimate foci of culture contact often have more community of interest and more frequent contact with other Whites outside the Navaho Reservation than they have with one another (see "White Society at Shonto," pp. 165–167). On the Navaho Reservation there is no community level of integration in the American sociocultural system. Each White contact institution at Shonto is separately integrated into a broader synthesis in its own special field of interest (chart J). In other words every contact institution in the community is in theory a separate unit of society, and there are no structurally inherent cross-relationships among them.

Nevertheless communication and even a degree of functional interdependence among contact institutions is an inevitable response to the realities of Navaho life (see "Intracultural Orientations," pp. 248–253). Some of the more institutionalized channels of communication between and among Shonto institutions and Navahos are diagrammed in chart K. The extent of such communication depends partly on community or at least lack of conflict of interest, and partly on frequency of communication. It is apparent in chart K that the institutions which have the most regular or most extensive contact with the Navaho community are consistently employed as channels of communication by institutions with less frequent contact.

The trading post, the school, and the Tuba City Hospital may be said to constitute a central constellation of interacting institutions which are in fairly frequent contact (by telephone in the case of the hospital). School and hospital are both government operations devoted to different aspects of what the Bureau defines as the welfare of the community. The store has little overt interest in either, but is willing to cooperate in the interest of good community and neighbor relations. Both trading post and community school are regularly active in circulating medical information, posting hospital notices, and relaying messages between the hospital and Navahos. The hospital as well as the school communicate with Navaho adults through the store to a very large extent.

No other institution is as closely incorporated into the communication pattern as are the store, school, and hospital. The tribal councilman lives far from the trading post (and part of the time entirely outside the community), so that he is normally out of touch with the other contact institutions. His status among the White representatives of external influence in the community is a holdover from the days when the tribal council was a rubberstamp organization with no powers of its own: he is not taken seriously. His White neighbors imply that the Navahos are merely playing at governing themselves, like children, and the local councilman's lack of education and low status in the community (see "Social and Political Authority," pp. 65–68) help to perpetuate this impression among them. The antagonism aroused between traders and the Navaho tribe in connection with trading post ownership a few years ago (see "Shonto Trading Post," pp. 157–161) has left an aftermath of mutual suspicion such that it is not uncommon for the trader to disparage the activities of the councilman. There is not, at any rate, any feeling of community of interest as between the tribal councilman and any White institution.

The status of the tribal court at Tuba City is affected by similar considerations. White people at Shonto generally regard it with complete indifference as a purely Navaho affair and something of a caricature of American courts. In most cases where the court or law enforcement system threatens a member of the community, the trader in particular is likely to side with the Navaho individual for personal reasons. Both traders and schoolteachers are apt to disparage the efforts and competence of the Navaho police for not furnishing them any kind of protection.

Probably the ultimate basis for disparagement of the tribal organization in all its activities is the potential threat which it poses to the status system. Not only do all White people on the reservation enjoy a distinct status advantage as a result of the cultural and social subjugation of the Navaho (see "History of Contacts," pp. 237–244), but in many cases their continued institutional role depends on the continued subordination of the Navaho. Both traders and government officials (even, occasionally, schoolteachers) can be heard to remark that they like the Navahos as Navahos (cf. Leighton and Leighton, 1944, p. xvii), but that educated ones are no good. Ambivalent feelings toward Navahos are characteristic of many Whites, and particularly employees of the Bureau of Indian Affairs. It might be said that they want the Navahos to become like White people collectively, as is more or less the aim of the modern Bureau program, but to remain Navahos individually. At any rate resentment of Navaho attempts to imitate White behavior is leveled primarily at individuals rather than institutions. Individual acculturation threatens the overall status system and with it some of the authority enjoyed by traders, government officials, and even missionaries.

In folk-urban culture contact situations such as that at Shonto, the recurrent roles of administrator, entrepreneur and missionary have been identified repeatedly (e.g. Malinowski, 1945, p. 15; Summer Seminar on Acculturation, 1954, p. 981). The recurrence extends in many cases to the interrelation of these roles as well as to their relation to the subordinate culture. It may be said of missionaries

in particular that throughout the northwestern Navaho Reservation
they tend to be looked down on by other Whites as "do-gooders."
It is readily observable from charts J and K that Shonto's missionary has few relationships of any kind with the other contact institutions in and around the community, except to the extent that he
is utilized by Navahos themselves as a source of rides to the hospital.

The isolation of Shonto's missionary from the overall communication network, a common phenomenon in this part of the Navaho
Country (a similar situation was found by the writer to obtain at
Kayenta in 1950), undoubtedly harks back ultimately to his lack of
local orientations (see "Intracultural Orientations," pp. 248–253). As
an outsider he has little common background of experience and values
with other local Whites; he is likely to be somewhat unfamiliar with
local White institutions as well as with those of Navaho society. It
is believed to some extent by both traders and government officials that
a missionary has nothing to lose, and perhaps something to gain, by
siding with Navahos as against other Whites in all cross-cultural
relations, and there is sometimes suspicion that he will do so. "I
don't mind having a missionary around. They're bad for business,
though," expressed the feeling of an experienced trader in a community west of Shonto. Missionaries for their part recognize that
their success is likely to depend on their dissociating themselves from
any other White institution, which may be a focus of hostility and a
source of coercion. The Shonto missionary dissociated himself initially from both the store and the school by selecting a residence site
across the canyon from them. Throughout his residence in the community he seldom if ever visited the school, and set foot in the trading
post only to pick up his mail. Despite his own unfamiliarity with
the Navaho language he never employed the store as a channel of
communication with Navahos as did most other White institutions
(cf. chart K). The result, at Shonto, is an almost total lack of communication between missionaries and other contact institutions. Lack
of expressed approval from the trader and the schoolteachers was
probably a contributing factor to the failure of the efforts of Shonto's
missionary (see "Religion and Ritual," pp. 70–74).

Off-reservation contact institutions are, of course, not specifically
chartered to deal with Navahos, and are functionally independent of
them to a very large extent. This is particularly true with regard
to the town of Flagstaff, which has made very little effort to entice
Navaho trade—by comparison to Gallup, for example, where markets
and other retail stores offer a variety of premiums to Navaho customers, and advertise for several hours daily via Navaho-language
broadcasts; and where there are in-town trading posts which will buy
for cash anything the Navaho owns. Flagstaff is thus independent also
of the reservation communication network. There is, of course, out-

right competition between town merchants and trading posts. Shonto's owner (although he maintains a home there himself) often feels compelled to disparage Flagstaff as a corporate institution of White society, dwelling on the existence of such imputed evils as Mexican and Negro bootleggers, "gyp joints," and petty crooks who prey on the innocent Navaho. Insofar as it is regarded as the source of most of the liquor now consumed on the western part of the reservation, there is a tendency for not only traders, but Government officials and even missionaries to discourage Navaho visits to town. "Why go to town? We can give you everything you need right here on the reservation" expresses the attitude of most reservation Whites toward off-reservation towns as contact institutions.

The Santa Fe Railway employs large numbers of Navaho track laborers (see "Railroad Work," pp. 129–133), and to that extent might be characterized as functionally dependent on the Navaho. The normal channel of communication between railroad and reservation is an indirect and also a highly formalized one, involving as intermediaries both the Railroad Retirement Board and the trader as its claims agent. The economic welfare of the Navaho community is largely regarded as the trader's unchallenged sphere of influence by other contact institutions; hence there is no significant communication with the railroad except through the trader. Once they are off the reservation and at work, of course, the contact between Navahos and the railroad is direct.

In sum, it is the store, the school, and the hospital which most clearly recognize and respect the legitimacy of one another's interest in the Navaho community. Health, education, money, and material goods are agreed, from their point of view, to be the basic items which Navahos require from their White neighbors. To the extent that it is able, therefore, each of these institutions is willing to assist the others in providing such goods and services. Beyond these limits there is no general agreement as to "what's good for the Navaho"—on the contrary the trader, teacher, and doctor often like to believe that they are all he needs or should want. The integration of other contact institutions into the general communication network is therefore either tenuous, situational, or nil.

CROSS-CULTURAL RELATIONS

Above and beyond all of the variables which have been discussed in preceding pages, Navaho-White relations at the contact level are affected to a very large extent by purely internal, structural-functional features of the contact institutions and their role in the community. For purposes of the Shonto study some 20 variables have been identified as determining the cross-cultural influence of contact institutions. They are subdivided, to some extent arbitrarily, as historical factors, factors of access, factors of role, and factors of communication.

In chart L, each of Shonto's contact institutions is assessed in terms of the four classes of variables. It is intended that this schematic representation, although highly simplified, will obviate the necessity of any prolonged discussion of individual institutions in terms of history, role, etc. It remains, however, to discuss and clarify briefly the significance of the various factors set forth.

Among historical factors, it is observable that Shonto Trading Post has been in effective contact with the Navaho community for nearly a decade longer than any other contact institution, and for two decades longer than any other strictly White institution. These figures measure only the length of time during which there has been significant contact between the various institutions and Shonto. Both the Tuba City Hospital and the court and jail were founded a decade before Shonto Trading Post (see "Government Development," pp. 44–48), and the town of Flagstaff goes back to 1876. In 1940, however, hardly any Shonto residents had been to Flagstaff; it was not until the outbreak of World War II in the following year that real contact was established as a result of the opening up of jobs at the nearby ordnance depot. Shonto had virtually nothing to do with the Tuba City court until 1939 and 1940, when several individuals were hailed into court for their resistance to stock reduction. Acceptance of and regular contact with the hospital came some time during World War II.

It is notable in chart L as in chart H that only commercial and/or economic contacts were initially received with favor. As of 1955, however, there was widespread if not universal favorable acceptance of the school and hospital as well. An attitude of general hostility remains only toward the Tuba City court, and is connected with its efforts to enforce liquor prohibition.

Under "Factors of Access" (chart L) is measured the actual numerical significance of contact in terms of frequency, duration, and the numbers and kinds of Navahos chiefly affected. The entries throughout, like the discussion throughout the present section, refer to contact with adults only. As was stated earlier, it is impossible as of 1957 to measure the effect of intensive schooling on Shonto's present crop of children. Shonto Community School is included in the list of contact institutions on the basis of its frequent and direct contact with adults in the community.

In the case of railroad work, the duration and especially the significance of contact cannot be measured in terms of the duration of the job. The work situation of Navaho track laborers constitutes a contact only with an entirely esoteric segment of White culture, as unfamiliar to the average Anglo-American as it is to the average Navaho. In and of itself it has no more cultural significance than many Navaho wage jobs within the reservation, e.g., those at Betatakin (see "Rail-

CHART L.—Comparative analysis of Shonto contact institutions

	In Shonto Community				At Tuba City		Off-Reservation	
	Trading Post	Community School	Missionary	Tribal Councilman	Hospital	Court	Flagstaff Businesses	Railroad Extra Gangs
Historical Factors:								
Yrs. of freq. contact	40	21	1	31	14	16	14	8
Overall frequency	High	Moderate	Low	Low	Low	Low	Low	High
Initial reception	Friendly	Indiff	Indiff	Indiff	Hostile	Hostile	Friendly	Indiff
Overall Navaho reaction	Friendly	Friendly	Indiff	Indiff	Friendly	Host.-indiff	Friendly	Friendly
Factors of Access:								
Avg. freq. of contact	6 X mo.	4 X mo.	2 X mo.	1 X mo.	1 X 2 yrs.	(Very low)	1 X yr.	1 X yr.
Avg. dur. of contact	3 hrs.	½ hr.	2 hrs.	2 hrs.	1 hr.	2 hrs.	½ day	(Not measurable)[1]
Pct. of households affected	100	45	25 ?	100	60	40 ?	80	65
Areas of contact:								
Age groups	15 up	20–40	20 up	35 up	All	15–40	All	21–50
Sexes	Both	Prim. women	Both	Men	Both	Mostly men	Both	Men
Interest groups	All	Parents	Educ. ind.	HH heads	All	All	All	Workers
Factors of Role:								
Operative charter	Commercial	Govt.	Religious	Govt.	Governmental	Governmental	(Unchartered)[2]	(Unchartered)[2]
Navaho dependence	Very high	Limited[3]	None	None	Moderate	Low	Low	High
Econ. dep. on Navaho	Very high		None	None	None	None	Very low	Very low
Navaho integration	High	Moderate	None	Moderate	Moderate	Low	Low	Moderate
Coercion	Indirect	Moderate	None	Slight	Low	High	None	Indirect
Areas of interest	Comm., econ.	Education	Religion	No special	Medicine	Common law	Commerce	Labor
Factors of Communication:								
Character of relations	Personal	Instrum.	Intermed.	Personal	Instrumental	Instrumental	Instrumental	Instrumental
Accessibility	High	Low	Variable	Variable	Low	Low	Low	Low
Privacy	High	Low	Variable	High	Low	Low	None	None
Primary language	Navaho[4]	English[3]	English[6]	Navaho	English[5]	Navaho	English	English[5]

[1] Work situation involves little direct contact.
[2] I.e., not chartered specifically as contact agencies.
[3] Dependence primarily to feed and house children.
[4] "Trader Navaho."
[5] Normally through interpreter.

road Work" and "Local Wage Work," pp. 127–133). Navaho railroad workers live and work among nothing but Navahos and speak nothing but Navaho from week to week.

It is apparent from chart L that there is an enormous variation in the extent and frequency of Navaho-White contact among the different institutions. Most of them are aimed primarily at particular age or interest groups within the community. Only the trading post, the hospital, and Flagstaff are of potential interest to all adults, and of these only the store has anything approaching regular contact with them.

Under "Factors of Role" (chart L) are functional characteristics which affect cross-cultural relations. The first of these concerns the basic charter or raison d'etre of the contact institution. It has been noted elsewhere that:

. . . particular roles demand specific purposes and entail specific expectations. In the expansion of western European culture, the roles of the administrator, the entrepreneur, and the missionary have established a stereotype in accordance with the principal incentives activating the expansion. Important subsidiary roles in this movement have been those of the educator and the physician. [Summer Seminar on Acculturation, 1954, p. 981.]

Each of the three "stereotyped" roles, as well as both of the subsidiary roles, is represented in the Shonto contact situation. The significance of this differentiation may be expressed in considerable part by the observation that commercial and charitable institutions, in contrast to governmental ones, have to depend on the good will of the subordinate group for effective operation and that commercial institutions furthermore have to pay their own way.

The culture contact situation at Shonto offers, in nearly every area of life, alternative institutions in Navaho and in Anglo-American with overlapping functions (see "Summary," pp. 93–94). It is this condition which is expressed in the variability of Navaho dependence on different contact institutions to perform their overt functions. The measure of Navaho dependence on any contact institution is the negative measure of effective alternates in purely Navaho life. Dependence on the trading post is high because it performs functions on which the community depends, and which are not duplicated by any Navaho institution. The functions of the school and the hospital are equally necessary, but in each case there are also alternative Navaho institutions. The effectiveness of native religion for its own purposes is generally regarded as so high that it is felt in this case that the White institution does not offer a satisfactory alternative, in profound contrast to conditions elsewhere in the Navaho country (see Rapoport, 1954).

Inasmuch as they are chartered deliberately to deal with Navahos in one way or another, it might be said that all contact institutions on the Navaho Reservation depend on the Navahos for their very existence. This, however, is not a legitimate measure of functional dependence. Of all contact institutions on the Navaho Reservation it is only the trading post which has to pay its own way in cross-cultural relations. Therefore Shonto Trading Post and Shonto community stand in a relation of interdependence which is almost total (cf. "Navaho Economics," pp. 94–148; and "Retail Trade," pp. 184–214), and which is in profound contrast to the situation of every other contact institution. The trader's continued operation is contingent not merely on his performing his assigned function, but on his performing it effectively and successfully.

Among the factors of role must be counted the extent to which any contact institution and its operation have become integrated into the overall life of the community. Such integration may result from dependence on the institution in its overt role, or in some secondary or even unintentional role. For example, most Shonto men depend on the tribal councilman as a source of information on new government policies and programs that may affect them, and his activities are integrated into the life of the community to that extent. On the other hand he is not generally accepted as a representative of the community at the seat of government and thus as an instrument of its will, although that is his theoretical function (see "Social and Political Authority," pp. 65–68). Extent of integration, in addition, must be measured in terms of the number or percentage of people who depend on the contact institution as well as on the extent of their dependence. It is highest in the case of the trading post, upon which every household in the community is heavily dependent.

Coercive power plays an important and obvious part in the role of any contact institution (cf. Redfield, Linton, and Herskovits, 1936, p. 150). Insofar as their operation is legally ordained, all governmental institutions have a certain amount of direct coercive power. The hospital can threaten prosecution for refusal to submit infectious conditions to treatment, and the school for refusal to send children to school. Both, moreover, can threaten welfare recipients with loss of their benefits for either cause.

Since he is not officially responsible for the enforcement of the directives of the Navaho Tribal Council, the councilman has no constitutional coercive power. He can, however, implement the activities of the tribe within the community by threatening prosecution to those who resist them.

The trading post, although not legally ordained, has an enormous indirect coercive power as a result of the community's economic dependence. Its sources and the ways in which it can be exerted are described in "Retail Trade," pp. 184–214. The railroad has a similar power as regards those who work for it.

Of all contact institutions within Shonto community, only the missionary had no effective sanctions of any kind; his operation, like that of all missionaries in recent years, was hedged with restrictions drawn up by the Navaho tribe. Nevertheless, on one occasion in 1955 a young Shonto man said to the missionary, "They told you down at Window Rock you're not supposed to do anything against the old Navaho ways—just preach your ways. Then how come you're going around telling everybody they're going to hell?" Apparently, the missionary too felt the need of coercive sanctions.

The last entries in chart L are those which affect the capacity of a contact institution to communicate cross-culturally, regardless of its opportunities to do so. The first of these factors, "Character of Relations," largely determines the range of subjects which may appropriately be discussed in any verbal contact between Navaho and White. In their "Folk-Urban Continuum," Redfield and his followers have recognized personal relations as one of the features of folk society as contrasted to primarily instrumental interpersonal relations in urban society (see, e.g., Redfield, 1947; Miner, 1952). Where relations are personal there may be conversation on virtually any subject; instrumental relations on the other hand are instrumental to a common interest or end and limited accordingly.

It has already been observed that in spite of their special ordination as contacts with Navaho society, the character of all Bureau of Indian Affairs agencies among the Navaho remains essentially urban (see "Intracultural Orientations," pp. 248–253), like Government agencies everywhere. In keeping with this quality, the character of interpersonal relations between Navahos and Government installations is strictly instrumental. A Shonto Navaho is likely to contact the schoolteachers only to discuss immediate educational problems; the hospital only in connection with health, and so on.

The interpersonal relations maintained by missionaries in different parts of the Navaho Reservation probably vary to a large extent according to the individual personalities involved. Insofar as they are free from restrictions of fiat and protocol, and also have the ability to move around from hogan to hogan, missionaries are potentially in a position to establish strongly personal relations. Shonto's missionary attempted to do so, but was hampered by his ignorance of the Navaho language and of native culture and society. Of all Shonto's contact institutions, only the tribal councilman and the trader have sufficiently personal relations with the Navaho members of the community so that it is possible for the latter to take up any question with them.

The character of relations as well as certain factors of role have important bearing on the social accessibility of the contact institution to Navahos. Wherever relations are instrumental, accessibility is low as a corollary. The schoolteachers are readily accessible only to the parents of schoolchildren; the hospital is concerned only with health problems, and so on. Furthermore, the duties of the various Government officials involved do not include time for anything like prolonged discussion or debate even within the field of instrumental relations. An interview between parents and schoolteachers, for example, must be specially arranged and must take place during time specially set aside.

The social accessibility of the missionary and the tribal councilman is diminished by the fact that their physical accessibility is sometimes low. Also, in the case of the missionary, it is affected by the difficulty of communication in many cases. The trader, because of the nature of his work and his ultimate dependence on the goodwill of the community, is accessible at all times.

The willingness of Navahos to communicate with any contact institution, or to receive communications from or through it, may be affected in some cases by the privacy in which such communication can be made. An example is the fact that many Navahos wish to conceal from certain of their relatives the fact that they have received money, so that there will be no pressure on them to share it. Although to a degree wealth is a source of pride, some of Shonto's well-to-do men consistently belittle their wealth before Whites and even before each other, possibly for fear of any suspicion of witchcraft (cf. Hobson, 1954, pp. 7–9, 17–20). In any such concealment the collusion of the trader is likely to be required.

For most of Shonto's adults there can be little or no privacy in any relationship in which an interpreter is required; i.e., in any situation where only English is spoken. In the case of Government agencies the possibility of privacy is further precluded by the instrumental character of relations. In effect, only the trading post and the tribal councilman are left as potentially private cross-cultural contacts. The facility of private communication is normally afforded to any trading-post customer who has a legitimate reason for requesting it. Trader and customer retire to the living room of the trader's residence in such circumstances.

Finally, the language of communication plays an obvious part in relation to cross-cultural influences. It may be recalled that less than one-third of Shonto's adult Navahos have sufficient control of English to use it for practical communication (cf. table 13, p. 92). Yet the trading post and the various functionaries of the Navaho tribe are the only contact institutions capable of communicating in the Navaho language. The "Navaho" spoken by the trader is more properly a trade jargon or pidgin (see "Communication," pp. 212–214), but at all events it is true that the trading post is the only White contact institution which normally communicates with Navahos in a language better controlled by them than by it. The contribution of this one factor to the overall influence of Shonto Trading Post is undoubtedly enormous.

THE INFLUENCE OF SHONTO TRADING POST

It is not necessary to elaborate further on chart L to establish the fact that Shonto Trading Post is the principal source of cross-cultural influence in Shonto community. The influence of the store is consistently greater than that of any other contact institution; in the fields of material culture, commerce, and economics it is greater than that of all others combined. The various and diverse sources of this influence, as set forth in preceding pages, may be reviewed and summarized here in a few paragraphs.

INTRACULTURAL ORIENTATIONS

Shonto Trading Post has a greater number and variety of contacts with areas and institutions within its own sociocultural system than do other contact institutions at Shonto. Because of this as well as its high frequency of communication with most members of the Navaho community, the store is employed regularly or occasionally by all manner of outside institutions as a channel of communication with Navahos, and by Navahos for the reciprocal purpose. It is Shonto's foremost line of communication with the outside world.

INTRACULTURAL RELATIONS AT THE CONTACT LEVEL

The position of the trading post with regard to other contact institutions is not essentially different from its external relations with the American sociocultural system. The store has more, and more frequent, contact with Shonto's other contact institutions than they have with one another, and is used as a channel of communication by them as well as by outside organizations.

CROSS-CULTURAL RELATIONS: HISTORICAL

Shonto Trading Post was in operation nearly 20 years before any other effective instrument of contact between Shonto and the White world was established. During that time its Navaho neighbors developed a pattern of dependence on the store in all their dealings with the American sociocultural system which has persisted to a large extent even after the establishment of other channels. Navaho reaction to the store was friendly from the start and remained so, whereas it was initially hostile or indifferent in the case of many other contact institutions.

CROSS-CULTURAL RELATIONS: ACCESS

As a result of its integration into the life of the community Shonto Trading Post has more, and more frequent, contact with its Navaho neighbors than has any other White institution. Its contact and influence reach all age groups, all interest groups, and both sexes.

CROSS-CULTURAL RELATIONS: ROLE

The foundation of the trading post's position of paramount influence in Shonto community is undoubtedly to be found among the factors of role. The store is the only contact institution upon which Navahos are almost totally dependent for their livelihood; and is, at the same time, equally dependent on them on the same terms. There is thus established a condition of interdependence which is lacking in all other contacts, and which has important effects on the trader's social accessibility and communicative role.

CROSS-CULTURAL RELATIONS: COMMUNICATION

Shonto Trading Post has a unique capacity to communicate with the Navaho community by contrast to other White institutions, not only because of its high frequency of contact, but also because of its personal relations with the clientele, its high social accessibility and potential privacy, and above all its use of what passes for the Navaho language in communication.

These are the sources of Shonto Trading Post's cross-cultural influence. They are causes, not effects, and therefore cannot serve to measure influence as felt by the community. They can and do allow the conclusion that Shonto Trading Post, far above and beyond any other contact institution, has an important power either to induce or to prevent changes in the attitudes and behavior of Navaho individuals in Shonto community over a period of days, months, or years.

THE HISTORICAL MEASURE OF INFLUENCE

Cross-cultural influence can be estimated in terms of significant contributing factors, as was done above. It cannot actually be measured, however, except through cross-cultural effects. In other words, in the final analysis it can only be tested historically, in terms of culture change or adaptation. In a synchronic analysis such as the one undertaken here, no such measurement is possible. Nevertheless a sort of rough check on the comparative influence of different contact institutions may be obtained by examining each in the light of the general pattern of Navaho-White cultural adjustment in its field of special interest or activity.

In "Navaho Life" (pp. 53–94) modern Navaho life at Shonto was described in terms of a discrete series of adjustments to White cultural influences in different areas of culture. It was suggested that the overall pattern of such adjustments was by no means constant from one part of the Navaho Reservation to another, but would be likely to vary according to the range and intensity of contacts presented to each individual community or area (see "Summary," pp. 93–94). The pattern of adjustment to be found in each particular area of culture would therefore be the best historical index of the continuing cross-cultural influence of whatever contact institution was operative in that field.

The general pattern of cross-cultural adjustments at Shonto is set forth in chart M. Information entered therein is contained in the relevant portions of "Navaho Life," pp. 53–94. Individual adjustments may be summarized here in a few paragraphs.

SOCIAL ORGANIZATION

There has been no attempt on the part of any contact institution to modify the native social fabric with its dual structure of residence groups and households. These survive structurally and functionally (see "Economic Interdependence," pp. 103–108) intact.

CHART M.—General patterns of Navaho cultural adjustment at Shonto [1]

Area of culture	Principal contact institution	Status of Anglo traits	Status of Navaho traits	Pattern of adjustment
Social organization_	None_____	Not introduced_____	Retained_____	None.
Material culture___	Trading Post_____	Almost total acceptance.	Largely lost_____	General replacement.
Economics_____	Trading Post_____	Selected high acceptance.	Largely retained__	Essential supplementation.
Government_____	Tribal Councilmen_	Largely rejected_____	Largely retained__	Very slight replacement.
Law_____	Tribal Court and Police.	Selected acceptance	Largely retained__	Alternatives.
Education_____	Community School_	Accepted_____	Retained_____	Complementation.
Medicine_____	B.I.A. Hospital_____	Accepted_____	Retained_____	Altern. and complement.
Religion_____	Missionary_____	Generally rejected___	Retained_____	None.
Recreation_____	None_____	Not introduced_____	Retained_____	None.

[1] For detailed discussion, see appropriate portions of pp. 53–94.

MATERIAL CULTURE

Modern Navaho material culture is basically American of 50 to 100 years ago, with a few more up-to-date items thrown in. Native material culture survives only in a handful of items associated with native esoteric practices, i.e., singing and craft manufacture. The trading post is practically the community's sole source of American material goods.

ECONOMICS

Modern Shonto derives four-fifths of its income directly from White sources (cf. table 21, p. 137) as against one-fifth from what may be termed native resources. Nevertheless the latter continue to take precedence. Navahos behave as if they were actually living on their native resources, supplemented voluntarily by wagework, relief, and the like. In actual practice few families could survive without a considerable amount of such supplementation, whereas many if not most could now survive without native resources of any kind. The overall pattern of adjustment is termed "essential (i.e., necessary) supplementation" (see "Summary," pp. 93–94).

GOVERNMENT

Lines of traditional social authority remain strong. There has been no acceptance of formal government in replacement of these, although there is unwilling submission to the authority of government, both tribal and Federal, in certain areas. The tribal councilman is accepted as its local representative and is listened to but never consulted.

LAW

The operation of tribal (i.e., White-modeled) law is not automatic, but must be invoked at the initiative of persons within the community, by swearing out a complaint and calling out the police from Tuba City. Tribal law therefore serves to provide an injured party with additional retributive sanctions in case he is unable to secure satisfaction through native channels. Any person may elect either to try for redress through the Navaho system or through the courts. The two systems are essentially alternatives.

EDUCATION

School education is recognized as necessary for success in contacts with the White man's world, but does not replace native education for life in the Navaho world, which survives both in the preschool years and during summer visits of schoolchildren to their homes.

MEDICINE

There is widespread acceptance of the efficiency of both White and Navaho medicine, and little sense of conflict between them. Each has its specific virtues. White medicine has gone farthest toward replacing the native practice where the latter was always and admittedly weakest: in treating painful and infectious conditions. There are strong indications that Navaho singers are glad to be relieved of these inevitably dubious cases. On the other hand there is some overt recognition of the psychiatric value of Navaho medicine, so that the two practices are to a considerable extent complementary.

RELIGION

There are only two professing Christians at Shonto. Acceptance of Christianity is confined to a few vague beliefs and no practices. The efforts of the community's missionary were met with indifference, and a permit for a permanent establishment was denied.

RECREATION

White recreations are beginning to filter into Shonto community indirectly through the influence of other Navahos. The principal of these are drinking and listening to the radio. They are not introduced by any direct contact institution. There is no organized recreation in the American fashion, such as baseball or basketball. Both sports are popular in other parts of the reservation.

SUMMARY

There can be no doubt that the highest degree of culture change at Shonto has taken place in the fields of material culture and economics. The almost total replacement of Navaho material culture and the successful shift from a primarily subsistence to a primarily market economy are the crowning features of Shonto's cultural adjustment to the White world. Both of these have taken place in fields of interest which are dominated by the trading post, and both can certainly be attributed heavily to its influence. It would seem, therefore, that the structurally inherent cross-cultural influence of Shonto Trading Post in the modern Navaho community is borne out by the observable facts of culture history. It remains, in the section which follows, to discover how cross-cultural influence is exerted from day to day in the lives of modern Navahos.

CROSS-CULTURAL ROLE

The foregoing discussion of Shonto Trading Post as a contact agency has focused upon the "cross-cultural status" of the store (cf., "The Structure of Contact," pp. 231–267) as determined by its own charter and by the social structure of the contact situation at Shonto. In one sense, therefore, the role of the trading post has also been established, insofar as *role* is often conceptualized simply as the behavioral aspect of *status*. Both terms are defined with regard to cultural expectation rather than observed behavior.

There is, however, another aspect of role which remains to be explored. Whatever the "ideal role" (cf. Levy, 1952, p. 160) of Shonto Trading Post, the actual behavior of the trader is not determined entirely by the expectations of either Navahos or Whites, but by his own motivations. Before going on to consider role in this light it is necessary to clarify the concept of role as employed in the present study, and particularly as between its structural and processual aspects.

THE CONCEPT OF CROSS-CULTURAL ROLE

LEVEL OF ABSTRACTION

Linton (1936, p. 114) noted that—

. . . the term role is used with a double significance. Every individual has a series of roles deriving from the various patterns in which he participates and at the same time a *role*, general, which represents the sum total of these roles and determines what he does for his society and what he can expect from it.

In practice anthropologists seem to have used the term at nearly every level of abstraction without any very clear specification. A recent theoretical study of acculturation (Summer Seminar on Acculturation, 1954, p. 981) asserts that contact agencies "may adopt a complex but limited number of roles," while a number of other writers (e.g., Paul, 1953, pp. 431–434; Kennard and Macgregor, 1953, p. 837; Forde, 1953, pp. 859–861) apparently take the view that they have only a single role.

Throughout the present study the term "role" is employed only in its most general sense, as applying to a single overall social position and set of behaviors associated with Shonto Trading Post. In its more specific connotations the term has been replaced by "function" and "activity" respectively (cf. "A Note on Terminology," pp. 214–216).

THE DEFINITION OF ROLE

Role, according to regular anthropological usage, is the dynamic aspect of *status*. Notwithstanding the extreme frequency with which this definition has been reiterated (e.g., Linton, 1936, p. 114; Davis, 1942, p. 311; Gillin, 1948, p. 349; Hoebel, 1949, p. 288; Parsons, 1949, p. 43; Bennett and Tumin, 1952, p. 96), there is quite evidently no general agreement as to whether it is actually meant in a structural or in a processual sense. To some writers (e.g., Gillin, 1948, p. 349; Bennett and Tumin, 1952, pp. 96–101) "the dynamic aspect of status" consists of the behavior culturally expected of a person or agency occupying any given status. The term "status" itself thereby becomes no more than a label for a social position, all of whose behavioral referants are subsumed under "role." The two terms are, in this sense, completely interchangeable, as when Davis (1949, p. 11) speaks of "the dual role of the social scientist," Linton (1936, p. 480) describes "the warrior role," and Parsons (1949, p. 43) mentions "the role of the surgeon." In referring to expected rather than observed behavior, *role* cannot genuinely be classed as a dynamic concept.

In spite of the usages quoted, however, the same writers have elsewhere conceived of role as "the manner in which an individual actually carries out the requirements of his position" (Davis, 1942, p. 311; see also Linton, 1936, p. 114, and Parsons, 1949, pp. 34, 43). This is obviously a very different matter from the way in which others expect he will carry out the requirements of his position. This usage of role can only apply to empirically observable behavior, not to expectation. Thus, as Levy (1952, p. 159) observes, "If the term 'role' is used consistently with its definition there can be no talk of people acting in terms of roles. Their actions *are* their roles."

It is apparent that the term "role" is being employed in both structural and processual senses to designate the behavioral (not necessarily dynamic) aspect of status. Levy (1952, pp. 159–160) resolves the discrepancy between the two usages by referring to the former, connotating expected behavior, as "ideal role," and the latter, involving observed behavior, as "actual role." He notes also that "ideal role" is properly an aspect of status (Levy, 1952, p. 160).

In the present study, the ideal role of Shonto Trading Post has already been identified in terms of a complex of functions and activities as described in pages 184–230. The term "role" as employed throughout the present discussion, however, refers to "actual role"— to the way in which the trading post actually performs, and in a few cases does not perform, its complex of stipulated functions. Further, since the study is concerned with the behavior of the trader with specific reference to his Navaho clientele, said behavior may be appropriately said to constitute the cross-cultural role of the trader.

THE ANALYSIS OF ROLE

The distinction between ideal and actual role, significant in many cases (cf. Levy, 1952, p. 160; also Merton, 1949, pp. 61–63 on "manifest" vs. "latent" functions), becomes of profound importance in situations of culture contact. Where there is imperfect cross-cultural communication and no uniformity of values, there is likely also to be no uniformity of expectation. In these circumstances actual behavior may be freer from the dictates of social expectation than is normally true in intracultural situations. If "intercultural roles" are defined as "constellations of behavior which are appropriate to particular situations" (Summer Seminar on Acculturation, 1954, p. 981), it is necessary to discover from whose point of view they are appropriate.

It was noted earlier ("Ancillary Functions," pp. 220–230) that perceptions of the true purpose and proper functions of the trading post vary considerably as between Navahos and Whites. There is not even any uniform conception among Whites themselves as to the status of the store (cf. "Intracultural Relations at the Contact Level," pp. 253–256). In other words Shonto's trader has no one clearly defined ideal role, but a series of partly conflicting ones. These circumstances allow him considerable leeway in "the manner in which (he) actually carries out the requirements of his position," (Davis, 1942, p. 311).

In the case of Shonto Trading Post, and probably in many other cases as well, the factor which primarily serves to differentiate actual from expected behavior is that of covert motivation. Every individual and agency has recognized overt motivations which are part of its status and help to determine its ideal role. It is also undoubtedly true that all, or nearly all, individuals and agencies have additional perceptions of self-interest which, possibly because of conflict with the perceived self-interest of others, are not shared with society. Being covert, such motivations do not figure in recognized status nor in expected behavior, but they may, nevertheless, play an important part in determining actual behavior. In a general sense, therefore, covert motivation may be taken as the measure of divergence between ideal and actual roles.

It should be apparent that the actual cross-cultural role of Shonto Trading Post cannot be ascertained or predicted from its status or ideal role as seen by either Navahos or Whites. It can be ascertained only by identifying the overt and covert motivations of the trader himself, and by studying his actual cross-cultural behavior with reference to those motivations. In other words it is necessary to consider the ways in which the manifold functions of the trading post are made to serve the interest, not of Navahos and other Whites as outlined in "Community Services," pp. 214–230, but of the trader.

MOTIVATION

In "Community Services," (see "Charter," p. 215) it was stated that the fundamental motivation for the operation of Shonto Trading Post is that of maximum sustained profit. The desire and need for *sustained* profit serves to differentiate the average trading post of today from that of the 19th century (see "Early Trading Posts," pp. 150–154) and has been an inevitable byproduct of increasingly stabilized social and economic conditions. Many of the first Navaho traders, were out for quick riches in the commodity market (see, e.g., Underhill, 1956, p. 183) and were quite willing to impoverish their Navaho clientele in the process. It was only as the opportunities for lucrative commodity speculation were gradually eliminated that traders were forced to settle for long-range profit.

A few modern traders are still primarily concerned with immediate profit; particularly those who feel themselves to be losing out to town competition. These operators are faced with the specter of declining investment value of their properties, and, believing their days to be numbered, are avowedly out to squeeze the last dollar out of the Indian trade while they have the chance. Particularly in the vicinity of Gallup, where supermarkets and other efficient and modern businesses have captured a great deal of the Navaho trade, and even the credit trade, most traders are out to salvage what they can at any cost.

Stores in this area advertise prominently their willingness to buy mature sheep and other Navaho productive assets for up to 50 percent cash. "We'll buy anything they got" the trader at Ganado informed the writer.

There is, of course, no significant profit to be made from the resale of sheep, saddles, rifles, and other Navaho assets bought by Gallup traders. The basis of these transactions is the 50 percent merchandise stipulation, which in other regards figures also in the system of commodity exchange at Shonto Trading Post (see "Direct Exchange," pp. 199–201). Gallup traders take advantage of the common Navaho desire for liquor, and need for money to buy it, by affording them a ready opportunity to convert their assets into cash—at the cost of having to receive half its value in merchandise at very high markups. The impact of several years of such trading operations in the Gallup area is readily observable: livestock holdings have been declining steadily and markedly, at the same time that they have been greatly on the increase at Shonto and throughout the northwestern Navaho country (cf. Young, 1955, pp. 191–192.)

Another feature of trading for short-term profits, as found in the Gallup area, is the deliberate promotion of great quantities of dead pawn through a policy of allowing cash loans against any piece of jewelry from any applicant, whether or not known to the trader. Dealers in Indian arts and crafts can readily confirm the fact that the great majority of dead Navaho pawn comes not from the reservation but from a handful of off-reservation traders, particularly in the east. Invariable symptoms of the quick-profit trader are pawn racks filled largely with Pendleton blankets and saddles. These are the last remaining pawnable assets of many Navahos in the Gallup area, who have already lost most or all of their jewelry in the form of unredeemed pawn.

The majority of modern trading posts, however, and particularly those which still enjoy significant territorial monopoly, are geared to long-term operation for sustained though moderate profits. This is particularly true of Shonto and other stores in the more remote portions of the reservation. These enterprises are continually concerned not only with sustaining sales, but also with sustaining and increasing the buying power of their clientele by the preservation and increase of Navaho productive resources (cf. Collier and Collier, 1953, pp. 219–220; Sanders, et al., 1953, p. 233). Trademarks of the sustained-profit trading post are conservative pawn policy, aimed at maximum redemption; minimum cash loans; refusal to buy mature sheep, ewe lambs, jewelry, and other productive resources; and a complex of activities designed to assist the community to a higher income level (see "Charter Functions," pp. 216–220). Above all, the sustained-profit operation strives to keep the resources of the community as much as possible in the community. All of these activities are characteristic of Shonto Trading Post. Perhaps the clearest signification of the trader's intention, however, is that in 1956 he declined an opportunity to sell the store at a 50 percent profit.

The basic motivation of maximum sustained profit is translated into a series of concrete operational objectives which go far to determine the behavior, hence the role, of the trader. The more overt objectives, underlying the charter functions of the store, were identified in "Community Services" (cf. chart E): minimum competition, maximum sales, and maximum community income. These objectives are generally recognized, especially by Navahos, as appropriate to the store, and are part of its status and ideal role.

There is, however, another and equally basic objective of Shonto Trading Post which, although implicit in the concept of sustained profit, is essentially covert. This is the objective of maximum and continuing Navaho dependence on the trading post (cf. Coolidge and Coolidge, 1930, p. 68; Kluckhohn and Leighton, 1946, p. 39). It is, of course, furthered to some extent by all of the overt objectives of the trader. Even more, however, it is served in a series of more subtle ways through the behavior of the trader as a representative of and spokesman for the White world.

The behavior and role of Shonto's trader, and of most other traders in this remote region, can only be fully understood in terms of the covert objective of perpetuating Navaho dependence, which in many instances takes precedence over all others. In this respect the trader has been and is unwilling to sell the future short for the sake of immediate profit, and it is here that the essential difference between his overt and covert roles lies.

PERFORMANCE OF FUNCTIONS

In "Retail Trade," pp. 184–214, and "Community Services," pp. 214–230, the cross-cultural functions and activities of Shonto's trader were defined and classified according to Navaho expectations, as well as the expectations of Whites other than the trader. The purpose of the present discussion is to reexamine and reclassify the same series of functions, and particularly the way in which they are performed, as determined not by the expectation of others but by the objectives, overt and covert, of the trader himself.

MINIMUM COMPETITION

The competitive position of Shonto Trading Post is based initially on a significant territorial monopoly (cf. "Market Control," pp. 169–170). The store's nearest competitor is located some 8 miles away by airline, and nearly 20 miles away by road (see "Trading," pp. 42–43; also map 2). With Navaho mobility increasing steadily through the introduction and use of trucks, however, territorial monopoly alone is no longer sufficient to insure a monopoly of trade. In these circumstances, as noted earlier ("Market Control," pp. 169–170), Shonto and many other trading posts have developed the technique of credit saturation as an effective device to control the consumer market (see also Kluckhohn and Leighton, 1946, p. 39).

The most direct way to eliminate competition, however, is to discourage and impede mobility on the part of the clientele. Shonto's trader is able to accomplish this in a variety of ways. Most significantly, he discourages in every way possible the purchase and use of automobiles, both by precept and action. He is the only credit reference whom Shonto Navahos can furnish, and he has on several occasions given unsatisfactory references when consulted by Flagstaff auto dealers (see "Ancillary Functions for Whites," pp. 227–229). He has also and repeatedly refused to lend money for the purchase of cars or to meet payments on them, even to avoid repossesssion. Although required by his lease agreement to sell gasoline, he re-orders so tardily and infrequently that the tank is empty, or reputedly so, a great deal of the time. Gasoline, moreover, is sold only on strictly cash terms.

The trader also discourages the use of cars by precept. He dwells on the uncertainty and especially the expense of operating them (both considerable in the Navaho Country), asserting that he would not have one himself if he did not need it to go in and out of town. He has even been known to state that the store truck is his biggest operating expense, and "the reason I don't make any more money." He can and does also point to the evil moral influence of the automobile: the fact, popularly alleged by traders, that most of the pickups are owned by bootleggers and drunkards (see "Native Commercial and Professional Enterprise," pp. 125–127). Similar sentiments regarding the automobile were often voiced by the old country storekeeper during the last stages of his losing competition with town merchants (see Carson, 1954).

Through his complex of ancillary functions Shonto's trader has various other opportunities to impede and minimize competition. He makes it a regular policy to intercept and eliminate competitive advertising, by removing from the mails and destroying brochures and even mail-order catalogues. He also refuses to assist or to post orders to mail-order houses. Although it has often been requested, he will not allow Shonto residents to listen to Navaho-language broadcasts on the store radio, because they advertise low prices offered by town merchants.

Finally, as a source of information about the White world in general, the trader is often able to disparage his competitors with little fear of rebuttal. He is particularly fond of quoting Shonto flour and shoe prices as against the alleged (and sometimes fictitious) prices charged by competing merchants for the same items. His most common sales pitch is: "It would cost you more in town." Similarly, when Navahos complain about high prices, as is not uncommon, his invariable reply is: "It's just the same in town. Things are going up everywhere."

By comparison to his own store, the trader is able to say about nearly every competitor either that its retail prices are too high, its commodity prices too low, its merchandise inferior, or its proprietor dishonest. His most vociferous disparagement, however, is reserved for Flagstaff; not so much for competing merchants as for the town itself. He dwells on the presence of bars and bootleggers, prostitutes, and petty thieves, and other evils designed especially to victimize the unwary Navaho (cf. "Intracultural Relations at the Contact Level," pp. 253–356). This type of propaganda has the effect of making the Flagstaff merchants guilty by association; implying that their admittedly attractive advertising serves only to draw Navahos into the clutches of town predators.

MAXIMUM SALES

Traders have long since discovered that Navahos, like other people, generally find it much easier to spend money which they do not have than money which is actually in their possession. For this reason they have concentrated on credit saturation as their primary technique of sales promotion (see "Sales Promotion," pp. 180–182; also Kluckhohn and Leighton, 1946, p. 39). Ancillary functions of the trading post assist this practice in several ways. First of all, the trader's functions as channel of communication, as well as mail distributor, frequently furnish him with advance information about Navaho income, allowing him to grant credit against it and thereby encumber it before it actually arrives.

As claims agent (see "Railroad Work," pp. 129–133) the trader has official information as to when his clients will begin to receive unemployment compensation, and how much they will receive. He obtains the same kind of advance information with regard to welfare income by intercepting and opening letters addressed to Shonto Navahos by the State Department of Public Welfare.[24]

---

[24] The action of the trader as agent for welfare claimants is in every way parallel to his function as claims agent for railroad workers, except that it is without official sanction of any kind. Nevertheless it has become so completely institutionalized that both Navahos and traders themselves have come to regard it as one of their official functions. Shonto's trader argues openly that his intercession is necessary in securing benefits— that his clients would never get on relief without his help—and that therefore he is entitled to the same perquisites that he enjoys as claims agent. At any rate few if any Shonto Navahos realize that communications regarding their welfare status are actually addressed to them and not to the trader.

The trader has also a more direct source of information with regard to welfare accounts. Since the store is utilized by caseworkers as a contact point in interviewing their Navaho claimants (see "Ancillary Functions for Whites," pp. 227–229), he is sometimes able to obtain information face-to-face. His relations with caseworkers have in one or two cases been sufficiently cordial so that the latter have been willing to furnish him with private information about increases or decreases in welfare payments, so that he could make the necessary adjustments in their credit accounts. Speaking of a woman recipient of Aid to Dependent Children, a caseworker in 1953 told Shonto's trader "you'd better clean her up; I'm going to cut her off;" i.e., "you'd better close out her credit account now because her next relief check will be her last."

Successful credit saturation depends largely on obtaining advance information of this kind. Where information is lacking or where the individual involved is slow in accumulating debt, however, it can also be furthered by the practice of delaying the delivery of checks and money orders until most of their face value has been exhausted in credit. As mail distributor for the community, Shonto's trader always has first notice of the arrival of any income. In sorting the mail for delivery (which is always done in the privacy of his own living room) his first act is to take out all checks and money orders, and determine the amounts thereof. Most of these are nowadays mailed in window-type envelopes and are thus readily identifiable, and face values can be read by squeezing the envelope at the sides so that most of the check is visible through the window. Other letters suspected of containing checks (e.g., letters written home by railroad workers) are held to the light to ascertain their contents.

The great majority of checks arriving in any given mail delivery are certain to have been anticipated by the trader as a result of his various sources of information, and their face value will have been duly exhausted in credit. These can therefore be earmarked for immediate distribution. Checks which arrive unexpectedly, on the other hand, can be "lost" (i.e., set aside) until sufficient credit has been allowed against them.[25]

---

[25] Only one instance is on record when Shonto's owner was caught completely off guard by the arrival of a large sum of money in the community. A woman recipient of Aid to Dependent Children opened her regular check envelope and discovered not one but three checks for $85.00 each; the two extras having been inserted to cover a period when benefits were withheld by mistake. The trader was entirely unprepared for this development, and realized that it was now too late to transform the windfall into store profit by any device other than old-fashioned high-pressure salesmanship. The result was an extreme but not unheard-of example of trade ingenuity. Since the crowded atmosphere of the store is seldom conducive to effective salesmanship, Shonto's owner solved the problem by closing the store, giving as a pretext the fact that a meeting was going on outside. He then secretly readmitted the woman, thereby locking her in and all other customers out, and had over 2 hours in which to concentrate his salesmanship on her without interruption. Eventually he sold her a wagon, the full value of which came to considerably more than the value of the two unencumbered checks.

Economically, the overall effect of trading post policy in maximizing sales is to keep to a minimum the amount of liquid cash circulating in the community. In this way the trading post is perpetuating a sort of commodity and barter economy by eliminating capital and by treating cash income as though it were scrip negotiable only for merchandise at the store. In this scheme of operation it is not surprising that a relief or railroad check is conceived by both Navahos and the trader as little different from a due bill, to be paid out in merchandise over a period of time (see "Direct Exchange," pp. 199–201).

MAXIMUM COMMUNITY INCOME

Since the beginnings of the Navaho trade it has been the historic function of the trader to develop new and increased sources of income for his clientele (cf. Sanders et al., 1953, p. 233; Underhill, 1956, p. 181). The overall contribution of traders to the modern Navaho economy has undoubtedly far outstripped that of Government programs and of other White agencies. Such diversified but regular sources of Navaho income as lamb and wool sales, craft production, railroad wages, and unemployment compensation have all come into being through the initiative or intercession of traders. The trader's stake in the Navaho economy is widely recognized, and is expressed in a series of functions which were described in pp. 214–230.

In addition to his officially sanctioned activities, Shonto's trader is often able to act unofficially in such a way as to extend the benefits of railroad work and unemployment compensation, as well as state welfare, somewhat beyond their officially stipulated limits. In all of his activities on behalf of community income the trader's essential motivation is more closely allied to that of his Navaho clientele than to the stated objectives of the White agencies with and for which he is working. In these respects Shonto's trader feels and avers that he is merely adapting the inflexible and unrealistic criteria of eligibility for employment and benefit programs to the special realities of Navaho life.

Most traders take considerable liberties with their duties as claims agents for the Railroad Retirement Board. At Shonto, age records and information have been withheld and even falsified, allowing a considerable number of men both above and below the official age limits to work on the railroad each year (see "Railroad Work," pp. 129–133).[26] Other information potentially deterimental to employment, such as police records and unsatisfactory work histories, is commonly withheld not only from the Railroad Retirement Board but from all other potential employers.[27]

---

[26] One Shonto man actually worked until he was 63—13 years over the current maximum age limit for track laborers.

[27] One of the regular employees of Navajo National Monument once informed the writer that he had served 2 weeks in jail for having too many sheep, although this information if officially divulged could have cost him his job.

In deference to the difficulties of travel in the Navaho Country, Shonto's trader occasionally permits unemployment claimants to sign their unemployment affidavits on days other than that officially designated by the R.R.B. (see "Railroad Work," pp. 129–133). No phase of his activity as claims agent, however, causes the trader more difficulty than the requirement that claimants, in order to receive benefits, must certify themselves ready and willing to go to work. The trader has explained repeatedly that the query "Are you ready to go to work?" is merely a matter of form, and must be answered in the affirmative, also as a matter of form, in order to qualify for benefits. Nevertheless the tendency of Navahos to take things literally is so strong (cf. Kluckhohn and Leighton, 1946, p. 231) that claimants frequently interpret the question as an offer of employment, and answer truthfully in the negative. As a result nearly all traders simply dispense with the question, certifying their unemployment claimants as eligible without bothering to consult them. If the question is asked, the trader is likely to tell the individual how to answer it in the same breath. If he still receives a negative answer he will nevertheless enter it on paper in the affirmative, with an admonition to the claimant to "quit kidding." At no time in the writer's experience has any Shonto man ever been officially certified as unwilling to accept work if offered, and therefore ineligible for unemployment compensation.[28]

Traders find additional occasion to use their own discretion in their efforts on behalf of relief applicants. Most of them believe, or profess to believe, that the official standards of eligibility for welfare benefits are too severe, especially since it is thought that any Navaho with steady income "has to support half his relatives all the time" (cf. "Economic Interdependence," pp. 103–108). Shonto's trader, like most others, often withholds information about the economic status and resources of his welfare applicants which might be detrimental to their claims. He is unwilling to accept valuable pieces of jewelry in pawn for them, since they might be spotted in his vault by visiting caseworkers. In acting as interpreter between Navahos and caseworkers, moreover, the trader can and does prompt the former in their replies to some extent so as to emphasize their economic plight. Questions can be phrased in such a way that the appli-

---

[28] For its part, the Railroad Retirement Board is not entirely unaware of the ways in which traders discharge their functions as claims agents. The chief of the Winslow office, in fact, has become so suspicious of them that he makes periodic spot checks on his traders during their signup days. These surprise visits have occasionally provoked considerable consternation at Shonto, where the affidavits of eligibility which have been carefully prepared in advance must all be hidden and destroyed, and new ones drawn up in the presence of the claimant. Nevertheless the trader's command of "Trader Navaho" (cf. "Communication," pp. 212–214) usually enables him to brief his claimants on how to behave and what to say without the knowledge of the inspector. The question of eligibility is likely to be phrased in Navaho as "You're willing to go to work, aren't you—say 'yes' or you won't get a check—?" If it is not too obvious it is also possible for the trader to mistranslate a negative answer.

cant names only his or her own personal resources (instead of all those of the household as required by law), but at the same time lists all the members of the residence group as partial dependents.

Because of the scarcity of overnight accommodations, caseworkers for the Nava-Hopi Unit of the State Department of Public Welfare, like many other travelers in the Navaho Country, were often forced to accept the hospitality of traders while making their rounds of contacts. The inherent advantages in the role of host were exploited to the full by numerous traders, who tried to suggest in various ways that they would be amply repaid for their hospitality if certain claimants were certified as eligible for relief. One caseworker was heard to say that he would rather sleep on the ground, or drive a hundred miles to the nearest hotel, than have to spend his evenings continually listening to traders pleading on behalf of erstwhile relief cases. At the present time the State government, following the Railroad Retirement Board, has become so suspicious of the activity of traders that it no longer allows its caseworkers to accept their hospitality.

Another area in which the activities of Shonto's trader sometimes exceed the expectations of his clientele is in his function as a public scribe. Letters written to absent wageworkers on behalf of their families will sometimes be found to contain gratuitous passages of sage advice such as to stay on the job, not to spend too much money off the reservation, and to send home a money order as soon as possible. Recipients of such letters have undoubtedly come to recognize the trader's special touch in these matters.

DEPENDENCE ON THE TRADING POST

All of the activities so far mentioned contribute their part to Navaho economic dependence on the trading post. Together, however, they constitute only one aspect of the condition of dependence which the trader consciously or unconsciously strives to create and to perpetuate. Just as many modern businesses find that it is safer and easier to meet competition by offering various services and premiums rather than by lowering prices (see, e.g., Brown and Davidson, 1953, pp. 474–475; Dolva and Beckley, 1950, p. 286), so modern Shonto Trading Post attempts to forestall competition from town merchants by offering services which the latter cannot duplicate. Thus the whole complex of ancillary functions described earlier (pp. 220–230) is sustained by the trader, not merely because they can be made to serve the interests of immediate profit, but also because in a more general way they contribute to continuing Navaho dependence on the trading post.

Many traders recall with undisguised nostalgia the "agency era" prior to 1930 (see "Government Development," pp. 44–48), when the trader held unchallenged sway throughout much of the Navaho Reservation, and the trading post for many Navahos was the beginning and the end of the White world (see Kluckhohn and Leighton, 1946, p. 79; Sanders et al., 1953, p. 233). As one trader of over 40 years' experience put it, "In the old days the Government minded its own business and left the traders alone." Those were the days when, so long as wool prices held up, "all you had to do to make a profit was to open the doors," in the words of the same informant, and it was not necessary to keep any books.

The years since 1930 have seen a general broadening of the area of contact between the Navaho and White worlds, accompanied by increasingly unstable social and economic conditions on the reservation. These processes are clearly recognized as a threat to the Navaho trading post no less than to the economic complex to which it is adapted. To counteract them most traders try in a variety of ways to preserve the conditions and relationships which prevailed before 1930, and especially to preserve their own paramount position in the structure of cultural contact (cf. pp. 231–267).

It was noted earlier ("Intracultural Relations at the Contact Level," pp. 253–256), however, that in recent years Shonto Trading Post has admitted the community school and the Tuba City Hospital to partnership as representatives of the White world. These three institutions recognize the legitimacy or at least the inevitability of each other's interests and motivations, and are thus enabled to work in consistent harmony. The school and the hospital remain at the present time, however, the only agencies with which Shonto's trader is willing to share the responsibility of first-hand culture contact. He noticeably does not encourage Shonto Navahos to seek out other White individuals or agencies; on the contrary by precept and performance he encourages them to leave all such contacts in his hands. He openly avows that his special familiarity with the White world, coupled with his special sympathy with Navaho interests, makes him better able to look after the welfare of his clients than are they themselves. So far as the writer's knowledge goes, no Shonto Navaho has ever been advised or encouraged by the trader to go to Tuba City or Flagstaff for any purpose except to go to the hospital. He is likely to suggest that all other functions be left in his hands.

Above all, the trader discourages mobility. This objective involves not only various positive sanctions such as impeding the purchase and use of cars, but also the effort to see that as many as possible of the community's wants are satisfied *in* the community. It means that he must perform himself the functions for which Navahos would otherwise have to go elsewhere. In a sense it also involves him in the effort to keep the community's wants restricted to those things which he can supply. Shonto's trader freely expresses his fear of creating new demands which might be as well or better satisfied by others, thereby increasing his area of competition with town merchants. To this end he discourages the circulation of any sort of advertising material in the community.

Like many modern traders, Shonto's owner is generally reluctant to introduce new and improved products (in marked contrast to early Navaho traders—see Sanders et al., 1953, p. 233; Underhill, 1956, p. 179). Regular salesmen from the wholesale houses of Flagstaff and Farmington assert that it is all they can do to persuade their trading post customers to stock new items and lines even on a trial basis. "Navvies like everything just so; changing around upsets them" is the rationale offered for this policy.

The functions of the trader in promoting and encouraging wage work do not in practice conflict with his need to limit Navaho mobility. In railroad way labor, he has discovered the ideal compromise between the two objectives. Everything about the structure of railroad work exactly suits the purposes of the trader. First, he himself is the officially designated recruiter and benefit agent, so that to that extent Navaho dependence on the store is not only furthered but institutionalized (see "Railroad Work," pp. 129–133). Secondly, Navahos are employed in large gangs and in remote areas, so that the actual work situation involves an absolute minimum of culture contact, and also affords few opportunities to spend earnings (see "Points of Contact," pp. 248–263). Thirdly, the work (unlike agricultural labor) involves men only; the wives and families are left behind more or less under the trader's care, and draw credit against the worker's wages. Finally, the trader's capacity as claims agent furnishes him officially and legally with advance information about unemployment compensation which enables him to practice credit saturation to the full.

As Shonto's trader once remarked, the fact that he actually gets paid (at 50 cents per claim affidavit) for discharging his duties as claims agent seems almost too good to be true, since he would be quite willing to pay for the same privileges. There can be no doubt that the overwhelming preponderance of railroad work over all other wage labor, not only at Shonto (table 21, p. 137) but throughout the Navaho Reservation (see Young, 1955, p. 65), is due in large measure to the eagerness and persistence with which traders have promoted this type of employment for their clientele.

Shonto's trader is thoroughly selective in his promotion of wage work. He does not encourage his clients to leave the reservation in whole family groups, nor to migrate to areas where they will come into intensive contact with White society and culture. In spite of his supposed cooperation with the State Employment Service field office at Tuba City (see "Ancillary Functions for Whites," pp. 227–229), in actual fact the trader, along with nearly all his neighbors, consistently discourages Navaho agricultural labor. He may post clearance orders on the bulletin board at the request of the field office, but he never announces them on the "headline slate" (see "Information Agency," pp. 221–223). Moreover, he consistently advises verbally against taking these jobs on the ground that they do not pay, and that agricultural employers abuse and cheat their Navaho field hands.

The trader has never actually assisted in recruiting agricultural labor. For the most part, on the contrary, he simply declines to pass along information which reaches him about employment opportunities of this sort. If individual Navahos inquire about farm jobs they are likely to be told that there are none available. The profound decline in agricultural work undertaken by Navahos from the northwestern area since 1950 (see "Other Wage Work," pp. 134–135) is certainly attributable largely to the behavior of traders in discouraging such employment.

Naturally enough, the trader does not favor permanent off-reservation relocation as a general principle. In any case few of his customers have the requisite education and experience. The trader generally takes the position that Navahos should remain Navahos or else should give up their Navaho ties altogether. Those individuals whose superior education makes them desirous of a higher standard of living (and hence are something of a threat to the old ways in the community) he feels should leave the reservation behind entirely. The great uneducated majority, on the other hand, should be satisfied to live in the community as Navahos without aping their White neighbors.

PERCEPTIONS AND VALUES

It has been asserted repeatedly, here and elsewhere (e.g., Coolidge and Coolidge, 1930, p. 67; Luomala, 1938, p. 5; Kluckhohn and Leighton, 1946, p. 79; Sanders et al., 1953, p. 233) that the trading post remains the primary spokesman for the White world in most Navaho communities. The trader is consistently called upon to interpret not only Government policy and programs, but all manner of White behavior, beliefs, and values (cf. chart F, p. 221). It was also noted, however ("Intracultural Relations at the Contact Level," pp. 253–256) that there is no real uniformity or continuity of values and interests as among the different agencies in contact with Shonto community. In these circumstances it is not surprising that the trader, in his capacity as spokesman for his society and culture, actually speaks for himself. The White world and the place of Navahos in it are portrayed as the trader would like to see them, and the values expressed are the trader's own.

If motivation spells an important difference between the expectations of Navahos and the actual behavior of the trader (see pp. 270–272), it results in an equal difference in outlook and behavior as between the trader and all other White contact agencies. As regards the place of the Navaho in the modern world, the trader's values are in many respects closer to those of Navahos themselves than they are to the values of his White neighbors. Government policy, although it has fluctuated considerably over the years, has been and remains essentially "assimilationist" (cf. Summer Seminar on Acculturation, 1954, pp. 988–990). In a more limited sphere, the objective of missionaries and of town merchants is the same. At the opposite extreme, a strong body of popular American sentiment favors Navaho "reactive adaptation" to White contact (see Summer Seminar on Acculturation, 1954, p. 987; also Redfield, Linton and Herskovits, 1936, p. 152). Between these two extremes, both of which he constantly disparages, the trader holds fast to the ideal of "stabilized pluralism" (Summer Seminar on Acculturation, 1954, p. 990) upon which his operation is structurally dependent.

The trader's special ideal in Navaho-White relations colors his own perception of them, and even more the view which he passes along to the Navaho community. As a result, the behavior and objectives of others are consistently reinterpreted, both deliberately and subconsciously, to conform to the trader's own ideals. Shonto's Navahos thereby form an impression as to what the White world expects of them which is, in fact, unique to the trading post, and at considerable variance from the actual expectations of other Whites.

THE WHITE WORLD IN GENERAL

Shonto's trader resolves the inevitable conflict between the ideals of stabilized pluralism on the one hand and intensive education for Navahos on the other by taking the view that there is no acceptable middle ground between "traditional" Navaho and White culture, although either extreme is acceptable. The White people as a group, he avers, want Navahos either to remain as traditional Navahos or else to make the complete cultural transition and give up all traces of Navaho culture and society. This is a safe enough position from the point of view of the trader's vested interest, since the condition of total acculturation is far beyond the reach of any Shonto Navaho in the present generation (see "Acculturation," pp. 90–93). As a result, the trader is able to uphold the ideal of education in theory, while in practice disparaging educated Navahos for not being perfectly acculturated—for being poor imitation Whites. This is a position which traders can be heard to take again and again, and is expressed by such sayings as "I'm all in favor of education if the Navvies will just make something out of it and get ahead on the outside instead of coming back here with a lot of crazy ideas." "These educated Indians around here are no good; they think they're too good to do any honest work. Give me the old-time longhairs every time."

In spite of the expressed ideal of Navaho education, the frequent repetition of sentiments such as those quoted above subtly discourages it by suggesting that those Navahos who have tried to live more like White people are ludicrous failures because they have not perfectly succeeded. There is not, in a word, any acceptable middle ground. It is suggested that the White world is a complicated and dangerous place in which it takes special skills and knowledge to get along. It is implied that Shonto Navahos in their present state of development are presumably incapable of these skills, and are therefore better off remaining as Navahos and away from the dangers of the White world. Above all it is reiterated in one way or another that it is better to be a good Navaho than a poor White man; and the alleged failure of a majority of Navahos to become acceptable White men is never forgotten. The trader is thus perhaps not unlike certain Americans, in paying lip service to the ideal of education while disparaging the educated.

In any case, according to the trader, White people in general are perfectly content for Navahos to remain as they are. The White world requires no more of them than that they should work hard and pay their own way when and where they can. This view of the desirability of Navaho cultural independence is obviously endorsed, and therefore reinforced, by tourist visitors to Shonto community who are apt to show a quite obtrusive interest in and curiosity about the special features of Navaho culture and life. Shonto Navahos realize that many Americans admire them simply for being different.

GOVERNMENT ACTIVITIES

The Bureau of Indian Affairs, as interpreted by Shonto's trader, is concerned only with Navaho physical and material welfare and does not intend to alter or destroy Navaho culture and society. Most Government programs are, in fact, readily interpretable in this light. The sole purpose of Indian school education is to help Navahos to make more money; not to make White people out of them. Those aspects of Government policy or activity which actually do threaten the traditions of Navaho society are condemned in terms of individual stupidity or ignorance. This view of the matter allows the trader the same sort of dualistic sophistry as in the case of education; if necessary he can always say that "the Government's all right—it's the stupid people in it that are bad." The Government is good to the extent that it contributes to Navaho material welfare, while individual administrators are bad when and where they threaten Navaho culture and society. According to the trader, the Government, like the rest of the White world, wants Navahos to remain culturally and socially independent.

OTHER CONTACT AGENCIES

Shonto's trader more or less openly disparages the activities of individuals or contact agencies which seek to promote Navaho culture change for other than material purposes. Primarily involved in this category are missionaries and law enforcement agencies. It is implied that these individuals pervert the American ideal, which is simply the promotion of material welfare without disturbing moral and spiritual values. The suggestion is likely to be given that missionaries and their ilk are simply individual cranks or crooks, deviant from the norms of their own society.

"There's missionaries and missionaries," as traders have observed. Relations with evangelistic missionaries such as the one who operated at Shonto (see "Religion and Ritual," pp. 70–74) are likely to be particularly guarded and suspicious, especially in the presence of Navahos. Missionaries who offer welfare programs of one sort and another and who show a healthier regard for the blessings of this world will usually be found to maintain much more cordial relations with their trader neighbors.

THE TRADING POST

Among all the agents of the White world, it is the trader, according to his own view of matters, who best understands the Navahos and has their interests most at heart. He alone successfully bridges the gap between the two societies and cultures; therefore he knows best of all "what's good for the Navaho." Individual Navahos should leave the management of their cross-cultural relations in his hands. It is part of his moral duty to protect Navahos against the disruptive influences of the outside world—to see that their material standard of living is raised to its highest point without threatening traditional social and cultural values. In cases of actual culture conflict he is on the Navahos' side.

Shonto's trader certainly believes himself and his fellow traders to be the truest and most dedicated "friends of the Indian" in the whole fabric of intercultural relations. This belief is frequently reiterated for the benefit of the Navaho community. By way of illustrating his special sympathy with Navaho interests, the trader makes it a point to wink at and even tacitly encourage such officially deplored Navaho practices as plural marriage, private revenge, and even tulapai making (cf. "Native Commercial and Professional Enterprise," pp. 125–127), while visibly disparaging and impeding the activities of visionary "do-gooders" and "reformers" such as the missionary and the forces of Tribal Statute.

THE NAVAHO TRIBE

Of all the forces and institutions of the modern world, none, in the eyes of traders, poses a greater threat to traditional Navaho life and Navaho-White relations than the tribal organization of the Navahos themselves. Consequently, no agency is more consistently or vehemently disparaged. The Navaho Tribal Council and its functionaries are regarded with considerable justification as the strongest organized force behind Navaho culture change today, and the most avowedly assimilationist of all contact agencies.

Shonto's trader attempts in various ways to provoke suspicion and distrust of the tribal government. In particular he aims to transfer Navaho hostility toward "government" in general (see "Social and Political Authority," pp. 65–68), specifically to the tribal government. The tribal council and particularly its leaders are represented to be unscrupulous, dishonest, and half-educated individuals who are preying on their own people for their own ends. Individual tribal councilmen from Shonto, Inscription House, and Kayenta, who because of various profiteering activities are highly unpopular in the community, are held up as examples of the caliber and intentions of the tribal organization.

Most of all, the onus of stock reduction is used to condemn the tribal organization. The fact that tribal authorities have assumed the burden of enforcing not only range capacities but also liquor prohibition is advanced as suggesting that tribal leaders are not really interested in the desires of their own people, but are simply working on behalf of reactionary and hostile elements in "government" for selfish and purely personal rewards.

If "Washindoon" (see "Social and Political Authority," pp. 65–68) is the universal Navaho scapegoat (cf. "History of Contacts," pp. 237–244; also Spicer, 1952, p. 203), it is equally true that Window Rock has become the trader's scapegoat on the same terms.[29] As Navahos blame the Federal Government indiscriminately for most of their woes, so the trader finds Window Rock a handy excuse for many conditions the cause of which he knows quite well to lie elsewhere. Thus he regrets that he must decline to loan cash to Navaho applicants because Win-

---

[29] The two cases are not dissimilar in many respects. The threatened tribal expropriation of traders' properties in the early 1950's had the same sort of symbolic impact as did stock reduction on the Navaho a decade earlier, and has left much of the same sort of bitterness. Just as today it is difficult for Navahos to talk to a White man for any length of time without coming around to the subject of stock reduction, so it is still difficult for traders to keep from alluding to the "tribal takeover" at every opportunity. In this respect the trader at Shonto feels that he and the Navahos are even, although each absolves the other of specific responsibility on the grounds of dissociation from the respective governments.

dow Rock won't allow it"; prices are high because he has to pay such a high rental fee to the tribe; or he would like to modernize the store building but it does not really belong to him.

THE IDEAL NAVAHO

Many traders express the opinion that Navahos are congenitally indolent, so that there is not, from their point of view, any such thing as an "ideal Navaho." Shonto's trader, however, is actually able to point to an "ideal Navaho" in the community. This individual is cited and extolled repeatedly (though not in his own presence) as embodying all of the qualities which the White world expects and values in a Navaho. So far as the trader is concerned he sets the standard of behavior for the whole community.

Shonto's "ideal Navaho" is a man of 44 who is, it is hardly necessary to add, one of the community's most unusual personalities as regards the personal adjustment which he has made between Navaho and White values. He has been a regular seasonal employee of Navajo National Monument for some 20 years, and has acquired a wide variety of job skills, from road grading to stonemasonry, all of which he performs with extreme competence. He is a completely reliable worker—punctual in arriving and constantly industrious on the job. He is always available for work when needed, and does not take time off without obtaining prior permission.

He is equally unusual in his relations with the store. Although, like his neighbors, he lives to a large extent on credit, he keeps close track of his account and budgets himself so that he never quite reaches his limit and has to be "cut off." He is the only regular and extensive recipient of credit in Shonto community whose credit has never, in the writer's knowledge, been stopped for any reason. Finally, he is thoroughly conscientious in paying his bill in full whenever he receives his paycheck. In short, his economic values correspond to White ideals.

In all other respects Shonto's "ideal Navaho" hews close to traditional Navaho ideals. He lives in an ordinary hogan with his wife and seven children, wears long hair, and speaks no English (although he is reputed to understand a good deal of it from his long work experience at Betatakin). He has never been to school. He has a very large flock of sheep, sells his lambs and wool to the store every year, and is an assiduous farmer. He is orderly in his behavior, does not drink or fight, and regularly attends and participates in native religious performances. He seldom if ever goes to Flagstaff.

This individual, who seems to have made a deliberate decision to remain an unacculturated Navaho in matters other than economic, has made the sort of personal adjustment between two worlds which corresponds to the trader's ideal for the whole Navaho tribe. His

behavior is approved and praised above that of other Navahos
of superior education who have actually achieved a higher income
and a considerably higher material standard of living in the outside
world.

SUMMARY

Although he endorses to some extent the functions of other contact agencies, Shonto's trader is sincerely convinced that he is the
truest advocate and practitioner of the American ideal in the Navaho
community. That ideal, as he himself interprets it and as he exempli-
fies it to his Navaho clientele, is simply the individual pursuit of
material well-being. In all other matters, spiritual, moral, and
esthetic, individual taste and individual judgment must be respected,
and no uniform ideal should be enforced. Right and wrong are, in
the last analysis, measurable only in dollars and cents: this is the
only legitimate yardstick by which the White man's part in Navaho
life and influence on Navaho behavior can be justified.

INTERPERSONAL RELATIONS

No analysis of the role of the trader would be complete without
some consideration of the systems of interpersonal behavior as between traders and Navahos, and through which the former influence
the actions and perceptions of the latter. It was noted in "Trader
Behavior" (pp. 210–212) that the trader has an inherent status advantage over his clientele which is maintained in such a way as to
emphasize the subordination and dependence of the Navaho. Within
this overall structure of relationship, however, there are several types
of approved reciprocal behavior patterns which are appropriate to
particular circumstances.

JOKING

As far as traders are concerned, the most approved behavior as
between trader and customer is a kind of avuncular joking relationship (see Lowie, 1948, p. 75), with the trader in the superordinate
avuncular role. Navahos are believed to appreciate highly a ready
wit and rabelaisian sense of humor (cf. Hill, 1943, and Kluckhohn
and Leighton, 1946, pp. 52-54), and these qualities are considered valuable assets in a trader. The most common joking relationship between
Shonto's trader and his male customers involves a kind of reciprocal
patterned teasing about one another's imputed recourse to prostitutes,
and particularly Negroes. The trader teases his women customers
about what their husbands are doing while they are out on the railroad, while they retaliate by wondering aloud what his wife is doing
in Flagstaff while he is at Shonto.

Joking behavior is not only the most approved way of passing the
time in the store, but is also permissible throughout routine trading

(cf. Sanders et al., 1953, p. 234). There is, however, a profound difference between the permissible latitude in joking as between trader and Navaho. The trader may be teased only on the crudest physical and physiological subjects. Even in jest any impugnment of his honesty, capability, or authority is strictly tabu, and will result in an immediate angry reaction. Also, any joking aspersions on the ideals of industriousness and wealth, and behavior connected therewith, are forbidden. Finally, Navahos may not touch the trader or play any practical joke on him.

The trader, on the other hand, can and does tease the Navaho on nearly all subjects (although he generally avoids offending Navaho religious beliefs as best he can), and also plays practical jokes on them, slaps them on the back, and the like. He is particularly fond of reminding individuals (and everyone else within earshot) of their troubles with the police, employers, and other agents of the White world. In this way Shonto's trader capitalizes on his joking relationship not only, in his own view, to further his popularity as "one of the gang" (cf. Underhill, 1956, p. 180) but even more to emphasize his paternal relationship to the community and its inherent status advantage.[30] Finally, since it is legitimate on nearly all occasions, the trader often finds a joking response a convenient device with which to meet Navaho hostility, suspicion, or inconvenient queries or assertions.

SINCERITY

Sincerity in Navaho-trader relations is permitted on all matters except highly personal ones, which are subject to joking only. In idle discourse as well as in actual trading sincerity is an allowable alternative to a joking relationship, although not as highly valued by the trader. A straightforward relationship does not emphasize the superior status of the trader in the same way as does the established joking pattern, and Navahos who do not want to joke are apt to be ridiculed much as are children who are "too serious." The trader may take special pleasure in trying to get a rise out of them in spite of their disinclination to be teased.

There are some subjects, however, upon which sincerity is the only allowable behavior. These are the areas in which the trader feels it his special duty to teach and guide his Navaho neighbors for their own good. Particularly as regards the sacred ideals of wealth and industriousness, no slighting allusions or buffoonery are allowed. The superior status of the trader is similarly above profanation, and must be respected at all times.

---

[30] In this regard it may be significant to note that in his institutionalized teasing about sex the trader is literally playing the avuncular part in Navaho life. See Kluckhohn and Leighton, 1946, p. 53.

NONRECIPROCAL BEHAVIOR

From the trader's own point of view, approved Navaho behavior in the trading post is confined to a special teasing pattern or to matter-of-fact relations. Any deviation from these limits is very likely to provoke an angry reprimand. The trader himself, on the other hand, can and does behave toward Navahos in various other ways which may not be reciprocated.

Shonto's trader may freely condemn Navahos, publicly or privately, for any behavior which does not meet his approval. In circumstances of extra "provocation" he does not feel it incumbent upon him to hold his temper; on the contrary he may even simulate anger by way of reinforcing his disapproval. Conversely he can and does openly praise and reward individuals for especially meritorious behavior—candy and soda pop being the traditional rewards. These behaviors are, of course, permitted to the trader only. His infallibility is such that Navahos may not presume either to praise or to criticize him.

In appropriate circumstances the trader may threaten Navahos in a variety of ways. It was noted earlier that the threat of credit refusal is basic to the commercial operation of the trading post, and is never absent from Navaho-trader transactions (see "Book Credit," pp. 188–195). This particular sanction is so constantly associated with the trading post and is so inseparable from it that it seldom has to be verbalized. Whenever necessary or desirable, however, the trader feels free to coerce Navaho behavior into acceptable channels by voicing such threats as withdrawal of credit, or refusal to perform any of his various ancillary functions on behalf of the individual involved.

Particularly in response to drunken and disorderly behavior, the trader may even threaten his Navaho customers with physical violence. Shonto's trader keeps a very large blackjack under the counter for this purpose, and there are also firearms on the premises. On the other hand, the trader never under any circumstances backs up his threats with sanctions other than his own. He is, so far as the community is concerned, capable of dealing with any situation without outside assistance, and therefore does not invoke either the police or any other authority in his behalf.

Finally, Shonto's trader can and does give advice to his Navaho neighbors, freely and often without solicitation, on any and all phases of their relations with the White world. Here again, Navahos may not presume to reciprocate by advising the trader in any way, although they may furnish him with helpful information.

The recognized and approved response to these non-reciprocated behavior patterns are consistent with the overall pattern of Navaho subordination. Trading post customers are expected to receive condemnation with humility, reward and praise with gratitude, threats with fear, and advice with attention and assent.

SUMMARY

Virtually every aspect of Navaho-trader relations, as approved and sustained by the latter, is reminiscent of the parent-child relationship. Each particular behavior pattern, whether it be joking, sincerity, condemnation, threat, or advice, emphasizes in its own way the superordinate authority of the trader and disparages independence, initiative, and counter-authority on the part of the Navaho. The standard in judging and rewarding Navaho behavior is whether or not it corresponds to, and has been induced by, the expressed desire of the trader. In practice, Navahos are not thanked or rewarded for contributing to the trader's purposes unless their actions in his behalf have been suggested in some way, either explicitly or by precept, by the trader himself. Even for his own profit, Shonto's trader does not encourage individual initiative on the part of his clientele. In the long run, therefore, Navahos are rewarded more for simply recognizing and acknowledging the authority of the trader than for actually assisting him.

THE ROLE OF SHONTO TRADING POST

REVIEW AND SYNTHESIS

If the modern Navaho economy represents a significant adaptation of Navaho culture to the conditions of White contact (cf. pp. 94–148), it is no less true that the modern Navaho trading post, with its complex of unique features and functions, represents a special adaptation of American culture to Navaho contact (see "The Consumer Market," pp. 169–170). No other White agency in contact with Navaho society is as completely differentiated from its counterpart in purely American society as is the trading post. Conversely, no other White institution is as thoroughly integrated into Navaho life, or as much depended upon.

The two cultural institutions—White trading post and Navaho economy — are mutually complementary. Their historic and now almost total interdependence goes back over half a century (see "Early Trading Posts," pp. 150–154; also Amsden, 1934, pp. 178–182 and Underhill, 1956, pp. 179–195) and represents the one significant example of genuine cultural fusion (cf. Summer Seminar on Acculturation, 1954, pp. 987–988) arising out of Navaho-White contact. While Navaho life and institutions have "progressed" in the directions suggested by American models, only the trading post among all American institutions has "retrogressed" so as to meet them half way. Shonto Trading Post is today an anachronistic enterprise which is specially adapted to an anachronistic socio-economic system (see "The Consumer Market," pp. 169–170).

"Anachronism" in the case of the trading post is an expression of the fact that in adapting itself so thoroughly to the conditions of Navaho life, the store over the years has become increasingly isolated from and out of step with the American sociocultural system (see, e.g., "Finance," pp. 171–172; also Sanders et al., 1953, p. 234). The trading post of today could not compete for White trade or even for a considerable amount of Navaho trade in an open and unprotected consumer market (cf. Kluckhohn and Leighton, 1946, p. 39). Whatever its cultural origins, it is true today that Shonto Trading Post as a functioning institution is in closer harmony with the conditions of Navaho life, and better integrated into it, than with the conditions of modern American life even in the Southwest. To an extent not approached by other contact agencies, it has become a necessary institution of community life at Shonto (see "Cross-Cultural Relations," pp. 256–263).

"Anachronistic" as applied to the economy of Shonto community expresses the fact that Navaho productive enterprise, although expanding under the stimulus of White contact, has in many respects arrived only at a "colonial" stage of development (cf. "Market Characteristics," p. 169). The anachronistic adjustment of store and community economy therefore represents a halfway meeting ground between two sociocultural systems in the fields of economics and commerce.

Regardless of its historical and cultural origins, the unique and now outdated relationship between store and community is a function of the isolation and lack of economic and social development of the Shonto region (see "Physical Setting," pp. 31–36) and is perpetuated thereby. In the long run it is environmental limitation which retards a closer adaptation of both to the norms and continuing trends of modern American life. The Shonto area itself is too barren of productive resources (unless uranium or oil should be discovered) to support anything more than the present limited agricultural and livestock industry, pieced out with a necessarily restricted number of wage opportunities. It is also too far from more favored regions to permit regular commuting to high-paid jobs. The only possible compromise between increased income and continued residence in the community is the type of seasonal commuting which is now manifest in connection with railroad work (see "Railroad Work," pp. 129–133). In its present degree of economic development, therefore, the Shonto region condemns its permanent inhabitants to the type of seasonal, cyclic, and credit-structured economy in which the function of the trading post is absolutely essential (see "The Economic Cycle," pp. 141–145).

Shonto Trading Post is no less an economic victim of its under-developed environment. The combination of high freight rates, low volume, minimum capital, outmoded equipment and methods, heavy credit, and all the other special conditions which are inherent in the Navaho trade and in remote regions (cf. pp. 167–184) conspire not only to produce prices 10 to 15 percent higher than those found in off-reservation towns (see "Markup," p. 182; also Kluckhohn and Leighton, 1946, p. 39) but to create trading conditions detrimental and sometimes downright unpleasant to the consumer. Given the present condition of its territory, therefore, Shonto Trading Post is absolutely incapable today of competing with off-reservation merchants on a dollar-for-dollar basis.

It is apparent to the trader, however, that the environmental limitation is more extreme and more immutable in his own case than in that of the Navaho. If the Navaho is prevented from adapting himself more closely to the conditions and the benefits of the modern White world by the remoteness of his community, he has always the ultimate choice of leaving it and establishing himself in some more developed region. In other words the Navaho, given the desire, has the undeniable right and opportunity to free himself from the economic limitations of traditional Navaho life with its inevitable consequence of dependence on the trader. The latter, on the other hand, is stuck with his location and its consequence of dependence on the Navaho and on the traditional, uncapitalized Navaho economy. *Of all the individuals and agencies involved in Navaho-White culture contact today, it is the trader and the oldest and least-educated Navahos who are least able to adapt to changing conditions and times.* Both are condemned to the reservation, and to the limitations of reservation life, by their inability to compete, each in his own way, with their White counterparts in the outside world. They are, therefore, condemned to their utter dependence on one another.

In view of the foregoing, and of the entire analysis of trading post and community which has preceded, it is perhaps superfluous to state that the primary objective of Shonto Trading Post as a contact agency, time and again, is to retard, divert, or prevent culture change rather than to promote it. Any threat to the cultural and social status quo in Shonto community is a threat to the well-being of the trader no less than to Navahos themselves, and is consciously or unconsciously recognized as such. The wellsprings of Navaho resistance to continued White cultural and social encroachment are to be found in the trading post as much as in Navaho culture itself.

Such has been the historic role of Shonto Trading Post in the Navaho community. The store has consistently sought to increase the material standard of living and the income level of its Navaho clientele (cf. Amsden, 1934, p. 179; Underhill, 1956, p. 180) without disturbing the framework of their native sociocultural system, which carried with it the condition of dependence on the trading post. As a contact agency, and in a position of pre-eminent cross-cultural power, the trader has been able to divert and restrict the impact of American culture upon Navaho culture largely to economic and material channels which would benefit the store, while minimizing or forestalling any more general assimilation or acculturation which would weaken Navaho dependence on him. To this end he has exercised a constant selection, modification, and reinterpretation in transmitting the impulses of the outside world to the Navaho community. He has shown his clientele a picture of the world and their place in it, not as it exists but as he wishes it to be.

It has been observed repeatedly, here (see pp. 53–148) and elsewhere (e.g., Kluckhohn and Leighton, 1946, p. 28) that Navaho acculturation and the replacement of native patterns has been most extensive in the areas of economics and material culture (see also Chart M, p. 265). Throughout the past century the Navaho economy has undergone a series of progressive adaptations (cf. Summer Seminar on Acculturation, 1954, p. 987) to changing economic and market conditions in the outside world, but with no very profound effect on the basic fabric of Navaho life (cf. Kluckhohn and Leighton, 1946, p. 28). Wool production, weaving, and other craftwork, lamb production, and finally wagework have come along, each in its turn to play its part in the changing Navaho economy. This process of economic adaptation has been guided at every turn by traders (see especially Underhill, 1956, p. 181), who have carefully selected and promoted the new subsistence activities with an eye to their own future—in other words in such a way as to perpetuate the seasonal, uncapitalized cycle with its inevitable dependence on trading post intercession and credit.

A recent theoretical consideration of the processes of acculturation (Summer Seminar on Acculturation, 1954, pp. 977–979) has called attention to "self-correcting mechanisms," and to the differential ability of different cultural systems to adapt themselves to the altered conditions brought about by culture contact. Navaho culture stands out markedly in this regard. Over the centuries it has shown itself capable of absorbing all manner of alien impulses and culture patterns without sacrificing its unique core configuration. This quality of adaptability is thought to be more distinctive of the Navaho cultural system than is any particular complex of behavior patterns (see, e.g., Kroeber, 1928, p. 386; Luomala, 1938, p. 16; Kluckhohn and Leighton, 1946, p. 28; Underhill, 1956, p. ix).

Navaho cultural adaptability undoubtedly continues to be manifest in many aspects of modern life. It might be argued from this that the type of relatively conflict-free intercultural adjustment (cf. Leighton and Kluckhohn, 1948, pp. 139–143) which has taken place at Shonto, confined largely to economics and material culture (cf. chart M, p. 265; also Kluckhohn and Leighton, 1946, p. 28), is due entirely to the "self-correcting mechanisms" (Summer Seminar on Acculturation, 1954, p. 977) of Navaho culture itself. A glance at the total Navaho picture, however, immediately reveals that the pattern of Navaho-White cultural relations is far from consistent throughout the reservation. In a great many areas culture contact is anything but free from conflict, and has wrought such non-assimilative conditions as cultural disintegration (see, e.g., Leighton and Kluckhohn, 1948, pp. 129–133; Rapoport, 1954, pp. 71–77) and nativistic reaction (e.g., Leighton and Kluckhohn, 1948, pp. 122–126; Underhill, 1956, pp. 247–249).

As was stated in an earlier section of this work ("Summary," pp. 93–94), the difference in cultural adaptation as between one area of the Navaho country and another is attributable not to regional variations in native Navaho life, but to quantitative and qualitative variations in the structure of culture contact. In a general way, it is observable that cultural change has been least, and most free from conflict, in the northwestern portion of the Navaho Reservation, where the Anglo-American sociocultural system has been represented largely or exclusively by trading posts (cf. Kluckhohn and Leighton, 1946, pp. 29–30, 55; Leighton and Kluckhohn, 1948, pp. 122, 139–43). If the continued flourishing of sheep-raising can be taken as an index, both symbolic and economic, of the persistence of Navaho cultural independence, then it may be appropriate to note that all but one of the six land-management districts in which actual range use still exceeds permitted capacity are those around and adjacent to Shonto, in the northwestern Navaho Country (see Young, 1955, pp. 190–191). This is the region which remains preeminently the domain of the trader. In short, an important "correcting mechanism" of modern Navaho culture, helping to maintain its equilibrium in the face of continued White cultural encroachment (see Summer Seminar on Acculturation, 1954, pp. 977–978) is none other than the trading post.

SUMMARY

Shonto Trading Post is by formal charter the principal and often the sole exchange agency where the gainful products of Navaho native enterprise and Navaho labor are exchanged for the material products of modern American industry. By operational charter it is also the principal and often the sole point of contact and channel of communication between Shonto Navahos and the White world which surrounds and impinges on them. As a result of various factors in the history as well as the present structure of Navaho-White contact, the trading post has a power to influence adult Navaho perceptions, behavior, and attitudes which is unrivaled by any other White agency.

This "cross-cultural power" of the trading post is exerted overtly and covertly to further its own purpose of maximum sustained profit. As a contact agent the trader both deliberately and subconsciously selects and reinterprets the elements and influences of White culture which are presented to the Navaho community, in such a way as to divert the impact of culture contact very largely into material and economic channels. On the one hand, the trader assists Navahos in taking advantage of the added economic opportunities resulting from contact with the White world. On the other hand, he opposes and resists any concomitant changes in other aspects of the Navaho sociocultural system which would threaten its historic and structurally inherent dependence upon the trading post. By precept and action he strives for the goal of stabilized pluralism in Navaho-White relations (see Summer Seminar on Acculturation, 1954, p. 990).

Historically, the influence of Shonto Trading Post upon its Navaho clientele can be measured in two respects. First, the presence and activities of the trader have significantly altered the material culture complex and raised the material standard of living in the community without bringing about any comparable change in other native traditions (cf. pp. 53–94 and chart M, p. 265). Secondly, the trader's activities have greatly expanded the economic base of the community without altering its essentially seasonal and subsistence nature. Expansion of the Navaho economy under the aegis of the trader has produced neither capital nor wealth, but simply a much higher level of material consumption. The economy of Shonto community today remains essentially a vast redistribution system in which the trader is the direct or indirect source and also the ultimate recipient of all of the financial benefits derived from contact with the White world.

THE QUINTESSENCE OF PATERNALISM

Critics of Indian Bureau policy, particularly on the Navaho Reservation, have sometimes been wont to accuse the Government of "paternalism" (see, e.g., Phelps-Stokes Fund, 1939, pp. 27–38). This is especially the view taken by assimilationists. It is argued that the Government "babies" the Indians, protects them from the hard realities of modern life, and thereby stifles their initiative. "The Indian should get out and sink or swim like the rest of us," as a Flagstaff resident expressed it.

Such critics either are not fully familiar with the reservation scene or, as is equally probable, do not comprehend the real meaning of "paternalism." In most respects Washington is no more "Great White Father" to Navahos than to other citizens. Although the Federal Government must perform for Navahos nearly all of the functions normally allocated to Federal, State, county, and local governments in White society (cf. Kluckhohn and Leighton, 1946, p. 86), the complex of such functions in education, health, welfare, and the like is generally comparable to those performed by various governments for non-Navahos of low income levels. Concern with the physical and material welfare of all citizens is one of the recognized functions of modern government.

Furthermore, Government dealings with Navahos as with other citizens are on a strictly instrumental rather than a personal basis (cf. chart L, p. 258). Under the rigid protocols of administration Navahos are inevitably treated as cases rather than as individuals. What they may receive from the Government in any case is determined by formally established criteria of eligibility which may or may not have anything to do with personally defined need.

In all these respects the contrast between the role of the Indian Bureau and that of the trader is profound. It is the trader, not the Government, whose relations with Navahos are personal, colored by personal value judgments, and not confined to instrumental contexts. It is the trader who tries to obtain jobs or relief for individuals, not because they are formally qualified but because in his opinion they need them, and it is he who does favors and performs services for his clientele not because he gets paid for it but for more indirect benefits and in the interest of personal friendship and community goodwill. Above all it is the trader who attempts, in his own interest, to soften the impact of culture contact; to protect his Navaho neighbors from the disruptive influences of the White world (cf. Kluckhohn and Leighton, 1946, p. 79) with which, in his opinion, they are not strong enough to deal; and who protects them even from Government agencies. Finally, it is the trader who literally treats the Navahos like children (see "Interpersonal Relations," pp. 287–290), even to the extent of talking a sort of baby-talk to them (cf. "Communication," pp. 212–214).

In short, it is the trader, not the Indian Bureau, whose role represents the epitome of paternalism in Navaho-White relations. He, if anyone, deserves the epithet of "White Father."

THE ENTREPRENEUR IN CULTURE CONTACT

According to a recent analysis of the general phenomena of culture contact—

Intercultural role playing reflects the interest areas that are shared by the two groups in contact, whether attention to these areas is cultivated or enforced by unilateral demands, or whether the areas represent a convergence of aspirations or needs. . . . Particular roles demand specific purposes and entail specific expectations. In the expansion of Western European culture, the roles of the administrator, the entrepreneur and the missionary have established a stereotype in accordance with the principal incentives activating the expansion. (Summer Seminar on Acculturation, 1954, p. 981; cf. also Malinowski, 1945, p. 15).

So long as Euro-American colonial expansion is motivated chiefly by merchantile considerations, the trader must inevitably remain one of its foremost pioneers. Throughout the primitive world he has instituted the earliest contact with tribal peoples, or has followed close on the heels of first contact. The Navaho trader even today remains only one of a vast army of private entrepreneurs who have penetrated beyond the limits of their own societies in search of profit in every part of the globe. They are or have been wherever European and native tribal cultures are in contact.

It was stated at the beginning of the present study (see "Definition and Delimitation," pp. 1–2) that the intercultural social system of modern Shonto community was to be examined first of all for its own sake. Neither the community nor the trading post was assumed to be a "sample," or to be representative of some larger social unit or institution. However, the suggestion has been put forward that the trader's role in culture contact is more or less constant or "stereotyped" (Summer Seminar on Acculturation, 1954, p. 981; Malinowski, 1945, p. 15). It may therefore be appropriate as an epilogue to the Shonto study to consider how far Shonto's trader may stand as representative of his fellow cross-cultural entrepreneurs in other parts of the world.

It is hardly necessary to observe that no detailed comparison of traders' roles and activities can be undertaken. For the most part the entrepreneur has fared no better at the hands of anthropologists elsewhere than he has in the Navaho country (see "The Trader in Literature," pp. 5–8). Historically he has been blamed for a variety of disruptive changes in native cultures (e.g., Keesing, 1928, p. 42; Price, 1950, passim; Hogbin, 1951, p. 187), yet the structural basis of his influence has received scant attention. The anthropological literature contains no more than a suggestion here and a hint there from which the "stereotyped" role of the trader can be reconstructed.

THE ENTREPRENEUR IN LITERATURE

HISTORIC ROLE

It has been noted earlier ("Theoretical Foundations," pp. 10–12) that anthropologists have generally interested themselves in culture contact primarily for the sake of its effects in terms of culture change. To the limited extent that they have given attention to the historical role of traders, therefore, it is not surprising that they have sought to measure their influence by the yardstick of changes in native subsistence patterns and material culture.

The replacement of aboriginal material culture by items of European manufacture is easily and widely recognized, and can be laid to the door of the trader with little fear of contradiction (see, e.g., Barnes, 1951, p. 244; Hogbin, 1951, p. 187; Keesing, 1928, p. 42; Lewis, 1942, pp. 60–61; Wilson, 1951, p. 62). Changes, or at least shifts of emphasis, in economic patterns (cf. Lewis, 1942, pp. 60–61; Mandelbaum, 1940, p. 187), including the deliberate promulgation of wagework (Barnes, 1951, p. 244; Hogbin, 1951, p. 187; Reed, 1943, p. 122; Wilson, 1951, p. 62) are also seen as overt effects of trader-native contacts. So far as anthropological studies go, these are in actuality the only influences in native life which have been traced to the direct and deliberate intervention of traders.

All of the other purported effects of entrepreneurs upon aboriginal life, as determined by students of culture history, have been indirect and often accidental ones, resulting from changes in material culture and subsistence patterns. They are developments which may well have been as unexpected by the trader as by the tribal group itself. They have included, for example, the breakdown of traditional status systems resulting from substitution of cheap manufactured goods for prestige items of native manufacture (e.g., Keesing, 1941, p. 68; Sharp, 1952); and the disintegration of native authority through the removal of its economic sanctions (Hogbin, 1939, p. 166; Keesing, 1928, p. 42). Most significantly, they have included the intensification of conflict between tribal groups through the introduction of firearms (Keesing, 1928, p. 42; 1941, p. 58; Lewis, 1942, pp. 60–61; Mandelbaum, 1940, p. 187). Such has been the historical role of the trader as determined by cultural anthropologists.

MODERN ROLE

In North America, trading between Anglos and natives is found primarily on the Navaho Reservation and in the more remote portions of Canada and Alaska. The celebrated Hudson's Bay Company continues to maintain slightly over 200 trading posts in various parts of Canada (see Bonnycastle, 1943, p. 70)—about equal to the number of posts in the Navaho country (cf. Kluckhohn and Leighton, 1946,

p. 39). The former have been described in general by Bonnycastle (of the Hudson's Bay Company's fur-trade division) in terms generally suggestive of Shonto (Bonnycastle, 1943, pp. 62–66). He discourses on the advantages to the natives of a "benevolent monopoly," and notes how "the problem of enabling Indians to become self-supporting is of vital interest to the trader." Among the benefits brought by the latter are enumerated the material products of civilization, law and order, medical assistance, and the benefit of having a "trained advisor and friend."

One Hudson's Bay Company store, at Great Whale River on the east shore of Hudson's Bay, has been studied in detail by an anthropologist (Honigmann, 1952). According to the author of the study:

> Considerable social power is linked with the status of company manager in a northern community like Great Whale River. While such power is not limited to trading, its expression is conditioned by the fact that natives who are dependent on the manager for employment or credit can hardly help but listen to, and sometimes obey him. The trader scolds laziness and other deviations from the norms he values. When these norms are also shared by natives, the sanctions of the "boss" meet with warm approval. The trader influences the annual cycle of the Eskimo through the amount of labor he makes available to them in the post during the summer or at Christmas. Additional power is invested in the trader as a result of government agencies relying on him to execute administrative procedures communicated by mail or radio. [Honigmann, 1952, pp. 514–515. A similar account of the Hudson's Bay trader's role is given in a letter quoted by Bonnycastle, 1943, p. 72.]

No comparable situation has been described anywhere south of the Rio Grande. This is par excellence the land of the wide open market—of regular market days and a pattern of native commerce which goes far back into colonial and probably pre-contact times (cf. Beals, 1952, p. 70; Tax, 1952 b, pp. 52–56). According to Tax (1952 b, p. 55): "In regions where the market economy predominates, among Ladinos and Indians alike there is an economic individualism and tendency toward opportunism." In the face of this type of native commercial pattern, European traders have apparently not been able to acquire a sufficient monopoly of supply and markets to establish a trading pattern similar to that found in North America.

The free market economy is probably characteristic of most of the areas of Latin America which supported high cultures in aboriginal times (cf. Gillin, 1947). It is apparently less developed in the southern and eastern portions of South America. In these areas, however, pioneer traders, if they ever gained a foothold at all, were speedily supplanted by the development of the encomienda if not of outright slavery (cf. Frazier, 1957, pp. 101–109). The private entrepreneur necessarily gave way to the company store or commissary (cf. Wolf, 1956, pp. 240–241). On the Puerto Rican hacienda, however, social functions closely comparable to those found at Shonto Trading Post ("Community Center," pp. 229–230) have been described

(Manners, 1956, p. 133; Wolf, 1956, p. 241). Credit saturation is also described from Puerto Rico: "Storekeepers feel that as long as they extend credit, people have an incentive to pay past debts. If credit is cut off they shift their allegiance to another store" (Wolf, 1956, p. 240).

In Africa, Malinowski (1945, p. 15) noted that, "... the missionaries and the administrators, the settlers and the entrepreneurs, are indeed the main agents of change." Nevertheless the entrepreneurs, in particular, have received little attention from anthropologists. It has been noted here and there (e.g., Barnes, 1951, p. 244; Hunter, 1936, p. 5; Wilson, 1951, p. 62) that they provide the stimulus as well as some opportunities for wagework by creating a desire for European goods.

The social functions of the store persist here also.

The trader's store is a social center to which young and old come to gossip and flirt, beg tobacco, and inquire as to the whereabouts of beer. Often a youth spends a whole morning at a store, talking to girls, chaffing with his contemporaries, and perhaps letting off steam in a stick-fight with a friend. Young men just back from the mines with money to burn treat their girl friends to sugar; parties of four or six squat on the verandah of the store, and quickly dispose of pound packets. The men inspect every girl who comes in. . . . [Hunter, 1936, p. 356.]

It is apparent, however, that in many parts of Africa as in Latin America a plantation economy has superseded the free trader (cf. Hunter, 1936, p. 2; Malinowski, 1945, pp. 118–120).

Trade and trade relationships have long been the focus of anthropological studies in Oceania, and only here has the European trader received significant attention. Here, too, a plantation economy has developed in many regions (see, e.g., Hogbin, 1951, pp. 183–203; Reed, 1943, pp. 98–105) and particularly in Indonesia (Furnivall, 1944, passim). Nevertheless, according to Keesing (1941, pp. 68, 121–122):

A . . . figure of great importance to the modern experience of indigenous peoples has been the trader. In many regions the earliest to arrive on the scene, he brought the native into touch with the larger markets of the world and gave him his primary education in the economics of civilization. History shows the trader as quickly becoming indispensable to native communities, even though under some circumstances he was judged a sinister influence. . . . Now, after decades of trial and give-and-take, the results can be seen in the trade store of today. Over the counter pass baskets of copra, shell or other products, and out come cloth goods, matches and kerosene, a variety of tools, canned goods, soap, and quite a long list of other products that have become either necessities or luxuries.

The trader has not been particularly concerned about contrasts in economic philosophy. Once he found out what goods suited the native needs and tastes, he continued to supply these.

All trade goods, indeed . . . tend to be fitted into the indigenous system of life in this way. As some put it, they become nativized, taking on meanings and functions of a local character.

The role of the missionary is contrasted. "With the trader, and in some places ahead of him, went the missionary . . . Not content to let the indigenous peoples pick and choose from his wares, he sought vigorously to refashion traditional belief and behavior." (Keesing, 1941, p. 68.)

In New Guinea,

Use and appreciation of European goods are fostered by trader and missionary, and in some instances demanded by Government officials. They all have something to gain from the rising consumption of European goods. The trader—be he the representative of a large commercial house, an Asiatic shopkeeper, or a recruiter who carries trade-goods as a sideline—is a vital link in the chain which binds the native into the new economic system. [Reed, 1943, p. 208].

Trader and missionary are again contrasted in New Guinea.

Traders and planters were interested in the natives economically: the latter's services and what they produced were of primary importance to them. Native folkways which had no apparent bearing on their new duties could be disregarded so long as the natives brought copra and shell to exchange for knives, calico and beads, and furnished "boys" for work whenever they were needed. While these conditions were fulfilled, the planter-trader could abide by a policy of laissez-faire.

Not so the missionary. He had to exert his authority over other aspects of the native culture, and among people whom the planter-trader had not approached. More conscious attempts to control all departments of native life were made by the mission than by other White groups. [Reed, 1943, p. 122].

On the Solomon Islands, it was observed that,

Unlike the administration, commerce is not concerned, even ostensibly, with native well-being. Plantations and trading stores have been established only because money is to be made, and the Europeans involved are interested in the islanders solely in so far as they supply the demand for labor and the market for goods. . . . I have often heard the argument seriously advanced that the one chance of native salvation lies in an insistence that they shall work for Europeans as laborers during a portion of their time. [Hogbin, 1939, p. 160].

SOME GENERAL CONCLUSIONS

THE DISTRIBUTION OF ENTREPRENEURS

It is apparent that free traders—private entrepreneurs who are engaged basically in marketing and only indirectly in production— are not found in all parts of the world where European enterprise has penetrated into tribal areas. They are, and perhaps always have been, absent throughout much of Latin America (cf. Tax, 1952 b, pp. 52–56) and apparently also in many parts of Africa and Oceania (cf. Malinowski, 1945, pp. 118–119). In some cases the absence of traders may well be due to structural features of the native economy, as where the innumerable free markets and extensive aboriginal trade of Mesoamerica have seemingly prevented European merchants from acquiring any effective control over supply and distribution (cf. Tax, 1952 b, pp. 52–56).

More often than not, however, the presence or absence of traders in modern contact situations has been determined by environment. The peaceful penetrations of Europeans and Americans into most of the primitive areas of the world has undoubtedly been initiated by a period, however brief, of direct barter (cf. Hunter, 1936, pp. 2–3; Keesing, 1941, p. 29; Reed, 1943, pp. 74–82). The extent of additional penetration, however, undoubtedly depended very largely upon the productive potential of the region. In many areas, and particularly wherever agriculture could be practiced extensively, permanent settlers followed the trader, and control of raw material production passed rapidly into their hands. The native, dispossessed of his land and traditional means of subsistence, lost his status as an independent producer and became instead a wage laborer (cf. Malinowski, 1945, pp. 118–120) if not a slave (Frazier, 1957, pp. 101–109).

Under the plantation economy which thus developed, and the substitution of cash for a commodity consumer market, control of commerce with natives inevitably passed from the man who marketed their native products to the man who paid and thus controlled their wages. The free trader gave way to the company or hacienda storekeeper or commissary (cf. Reed, 1943, p. 122; Wolf, 1956, p. 241). His role was for the most part reduced to a purely commercial and instrumental one, as ancillary functions (see pp. 220–230) were assumed by overseers or other Europeans in the plantation system. In some cases, particularly in Oceania, the trader himself became a planter (cf. Reed, 1943, p. 122).

European and American colonial economies throughout the world can probably be roughly divided as between plantation and non-plantation patterns. The former is found whenever environmental conditions are suitable to intensive agriculture. Here the native is rapidly dispossessed and becomes a wage or indentured laborer, if not actually a slave. Non-plantation economies occur where environments are not suitable to plantation agriculture; where the economic base is some other exploitative industry, and particularly one to which natives are as well or better adapted than Europeans. Examples of the latter are the fur trade (Mandelbaum, 1940, pp. 172–187; Lewis, 1942, pp. 60–61), native craft manufactures (Hunter, 1936, pp. 139–143; Keesing, 1941, p. 68; Underhill, 1956, pp. 185–190), and the gathering of wild plant and other products (Keesing, 1941, p. 68; Reed, 1943, p. 122). Most commonly, perhaps, non-plantation economies are found where native populations have been protected from dispossession by Government edict—i.e., on reserves or reservations.

The free trader is undoubtedly the key figure in the nonplantation economy as is the planter himself on the plantation. The trader not only markets the products of native industry, but also helps his clientele to augment such subsistence with seasonal wagework (Barnes, 1951, p. 244; Honigmann, 1952, p. 215; Hunter, 1936, p. 5; Hogbin, 1939, p. 160; Wilson, 1951, p. 62). It is apparent, as developed in the foregoing discussion, that entrepreneurs whose role and functions are comparable to those of the Shonto trader are to be found largely in areas of nonplantation colonial economies, and particularly on or near native reservations (Barnes, 1951, p. 244; Bonnycastle, 1943, p. 70; Wilson, 1951, p. 62).

HISTORICAL INFLUENCE OF ENTREPRENEURS

In spite of the great and even cataclysmic culture changes which have been attributed to the influence of European entrepreneurs (cf. Keesing, 1928, p. 42; 1941, p. 58; Price, 1950, passim), it has not been shown that traders, at Shonto or elsewhere, have deliberately fostered change in areas of culture other than subsistence and material culture. They have not, for example, endorsed or assisted the efforts of missionaries or educators in most instances. On the contrary, the roles of trader on the one hand and of other contact agencies on the other have been clearly contrasted in several instances (e.g., Hogbin, 1939, p. 160; Keesing, 1941, p. 68; Reed, 1943, p. 122). It would seem that, as at Shonto (see "The Role of Shonto Trading Post," pp. 290–297), the trader has seldom been an assimilationist.

Moreover, it is apparent that in those instances where the influence of traders has inadvertently wrought profound changes in native cultures, these have not been of an assimilative nature. Often they have been purely disruptive. Circulation of certain material goods has indirectly caused the breakdown of aboriginal social and political organization without any replacement by European patterns (cf. Keesing, 1928, p. 42; 1941, p. 68; Hogbin, 1939, p. 165; Price, 1950, passim). Such consequences can hardly have been anticipated by traders; on the other hand they themselves have done nothing to introduce new traditions to replace those which were disrupted.

In other and perhaps equally numerous cases the influence of the trader has been to bring about reorientations in native culture accompanied by new cultural vigor and social expansion. This has manifestly been the case among the western Navaho (see "The Role of Shonto Trading Post," pp. 290–297). It has also been true in various other areas (e.g., Keesing, 1941, p. 121; Lewis, 1942, pp. 60–61; Mandelbaum, 1940, p. 187). Even the much-noted intensification of conflict among aboriginal groups in various parts of the world (e.g.,

Keesing, 1928, p. 42; 1941, p. 58; Lewis, 1942, pp. 60–61; Mandelbaum, 1940, p. 187), resulting both from the sale of firearms and from the stimulus to competition for trade goods, has not always been an entirely disruptive influence. It, too, has brought about some surprising adaptations of native life. On the Great Plains of America, for example, it led directly to the celebrated hunting-and-warfare complex (Lewis, 1942, pp. 60–61; Mandelbaum, 1940, p. 187) which to the layman has become nothing less than the stereotype of American Indian culture.

MODERN ENTREPRENEURS

As the report of the Summer Seminar on Acculturation (1954, p. 980) observes: "Cultures do not meet, but people who are their carriers do. That part of their cultural inventory which they . . . transmit is conditioned primarily by their reasons for making the contact . . . ." Literature on culture contact situations (see "The Entrepreneur in Literature," pp. 298–301) consistently points up the differentiation in role between the trader and other agents of culture contact. In Canada, for example, he has eliminated competition from rival trading companies and from White trappers "to enable the native population to become self-sustaining" (Bonnycastle, 1943, p. 62). He has also "worked wholeheartedly for conservation of fur with a view to continuing as long as possible the normal living conditions of the Indian. This is, in fact, his plain and selfish interest" (Bonnycastle, 1943, p. 64).

In Oceania, the trader, unlike the missionary, has "let the native pick and choose from his wares" (Keesing, 1941, p. 68). In New Guinea, he is content to "abide by a policy of laissez-faire" (Reed, 1943, p. 122), and in the Solomon Islands "Unlike the administrator, commerce is not concerned, even ostensibly, with native well-being" (Hogbin, 1939, p. 160). All of these observations seem to express in one way or another the idea that traders are not working to promote native assimilation or social change. Their purpose is simply to assist the aborigine to exploit the resources of his native territory to the utmost, that he in turn may be exploited to the utmost by the trader.

In this regard the interest of the trader is clearly differentiated from that of his White neighbors. The missionary, for example, "sought vigorously to refashion traditional belief and behavior;" (Keesing, 1941, p. 68), and "more conscious attempts to control all departments of native life were made by the missionary than by the other White groups" (Reed, 1943, p. 122). The administration, unlike the trader, "is concerned with native well-being" (Hogbin, 1939, p. 160).

Wherever traders have introduced a cash economy, they have consistently taken care to deprive it of any added economic freedom for the consumer by the technique of credit saturation (see "Market Control," pp. 169–170). The practice has been noted in Canada (Bonnycastle, 1943, p. 65), Puerto Rico (Wolf, 1956, p. 240), in Africa (Hunter, 1936, p. 143), and in Oceania (Keesing, 1941, p. 123; Reed, 1943, p. 208).

In short, the trader appears as a conservative force by comparison to his White neighbors time after time. It may have been true "... that the European residents, the missionaries and the administrators, the settlers and the entrepreneurs, are indeed the main agents of change" (Malinowski, 1945, p. 15). If so, the entrepreneur appears to be the most easily satisfied of the four in this regard. Once his chartered objective of promoting maximum economic exploitation and consumption of manufactured goods is attained, he often becomes a force not for change but for stability and the preservation of native social integrity. In cases of advanced culture contact, as at Shonto, the trader may become the most significant "correcting mechanism" in the native culture (cf. "Summer Seminar on Acculturation," 1954, p. 977).

HYPOTHETICAL REGULARITIES IN TRADER-NATIVE CONTACT

In view of the limited interest devoted to traders by anthropologists, and the paucity of literature on the subject, the foregoing considerations are necessarily mere speculations. The suggestion that there is any such thing as a "stereotyped" trader role in culture contact, as suggested by the Summer Seminar on Acculturation (1954, p. 981), cannot be considered as more than an unproved hypothesis.

The hypothesis of a generalized trader role similar to that found at Shonto is based on the assumption of certain common factors in the history and environment of European contact with indigenous populations. Following the example of a recent exhaustive survey of culture contact and its consequences (Steward et al., 1956, pp. 503–512), I may appropriately conclude by summing up the foregoing discussion with a statement of the hypothetical processes by which the special and unique role of the trader may become developed and differentiated in any native community.

1. The peaceful penetration of Europeans into aboriginal territories is commonly spearheaded by traders (cf. Bonnycastle, 1943, pp. 59–60; Hunter, 1936, p. 2; Keesing, 1941, p. 29).

2. In a few areas Europeans may encounter a native market economy so well developed that they cannot effectively control it, and no general pattern of free trade can be established (e.g., Tax, 1952 b, pp. 52–55).

3. In most primitive areas, Europeans encounter only some form of subsistence economy. Here the earliest pattern of intercultural commerce and industry involves direct barter between pioneer traders and natives, as European manufactured goods are exchanged for the products of native enterprise (Hunter, 1936, p. 2; Keesing, 1941, p. 121; Reed, 1943, p. 96).

4. Pioneer traders are accompanied or shortly followed by other Europeans: missionaries, administrators, and settlers (Hunter, 1936, p. 2; Keesing, 1941, p. 68; Reed, 1943, pp. 105–116).

5. In environments favorable to intensive agriculture, the advent of European settlement speedily results in territorial dispossession of the natives and the development of a plantation economy under European control (cf. Malinowski, 1945, pp. 118–119).

6. Under a plantation economy the native subsistence base is largely destroyed, and the individual native becomes a wage or indentured laborer, or even a slave (Hogbin, 1939, pp. 160–165; Hunter, 1936, pp. 2–3; Keesing, 1941, pp. 129–131; Reed, 1943, pp. 98–105; Frazier, 1957, pp. 101–109).

7. Control of native commerce is largely destroyed along with native subsistence patterns and manufactures under a plantation economy. The earlier role of the trader shifts to the planter and to the company store (cf. Reed, 1943, p. 122; Wolf, 1956, pp. 240–241).

8. The early patterns of barter between Europeans and natives (cf. No. 3, above) persist in environments unfavorable to agriculture and in regions where native territorial integrity is preserved by fiat (Bonnycastle, 1943, p. 70; Honigmann, 1952, p. 215; Wilson, 1951, p. 62).

9. In the earliest phases of contact all Europeans are concerned with altering indigenous culture patterns in one way or another, and all are agents of culture change (Hunter, 1936, p. 5; Keesing, 1941, p. 69; Malinowski, 1945, p. 15; Reed, 1943, p. 208).

10. However, the ideals and purposes of different European contact agencies with regard to native culture and the alteration thereof are far from uniform (Keesing, 1941, p. 68; Reed, 1943, p. 122; Summer Seminar on Acculturation, 1954, p. 981).

11. The trader is directly concerned only with changing or augmenting the subsistence patterns and material culture of native peoples, and is quite content to have them stay as they are in other respects (Bonnycastle, 1943, p. 64; Keesing, 1941, p. 68; Reed, 1943, p. 122).

12. Therefore, of all European contact agencies, the trader perhaps demands least from the native, and his demands are most easily and quickly satisfied (cf. Summer Seminar on Acculturation, 1954, p. 990).

13. At the point when he has created a satisfactory market for manufactured goods and a high development of native enterprise, the trader is no longer concerned with or desirous of promoting further change in native culture, which might tend in the direction of a free market or free cash economy and weaken his own position (Bonnycastle, 1943, p. 64; Keesing, 1941, p. 68; Reed, 1943, p. 122).

14. Therefore, at a certain stage of development of native-European contact, the trader ceases to be an agent of culture change. He becomes instead an advocate and promoter of stability and the status quo, even while other White agencies—missionaries and administrators—are continuing to work for additional acculturative changes in the native population (Hogbin, 1939, p. 160; Keesing, 1941, p. 68; Reed, 1943, p. 122).

15. At a further stage in intercultural relations the native himself may become desirous of acculturation; that is, he may himself become an agent of culture change (Bonnycastle, 1943, p. 66; Hunter, 1936, p. 143; Keesing, 1941, pp. 69–70).

16. The trader, however, continues to be a conservative force, since his special position as intermediary depends on the continued economic and social separation of the two groups in contact. In advanced stages of culture contact, therefore, the trader may become the most influential single agent, either European or native, for the preservation of indigenous culture. Such appears to be true of Shonto today.

BIBLIOGRAPHY

ADAIR, JOHN, and VOGT, EVON Z.
    1949. Navaho and Zuni veterans. Amer. Anthrop., vol. 51, pp. 547–561.
ADAMS, WILLIAM Y.
    ——— Archaeology and culture history in the Navajo country; Report on
        reconnaissance for the Pueblo Ecology Survey, 1951. MS. on file
        at the Museum of Northern Arizona, Flagstaff.
ALBRECHT, A. C.
    1946. Indian-French relations at Natchez. Amer. Anthrop., vol. 48,
        pp. 321–353.
AMSDEN, CHARLES A.
    1934. Navaho weaving. Santa Ana, Calif.
ATHERTON, LEWIS E.
    1939. The pioneer merchant in mid-America. Univ. Missouri Stud., vol.
        14, No. 2.
BAILEY, FLORA L.
    1940. Navaho foods and cooking methods. Amer. Anthrop., vol. 42,
        pp. 270–290.
    1950. Some sex beliefs and practices in a Navaho community. Pap. Pea-
        body Mus. Amer. Archeol. and Ethnol., Harvard Univ., vol. 40, No. 2.
BARNES, J. A.
    1951. The Fort Jameson Ngoni. In "Seven Tribes of British Central
        Africa," E. Colson and M. Gluckman, editors, pp. 194–252.
BEALS, RALPH.
    1952. Acculturation, economics and social change in an Ecuadorian vil-
        lage. In "Acculturation in the Americas," Sol Tax, editor, pp. 67–73.
BEALS, RALPH; BRAINERD, GEORGE W.; and SMITH, WATSON.
    1954. Archaeological studies in northeast Arizona. Univ. California
        Publ. Amer. Archaeol. and Ethnol., vol. 44, No. 1.
BECKMAN, THEODORE N., and ENGLE, NATHANAEL H.
    1951. Wholesaling. New York.
BENEDICT, RUTH.
    1934. Patterns of culture. New York.
BENNETT, JOHN W., and TUMIN, MELVIN M.
    1952. Social life. New York.
BLACK, HENRY C.
    1951. Black's law dictionary. 4th ed. St. Paul, Minn.
BONNYCASTLE, H. G.
    1943. The role of the trader in Indian affairs. In "The North American
        Indian Today," by C. T. Loram and T. F. McIlwraith, pp. 59–76.
BROWN, PAUL L., and DAVIDSON, WILLIAM R.
    1953. Retailing principles and practices. New York.
BUNKER, ROBERT.
    1956. Other men's skies. Bloomington, Ind.
CARR, MALCOLM; SPENCER, KATHERINE; and WOOLLEY, DORIANE.
    1939. Navaho clans and marriage at Pueblo Alto. Amer. Anthrop.,
        vol. 41, pp. 245–257.

CARSON, GERALD.
    1954. The old country store. New York.
COLLIER, MARY, and COLLIER, JOHN, JR.
    1953. Navajo farmer. *In* "Societies around the World," by Irwin T.
        Sanders et al., vol. 1, pp. 218–225.
COLSON, ELIZABETH, and GLUCKMAN, MAX, EDITORS.
    1951. Seven tribes of British Central Africa. London.
COMISH, NEWEL H.
    1946. Small scale retailing. Portland, Ore.
COOLIDGE, DANE.
    1925. Lorenzo the magnificent. New York.
COOLIDGE, DANE, and COOLIDGE, MARY R.
    1930. The Navajo Indians. New York.
CORBETT, PEARSON H.
    1952. Jacob Hamblin, the peacemaker. Salt Lake City.
CUERVO Y VALDEZ, FRANCISCO.
    1706. Letter Translated in "Historical Documents Relating to New Mexico,
        Nueva Viscaya, and approaches thereto, to 1773," by Charles W.
        Hackett, vol. 3, pp. 381–383. 1937.
DAVIS, KINGSLEY.
    1942. A conceptual scheme of stratification. Amer. Sociol. Rev., vol. 7,
        pp. 309–321.
    1949. Human society. New York.
DE L'ISLE, GUILLAUME.
    1700. L'Amerique septentrionale. Amsterdam.
DOLVA, WENZIL K., and BECKLEY, DONALD K.
    1950. The retailer. New York.
DURKHEIM, ÉMILE.
    1897. Le suicide. Paris.
DYK, WALKER.
    1938. Son of Old Man Hat. New York.
    1947. A Navaho autobiography. Viking Fund Publ. in Anthrop. No. 8.
EATON, J. W.
    1952. Controlled acculturation: a survival technique of the Hutterites.
        Amer. Sociol. Rev., vol. 17, pp. 331–340.
EKVALL, ROBERT B.
    1939. Cultural relations on the Kansu-Tibetan border. Chicago.
ESCALANTE, FRAY SILVESTRE de, and DOMINGUEZ, FRAY FRANCISCO.
    1776. Diary and travels; to discover a route from the presidio of Santa
        Fe, New Mexico, to Monterey in Southern California. Translated
        in "The Catholic Church in Utah," by W. R. Harris, pp. 125–242,
        1909.
FARMER, MALCOLM F.
    1941. The growth of Navaho culture. San Diego Mus. Bull., vol. 6, pp.
        8–16.
FAUNCE, HILDA.
    1934. Desert wife. Boston.
FIELD, THOMAS P.
    1953. Climate. *In* "Societies around the world," by Irwin T. Sanders et al.,
        vol. 1, pp. 208–214.
FORDE, C. DARRYL.
    1953. Applied anthropology in Government: British Africa. *In* "Anthro-
        pology Today," A. L. Kroeber, editor, pp. 841–865.

FORTES, MEYER.
    1936. Culture contact as a dynamic process. Africa, vol. 9, pp. 24–55.
             London.
FOULKE, ROY A.
    1941. The sinews of American commerce. New York.
FRANCISCAN FATHERS.
    1910. An ethnologic dictionary of the Navaho language. St. Michaels, Ariz.
FRAZIER, E. FRANKLIN.
    1957. Race and culture contacts in the modern world. New York.
FURNIVALL, J. S.
    1944. Netherlands India. Cambridge, England.
GARRIDO Y DURAN, PEDRO.
    1786. Account translated in "Forgotten frontiers: a study of the Spanish
             Indian policy of Don Juan Bautista de Anza, Governor of New
             Mexico, 1777–87," by Alfred B. Thomas, pp. 345–351, 1932.
GILLIN, JOHN.
    1947. Modern Latin American culture. Social Forces, vol. 24, pp. 243–248.
    1948. The ways of men. New York.
GILLMOR, FRANCES, and WETHERILL, LOUISA W.
    1934. Traders to the Navajos. New York.
GLUCKMAN, MAX.
    1940. Analysis of a social situation in modern Zululand. Bantu Studies,
             vol. 14, pp. 1–30, 147–174.
GREGORY, HERBERT E.
    1916. The Navajo country; a geographic and hydrographic reconnaissance
             of parts of Arizona, New Mexico, and Utah. U.S. Geol. Surv.,
             Water-Supply Pap. 380.
    1917. Geology of the Navajo country; a reconnaissance of parts of Arizona,
             New Mexico, and Utah. U.S. Geol. Surv., Professional Pap. 93.
HACK, JOHN T.
    1945. Recent geology of the Tsegi Canyon. In "Archaeological studies in
             northeast Arizona," by Ralph Beals, George W. Brainerd, and
             Watson Smith, pp. 151–158.
HACKETT, CHARLES W., EDITOR.
    1937. Historical documents relating to New Mexico, Nueva Viscaya, and
             approaches thereto, to 1773. Vol. 3.
HAILE, FR. BERARD.
    1935. Religious concepts of the Navajo Indians. Proc. 10th Ann. Meeting
             Amer. Catholic Philosoph. Assoc., pp. 84–98.
    1938 a. Navaho chantways and ceremonials. Amer. Anthrop., vol. 40,
             pp. 639–652.
    1938 b. Origin legend of the Navaho Enemy Way. Yale Univ. Publ.
             Anthrop. No. 17.
HANNUM, ALBERTA.
    1946. Spin a silver dollar. New York.
HARRIS, W. R.
    1909 The Catholic Church in Utah. Salt Lake City.
HERSKOVITS, MELVILLE J.
    1938. Acculturation. New York.
    1952. Economic anthropology. New York.
HILL, W. W.
    1937. Navajo pottery manufacture. Univ. New Mexico Bull., Anthrop.
             Ser., vol. 2, pp. 5–23.

HILL, W. W.—Continued
  1938.   The agricultural and hunting methods of the Navaho Indians.   Yale
          Univ. Publ. Anthrop. No. 18.
  1940 a. Some aspects of Navajo political structure.   Plateau, vol. 13, pp.
          14–19.
  1940 b. Some Navaho culture changes during two centuries.   Smithsonian
          Misc. Coll., vol. 100, pp. 395–416.
  1943.   Navaho humor.   General Ser. Anthrop. No. 9.
  1948.   Navaho trading and trading ritual.   Southwestern Journ. Anthrop.
          vol. 4, pp. 371–396.
HOBSON, RICHARD.
  1954.   Navaho acquisitive values.   Pap. Peabody Mus. Amer. Archeol. and
          Ethnol., Harvard Univ., vol. 42, No. 3.
HOEBEL, E. ADAMSON.
  1949.   Man in the primitive world.   New York.
HOGBIN, H. IAN.
  1939.   Experiments in civilization.   London.
  1951.   Transformation scene.   London.
HOIJER, HARRY.
  1945–49. The Apachean verb.   Internat. Journ. Amer. Linguistics, vol. 11,
          pp. 193–203; vol. 12, pp. 1–13, 51–59; vol. 14, pp. 247–259; vol.
          15, pp. 12–22.
HONIGMANN, JOHN J.
  1952.   Intercultural relations at Great Whale River.   Amer. Anthrop., vol.
          54, pp. 510–522.
HULSIZER, ALAN L.
  1940.   Region and culture in the curriculum of the Navaho and the Dakota.
          Federalsburg, Md.
HUNTER, MONICA.
  1936.   Reaction to conquest.   London.
HYMES, D. H.
  1956.   Na-Dene and positional analysis of categories.   Amer. Anthrop., vol.
          58, pp. 624–638.
JEFFERYS, THOMAS.
  1775.   The American atlas.   London.
KAPLAN, A. D. H.
  1948.   Small business: Its place and problems.   New York.
KEESING, FELIX M.
  1928.   The Changing Maori.   Mem. Board Maori Ethnol. Res. 4.
  1941.   The South Seas in the modern world.   New York.
  1953.   Culture change.   Stanford Anthrop., Ser. No. 1.
KELLY, WILLIAM H.
  1953.   Indians of the Southwest.   Bur. Ethnic Res. Ann. Rep. No. 1.   Tucson.
KENNARD, EDWARD A., and MACGREGOR, GORDON.
  1953.   Applied anthropology in Government: United States.   In "Anthro-
          pology Today," A. L. Kroeber, editor, pp. 832–840.
KIMBALL, SOLON T., and PROVINSE, JOHN H.
  1942.   Navaho social organization in land use planning.   Applied Anthrop.,
          vol. 1, pp. 18–25.
KIRK, RUTH F.
  1953.   Navajo silver work.   In "Societies around the World," by Irwin T.
          Sanders et al., vol. 1, pp. 240–243.

KLUCKHOHN, CLYDE.
1938. Participation in cermonials in a Navaho community. Amer. Anthrop., vol. 40, pp. 359–369.
1944. Navaho witchcraft. Harvard Univ., Peabody Mus. Pap., vol. 2, No. 2.

KLUCKHOHN, CLYDE, and LEIGHTON, DOROTHEA.
1946. The Navaho. Cambridge, Mass.

KLUCKHOHN, CLYDE, and SPENCER, KATHERINE.
1940. A bibliography of the Navaho Indians. New York.

KLUCKHOHN, CLYDE, and WYMAN, LELAND C.
1940. An introduction to Navaho chant practice. Amer. Anthrop. Assoc. Mem. 53.

KLUCKHOHN, FLORENCE R.
1940. The participant observer technique in small communities. Amer. Journ. Sociol. vol. 46, pp. 331–343.

KROEBER, A. L.
1928. Native culture of the Southwest. Univ. California Publ. Amer. Archaeol. and Ethnol., vol. 23, pp. 375-398.

KROEBER, A. L., EDITOR.
1953. Anthropology today. Chicago.

KRUG, J. A.
1948. The Navajo. Washington, D. C.

LANDGRAF, JOHN L.
1954. Land-use in the Ramah area of New Mexico. Pap. Peabody Mus. Amer. Archeol. and Ethnol., Harvard Univ., vol. 42, No. 1.

LEE, JOHN D.
1955. A Mormon chronicle; the diaries of John D. Lee, 1848–1876. Edited and annotated by Robert G. Clelland and Juanita Brooks. 2 vols. San Marino, Calif.

LEIGHTON, DOROTHEA, and KLUCKHOHN, CLYDE.
1948. Children of the people. Cambridge, Mass.

LEIGHTON, ALEXANDER H., and LEIGHTON, DOROTHEA.
1944. The Navaho door. Cambridge, Mass.

LEVY, MARION J.
1952. The structure of society. Princeton, N.J.

LEWIS, OSCAR.
1942. The effects of White contact on Blackfoot culture. Amer. Ethnol. Soc. Mem. 6.

LINTON, RALPH.
1936. The study of Man. New York.

LINTON, RALPH, EDITOR.
1940. Acculturation in seven American Indian tribes. New York.

LIPPS, OSCAR H.
1909. The Navajos. Cedar Rapids, Iowa.

LORAM, C. T., and MCILWRAITH, T. F.
1943. The North American Indian today. Toronto.

LOWIE, ROBERT H.
1948. Social organization. New York.

LUOMALA, KATHERINE.
1938. Navaho life of yesterday and today. Berkeley, Calif.

MCALLESTER, DAVID P.
1954. Enemy Way music. Pap. Peabody Mus. Amer. Archeol. and Ethnol., Harvard Univ., vol. 41, No. 3.

MCCLINTOCK, JAMES H.
1921. Mormon settlement in Arizona. Phoenix.

McCombe, Leonard; Vogt, Evon Z.; and Kluckhohn, Clyde.
    1951. Navaho means people. Cambridge, Mass.
Mair, Lucy P., Editor.
    1938. Methods of study of culture contact in Africa. Intern. Inst. African
        Languages and Cultures, Mem. 15.
Malinowski, Bronislaw.
    1945. The dynamics of culture change. New Haven.
Mandelbaum, David G.
    1940. The Plains Cree. Amer. Mus. Nat. Hist., Anthrop. Pap., vol 37, pt. 2.
    1941. Culture change among the Nilgiri tribes. Amer. Anthrop., vol. 43,
        pp. 19–26.
Manners, Robert A.
    1956. Tabara: Subcultures of a tobacco and mixed crops municipality. *In*
        "The People of Puerto Rico," by Julian H. Steward et al., pp.
        93–170.
Matthews, Washington.
    1902. The night chant. Amer. Mus. Nat. Hist. Mem. 6.
Merton, Robert K.
    1949. Social theory and social structure. Glencoe, Ill.
Mindeleff, Cosmos.
    1898. Navajo houses. 17th Ann. Rep. Bur. Amer. Ethnol., pt. 2, pp. 469–517.
Miner, Horace.
    1952. The folk-urban continuum. Amer. Sociol. Rev., vol. 17, pp. 529–537.
Mitchell, F. G.
    n.d. Dineh Bizad. Published by the Board of National Missions of the
        Presbyterian Church in the U.S.A., 156 Fifth Ave., New York City.
        (Copies available from Ganado Mission, Ganado, Ariz.)
Morgan, William.
    1931. Navaho treatment of sickness; diagnosticians. Amer. Anthrop., vol.
        33, pp. 390–402.
    1936. Human-wolves among the Navaho. Yale Univ. Publ. Anthrop. No. 11.
Nystrom, Paul H.
    1930. Economics of retailing. 3d ed. New York.
Officer, James E.
    1956. Indians in school. Bur. Ethnic Res. Amer. Indian Ser. No. 1.
Page, Gordon B.
    1937. Navajo house types. Mus. Northern Arizona, Mus. Notes, vol. 9, No. 9.
Parsons, Talcott.
    1949. Essays in sociological theory. Glencoe, Ill.
    1951. The social system. Glencoe, Ill.
Paul, Benjamin D.
    1953. Interview techniques and field relationships. *In* "Anthropology
        Today," A. L. Kroeber, editor, pp. 430–451.
Phelps-Stokes Fund.
    1939. The Navajo Indian problem. New York.
Powell, Richard R.
    1949. The law of real property. Vol. 1. New York.
Price, A. Grenfell.
    1950. White settlers and native peoples. Melbourne, Australia.
Radcliffe-Brown, A. R.
    1940. On social structure. Journ. Royal Anthrop. Inst., vol. 70.

RAPOPORT, ROBERT N.
    1954.   Changing Navaho religious values. Pap. Peabody Mus. Amer. Archeol.
            and Ethnol., Harvard Univ., vol. 41, No. 2.
REAGAN, ALBERT B.
    1934.   A Navaho Fire Dance. Amer. Anthrop., vol. 36, pp. 434–437.
REDFIELD, ROBERT.
    1947.   The folk society. Amer. Journ. Sociol., vol. 52, pp. 293–308.
REDFIELD, ROBERT; LINTON, RALPH; HERSKOVITS, MELVILLE J.
    1936.   Memorandum on the study of acculturation. Amer. Anthrop., vol.
            38, pp. 149–152.
REED, STEPHEN W.
    1943.   The making of modern New Guinea. Amer. Philos. Soc. Mem. 18.
REICHARD, GLADYS A.
    1928.   Social life of the Navajo Indians. Columbia Univ. Contrib. Anthrop.
            No. 7.
    1936.   Navajo shepherd and weaver. New York.
    1949.   The Navaho and Christianity. Amer. Anthrop., vol. 51, pp. 66–71.
    1950.   Navaho religion. 2 vols. New York.
REINECKE, JOHN E.
    1938.   Trade jargons and Creole dialects as marginal languages. Social
            Forces, vol. 17, pp. 107–118.
ROBERTS, JOHN M.
    1951.   Three Navaho households. Pap. Peabody Mus. Amer. Archeol. and
            Ethnol., Harvard Univ., vol. 40, No. 3.
ROESSEL, ROBERT A., JR.
    1951.   Sheep in Navaho culture. M.A. thesis, Washington University,
            St. Louis, Mo. Mimeographed.
SANDERS, IRWIN T., et al.
    1953.   Societies around the world. Vol. 1. New York.
SCHMEDDING, JOSEPH.
    1951.   Cowboy and Indian trader. Caldwell, Idaho.
SHARP, LAURISTON.
    1952.   Steel axes for Stone Age Australians. In "Human Problems in
            Technological Change," Edward H. Spicer, editor, pp. 69–90.
SPICER, EDWARD H., EDITOR.
    1952.   Human problems in technological change. New York.
SPINDLER, GEORGE D., and GOLDSCHMIDT, WALTER.
    1952.   Experimental design in the study of culture change. Southwestern
            Journ. Anthrop., vol. 8, pp. 68–83.
STEWARD, JULIAN H.
    1950.   Area research, theory and practice. Social Sci. Res. Council
            Bull. 63.
    1951.   Levels of socio-cultural integration. Southwestern Journ. Anthrop.,
            vol. 7, pp. 374–390.
    1955.   Theory of culture change. Urbana, Ill.
STEWARD, JULIAN H., et al.
    1956.   The people of Puerto Rico. Urbana, Ill.
STEWART, OMER C.
    1938.   The Navajo wedding basket—1938. Mus. Northern Arizona, Mus.
            Notes, vol. 10, No. 9.
SUMMER SEMINAR ON ACCULTURATION.
    1954.   Acculturation: an exploratory formulation. Amer. Anthrop., vol.
            56, pp. 976–1002.

TAX, SOL, EDITOR.
  1952 a. Acculturation in the Americas. Proc. and Selected Pap. 29th
           Intern. Congr. Americanists.
  1952 b. Heritage of conquest. Glencoe, Ill.
THOMAS, ALFRED B.
  1932.   Forgotten frontiers; a study of the Spanish Indian policy of Don
          Juan Bautista de Anza, Governor of New Mexico, 1777–87.
          Norman, Okla.
THOMPSON, LAURA.
  1950.   Personality and government. Pt. 2. America Indigena, vol. 10,
          pp. 135–78.
TSCHOPIK, HARRY.
  1941.   Navaho pottery making. Pap. Peabody Mus. Amer. Archeol. and
          Ethnol., Harvard Univ., vol. 17, No. 1.
  1942.   Navaho basketry: A study of culture change. Amer. Anthrop., vol.
          44, pp. 444–462.
UNDERHILL, RUTH.
  1953.   Here come the Navaho! U.S. Indian Service, Branch of Education,
          Indian Life and Customs Publ. 8.
  1956.   The Navajos. Norman, Okla.
VAN VALKENBURGH, RICHARD.
  1936.   Navajo Common Law I. Mus. Northern Arizona, Mus. Notes, vol. 9,
          No. 4.
  1937.   Navajo Common Law II. Mus. Northern Arizona, Mus. Notes, vol. 9,
          No. 10.
  1938.   Navajo Common Law III. Mus. Northern Arizona, Mus. Notes, vol.
          10, No. 12.
  1941.   Dine Bikeyah. Window Rock, Ariz.
VAN VALKENBURG, RICHARD, and MCPHEE, JOHN C.
  1938.   A short history of the Navajo people. Window Rock, Ariz.
VOGT, EVON Z.
  1951.   Navaho veterans. Pap. Peabody Mus. Amer. Archeol. and Ethnol.,
          Harvard Univ., vol. 41, No. 1.
WILSON, GODFREY, and WILSON, MONICA H.
  1945.   The analysis of social change. Cambridge, England.
WILSON, MONICA H.
  1951.   Good company. London.
WOLF, ERIC R.
  1956.   San Jose: Subcultures of a "Traditional" coffee municipality.   In
          "The People of Puerto Rico," by Julian H. Steward et al., pp.
          171–264.
YOUNG, ROBERT W.
  1954.   The Navajo yearbook of planning in action; calendar year 1954.
          Window Rock, Ariz.
  1955.   The Navajo yearbook of planning in action; calendar year 1955.
          Window Rock, Ariz.
YOUNG, ROBERT W. and MORGAN, WILLIAM.
  1943.   The Navaho language. Washington, D.C.
  1946.   The ABC of Navaho. Washington, D.C.
YOUNGBLOOD, B.
  1937.   Navajo trading. In "Survey of Conditions of Indians in the United
          States, Hearings before a Subcommittee of the Senate Committee
          on Indian Affairs." 75th Congr., 1st sess., pp. 18036–18115.
          Washington, D.C.

a, Tsegi Canyon, typical of the topography of the Shonto region. (Courtesy Parker Hamilton.) *b*, Betatakin ruin, Navajo National Monument. (Courtesy Christy G. Turner II, Museum of Northern Arizona.)

a, Winter in Shonto Canyon: the trading-post grounds.   *b*, The road into Shonto Canyon
from the west.

a, The Government corral, Shonto Canyon.   *b*, In Shonto Canyon. (*a* and *b*, Courtesy
Bud DeWald, Arizona Days & Ways, The Arizona Republic.)

a, Modern Navaho material culture, illustrating the influence of the trading post.   *b*, Pawning a belt.   (*a*, *b*, Courtesy Bud Dewald, Arizona Days & Ways, The Arizona Republic.)

a, Setting of the trading post. (Courtesy Christy G. Turner II, Museum of Northern
Arizona.) *b*, The trading post. Warehouse to left, store in center, living quarters to
right. Electric gasoline pump installed, 1957. (Courtesy Bud DeWald, Arizona Days &
Ways, The Arizona Republic.)

a, Entrance to the store.   (Courtesy Bud DeWald, Arizona Days & Ways, The Arizona
Republic.)   *b*, Shipping cattle from the Government corral.

a, In the pawn vault.   Rugs taken in trade are also stored here.   Dial telephone installed, 1956.   *b*, Inside store, looking toward the grocery counter.   (*a*, *b*, Courtesy Bud DeWald, Arizona Days & Ways, The Arizona Republic.)

a, *b*, Trading at the grocery counter.

a, Navajo National Monument, a source of employment for Shonto Navahos.   *b*, Police visit to Shonto Trading Post.   (*a*, *b*, Courtesy Bud DeWald, Arizona Days & Ways, The Arizona Republic.)

a, Listening to speeches at community meeting.   *b*, Indoor community meeting at Shonto.
(*a*, *b*, Courtesy Arthur H. White.)

INDEX

Abiquiu, 40
Accounting firms., 183
Accounts receivable, 190, 197
Acculturation, 90–93, 223, 233, 246, 282
Acknowledgments, personal, 27–29
Activity, definition of, 216
Adahooniligii, Navaho language paper, 222
Adair, John, and Vogt, Evon Z., 233
Adakai, Ruth, informant, 28
Adams, Ernest, 28
Adams, Lucy W., 27
Adams, Nettie, 29
Adams, William Y., 36
Administrative subagency, 247
Administrators, 306, 307
Adobe, blue, 35
Adolescence, later, 87, 90
Advice, 290
Advisory (executive) Committee, 48, 67
Aeolian sand, 34
Affidavits, benefit claim, 202
Africa, 301, 305
Agriculture, 123–124, 141, 302
    employers, 217
    equipment, 89
    income from, 124, 147
    labor, 281
Aid to Dependent Children, 48, 88, 136, 226, 275
Aid to the Blind, 48, 136
Alamosa, Colo., 152
Albrecht, A. C., 233
Albuquerque, N. Mex., 177
Alcoholic beverages, use of, 76, 247
Alfalfa, 123
Alka-Seltzer, 74
Alluvial deposits, 34
American cultural system, 250, 263
American culture products, 246, 247, 265
American Indian culture, 304
American social structure, 245
Amsden, Charles A., 6, 7, 83, 121, 124, 199, 204, 220, 290, 293
Anachronism, definition of, 291
Anasazi Indians, 36
Anglo-American culture, 90, 91, 93, 94, 140, 244, 250, 252, 257, 259, 294
    influence, 9, 31, 40, 54, 70, 75, 76, 85, 90, 241, 242
Anglo-Americans, 61, 70, 124, 128, 149, 238
Anthropologists, relations to culture changes, 298, 300, 305
    relationship with Navahos, 25
Apache, 71, 149
    Western, 38, 126

Apple trees, 123
Arizona State Department of Public Welfare, 19, 48, 56, 136
    Nava-Hopi Unit of, 15, 19, 218, 278
Arizona State Employment Service, 135, 217
Arizona State Government, 48
Arts and crafts, 82–84
Aspen, 35
Assault and battery, 70, 73
Assembly of God mission, 49, 73
Aspirin, 74
Atherton, Lewis E., 21, 167, 168, 180
Atlantic and Pacific Railroad, 42
Aubuchon, Mr. and Mrs. John A., 28
Authority, social and political, 65–68
Automobiles, see Motor Vehicles.
Awatovi, Hopi settlement, 39
Axes, 89
Awls, wooden, 84

Babbitt Bros. Trading Co., 155, 156
Bailey, Flora L., 77, 81, 82, 84, 85, 87
Baking powder, 207
Bank, function of trading post, 216, 220
Barnes, J. A., 298, 301, 303
Barter, see Exchange, 199, 200, 306
Baseball, 267
Basketball, 267
Baskets, 71, 82, 83, 125, 126, 201
    makers of, 62
    making, 97, 124
    pitched water, 83, 173, 201
Beads, 196, 198, 208, 301
    silver (squash blossom), 81
    turquoise, 81
Beals, Ralph, 299
Beatings, punishment for offenses, 69, 70, 72
Beckley, Donald K., 182, 204, 278
Beckman, Theodore N., and Engle, Nathanael H., 21, 171
Bedding, 96
Beds, 78
Begay, Dana Natani, informant, 28
Behavior, nonreciprocal, 289–290
Belts, 79, 208
    Concho, 81
    silver, 196, 197, 198
Benedict, Ruth, 68
Benefit agent, Shonto Trading Post, as, 216, 218–220, 224–225, 228
    See also Arizona State Department of Public Welfare.
Benefit checks, credit on, 109
Bennett, John W., and Tumin, Melvin M., 268

U.S. GOVERNMENT PRINTING OFFICE:1963

Date Due